THE TEACHING OF ENGLISH

THE TEACHING OF ENGLISH

The Seventy-sixth Yearbook of the National Society for the Study of Education

PART I

By
THE YEARBOOK COMMITTEE
and
ASSOCIATED CONTRIBUTORS

Edited by
JAMES R. SQUIRE

Editor for the Society
KENNETH J. REHAGE

19 NSSE 77

Distributed by THE UNIVERSITY OF CHICAGO PRESS • CHICAGO, ILLINOIS

The National Society for the Study of Education

The purposes of the Society are to carry on investigations of educational problems and to publish the results of these investigations as a means of promoting informed discussion of important educational issues. The two volumes of the seventy-sixth yearbook (Part I: *The Teaching of English* and Part II: *The Politics of Education*) continue the well-established tradition, now in its seventy-seventh year, of serious effort to provide scholarly and readable materials for those interested in the thoughtful study of educational matters. The yearbook series is planned to include at least one volume each year of general interest to all educators, while the second volume tends to be somewhat more specialized.

A complete list of the Society's past publications, including the yearbooks and the recently inaugurated series of paperbacks on Contemporary Educational Issues, will be found in the back pages of this volume.

It is the responsibility of the Board of Directors of the Society to select the subjects to be treated in the yearbooks, to appoint committees whose personnel are expected to insure consideration of all significant points of view, to provide for necessary expenses in connection with the preparation of the yearbooks, to publish and distribute the committees' reports, and to arrange for their discussion at the annual meeting. The editor for the Society is responsible for preparing the submitted manuscripts for publication in accordance with the principles and regulations approved by the Board of Directors.

Neither the Board of Directors, nor the Society's editor, nor the Society is responsible for the conclusions reached or the opinions expressed by the Society's yearbook committees.

All persons sharing an interest in the Society's purposes are invited to join. Regular members receive both volumes of the current yearbook. Those taking out the "comprehensive" membership receive the yearbook volumes and the volumes in the current series of paperbacks. Inquiries regarding membership may be addressed to the Secretary, NSSE, 5835 Kimbark Avenue, Chicago, Illinois 60637.

Library of Congress Catalog Number: 76-44918

Published 1977 by

THE NATIONAL SOCIETY FOR THE STUDY OF EDUCATION

5835 Kimbark Avenue, Chicago, Illinois 60637

First Printing, 9,000 Copies

Printed in the United States of America

Officers of the Society
1976-77
(Term of office expires March 1 of the year indicated.)

JEANNE CHALL
(1977)
Harvard University, Cambridge, Massachusetts

N. A. GAGE
(1979)
Stanford University
Stanford, California

JACOB W. GETZELS
(1978)
University of Chicago, Chicago, Illinois

A. HARRY PASSOW
(1978)
Teachers College, Columbia University, New York, New York

KENNETH J. REHAGE
(Ex-officio)
University of Chicago, Chicago, Illinois

HAROLD G. SHANE
(1979)
Indiana University
Bloomington, Indiana

RALPH W. TYLER
(1977)
Director Emeritus, Center for Advanced Study in the Behavioral Sciences
Stanford, California

Secretary-Treasurer

KENNETH J. REHAGE
5835 Kimbark Avenue, Chicago, Illinois 60637

v

The Society's Committee on the Teaching of English

JAMES R. SQUIRE

(Chairman)
Senior Vice-president and Publisher
Ginn and Company
Lexington, Massachusetts

MARGARET J. EARLY

Professor of Education
Syracuse University
Syracuse, New York

RONALD T. LA CONTE

Professor of English Education
University of Connecticut
Storrs, Connecticut

JOHN C. MAXWELL

Deputy Executive Secretary
National Council of Teachers of English
Urbana, Illinois

WALTER T. PETTY

Professor of Education
State University of New York
Buffalo, New York

HAROLD G. SHANE

University Professor of Education
Indiana University
Bloomington, Indiana

Associated Contributors

JAMES N. BRITTON

Emeritus Professor of Education
University of London
London, England

GORDON. C. BROSSELL

Associate Professor of Education
Florida State University
Tallahassee, Florida

EVELYN M. COPELAND

Consultant for English and Humanities
Fairfield University
Fairfield, Connecticut

KENNETH L. DONELSON

Professor of English
Arizona State University
Tempe, Arizona

EDMUND J. FARRELL

Associate Executive Secretary
National Council of Teachers of English
Urbana, Illinois

MARY M. GALVAN

Educational Consultant
Austin, Texas

ALLAN A. GLATTHORN

Associate Professor of Education
University of Pennsylvania
Philadelphia, Pennsylvania

WILLIAM A. JENKINS

Vice-president for Academic Affairs
Professor of English and of Education
Florida International University
Miami, Florida

HELEN C. LODGE

Professor of Education
California State University
Northridge, California

ELISABETH MC PHERSON

Chairperson, Humanities Division
Forest Park Community College
St. Louis, Missouri

ANABEL P. NEWMAN

Associate Professor of Education
Director, Reading Practicum Center
Indiana University
Bloomington, Indiana

DOROTHY C. PETTY

Educational Consultant
Buffalo, New York

ALAN C. PURVES

Professor of English Education
University of Illinois
Urbana, Illinois

DEBORAH DASHOW RUTH

Head, Education Extension
University of California
Berkeley, California

ELOISE M. SKEEN

Assistant Professor of Education
State University of New York
Buffalo, New York

Editor's Preface

The three decades since the publication of the forty-third year-book, when the Society last looked at the teaching of English, have seen profound changes in the educational environment materially affecting the learning of language and literature in our schools. However evolutionary many of these changes have seemed, their cumulative impact can be suggested merely by reviewing a few of the major developments.

First, expansion of the school population, upward extension of the school leaving age, and growing sensitivity to the complex mosaic of cultural, social, and educational values that characterize contemporary America have continually confronted teachers of our native language and literature with the task of designing curriculum and instruction to satisfy the changing requirements of a pluralistic society.

Second, profound alteration in the nature of communication and in the accessibility of Americans to ideas and values transmitted through television and modern electronic media have altered the ways in which young people learn language and respond to imaginative experience. Staggering growth in the publication and distribution of inexpensive paperback books has made literature of all kinds instantly available to those who will seek it. Contemporary technology provides methods of quick duplication of all print-on-paper material and further extends the accessibility of our students to new ideas.

Third, the Civil Rights movement not only awakened educators to the need for providing quality education for all children in heterogeneous as well as homogeneous student groups, but to the unique problems of planning language and literary education for bilingual, bidialectal, and bicultural students. Supported by sociological studies, teachers increasingly found classroom decisions could no longer be isolated from community and home influences.

Fourth, studies in developmental, behavioral, and cognitive psychology provided critical new findings on the ways in which children develop and learn, as well as important new strategies for ensuring the effectiveness of learning.

Fifth, modern linguistic scholarship contributed new insights into the nature and structure of our language as well as into the ways in which language is learned.

Sixth, literary scholarship offered students tools and techniques for close reading and analytical study of texts and insights into the internal responses of readers to literature of many kinds.

Seventh, the boundaries of formal schooling in English expanded horizontally and vertically—the first through the continual broadening of subject matter at every level of study; the latter, through upward extension of English programs into the "open door" two-year college and downward to preschool and early childhood programs.

In the teaching of English, these have been decades of change. Through it all, one can discern at least three major periods of curriculum reform.

The first, best typified by the publication in 1952 of *The English Language Arts* by the Commission on the English Curriculum of the National Council of Teachers of English (NCTE), related the child study movement of those years to the *experience curriculum* of the 1930s and 1940s and focused on providing developmental experiences in reading, writing, speaking, and listening.

A period of academic reform initiated in 1969 by publication of *The Basic Issues in the Teaching of English* by NCTE and the Modern Language Association saw linguists, literary scholars, and rhetoricians from our universities join with teachers of English to focus on sequential instruction in the subject matter of language, literature, and written composition. Most influential during this period was the work of the Commission on English of the College Entrance Examination Board, the federally sponsored efforts to rewrite curriculum known as Project English, and the institutes for teachers supported by provisions of the National Defense Education Act.

But the rigors and restrictions of an academic, content-oriented education seemed inadequate for responding to the needs of the pluralistic, multiethnic student population found in many of the schools of the 1960s. Our nation's attention turned to reform of urban education and to satisfying the requirements of restless young people buffeted by the pressures of urban life and the conflict in values posed by an unpopular foreign war. Typically, much of the relevance demanded by the so-called romantic reformers of this period (Jonathan Kozol and John Holt, among others) focused on imperative changes in a child's school experience in English. Others pressed for strengthening language and reading instruction for linguistically different children. Bilingual and bicultural programs became a compelling national priority. Perhaps the seminal event in curricular reform in English was the Anglo-American Conference at Dartmouth College in 1966, which called for interactive approaches to language learning, relevant content, student involvement in decision making, and emphasis on student growth in language rather than coverage of subject matter. But concern for pluralizing the Anglo-Puritan tradition that dominated the traditional school curricula led also to area studies, including studies of minority concerns, the rapid spread of short courses and electives in our high schools, and an expansion of content to embrace film, drama, the oral tradition, and the literatures of the nonwestern world.

As the Yearbook Committee looked at the teaching of English in the mid-1970s, it seemed clear that English Education was in a period of transition. The ardor for a student-centered interactive approach emerging from Dartmouth seemed largely spent; no new major curricular thrust had yet significantly altered perceptions of ends and means.

Clearly, a conservative reaction is influencing many teaching decisions. Understandably concerned about the quality of their children's reading and writing, parents call for a return to basics. Accountability of the formal school system for children's mastery of essential skills has become a major concern. Some refinement in school priorities seems inevitable as a result of the present reexamination, yet not one which will see a full rejection of what has been learned about the ways in which children learn to read and write.

The explosion in subject matter has led, also, to overt, widely publicized controversy about the inclusion of content in the curriculum that many parents find objectionable; and in some ways the tension engendered by these local controversies mirrors ten-

sion in the social context in which the teaching of English occurs.
Robert F. Hogan, executive secretary of the National Council of
Teachers of English, in a report prepared for the Council's executive committee in the fall of 1975, forcefully describes the dilemma
that today's teachers of language and literature face when he writes
of community resistance to "intellectual and cultural bussing":

Except in some northern areas, bussing children to achieve racial
balance in public schools seems an accomplished fact. Since the authority
for bussing is constitutional, nothing short of an amendment to the
constitution or a radical shift in the composition of the Supreme Court
is likely to stall its northern drift. In Kanawha County, West Virginia,
most visibly, but also in Baton Rouge, Louisiana, and in a host of other
localities, another side of the bussing issue is surfacing. It is resistance
to intellectual and cultural bussing. In those communities it is all right
to bus black children into white schools. Even if it's not completely "all
right," it has the force of law. But it is as if these children must leave
their language, their culture, their values, and their history on the bus,
to be picked up after school on their way home.

There was a time when the defenders of books built their arguments
on first amendment rights and on principles of intellectual freedom and
growth. Most of the attacks on books took either or both of two clear
tacks. Some books, it was alleged, were inherently in violation of one
or more of the Ten Commandments (e.g., Thou shalt not take the name
of the Lord, thy God, in vain) or would incite behavior in violation
of one or more commandments (e.g., Honor thy father and thy mother).
Other books, the critics argued, were destructive of general social or
political values not covered by the commandments, but generally held
to be basic to our social and political systems.

But the situation has changed markedly. For one thing, publishers
in many instances have changed from textbook series to textbook systems. Although the superficial differences are in visuals, in related col-
lateral material, print and nonprint, a much more fundamental difference is in the construction of a pervasive philosophy that guides the
development of the system. For example, a literature system differs from
a literature series not so much in the graduated difficulty of materials
from year to year, but in its pervasive philosophy—e.g., that the study
of literature ought to be the study of our cultural heritage; or, on the
other hand, that the study of literature ought to reflect the cultural
diversity and cultural pluralism of the larger society. That latter, to
some, is an objectionable philosophy. So, too, in a textbook system on
language, is the principle that through language we can come to understand the values of other cultural groups and to examine our own
values.

At any rate, no longer is the attack being leveled fundamentally at a particular selection or a particular book even though particular selections are named in the attack. Cleaver, for example, will be named and his language cited. But that's only the surface problem. The real problem is that the overriding philosophy which governs selection is one the critic finds objectionable or threatening. And defenders of books can no longer reach for the First Amendment and for intellectual growth for their defense.

Local communities will resolve these issues surrounding the teaching of literature and language in different ways. So will they determine the extent to which renewed focus on basic skills will require changing priorities in classroom instruction. Hopefully, much of what has been learned about effective language and literary education from the experimentation of the past three decades will not be lost but will be integrated into a powerful new "field theory" or binding concept to unify our educational goals in the English language arts.

This yearbook not only attempts to analyze the present concerns and controversies but to summarize much of what has been learned from the three recent periods of curricular reform. It suggests guidelines and directions that must be considered in developing a powerful and unified curriculum in English from the preschool to the early college years.

In the opening chapter, James Britton discusses the processes through which children acquire initial competence in the uses of oral and written language. Gordon Brossell then considers the application of these processes to the upper grades and secondary school years where teachers and students strive for achieving power and expressiveness in writing and speaking. This emphasis on interactive processes in language learning is balanced in chapter 3 by an insistence from Walter Petty and his collaborators that out of such learning children and young people must acquire certain basic competencies.

The dramatic impact of new media and its place in the English classroom is analyzed by Deborah Dashow Ruth in chapter 4, followed by Helen C. Lodge's consideration of the inescapable responsibility of teachers of language and literature for nurturing personal, aesthetic, and ethical values.

Given the major emphasis in this yearbook on process-oriented learning, special consideration of changing subject matter seemed advisable. Chapter 5 presents five succinct reviews of new content in the humanities (Evelyn M. Copeland), in literature (Kenneth L. Donelson), in composition (Elisabeth McPherson), in language (Mary M. Galvan), and in reading in the secondary school (Margaret Early). As these reviews make clear, many of the current controversies relate directly to the expanded content now being introduced in English.

If the process and content of English instruction have changed dramatically over the past thirty years, so have the learning contexts in which teachers and students function. In chapter 7, Allan A. Glatthorn not only reviews classroom and schoolwide innovations for creating effective learning environments, but suggests a plurality of alternatives for tomorrow's schools.

Evaluation of pupil growth is discussed in chapter 8 by Alan C. Purves and the education of teachers for new and expanded responsibilities is treated by William A. Jenkins in chapter 9. In each case, the author carefully reviews historical antecedents of present practice and suggests contemporary needs.

The yearbook concludes with two contributions on the future of the teaching of English. Chapter 10 presents a condensed transcript of a discussion on societal and educational issues by leading English educators of various persuasions assembled by the yearbook committee to consider future developments. If their concern with modes of symbolization and states of consciousness offers insufficient fuel for futuristic planning, Edmund J. Farrell's concluding analyses of the social and cultural problems that impinge on and influence the study of English certainly guarantees that the changes of the next thirty years will be no less profound than those of the last.

In its total perspective, the yearbook presents a comprehensive review of the state of English teaching today—broadly based, exceedingly complex, intimately related to personal and social needs and concerns of individuals and groups. Language and literature inevitably reflect the values of a culture, and the teaching of language and literature inevitably reflects the conflicts and complexities of the culture in which the teaching occurs. It seems inevitable then that this yearbook presents no simplistic solution to solving the problems of English teaching in our pluralistic society; inevitable, too, that authors sometimes speak in conflict and opposition. But if the yearbook advances understanding of the complexity of English teaching and awakens readers to a serious consideration as to how major problems may be resolved, it will have served its purpose.

Any yearbook is a collective work involving a large number of individuals. As editor, I am particularly indebted to the members of the yearbook committee who contributed in important ways to shaping the design of the volume and to their succinct criticisms of individual chapters. Each contribution was also read by one or more independent consultant readers to assure adequacy of coverage and authenticity of content. Harold G. Shane initially persuaded the Board of Directors of the National Society for the Study of Education that a yearbook on the teaching of English was necessary. The National Council of Teachers of English, through Robert F. Hogan, executive secretary, and John C. Maxwell, deputy executive secretary, provided important assistance, especially in making available the resources of its ERIC Clearinghouse on Reading and Communication Skills. Herman G. Richey, formerly secretary-treasurer of the National Society for the Study of Education, prepared the index. For all this assistance, the authors and I are deeply grateful.

JAMES R. SQUIRE
Lincoln, Massachusetts
November, 1976

Table of Contents

CHAPTER I

Language and the Nature of Learning: An Individual Perspective

JAMES BRITTON*

Introduction

The question that lies behind all I want to say in this chapter is an easy one to ask: how do we as teachers make sense of our experiences of children's language development in school? I believe other readers who are not themselves teachers will profit from asking and attempting to answer the same question. For the teachers, there will remain a further question: given that I interpret my experiences this way or that, what do I now do about it in the classroom? I hope in what follows to suggest general implications to help answer this second question, but in the final analysis it is one that must be asked afresh, and given a particular answer, in every new teaching situation.

An effective teacher has to be a pragmatist in that he experiments to discover methods that achieve the results he desires. But he has also to be a theorist in a less direct mode. It is not enough to ask, "Does it work?" He must go on to ask, "Why does it work?" and "Why does it not work?" In this way he has to build a rationale that profits from both success and failure, investing, as it were, in an understanding that may serve to solve, one day, problems that have not yet arisen. Further, the criteria by which he judges success or failure are themselves liable to revision, and demand thinking of a particularly difficult kind, the questioning of objectives. If, in face of this range of problems, he succeeds in becoming an active and constant theorizer, psychological theories

* Consultant readers for this chapter have been Arthur N. Applebee, Tarleton High School, Lancashire, England; and Sara W. Lundsteen, Visiting Professor of Education, University of California, Irvine, and Pepperdine University.

(for example) will be of help to him; but, as teacher, he does not become a psychologist since his theorizing stops at a point nearer to the phenomenon than does the psychologist's—and the phenomenon in our case is the child using language to learn and to grow up. The teacher is thus something of a psychologist, something of a philosopher, linguist, sociologist—never one of these because always something of each of them. His level of theorizing, in fact, lies somewhere between that of the psychological thinking of a psychologist and that of the reasoning the same psychologist brings to solving his daily problems as a family man, a householder, a financial planner, a voting citizen, and so on. We cannot call such theorizing "interdisciplinary" without raising objections from those upholders of the disciplines who reserve that term for the collaboration of a full-fledged psychologist, say, with a full-fledged linguist. Perhaps we may call it "predisciplinary" without being misunderstood.

In case my views sound contentious, let me say here that no teacher in his right mind would deny the value of the social scientist's highly abstract taxonomies and the powerful theories they generate. Teaching has often enough been transformed by them; but we know that such effects take time, and meanwhile teachers must go on teaching. Working by hunch, they have to beg many of the questions that basic research has barely begun to tackle. The Report of the Study Group on Linguistic Communication, for example, in referring to the way writing and reading are learned, says: "At present, neither learning process is well enough understood to enable us to evaluate claims about their interrelations or about instructional tactics based on such interrelations."[1] Nevertheless, week in, week out, teachers are everywhere committed to fostering a child's efforts in learning to read and write, each process in some way related to the other. The argument here is for the necessity of both kinds of theorizing, the scientist's (or the philosopher's) and the teacher's, and it is the status of the latter that is in need of acknowledgment.

Both methods of inquiry, both levels of theorizing, are necessary

1. George A. Miller, ed., *Linguistic Communication: Perspectives for Research* (Newark, Del.: International Reading Association, 1974), p. 35. (Report of the Study Group on Linguistic Communication, George A. Miller, chairman.)

since they fulfill distinguishable and complementary purposes. To the scientist it is important that his theoretical categories at any level articulate well with the phenomena beneath them, the material under study; and equally well with the paradigm, the overarching theory that constitutes the mode of his discipline or his school of thought. The practitioner and "predisciplinary" theorist must comply with the first requirement, but not with the second; indeed, he cannot as teacher afford the fragmentation of his field of concern that results from articulation upwards into the frame of reference of a discipline or disciplines.

As to whether the educational theorist, in pursuit of the higher and more powerful abstractions governing thought in his domain, practices *a discipline* or works in an *interdisciplinary* mode is a question I shall leave open. I favor the latter view. However, the arguments on both sides would take us further than our present purposes require. As I have construed the terms, a move from predisciplinary theorizing either to a discipline or to an interdisciplinary field would mark change in a similar direction, and I am satisfied to leave it at that.

Choosing a Psychology

Educational thinking today suffers from a dualism in the psychological bases on which it principally rests. A report of a government Committee of Inquiry into Reading and the Uses of English (the Bullock Report), recently published in England, may illustrate the problem.[2] While the report in general stresses the importance of regarding reading as part and parcel of language uses that are inextricably interrelated, the sections that deal with reading specifically seem to me to reflect a predominately behaviorist psychology, while those specific to talking and writing are based very largely on cognitive schools of psychology. This dualism, and these particular areas of focus, could be widely paralleled. Can the distinction be justified on logical or empirical grounds, or am I right in suspecting that there is a conflict of ideologies leading to inconsistency in thought and practice?

2. Committee of Inquiry into Reading and the Uses of English (Sir Alan Bullock, chairman), *A Language for Life*, Report to the Secretary of State for Education and Science (London: Her Majesty's Stationery Office, 1975).

Behaviorist psychology has amply demonstrated its success in explaining and predicting animal behavior and, further, in modifying that behavior. Thence has come a learning theory that has been successfully applied to some forms of human behavior, and (more importantly from our point of view) that has provided a model with wide appeal to "outsiders" unfamiliar with the day to day detail of teaching and learning. Thus it is a model that has tended to dominate educational planning, theorizing, and experiment over a long period. We may cite, as an example of its effects, the strong move in recent years to establish a regime of behavioral objectives in American schools and colleges. In that campaign, teachers—often teachers of the humanities—have from time to time put forward the claim that there are certain areas of the curriculum where some of the objectives cannot be specified in behavioral terms nor evaluated by the observation and direct measurement of student behaviors. It is time we reversed this position. It is time we recognized the limited areas of human behavior to which the behaviorist model *does* apply and in which operant conditioning methods are appropriate.

Roger Brown's recent publication, *A First Language*, records his approving interest in two experimental attempts to train chimpanzees in the systematic use of symbols, one of them applying cognitive theories, the other operant conditioning. In doing so, however, he makes an interesting comment:

About ten years ago, in the laboratory of B. F. Skinner, pigeons were, by a clever training procedure, brought to play something that looked very like a game of table tennis. They did not, however, keep score or develop strategies for misleading one another. One might say that their performance was, in certain superficial ways, like that of humans playing a game of ping-pong but in other ways, which we think of as belonging to the essence of the game, the pigeon performance was not ping-pong. The pigeon ping-pong problem is a completely general one for experimental paradigms. The question always arises whether the paradigm preserves the essential properties of the process it is intended to represent.[3]

I am inevitably reminded of primary-school classrooms where children are learning to read, with the help of reading schemes, kits,

3. Roger Brown, *A First Language: The Early Stages* (London: George Allen & Unwin, 1973), p. 45.

and apparatus, from teachers trained in the prevailing "reading specialist" approach. It may be evident that they want to please their teachers, to outdo each others' performances, to satisfy their parents' ambitions for them, and that they enjoy some of the routines; but something is missing: it is clear that they have not yet discovered what reading *is*, what it is *for*, or grasped it imaginatively. Reading cannot therefore be for them *the behavior that they intend*. The infant who spins his own yarn, book in hand, *pretending* he is reading, may well be in one vital respect further on the road to success than these schoolchildren.

Piaget also acclaims Skinner's achievement in applying his methods to human learning, welcomes the advent of the teaching machine, and goes on to suggest that in the degree to which such machines can replace traditional teaching practices their presence may awaken teachers to their real task: not the eliciting of "correct repetition of what has been correctly transmitted," which may be left to the machines, but the fostering of initiative, free, active exploration, and cooperative intellectual effort.[4] Piaget's patient, methodical observations and tentative theorizing over a long period have, in fact, given us an alternative foothold, exploring the nature of processes outlawed under the behaviorist code, and so casting light upon the kind of teaching and learning he wants to see in schools. Now that there is developing a dialogue between the Genevan school and the psycholinguists whose inquiries were largely inspired by Chomsky's outspokenly antibehaviorist theories of language, that foothold is being strengthened and extended.

Bruner has without question been a key figure in that dialogue, and one way of observing its broad development is to compare his concerns in 1956 when he produced *A Study of Thinking*[5] (Brown's account of the role of language being then in an appendix) with the area of concern of *Studies in Cognitive Growth* in 1966.[6] Bruner's own introduction to the later book documents a growing collabora-

4. Jean Piaget, *Science of Education and the Psychology of the Child*, trans. Derek Coltman (London: Longmans, Ltd.), pp. 77-79.

5. Jerome S. Bruner et al., *A Study of Thinking* (New York: John Wiley & Sons, 1956).

6. Jerome S. Bruner et al., *Studies in Cognitive Growth* (New York: John Wiley & Sons, 1966).

tion: he tells of his term at Cambridge University with visits to Geneva; his more extended collaboration at Harvard with Inhelder, Luria, and Elkonin as visitors and Miller, Brown, Slobin, and McNeill as residents; and then of his own stay in Moscow. *Studies in Cognitive Growth* is dedicated to Piaget. Today, ten years after its publication, Bruner's work—on the cognitive precursors of speech, for example, or his revised version of "the spiral curriculum"[7]—keeps him in the center of a converging quest for a psychological framework relevant to teaching and learning.

Perversely enough, therefore, in choosing a psychology to provide a paradigm appropriate to education, I would begin with a name that does not appear in the books I have referred to in this section. First, however, let me make clear what I mean by "choosing a psychology." It would be crass to suppose that any interpretation of the nature of educational problems could dictate the hypotheses psychologists ought to frame for their experimental work. What concerns me here is what goes on *outside* laboratories and schools of psychology; it is the psychological contribution to theories of education as they flourish in the public domain, in the planning of administrators and the reflections of teachers and the initiation of entrants to the profession. Such a theory cannot of course flourish in a vacuum; without experimental inquiry and supporting evidence it must either wither away or survive anemically to mislead and delude us. There is a growing body of evidence—including new ways of perceiving and interpreting experience—indicating that the prevailing paradigm of vaguely behaviorist origin survives in just this way, and it is time we chose an alternative that ignores fewer of the available insights. The notion of "choosing" is precisely that which enters into the framing of a hypothesis. The effect upon the way teachers organize their interpretations of the experience of teaching, the consequent effects upon their students' learning; the effects upon administrative policy and consequent practice —these represent experimental outcomes by which we shall justify or amend or reject the theory we have chosen.

In the simplest beginning, we need a theory that sees human

7. Jerome S. Bruner, "Nature and Uses of Immaturity," *American Psychologist* 27 (August 1972): 687-708; idem, "Organization of Early Skilled Action," *Child Development* 44 (March 1973): 1-11; idem, Lecture at the University of London Institute of Education, February 27, 1975.

beings as creatures who take up *enterprises* that embody *intentions* and set up *expectations*. "Enterprises" would have to be variously seen as sequences of acts, as interactions with the environment, as encounters; as individual, or corporate, or in other ways inter-personal. "Intentions" would be seen as an indispensable key to the way we perceive and interpret human life, and yet the most elusive of the terms. "Expectations" would be seen as a word that implies an active principle locating knowledge in someone who knows, and conceiving of past experience not as gold in the coffers but as capital expertly invested. All this perhaps explains my perversity, with such notions in mind, in turning to George Kelly for enlight-enment. His personal construct theory, in its general outlines, seems an obvious starting point.

The twin pillars that give Kelly's theory its appeal are the ideas of "representation" and "anticipation." Although he himself devel-oped mainly the personality aspects, the framework seems equally appropriate to the kind of studies we have usually called "cognitive." In sharing this framework they may be freed from some of the limitations we have imposed on them.

Kelly's formulation "emphasizes the creative capacity of the living thing to represent the environment, not merely to respond to it."[8] But the representation, cumulatively constructed, becomes a source from which we draw hypotheses, expectations that enable us to make sense of fresh encounters. Our behavior is a series of experiments by which we refine our powers of anticipating. We refine our powers of anticipating "so that future reality may be better represented."[9] There is a strong sense in Kelly's writings that man's processes work towards the future, that we are drawn on by glimpses of possibilities ahead: hence our "intentions" that become embodied in "enterprises." Of all the data of the environ-ment open to our construing, the features we attend to and build into our constructions are those that nourish our enterprises, that is to say, those for which our past experiences provide expectations.

8. George A. Kelly, *A Theory of Personality* (New York: The Norton Library, 1963), p. 8. Cassirer would have said "the human being" rather than "the living thing"; for discussion of this point see John Shotter, "Men, the Man-Makers," in *Perspectives in Personal Construct Theory*, ed. Donald Bannister (New York: Academic Press, 1970), pp. 239-40.

9. Kelly, *A Theory of Personality*, p. 49.

"A person's processes, psychologically speaking, slip into the grooves which are cut out by the mechanisms he adopts for realizing his objectives."[10]

Making a rapid inventory of ideas that matter to us, we might see Kelly's theory as a suitable psychological starting point in a number of ways. First, the emphasis upon representation is consistent with all we have learned in the past forty years from Cassirer, Langer, and others concerning the role of symbolic behavior in human life; and it provides a perspective that, while it differs at times, does not distort the view of representation that Bruner takes, both in his own work and in interpreting the findings of Piaget.

Second, Kelly provides a psychological framework consistent with our views about the role of language for the user—all the more valuable, perhaps, because it is framed without language in mind. When Sapir made his classic statement that "language is primarily a vocal actualization of the tendency to see realities symbolically,"[11] he placed it as one among a number of ways of representing the world. In the section that follows we shall be referring to recent attempts to study the semantic aspects of language acquisition, and hence to establish a relation between nonlinguistic ways of construing experience and a child's first verbalizations. It is interesting to note here that Shotter, working with Newson on a study of mothers and infants, reports his feeling that they are "beginning to uncover processes at work by which they [mother and child] create a mutual construct-system between them before language proper develops."[12] Kelly's theory may indeed prove useful as a broad background to psycholinguistic studies, and may suggest new ways of construing familiar problems.

In the third place, the social aspects of Kelly's theory, represented principally in his Commonality and Sociality Corollaries, provide open access to some of the key ideas in sociological thinking in our times, from Mead's "symbolic interactionism" to ethnomethodological approaches. Mead stressed the importance of the interplay of *meanings* in human interaction as opposed to the inter-

---

10. Ibid.

11. Edward Sapir, *Culture, Language, and Personality* (Berkeley and Los Angeles: University of California Press, 1961), p. 15.

12. Shotter, "Men, the Man-Makers," p. 249.

play of outside forces to which the participants are exposed.[13] (Reduced to its simplest, Mead's theory states that I frame expectations regarding the behavior of those I encounter, and regarding their responses to my actions, at the same time as I monitor my actions in the light of what I take to be their expectations of me.) Kelly's Sociality Corollary reads: "To the extent that one person construes the construction processes of another, he may play a role in a social process involving the other person."[14] It could be said that the individual human being represents and interprets rather than simply responds. At a very general level it is this idea that allows a common perspective to be developed across the various theories.

Finally, Kelly's theory gives support to a view, rapidly gaining ground, that learning in school should merge and be part of an individual's total, purposeful, adaptive, living-and-learning. The view is strongly urged in the Report of the Study Group on Linguistic Communication to which we have already referred. It recommends that the National Institute of Education should "explore ways of relating the curriculum and the school to the child's home and peer culture," and in making its research proposals states that "a guiding principle has been the need better to connect what the child brings to his first grade and what the first grade presents to him."[15] Kelly claims to have "kicked learning theory upstairs." Where other theories have defined learning as a special form of human behavior, he regards it as human behavior at its most typically human.[16]

"Intentions," "enterprises," and "expectations" are notions we shall return to from time to time in such particular contexts as language acquisition, language in the curriculum, and reading. We shall draw upon the work of D. W. Harding, the British psychologist, to propose a development that may serve as link between Kelly's theory of personal constructs and Langer's philosophical

13. George H. Mead, *Mind, Self, and Society*, ed. Charles W. Morris (Chicago: University of Chicago Press, 1934).

14. Kelly, *A Theory of Personality*, p. 104.

15. Miller, *Linguistic Communication*, p. 6.

16. Kelly, *A Theory of Personality*, p. 76.

sketch for a "psychology of feeling" and a theory of art. Meanwhile, let us conclude this section by noting that it is entirely consistent with Kelly's ideas that we should have set out, responsibly, to "choose a psychology." The teacher, the student, the administrator, each on the model of a scientist, tries the theory experimentally. Each wears it as his "hopeful construction of the realities of nature" for as long as it continues to explain experiences, anticipate events, and so give him fuller control of his situation.

Infant Speech

When in 1926 Piaget addressed himself to the *Language and Thought of the Child,* and when some six or seven years later Vygotsky took up that theme and extended its range in *Thought and Language,* they served between them to open up for investigation a field of study that is today a central concern for psycholinguists all over the world.[17] As psychologists they were each influenced by original developments in sociological theory but found little support from contemporary linguistics. Each book was in its own way a seminal work, although the ground lay fallow for twenty-five years after they were written. It required a powerful injection of linguistic theory from Chomsky (*Syntactic Structures* was published in 1957)[18] before an effective working partnership could be established between linguists and psychologists; when it came, it led to a veritable outburst of activity.

Even so, for much of the work, it has been the linguists who have defined the research problems. As Hymes has pointed out, they have turned to acquisition studies for a better understanding of *what language is,* its rules and structures, rather than for a better understanding of its range of purposes and functions in social interaction within a social context.[19] In recent years, as sociological and

17. Jean Piaget, *Language and Thought of the Child,* rev. ed., trans. Marjorie Sabain (London: Routledge & Kegan Paul, 1959); L. S. Vygotsky, *Thought and Language,* trans. Eugenia Hanfmann and Gertrude Vakar (New York: John Wiley & Sons, 1962).

18. Noam Chomsky, *Syntactic Structures* (The Hague: Mouton, 1957).

19. Courtney B. Cazden, Vera P. John, and Dell Hymes, eds., *Functions of Language in the Classroom* (New York: Teachers College Press, 1972), p. xii.

anthropological perspectives have been developed, the exploration of infant speech has moved nearer to the concerns of educational practitioners.

To set out a synoptic view of language acquisition studies would be beyond the intentions of this chapter. Rather, I shall select some points of pedagogical interest and theoretical promise.

Perhaps the most dramatic evidence in support of a view of language learning held intuitively by many teachers lies in the discovery of young children's "transitional grammars." It has been shown that the two-year-old's early two-word utterances are constructed according to rules (that is to say, they are very far from a random pairing of the words at his disposal) and yet the rules are not partial imitations of the grammatical rules governing adult speech. Moreover, as the child grows, the rules evolve, taking successive steps, as it were, toward the adult grammatical system. To explain language acquisition in terms of *imitation* clearly fails to account for this evidence; some other process is at work. It has often been noted that once an infant has acquired, say, the rule for forming the past tense of a weak verb (*play*: *played*), he will overuse his rule, saying *goed* for *went* and *breaked* for *broke*. As Slobin has pointed out, this overgeneralizing will occur even *after* the child has begun to use correctly such forms as *went* and *broke*.[20] This seems to suggest that as he imitates linguistic items he has heard, he is able to organize the data (reducing its multiplicity the better to master it), and that of the two processes, imitating and organizing, the tendency to organize is the stronger. Or as Slobin puts it, "one cannot help but be impressed with the child's great propensity to generalize, to analogize, to look for regularities—in short, to seek and create order in his language." [21]

What is suggested is that the infant educes principles from the speech he hears and applies these principles in constructing his own utterances; he has thus "acquired rule-governed behavior," but without a knowledge of the rules. Chomsky has put it this way: "The child who learns a language has in some sense constructed the grammar for himself on the basis of his observation of sentences and non-

20. Dan I. Slobin, *Psycholinguistics* (Glenview, Ill.: Scott, Foresman & Co., 1971), p. 49.

21. Ibid., p. 50.

sentences (that is, corrections by the verbal community)," and he concludes with the comment, "Any theory of learning must cope with these facts." [22] Such evidence that even the very young child is able to *generate* a system for himself provides notable support for the many enlightened teachers who have acted in the belief that children will learn to use language primarily in the course of *using it to satisfy their own purposes.*

Supportive in a more general way is the impression we gain from many studies of the nature of the speech context afforded by the home, and in particular by the mother's relationship with the child. Language learning is seen as a *natural* process, if that is not too naive a way of putting it. We are reminded of the way Vygotsky viewed learning as, optimally, a cooperation between adult and child: "What the child can do in cooperation today he can do alone tomorrow." [23] Brown and Bellugi show how the mother, seemingly without conscious intention, modifies her speech in talking to her two-year-old; her sentences are short and simple, the kind of sentences, they suggest, that the child is likely to be using himself when he is a year or so older. [24] The relationship of partners in an enterprise is even more sharply focused in the case of the mother's frequent expansions of her child's "telegraphic" utterances. (Child: Baby high-chair. Mother: Baby is in the high-chair.) The researchers noted that when they themselves spoke to the child they found it natural to respond to the reduced or incomplete sentence with an expanded version. McNeill suggests this behavior may even be regarded as a kind of experiment on the part of the child; not yet being able to produce the structure that would match his understanding of a situation unambiguously, he produces his skeletal statement in order to elicit and attend to the expanded version. [25] Cazden believes, however, that expansions may be no more significant a factor in development than many other features of adult-child inter-

22. Noam Chomsky, "Review of B. F. Skinner, *Verbal Behavior*," *Language* 35, no. 1 (1959): 57.

23. Vygotsky, *Thought and Language*, p. 104.

24. Roger Brown and Ursula Bellugi, "Three Processes in the Child's Acquisition of Syntax," *Harvard Educational Review* 34 (Spring 1964): 133-51.

25. David McNeill, "The Creation of Language," *Discovery* 27, no. 7 (1966): 34-38.

action; indeed, that the rough and tumble of conversational exchange within the family may be more effective than deliberate or directed speech in revealing the structure of language to the child. The home is a language workshop in which the child serves an eager apprenticeship.[26]

Young children's syntactical resources have been investigated, not only by observing their spontaneous utterances, but also by studying their ability to imitate sentences offered to them. Ervin worked with five children at ages between twenty-two and thirty-four months and compared their spontaneous utterances with their imitations.[27] Her general conclusion supports what others have suggested, that children at this stage cannot imitate structures they are incapable of producing spontaneously: "We cannot look to overt imitation as a source for the rapid progress children make in grammatical skill in these early years." [28] Slobin and Welsh take the argument a stage further.[29] Studying a two-and-a-half-year-old girl (they christened her "Echo") they noticed that her spontaneous utterances were often surprisingly long and complicated; for example, "If you finish your eggs all up, Daddy, you can have your coffee." Then, using utterances such as this as models for her to imitate, they found that she was unable to repeat them correctly unless they were offered to her within about ten minutes of her original, spontaneous production. They conclude that an important aspect of language production must be "an intention to-say-so-and-so."

If that linguistic form is presented for imitation while the intention is still operative, it can be fairly successfully imitated. Once the intention is gone, however, the utterance must be processed in linguistic terms alone—without its original intentional and contextual support. In the

26. Courtney B. Cazden, *Child Language and Education* (New York: Holt, Rinehart & Winston, 1972), p. 128.

27. Susan M. Ervin, "Imitation and Structural Change in Children's Language," in *New Directions in the Study of Language,* ed. Eric H. Lenneberg (Cambridge, Mass.: M.I.T. Press, 1964), pp. 163-89.

28. Ibid., p. 172.

29. Dan I. Slobin and C. A. Welsh, "Elicited Imitation as a Research Tool in Developmental Psycholinguistics," in *Language Training in Early Childhood Education,* ed. C. S. Lavatelli (Urbana Ill.: University of Illinois Press for the ERIC Clearinghouse on Early Childhood Education, 1971), pp. 170-85.

absence of such support, the task can strain the child's abilities, and reveal a more limited competence than may actually be present in spontaneous speech.[30]

As a way of illustrating language acquisition processes, Chomsky set up a model, an abstraction he called a "Language Acquisition Device." [31] This is a device that receives as input a corpus of spoken utterances in a particular language and yields as output the competence by which (without a knowledge of the rules) a speaker produces grammatical utterances in that language. If the studies we have been considering are seen as attempts to explain the workings of a Language Acquisition Device, it is a notable discovery that "an intention to-say-so-and-so" appears to play a vital role.

Listening to a young child talking with his mother, we may sense that he verbalizes certain aspects of what he is doing, and what he sees going on around him; his verbalizations constitute a part of what he is doing and affect its course. At the same time, his mother's verbalizations constitute a part of what is going on and affect the course of events in the encounter. As the child's powers of speech production and comprehension grow, we should expect to find that in some situations interchanges come to be more and more dominated by verbal rather than nonverbal interactions, although, of course, what actually takes place continues to depend upon the situation. Wells and his colleagues set out to examine what aspects of a situation a child encodes in speech, that is, to classify the cognitive content of his utterances.[32] For this purpose they employ categories of clause-types worked out in collaboration with Slobin and Antinucci; substantially the same categories are being used in the Berkeley Cross-Linguistic Language Development Project.[33]

The data from the main experiment are still being recorded, but the analysis of scripts in the pilot study suggests very interesting possibilities. The earliest utterances are mainly of a kind that con-

30. Ibid., p. 175.

31. Noam Chomsky, *Aspects of the Theory of Syntax* (Cambridge, Mass.: M.I.T. Press, 1965). See also McNeill, "The Creation of Language."

32. Gordon Wells (Project Director), "Language Development in Pre-School Children," Second annual report (Bristol, England: University of Bristol School of Education, 1974).

33. Institute of Human Learning, University of California, Berkeley.

firms Piaget's developmental model, reflecting sensorimotor responses to physical aspects of the environment. However, there are also signs of a surprisingly early development of the notion of possession, a sociocultural response. If early utterances can be related in ways such as this to stages in preverbal cognitive development, important links may be established between the genesis of speech and the genesis of thought, and some light shed, perhaps, upon the precise nature of the innate predispositions that have been variously assumed to underlie both. I must note here that Brown and his associates have reported findings consistent with the observations in this discussion, and in a fascinating section of his latest book he discusses the relationship between his work and Piaget's model.[34]

What are we as teachers to make of all this detail on language acquisition? Is it right to assume that with institutionalized education and a teacher trained and paid to teach, we are into a whole new ball game? In the material so far analyzed, Wells has found that 70 percent of the verbal interactions recorded are initiated not by the mother but by the child. School, on this score, must certainly seem a whole new ball game to the first grader!

As a profession, we have grown accustomed to a conception of schools in which we now acquiesce: a conception of institutionalized learning as learning with special privileges for which a price must be paid in the sense that it is accepted that a child will have to adjust substantially to the school situation. Where teachers do not accept this conception of their situation, where the rhythms of learning that attend a learner's initiative are free to operate, there are real breakthroughs in learning and language development. Such situations are not common in my experience and they tend as yet to characterize a classroom rather than a school as a whole.

Talking to Learn

If there is one thing that language acquisition studies have taught us, it is that children are born learners. What is demonstrated is not only that they learn language but also that they use language as a means to a great deal of learning about the world. The task of learning to speak has been widely described as a major intellectual achievement, yet it is substantially achieved before the age of five.

34. Brown, *A First Language*, pp. 168-201.

A broader look at those first five years would make equally clear the striking development in mastery of the environment that marks the change from a virtually helpless infant to a self-possessed five-year-old. The two parallel achievements can only be explained by recognizing a means-end tie-up: self-possession as the end and speech as an essential means. Until we can emulate in school the directness of that tie-up we shall not succeed in fostering either language or learning as well as we might.

Anyone who has lived with a three-year-old could supply ample evidence of learning through language. An inventory of the questions asked would be one kind of evidence; but so would many of the infant's more freely offered comments about the world. These are often in fact hypotheses, put forward principally to test the reaction they will provoke and, hence, to test the extent to which they match the adult's ways of construing. He is thus able both to build his own representation of the world through his talk and to insure at least a minimum of congruity with the views of those around him. In Nemerov's words, it is talk "that makes the world his apple, and forces him to eat." [35]

The revolution that is asked of schools, and more particularly of secondary schools, in the light of so much recent discovery about language and learning in infancy is that by some means time should be found for pupil talk, classes so organized that they provide a context in which pupil talk becomes possible, and the curriculum envisaged and evaluated in terms of the learning processes involved rather than of "what has been taught." That this would constitute a revolution from prevailing current practice may be inferred from many studies of teaching styles and classroom procedures; overwhelmingly it is the teacher who talks most, and who specifies who talks when.[36] Pupil talk makes individual learning overt; by its means a good teacher is better able to engage in the dialogue that constitutes good teaching. Whatever he demonstrates or explains or

35. Howard Nemerov, "Life Cycle of Common Man," in *Five American Poets*, ed. Thom Gunn and Ted Hughes (London: Faber & Faber, 1948), p. 46.

36. Arno A. Bellack et al., *The Language of the Classroom* (New York: Teachers College Press, 1966), J. McH. Sinclair and R. M. Coulthard, *Towards an Analysis of Discourse: The English Used by Teachers and Pupils* (London: Oxford University Press, 1975).

expounds, he does it more effectively if his activity enmeshes with pupil responses that may lawfully find verbal expression. Further, pupil talk will in the end establish the learner as the chief protagonist in his own learning processes. It is no distortion of Hymes's comment on the way teachers should relate to researchers to apply it to the relation of pupils to teachers: "The point here is to stress that the importance of the participants in a situation is a matter, not of courtesy or rhetoric, but of scientific principle." [37]

Talking may, as we all know, be a way of wasting time. Traditionally we have not assigned any useful purpose to pupil talk in school and it is inevitable that, with the expectations we have helped to set up, many children will find it difficult to treat seriously any opportunity we now give them. We may have to work our way through that phase; there should be some consolation in the thought that when a class is divided into small groups, something like half a dozen channels are on the air at one and the same time.

It has to be recognized that the groups we have in mind are work-groups and not simply talk-groups. Heaven forbid that we should promote a model for schooling that represents an endless chain of committee meetings, their agendas supplied by the teacher as problems to solve or "topics" to "discuss"! Speech must be seen as one among a number of ways of representing and working upon experience and doomed to become sterile if it operates in isolation from these other modes.

Bruner's work has shaped our thinking over a number of years in this matter of the "representation" of experience. Some of his ideas break through to a new simplicity in his recent collaboration with Olson as it is reflected in a previous volume in this series.[38] Learning, they argue, derives from *performance*, and in performance both skills and knowledge are fundamentally and inseparably linked. Three major modes of gaining experience, which I would roughly describe as practical, by observation, and through symbolic com-

37. Dell Hymes, in Cazden, John, and Hymes, *Functions of Language*, p. xviii.

38. David R. Olson and Jerome S. Bruner, "Learning through Experience and Learning through Media," in *Media and Symbols: The Forms of Expression, Communication, and Education*, Seventy-third Yearbook of the National Society for the Study of Education, Part I, ed. David R. Olson (Chicago: University of Chicago Press, 1974), pp. 125-50.

munication, relate to what Bruner has previously termed the *enactive*, *iconic*, and *symbolic* modes of representation.[39] Learning is seen as accruing from performance in any of these modes, which "converge as to the knowledge they specify, but . . . diverge as to the skills they develop." [40] It is on account of this divergence in the skills developed that education must foster performances in a variety of culturally important media, including talk.

In referring to the revolution that seems demanded if teaching is to come into line with present understandings, I suggested above that curriculum must be seen in terms of learning processes rather than in terms of "what is taught." Olson and Bruner refer to the naive psychology reflected in much current educational practice, a psychology that assumes that "the effects of experience can be considered as knowledge, that knowledge is conscious, and that knowledge can be translated into words. Symmetrically, words can be translated into knowledge; hence, one can learn, that is one can acquire knowledge, from being told." [41] This aptly describes what lies beneath the self-enclosing curriculum that has imprisoned us, teachers and students alike, for a long time. By its terms, what is told is later recovered by our modes of evaluation, our tests and examinations, and the whole program may proceed without any noticeable interaction with the lives we lead and the learning that is a part of living.[42] What we have observed in the behavior of infants indicates quite other possibilities for the school curriculum. Probably the most immediate way of breaking into the closed system of teaching and testing "knowledge" is by providing opportunities for pupil talk. The initial effect might be, indeed, an improvement in learning even where that is conceived of and evaluated in the traditional way; but the long-term effect would surely be to remove from our thinking the psychological naiveté to which Olson and Bruner refer, and initiate a more realistic conception of the nature of students' learning and the nature of our objectives as teachers.

39. Bruner et al., *Studies in Cognitive Growth*, chapter 1.

40. Olson and Bruner, "Learning through Experience and Learning through Media," p. 132.

41. Ibid., p. 125.

42. For a forceful critique of examinations in education see Piaget, *Science of Education and the Psychology of the Child*, pp. 7-9.

Listening and Reading

Since, in Sapir's terms, the spoken language "is learned early and piecemeal, in constant association with the color and the requirements of actual contexts," [43] our speech establishes intimate connections with our firsthand experience, with the world in which we operate and to which all our meanings apply. This being so, it seems reasonable to assume that speech forms will always in some way intervene and mediate between the reader and the written text. Once committed to that principle, however, we must recognize that the incidence of the mediation and the forms it takes may vary widely according to the reader, his purposes, and the varieties of written discourse.

All that is known about the way meaning is derived from an utterance, by listener or reader, indicates that it is a highly subtle and complex process about which more remains to be discovered than is already known. We shall avoid the complexities here to take as simple a perspective on it as we can. Our ordinary experience as eavesdroppers, say in a railway carriage or a restaurant, would suggest to us that once we have identified the topic of a conversation and made out the situation (including the relationships of the participants), we shall "overhear" a great deal more than up to that point we had been able to. What has changed is the pattern of our expectations; we cannot fail to anticipate more effectively when the range within which to anticipate has been sharply reduced. An experiment carried out in Daniel Jones's phonetics laboratory in London some forty or fifty years ago illustrates this point. A mechanically distorted recording of conversation between two people could not be "heard" at all when played and replayed to a group of students; however, when a second group was told, between the two playings, that the recording was of a fitter and a customer in a tailor's shop, a good deal of the conversation was in fact picked up on the second hearing.

Since conversation is a social process, we might apply Kelly's Sociality Corollary and see the participants as engaged in "construing each other's construction processes." What is said is differently interpreted by each participant and differently interpreted by him ac-

---

43. Sapir, *Culture, Language, and Personality*, p. 10.

cording to who says it; that is to say, the utterance is referred to a frame of reference relating to the speaker. At one and the same time the utterance is interpreted in the light of the frame of reference and the frame of reference is confirmed, extended, or modified in the light of the utterance. A theoretical model that preserves this complexity and fluidity has recently been proposed by Barnes and Todd. They suggest that the meaning of an utterance in a conversation "lies not in the utterance itself but in the implicit hypotheses about it which shape the future history of the conversation." [44]

Berger and Luckmann have described what they call "reality-maintenance," in brief, the maintenance of an individual's subjective view of reality, of himself in society, in face of the demands made by society or by "reality as institutionally defined." [45] They go on to suggest that

the most important vehicle of reality-maintenance is conversation. One may view the individual's everyday life in terms of the working away of a conversational apparatus that ongoingly maintains, modifies and reconstructs his subjective reality. . . . It is important to stress, however, that the greater part of reality maintenance in conversation is implicit, not explicit. Most conversation does not in so many words define the nature of the world. Rather, it takes place against the background that is silently taken for granted.[46]

It is a simplification, but not I think a reductive one, to see such a process in Kelly's terms as the construing of others' construction systems in search of commonality at the level of implicit, unspecifiable meanings. We might describe it as a tentative exploration of what others who share our social milieu and our cultural pattern expect of us; an exploration in the hope of finding a similarity in what each perceives to be expected of him.

In speaking of the expectations that guide a listener, of relevant bodies of knowledge, of frames of reference, we have been moving within an area described in general terms as "context" in Lyons's study of semantic structure. The context of an utterance, he said,

44. Douglas Barnes and Frankie Todd, *Communication and Learning in Small Groups* (London: Routledge & Kegan Paul, forthcoming).

45. Peter L. Berger and Thomas Luckmann, *The Social Construction of Reality* (Harmondsworth, England: Penguin Books, 1971).

46. Ibid., p. 172.

"must be held to include not only the relevant external objects and the actions taking place at the time, but the knowledge shared by hearer and speaker of all that has gone before." [47] Throughout a conversation he sees the context as "constantly 'building up' from universe of discourse, taking into itself all that is relevant . . . from what is said and what is happening." [48] It seems reasonable to suggest here that when we speak of "expectations," implicit as well as explicit, we are employing a version of what Lyons and others have meant when they defined "context" as the *relevant* objects, events, areas of knowledge. But it is a version that stresses action rather than state. We might say that our expectations, initial and developing, as we listen to an utterance, are those parts of our "knowledge of all that has gone before" that are activated as we approach and as we participate in verbal interaction. (We should notice, moreover, that one model will serve as a basis both for verbal and nonverbal interactions. Gestalt psychology provides manifold evidence of the way our perceptions are affected by our expectations.)

Empson, in one of his critical writings, turns aside from his task to remark: "We could not use language as we do, and above all we could not learn it when babies, unless we were always floating in a general willingness to make sense of it." [49] I. A. Richards makes the same point in all practical seriousness when, in his little manual on *How to Read a Page*, he advises the reader faced with a difficult text to "read it as though it made sense." [50] In their anxiety about the reading difficulties of children in their classes, teachers have sometimes derided this advice as entirely unhelpful. It is interesting, therefore, to find that a researcher setting out to describe the behavior of a successful five-year-old reader sums up his performance in almost the same words. John was a black child from a working-class home who had taught himself to read before going to school. In her case study of John, Torrey writes:

When he did not understand what he was reading, he slurred over it, skipped words, converted it into something that was normal for him

47. John Lyons, *Structural Semantics* (Oxford, England: Blackwell, 1963), p. 84.

48. Ibid., p. 85.

49. William Empson, *Milton's God* (London: Chatto & Windus, 1961), p. 28.

50. I. A. Richards, *How to Read a Page* (London: Kegan Paul, 1943), p. 41.

to say or just rejected the task of reading it. He never did anything remotely like sounding letter by letter a sequence that wasn't a word he knew or calling word by word a sentence whose meaning escaped him. He read as though he always expected it to say something understandable.[51]

Among the expectations we bring to our reading, that anticipation of meaning is a very important one; however obvious that may seem to most readers, it is a point ignored in too many schools today.

Such an expectation is, of course, a mere threshold. Regarding the specific expectations that contribute to the reading of a particular text, I would like to start by quoting a document prepared by a group of London teachers some twenty-five years ago:

A Generalized Account of the Process of Reading

1. The reader *attends* to the passage, submits himself to the words written.
2. He calls upon his concepts of the terms used. His concepts will vary in adequacy, accuracy, richness, emotive power, etc.
3. From these as they accumulate in the reading he builds a pattern in his mind, building in accordance with the grammatical and rhetorical pattern of the writing and other signs or indications of relationship. The pattern will be vague and sketchy at first (an outline), but will become better defined and more complex as more and more of the meaning of the passage is assimilated. (*Emergent* pattern.)
4. The reader tests this pattern in its broad outlines by comparing it with familiar patterns of thought, by translating it into concrete examples, or by some other kind of analogy. Approval and disapproval begin to affect his interpretation. A faulty element will be seen to be a "discoloration" of the whole more often than as a missing or misplaced piece in the jigsaw puzzle.
5. He anticipates and welcomes (and is reassured by) concepts which fit easily into the pattern forming in his mind.
6. He is checked or jarred by elements which do not fit the pattern; he reads on with suspended judgment until further concepts met (by fitting or not fitting) demand that he should either concentrate on the recalcitrant element or reconsider his whole interpretation; or ignore the "check" and read on.
7. The pattern constructed in this way is not limited to ideas, sense, thought—to suppose this would be to believe in an unrealistic abstraction. (Richards's "neutral intellect fighting against the motives

51. Jane W. Torrey, "Learning to Read without a Teacher: A Case Study," in *Psycholinguistics and Reading*, ed. Frank Smith (New York: Holt, Rinehart & Winston, 1973), p. 156.

which make up its activity."[52]) The pattern involves sense, emotional responses, approval and disapproval both of what is read and of the writer's attitude or intentions.[53]

I would not, today, want to alter much of that account; some of its notions I think we have rediscovered toward the latter end of the twenty-five year gap. I would, however, want to add the idea that the pattern in the mind emerges as a modification of the expectations, the "all that has gone before," that the reader takes to the page. Let us say we take up a book because it has been recommended to us or because we have a good opinion of the author; or because the title suggests that it will give us information we need; and the appearance of the book itself indicates that it is not too long, the print is not too small, the words are not too unfamiliar for us to cope with. All these are a part of the expectations active in us as we approach the reading; and what we read will proceed to modify those expectations. It is likely that the first few words or paragraphs will make the sharpest modifications of all. They may quickly demonstrate, for example, that this is not the book we took it to be. Or, in the opposite case, where we find the book immediately rewarding and worth going on with, it is likely to be because the words have thrown new light upon notions that formed part of the expectations we brought to the page. Our successively modified expectations as we read constitute the meaning we take from the text. To deal in crude images, the process is less like a train appearing coach by coach out of a tunnel into view than it is like a photographic negative taking shape in a developing dish.

In reading, then, we process the words on the page and take away a meaning in the mind. To keep a distinction between the two, between the text and the message, is important. Polanyi suggests that we focus our attention, as we read, upon the emergent pattern, the message, while at the same time we are aware in a subsidiary way of (a) the words in the text that carry the message and (b) meanings those words have come to carry for us from past encounters.[54] Thus we show two kinds of awareness: focal aware-

52. Richards, *How to Read a Page*, p. 240.

53. Unpublished paper by a study group of the London Association for the Teaching of English, December 1950.

54. Michael Polanyi, *Personal Knowledge* (London: Routledge & Kegan Paul, 1958), p. 92.

ness of the message evoked by the text, subsidiary awareness of the *means* by which it is evoked. When the reading is over, it is the message that remains in mind, not the text. Thus, there is evidence that bilingual readers may derive the meaning of a text and, in a very short time, be so oblivious of the text that they cannot recall in which language it was written.[55] And Sachs reports experiments in which subjects were asked to identify sentences either excerpted or adapted from a text they had read less than a minute earlier; they were unable to detect quite substantial changes in form that left the meaning intact, but had no difficulty in recognizing minimal changes that resulted in a change of meaning. In her words, "The findings . . . are consistent with a theory of comprehension which contends that the meaning of a sentence is derived from the original string of words by an active, interpretative process. That original sentence which is perceived is rapidly forgotten, and the memory then is for the information contained in the sentence."[56]

The relation between text and message will vary in accordance with differing purposes in reading and kinds of discourse. In our examples we have had principally in mind reading for information. Most of us know books (usually on subjects we were in process of mastering) that yielded a great deal more on our second reading than on the first. What we have gleaned from the first reading, especially perhaps in highly general ways, has provided us with a more appropriate set of expectations with which to tackle the complexity of the detail. On the other hand, as Hebb has suggested, our expectations regarding the course of events in an adventure or detective story we had just read would effectively prevent us from enjoying a second reading, and this would hold until the "message" of our first reading had been substantially obliterated.[57] Again, we shall see in a later section that reading for meaning in the way we have described may be inadequate for a poetic text; compare,

55. Paul A. Kolers, "Three Stages of Reading," in Smith, *Psycholinguistics and Reading*, pp. 28-49.

56. Jacqueline Sachs, "Recognition Memory for Syntactic and Semantic Aspects of Connected Discourse," *Perception & Psychophysics* 2 (September 1967): 442.

57. D. O. Hebb, *The Organization of Behavior* (New York: John Wiley & Sons, 1949), p. 229.

for example, a situation in which I hear an interesting talk on the radio and effectively interest somebody else by retelling it, with the situation in which I am moved by a poem I hear but am powerless to communicate the effect to another person because I cannot recover the words of the text.

Language and the Organization of Experience

Langer takes experimental psychologists to task for their failure to deal constructively with the fact that sentient beings experience feelings.[58] In their study of the laws governing human reasoning they have tended to see emotion as a *disordering* factor; looking for one kind of order they have mistaken order of another kind for chaos. "No crasser oversimplification," she writes, "could possibly be made than the assumption that symbolic processes are either concerned with receiving, handling, and storing information, or with externalizing and working off emotions."[59] She suggests that an alternative ordering, obeying a different set of rules from those of discursive thought, is manifested supremely in works of art. It is my purpose here to pursue this idea of an alternative ordering, first by drawing upon Langer's work, then by distinguishing among the purposes to be discerned in the speech and writing of young children, and finally by applying some ideas from Harding.

Langer's major effort has been directed towards spelling out the laws by which an artist abstracts from experience to construct a work of art. Her association of the arts with human feeling is not likely to be disputed. However, to equate the one order with cognitive aspects of experience and the other with affective aspects would be a serious misinterpretation of what she proposes. I take it, rather, that the individual, particular, affective concomitants of our experiencing are ordinarily shed in "logical discourse," but that no such disjunction is at any point required in constructing a work of art. What is there organized is cognitive-cum-affective.

Following Cassirer, Langer sees the discursive symbolism of language as the characteristic instrument by which science, history,

58. Susanne K. Langer, *Philosophical Sketches* (Baltimore: Johns Hopkins University Press, 1962), chapter 1.

59. Susanne K. Langer, *Mind: An Essay on Human Feeling*, 2 vols. (Baltimore: Johns Hopkins University Press, 1967 and 1972) I, p. 80.

and philosophy are produced and sets over against it the *presentational symbolism* of the arts. In her first work she uses music to exemplify presentational symbolism, in clear contrastive relationship with discourse.[60] Very soon, however, she has to face the fact that discourse itself may submit to the rules of presentational symbolism and constitute a verbal object that is a work of art. Linguists sometimes speak of "poetic discourse": remembering that one lump of granite may serve as a farmyard gatepost while another becomes a Henry Moore sculpture may go some way toward helping us to accept the paradox of nondiscursive discourse. Langer uses the term more strictly. For her, the work of fiction or of poetry is not discourse but an illusory experience.[61] As we move from discourse to the language of literature, we have, as it were, to change gear: "the very first words of the poem effect the break with the reader's actual environment."[62] And if we fail to do so nothing of the illusory experience can be reconstructed.

In a recent statement, Olson seems to be endorsing the presentational/discursive distinction. He refers on the one hand to symbol systems, including language, which are characterized as having a small set of elements with "highly constrained rules for combining them," and on the other hand to symbol systems such as poetic language and the visual arts, which "cannot be analyzed in terms of such categories."[63]

The distinction between discourse and "nondiscursive discourse" seems striking enough to deserve the attention of linguists, and one might have supposed that it would be recognized at an early stage in any taxonomy of linguistic functions. This is not, however, the case. It is perhaps because linguists have tended to concentrate upon discursive material—the kind of language they principally employ—that their failure to recognize the distinction Langer makes has not yet become glaringly obvious.

Langer's treatment of the concept of "common sense" and its

60. Susanne K. Langer, *Philosophy in a New Key* (Cambridge, Mass.: Harvard University Press, 1960).

61. Susanne K. Langer, *Feeling and Form* (London: Routledge & Kegan Paul, 1953), pp. 252 and 297.

62. Ibid., p. 214.

63. Olson, *Media and Symbols*, p. 12.

relation to an individual's "coherent life of feeling"[64] suggests that she is willing to recognize not only discursive thought operating at less intense levels than logical reasoning, but also presentational symbolizing operating at a less intense level than is required to produce a work of art. It is this domain of the "art-like" in language usage that particularly concerns us here.

Several examples of young children's speech offer themselves for consideration in approaching the topic. Many children, given the encouragement of someone who will play the part of audience, will at times employ speech, not for conversational exchange (requiring an interlocutor), nor as "running commentary" (which may function even if no one is listening), but as *performance*, requiring a listener who will not interrupt, an "entertainee." Such utterances have been noted as the form of speech in which context-free elements make their earliest appearance (language, freed from its here-and-now bonds, being used to generate further language). A sense of performance may be heightened by rhythmical speaking, rhythmical movements, an incantatory tone of voice. One three-year-old, performing straight after her lunch, seems to recognize that what she is doing *is* a performance, and her parenthetical insertion was marked by a switch to conversational intonation:

> There was a little girl called May
> and she had some dollies—
> and the weeds were growing in the ground—
> and they made a little nest out of sticks
> for another little birdie up in the trees
> and they climbed up the tree—
> and the weeds were growing in the ground
> (I can do it much better if there's some food in my tum!)[65]

Storytelling is also a kind of performance, and may be clearly marked as such. A five-year-old boy spins a yarn about large sums of money, powerful racing cars, and other objects of ambition, and finishes: "That is the end of my story what I told you." Applebee has shown that children develop a "sense of story" at a surprisingly early age (at least as early as two and a half years), taking over

64. Langer, *Philosophical Sketches*, pp. 128-29.

65. James Britton, *Language and Learning* (Harmondsworth, England: Pelican Books, 1972), p. 84.

the formal conventions that mark fiction off from discourse proper.[66] Their performance in speech often leads to performance in writing. In fact, it is my experience that children who teach themselves to write before they get to school most commonly do so by making storybooks—a reflection of their concept of what the written language exists to do, and their personal contribution to the world's stock of storybooks.

The final example represents a highly sociable kind of performance. Bryant describes forms of oral performance found among members of black communities. She refers to "signifying," "playing the dozens," and sophisticated forms of storytelling.[67] She finds a developmental order in the appearance of the forms. Youngsters of four will begin to practice some form of "signifying" ("Ha Ha, mama broke your face!" as a taunt to a brother who didn't get his own way). By adolescence, they are expert at "playing the dozens" or at elaborate ritual insults; and the more sophisticated forms of storytelling are mainly performed by adults. A studied indirectness seems to be a principal characteristic; the speech has a formulaic quality, yet within it the individual is free to develop a vigorous style of his own.

Taking on the one hand examples of a range of performances in speech and writing, mainly by children, and on the other hand Langer's distinction between discourse and the language of literature, can we find a theoretical framework to bring the two levels into one perspective?

In 1937, Harding, who was at the time coeditor of *Scrutiny* with F. R. Leavis, contributed to that journal an article he called "The Role of the Onlooker." In 1962 he returned to the theme and developed it under the title "Psychological Processes in the Reading of Fiction."[68] It was his contention that the writer and the reader

66. Arthur N. Applebee, "The Spectator Role: Theoretical and Developmental Studies of Ideas about and Responses to Literature, with Special Reference to Four Age Levels" (Ph.D. thesis, University of London, 1973).

67. Betty Bryant, "The Relationship between Language Usage and Reading Skill" (Unpublished term paper, Harvard University, 1970), quoted in Cazden, *Child Language and Education*, pp. 201-2.

68. D. W. Harding, "The Role of the Onlooker," *Scrutiny* 6, no. 3 (1937): 247-58; idem, "Psychological Processes in the Reading of Fiction," *British Journal of Aesthetics* 2, no. 2 (1962): 133-47.

of fiction take up a role that may be likened to that of a spectator interesting himself in what other people are doing. A spectator's evaluations, both of the patterns events can take—the possibilities of experience—and of the patterns of other people's behavior, are more fully and more openly referred to his system of values and sentiments for the very reason that he remains outside the theater of operations and does not stand to gain or lose by what is taking place. Harding calls the role of spectator "a detached evaluative response" and suggests that evaluating in this way materially affects the kind of value systems we maintain and thus the kind of people we are.

He goes on to show that we vastly extend the opportunities afforded us for spectatorship by taking up the role in a range of modified forms. Watching a football match, a circus act, a state occasion are formalized "social spectatorship," and here evaluation is enhanced by verbal exchange: we jointly evaluate what we see, try out our judgments against those of others, and the way we feel about an incident or a performer is affected to some degree by the way other people feel. But what we persistently and habitually do is to take up "imaginary spectatorship," that is to say, we contemplate remembered or imagined experiences. When we go home in the evening we gossip about the day's events, reconstructing them in the imagination as we talk. It is by this means, Harding says, that we put a wide range of possible human experience on the agenda for contemplation and assessment. What we have selected as worth reconstructing constitutes one element in our evaluation, and the terms in which we describe it constitute another. We expect back from our listener his response both to the events recounted and to the explicit and implicit evaluations we have offered. To have our value systems thus sanctioned or challenged or modified by fellow members of our society represents, in Harding's view, a principal form of social satisfaction.[69]

If gossip about events stands at one end of a scale of "imaginary spectatorship" in a social setting, there lies at the other end the special form of dialogue that is carried on between writer and readers of a work of literature. The governing principles remain un-

69. D. W. Harding, *Social Psychology and Individual Values*, rev. ed. (London: Hutchinson's University Library, 1963), p. 15.

changed: "Fiction has to be seen, then, as a convention, a convention for enlarging the scope of the discussions we have with each other about what may befall."[70] Readers discriminate, accept, or reject the evaluations offered; where many find satisfaction in "going with" a writer, that writer's reputation and influence grow and the dialogue flourishes. The sophisticated reader "knows that he is in social communication of a special sort with the author, and he bears in mind that the represented participants are only part of a convention by which the author discusses, and proposes an evaluation of, possible human experience."[71]

Throughout Harding's consideration of spectatorship there has been implied the contrasting role of a participant. Let us sharpen the distinction now by limiting our concern specifically to the activity of using language. If we use language in a participant role, it is a means of getting something done, although what is done will cover a wide range: bargaining, persuading, briefing, planning, problem solving, handling information, giving evidence, categorizing, framing hypotheses, and so on. A participant may, of course, use language to reconstruct past events, as a witness in a court of law would have to do. If on the other hand an unusually talkative witness began to work up his narrative for his own and other people's enjoyment, he would very soon be ruled out of court. It is not enough, then, to say that in the spectator role we use language to reconstruct past events or to construct imagined ones: we have to add that we do this *for its own sake*—that is to say, for the satisfaction of doing so—and not for any ulterior end, any purpose that lies outside the activity itself. (That ulterior end, if there were one, would constitute a "context" delineating the sequence of events in which the speaker was *participating*.) We are back, then, in the vicinity of "play," of activities that occupy us solely because they *pre*occupy.

What is suggested, to restate Harding's principal point, is that the essential activity when we chat about experiences or when we read or write fiction is that of detached evaluation, characteristic of the role of a spectator. Among uses of language in that role for

70. Harding, "Psychological Processes in the Reading of Fiction," p. 139.

71. Ibid., p. 147. For a discussion of how the notion of a social bond between author and readers may be held to apply to authors no longer living, see D. W. Harding, *Experience into Words* (London: Chatto & Windus, 1963), pp. 163-74.

that purpose we include also the other verbal arts, poetry and drama, and the stories children tell and the oral performances they give. There is a spectrum, from informal and everyday uses of language at one end to the verbal arts of literature at the other.

The distinction between activity as a participant and as a spectator may be represented at a highly abstract level by picking up a comment from Sapir we have quoted earlier (p. 8). Setting out the theory that we represent the world to ourselves, Sapir suggested that we do not handle reality directly and *ad hoc* but "by the reduction of experience to familiar form." Cassirer made a similar claim when he pointed out that in man, for the first time in the evolutionary scale, a symbolic system is "shunted across" the receptor and effector systems that we share with the animals.[72] Now if we accept this model, it is clear that two modes of behavior are open to us: we may operate upon reality through the agency of the representation, or we may operate upon the representation itself without seeking outcomes in actuality. Since our world representation is our only conception of the world we live in it is important to preserve its coherence and unity, to keep it a world we are willing to go on living in. The maintenance of order in our conception of the world in total as we have experienced it becomes a principal concern for most of us, and this fact accounts for the readiness with which we take up the role of spectator. When we do so, we broaden the basis from which we contemplate until it is, potentially, "the way things are with us," the quality of our living. The topic may of course be trivial; we may nevertheless use it as a spy-hole through which we catch a glimpse of the "lifetime of feeling" of the speaker, or through which we reveal our own.

To be in the role of spectator is thus to be in a particular stance and I hope the reasons for valuing it are clear. But that is all that is claimed: imagination, creativity, passionate involvement, passionate commitment and purpose—none of these things is a prerogative of activity in either role, participant or spectator; all are equally appropriate and valuable to both.[73]

72. Ernst Cassirer, *Essay on Man* (New Haven, Conn.: Yale University Press, 1944), p. 24.

73. To speak of a "detached evaluative response" as that of the spectator is, of course, a technical accuracy; the spectator is detached in the sense that he is not participating in the events he contemplates. He may nevertheless be passionately involved in the memory, the dream, the fiction.

On the distinction we have been considering, the Schools Council Writing Research Unit in London[74] based the main divisions of a set of function categories for writings in school. Three principal categories were proposed: Transactional, Expressive, and Poetic. The central term, Expressive, is used in what is a generally accepted sense based on Sapir's statement that the ordinary face-to-face speech is mainly expressive, only to a limited degree referential.[75] We might define the governing convention as an assumption that in expressive uses of language the listener/reader is interested in the speaker/writer as well as in what he has to say about the world. Thus, expressive speech and writing rely on a shared context and are loosely structured to follow the preoccupations of the user. We have added a corollary—the notion that the informality, the mutual assumption of close relations between speaker and listener, constitute a situation in which speakers are willing to take risks; hence, that expressive speech will often be heuristic, the medium in which ideas are explored. And we would see a similar role for expressive writing.

Transactional language is developed to satisfy the demands of the participant role, that is to say, in broad terms, it is language to get things done. Verbal transactions will clearly be of many kinds. For the purposes of sustained written utterance the major categories were identified as informative and conative (substantially equivalent to Jakobson's "focus on the context" and "focus on the addressee").[76] The conative has two forms: *regulative* when compliance is assumed (usually by virtue of the status of the writer) and *persuasive* where compliance cannot be, or is not, assumed. The informative is, naturally enough, the most frequently used transactional category of writing. Subdivisions in informative writing were based upon Moffett's "abstractive scale," the movement from a near to a distant relationship between a writer and his topic.[77] The

74. The author acknowledges his colleagues in the Unit, Miss Nancy Martin, Dr. Harold Rosen, and Messrs. Tony Burgess, Dennis Griffiths, Alex McLeod, and Bernard Newsome.

75. Sapir, *Culture, Language, and Personality*, p. 10.

76. Roman Jakobson, "Linguistics and Poetics," in *Style in Language*, ed. T. A. Sebeok (New York: John Wiley & Sons, 1960), pp. 353 and 357.

77. James Moffett, *Teaching the Universe of Discourse* (Boston: Houghton Mifflin Co., 1968), pp. 33-59.

change of perspective they represent is one that Polanyi has commented on in connection with what he took to be the two operational principles of language, that of "representation" and that of "the operation of symbols to assist thinking."[78] As the second principle comes to dominate the first, he sees language changing in a way that is most clearly demonstrated in the distinctions between (a) the descriptive sciences (for example, biology), (b) the exact sciences (for example, physics), and (c) the deductive sciences (for example, mathematics). Thus he sees increasing "formalization" bought at the cost of decreasing contact with experience, precision of statement at the expense of concrete richness. Dixon similarly distinguishes "becoming involved" in order to explore experience personally from within, from "standing back" in order to gain in control and intellectual grasp of experience.[79] He goes on to point out how movements up and down this scale, within a single conversation or a piece of writing, may set up a kind of dialectic that makes the exploration of experience more subtle and more searching.

The spectrum from expressive to poetic represents language "in the role of spectator"; the more fully the demands of that role are met, the greater is the concern for form, for patterning, for organization into a verbal object, a work of art in language. Thus, both to writer and reader, it comes to constitute *an experience of order* consistent with the focal purpose we have attributed to it, that of maintaining the unity and coherence of our individually constructed representations of the world.

It may already be apparent that in the research model expressive writing is seen developmentally as a matrix from which other uses of language are achieved by a process of dissociation, or progressive differentiation. Add to this its heuristic facility, its role as the language of "work in progress," and its educational importance in all areas of the curriculum will be clear. Optimally, an all-purpose expressive writing, drawing freely upon language resources recruited through speech, and giving full rein to exploratory thinking, would progressively differentiate into specific forms to meet specific demands over a wide range of transactional and poetic tasks, and

78. Polanyi, *Personal Knowledge*, pp. 78 and 86.

79. John Dixon, *Growth through English*, rev. ed. (London: Oxford University Press, 1975), p. 117.

including also those developed forms of expressive writing itself in which, as adults, we maintain intimate relationships with those we love but are no longer with. An individual's progress in writing would therefore be reflected in a general decline in the amount of expressive in favor of transactional and poetic varieties; yet, at any stage, a new task or area of concern might demand a return to expressive writing as a starting point.

It must be added that the Writing Research Unit's initial findings regarding written work in all subjects in English secondary schools suggest that school programs are not yet structured to reflect this hypothesis.[80] An alternative hypothesis seems to hold, which might be formulated: "If you limp around long enough in somebody else's language you may eventually learn to walk in it." What does come through, however (from a limited sample of about two thousand scripts, the work of 500 boys and girls in 65 schools), is the firm nature of the association between Moffett's abstractive scale and progress through the years of schooling. Distribution of the informative scripts showed that his "generalizing" category was represented in the first, third, fifth, and seventh years of the secondary schools by the following percentages (of year totals): 19 percent, 28 percent, 46 percent, 62 percent; whereas the more *concrete* categories for those years contained the following: 34 percent, 26 percent, 7 percent, 4 percent; and the more *abstract* category: 0 percent, 1 percent, 3 percent, 14 percent. There were interesting differences between curriculum subjects. Generalizations are fully established in science and history by the fifth year; in geography, not until the seventh year; poetic writing, as might be supposed, came mainly in English, where it grew steadily until the fifth year and dropped off sharply in the seventh; it featured also in religious education and made an appearance in history. Expressive writing was more or less confined to English and religious education and provided in total no more than 6 percent of the scripts.[81]

Complementary to these broad indications of development over

80. James Britton et al., *The Development of Writing Abilities, 11 to 18* (London: Macmillan & Co., for the Schools Council, 1975).

81. Ibid., chapter 9. Since the Writing Research Unit covered the abstractive scale in seven divisions compared with Moffett's four, the distribution given above must be taken as approximate in relation to his model.

the secondary-school years, Applebee has made a detailed study
of the way children learn to produce and to respond to writing in
the spectator role from the earliest years to the age of seventeen.[82]
He relates acquisition of the conventions of spectator role discourse
in two to five-year-olds with Vygotsky's stages in concept development, and finds correspondences over a wider age range between
responses to literature and Piaget's preoperational, concrete operational, and formal operational stages of intellectual development.
In conclusion he suggests that developmental changes focus upon
(a) the changing relations between spectator role experience and
life experience, (b) progressive acquisition of spectator role conventions, and (c) the complexity of the experiences, primary and
secondary, over which an individual has mastery—a mastery that
relies upon spectator role activity to bring the whole corpus into
perspective and balance.

By way of conclusion to this part of the chapter, I want to
suggest that the two roles (participant and spectator) and the three
major functions (Transactional, Expressive, and Poetic) may be
related in a very general way to "rules of use" constituting part of
linguistic competence.

When we read a piece of transactional writing, we "contex-
tualize" it, or make its meanings our own, in a piecemeal fashion.
We take what fragments interest us, reject others because they are
overfamiliar, or because we find them unacceptable or incompre-
hensible; and we forge new connections for ourselves between and
around the fragments we take. But the writer of a poetic utterance
must resist such piecemeal contextualization by his reader. His
verbal object is a thing deliberately isolated from the rest of reality,
his own or the reader's. The appropriate response for a reader is
to reconstruct the verbal object in the terms in which it is presented—in accordance, that is, with the complexity of its internal
organization; and having done that to his satisfaction, to relate it
as a total construct to his own values and opinions. (If a novel has
"a message," say a social one, that message is in the work as a whole
and not in any fragment of it.) This process we have called "global
contextualization." Of course, as readers we may learn incidentally
a great deal about the world from fiction, and this will be a process

82. Applebee, "The Spectator Role."

of piecemeal contextualization. However, such incidental responses are to be distinguished from what is essential to the conventions of poetic writing and to the main purpose in hand.

Writing in the role of participant has a very evident and important educational function in all areas of the curriculum. We need to work for a better understanding of the learning processes it embodies on the part of all teachers, a recognition of the particular contribution of the expressive end of the spectrum. For the other spectrum, that from expressive to poetic, we need firm reminders of its educational value if it is to find a place in the curriculum at all in many schools. When students write in the spectator role, whether autobiographically or fictionally, whether in story or poem form, they are in search of satisfactions that are not easy to specify because they lie well below the surface; and any attempt to specify them is in danger of sounding like evangelical nonsense. Here, nevertheless, is such an attempt in brief:

1. When a child writes autobiographically he offers his experiences as a basis for forming a relationship with the reader he has in mind, a relationship of mutual interest and trust. (Martin Buber might have said that the child offers a version of the "I" in search of a relationship of "we" with the reader.) His satisfaction in the writing, if he succeeds, lies in the rewards of that relationship. Since for teachers this mutuality is in fact a *professional* relationship necessary to the kind of teaching and learning they seek to establish, the teacher will aim at cultivating it with every student he teaches.

2. When a child writes in the spectator role, whether autobiography or fiction, he exposes, by what he chooses to write about and the way he presents it, some part of his system of values, his feelings and beliefs about the world; and his satisfaction lies in having his evaluations corroborated, challenged, or modified. But this exchange of values is not indiscriminate: it is fostered by a relationship of trust and by a sense of shared values, both of which are necessary if the fullest satisfaction is to be derived.

3. In offering his evaluations the child is in fact presenting himself in the light he would like to be seen in. Acceptance of what he offers confirms for him that picture, and this is probably the deepest kind of satisfaction to be had from the whole process. Again, this is not an indiscriminate undertaking; it matters who plays the part of respondent.

4. There is finally the sheer satisfaction of bringing into existence a pleasing verbal object. ("What the child desires," wrote Martin

Buber, "is its own share in this becoming of things: it wants to be the subject of this event of production.")[83] Such satisfaction is likely to increase, obviously, as the writing moves toward the poetic end of the spectrum.[84]

A Conclusion

There lies ahead of us the enormous task of translating what we know of language acquisition, language development, and the nature of learning into structures by which teaching and learning in school may be organized. Too often today the call for "structure" takes the form of demanding the preservation of, or a return to, lockstep procedures that grew up in ignorance of the nature of learning and reflecting a mistaken view of knowledge, and hence of curriculum. In this task teachers must take a lead, both as to theory and as to practice, if the structures devised are to be workable and grounded in experience. The further participation of linguists, psychologists, and sociologists will be essential.

If the mistaken view of knowledge is corrected in Olson and Bruner's terms (see p. 17), and learning is seen to rest in performance in a range of culturally important media, schools will be free to be far more hospitable to children's own intentions than at present they are. Even the proposers of the notion do not seem to accept the full implications of the fact that speech, a vitally important cultural medium, is voluntarily and spontaneously acquired by children in pursuit of their own intentions. What we are increasingly discovering is that our intentions have the effect of unlocking tacit powers within us. To unlock these powers, we must, in Polanyi's terms, encourage a *focal* awareness of what it is desired to achieve through language, reserving a *subsidiary* awareness for the linguistic means of achieving it.[85] No doubt there will always be times when as teachers we need to awaken fresh intentions in a child. Good teachers already see their job very much in terms of being ready to fan a child's flame of interest, however flickering:

83. Martin Buber, *Between Man and Man* (London: Kegan Paul, 1947), p. 84.

84. A version of this statement on the satisfactions of spectator role writing appears in the Bullock Report, *A Language for Life*, pp. 165-66.

85. Michael Polanyi, *Knowing and Being* (London: Routledge & Kegan Paul, 1969), pp. 144-46.

that is, they are working upon intentions before attending to means. We need now to overcome our fears that someone will be burnt if children are free to contribute their own fires to the general display. For such a program to be effective throughout the years of schooling, we have to know a great deal more about the purposes served by language outside school—in the home, in the peer group, in the factory and the committee room, in the political community, and in a wide range of social contexts and conditions.

CHAPTER II

Developing Power and Expressiveness in the Language Learning Process

GORDON C. BROSSELL*

Introduction

Historically, the teaching of English has vacillated between two competing traditions, each with its own view of language learning. One tradition sees language as a subject to be studied, manipulated, and mastered, and stresses rhetorical knowledge and skill as determinants of linguistic competence and power. In this view, language is a tool for achieving the specific purposes and effects of its users.

The second tradition views language as a vehicle for learning and emphasizes the language user and his attempts to discover, define, and express himself and his relation to the world. Language in this view is less a tool for achievement than an instrument for personal and social growth.

An amalgam of the best of both traditions is a worthy goal for the teaching of English, but one not likely to be quickly and easily attained. Verbal power and expressiveness develop correlatively with cognitive growth and thus are subject as much to natural as to educative influences. Without reference to the natural process by which language learning occurs, language teaching becomes separated from its best source of guidance.

The process of language learning and some central strategies for promoting it in the classroom are the subjects of this chapter. The chapter will relate the primary process of language learning and the secondary process of language education in terms of natural human growth and will discuss that growth in terms of de-

---

* Consultant readers for this chapter were MaryAnn Hall, Professor of Education, Georgia State University; James Hoetker, Professor of English Education, Florida State University; and Bette J. Peltola, Associate Professor of Education, University of Wisconsin at Milwaukee.

velopmental stages. It will explore the organization of language education and set forth some major procedures and sequences for developing linguistic power and expressiveness. Following a consideration of talk and small-group process, two fundamental classroom activities, it will conclude with a discussion of the most significant language learning modes—drama, reading and responding to literature, and writing.

The Language Learning Process

PRIMARY AND SECONDARY PROCESSES

Human processes can be distinguished from one another in a number of ways and arranged in hierarchies of significance.[1] One basic and useful distinction is that between primary human processes that are constitutional and hereditary, and arise out of tendencies inherent in the organism, and secondary processes that are cultural and societal inventions. The first group includes the processes of physical and psychological maturation and intellectual and emotional growth—human processes that occur "naturally." The second group includes the processes that have been developed collectively over the course of time. These take their shape and direction from major social institutions and reflect the most significant practices, relationships, and organizations of a culture. They include, as examples, forms of government, dominant styles of life (for example, marriage and the family), and prevalent forms of socialization and enculturation, such as education.

Language learning is a primary human process, for the ability to acquire and use language and to gain knowledge, understanding, and skill through language is innate in every human being. Although language learning is one of the most subtle and complex of all human processes, it occurs regularly and informally, without instruction. Clearly, however, language learning (or any other kind of human learning) does not occur in a vacuum, but requires a social context. We learn language by interacting with others. Learning one's own language becomes a matter of realizing a human

1. The principle is the same as James Britton's, that "hierarchical categories are important means by which to organize expectations and regulate behaviour in the light of them." James Britton, *Language and Learning* (Coral Gables, Fla.: University of Miami Press, 1970), p. 198.

potential in terms particular to one's cultural and social conditions. And developing one's language becomes a matter of one's "cumulative experience as a member of innumerable human groups, from the family to the nation, and embracing all aspects of [one's] life." [2]

The same relationship exists between the primary process of learning and the secondary process of education. The innate potential for learning is actualized in the contexts of a multitude of educational settings ranging from the informal (undifferentiated personal experience) to the formal (schooling). The use of language for learning is a particular instance of language as cultural and social behavior, and language learning in school is a particular instance of language learning. For a teacher, the recognition of the interrelationship of the primary process of language *learning* and the secondary process of language *education* has powerful implications for classroom organization and procedure. The task is not how to teach language but how to enhance the language learning already taking place. Successful teaching grows out of a "careful consideration of the relationship between the processes every human being uses to extend his command of his language in the normal course of his daily life, and the deliberate attempts that teachers make in the classroom to achieve the same end." [3]

Three essential elements—language, learners, and language learning situations—determine the nature and impact of the educational process in a particular school setting. When their interaction is rich, varied, and meaningful, the learning process will be quickened and deepened. When the elements are fragmented and discordant and lack direction and purpose, the learning process will be impeded, slowed, and made to seem unnatural. Ideally, the language education process ought to broaden the capacity for receiving, producing, and responding to language and language matters.

In terms of language as social behavior, linguistic power is a matter of using language appropriate to various social contexts; thus, teaching for language growth becomes a matter of providing opportunities for experiencing and practicing increasingly differentiated language appropriate to new and different social situations.

2. Peter Doughty, John Pearce, and Geoffrey Thornton, *Exploring Language* (London: Edward Arnold, 1972), p. 112.

3. Ibid.

But language has personal as well as social uses. It is a unique means of apprehending and understanding our experience, of making sense of the world and our place in it—a means of assisting and modulating the process of becoming an individual. Language is a medium for exploring ideas, trying out roles, and generally, to borrow Piaget's term, committing oneself to possibilities. Growth in language reflects personal as well as social development, and thus teaching for language growth is, in the deepest sense, teaching for integrated human development, a conception that imbues the process of language education with deeper purpose than does a language-as-skill or language-as-knowledge model.

DEVELOPMENTAL STAGES OF GROWTH

Understanding any natural process requires a concept with which to organize meaningful patterns of relationships among the gradual changes that occur in it. The notion of developmental stages of growth is one of the most useful for this purpose and one which has gained considerable currency among the most influential theorists of personality and human behavior. Piaget's theories about the intellectual growth of the child, for example, involve the idea of a developmental continuum. A set of generalizations about the process of intellectual growth underlies his thought: that all developmental processes are continuous; that development takes place through differentiation and generalization; that each phase of development has its roots in an earlier phase and is itself the root of the next higher stage; that repetition of processes in different forms occurs in succeeding phases of development; that differences in organizational patterns constitute a hierarchy of experience and actions; and that individuals attain different levels within the hierarchy though theoretically capable of achieving all levels.[4]

Theoretical constructs of this sort are significant as *descriptions* of human growth and behavior. They provide a means of coming to a fuller understanding of learning and developing—what have been called primary processes here—as these occur in the context of our culture and society. Organizing principles such as the con-

4. S. B. Sells, "Personality," in *Encyclopedia of Educational Research*, 4th ed., ed. Robert L. Ebel (New York: Macmillan Co., 1969), pp. 938-39.

cept of developmental stages of growth offer a way of conceiving and directing secondary processes like education, so that the natural inclinations of individual human beings to learn and grow can be sustained in socially structured institutions like schools.

The whole question of whether society—or rather the power structure of society—*wants* education to operate in this way is another matter and, in a sense, is outside the scope of this chapter. But it is mentioned here out of recognition that there is always a point at which "purely academic" matters like developing power and expressiveness in language impinge upon sociopolitical issues like enculturating the youth of a nation. The conception of process-oriented language learning being presented here implies that greater emphasis in education should be consciously placed on human needs than on social values. Given the indisputable fact that schools are agents of enculturation, any notion of what should happen in them is, depending on its value orientation, either more or less disposed toward that end.

The idea of developmental stages of growth provides a conceptual framework for guiding the language learning process in school, a theoretical basis for a consistent, operational approach to teaching English/language arts from elementary through secondary school—a theoretical basis sorely needed in view of the territorial claims for curriculum and instruction arbitrarily staked out at various educational levels, usually on grounds no more substantial than historical accident, local preference, and the demand for tangible teaching guides.

It is possible to identify Piaget's notion of "decentering" as the primary dimension of human growth, and then view its manifestations as they occur in language learning, recognizing that such manifestations are not isolated language matters in themselves but significant representations of integrated human growth in both personal and social terms. Moffett takes this position:

The primary dimension of growth seems to be a movement from the center of the self outward. Or perhaps it is more accurate to say that the self enlarges, assimilating the world to itself and accommodating itself to the world, as Piaget puts it. The detailed forms which this movement takes are various and often paradoxical. In moving outward from himself, the child becomes more himself. The teacher's art is to move with this movement, a subtle act possible only if he shifts his gaze from the subject to the learner, for the subject is the learner.[5]

The fact that the "detailed forms" of human growth are "various and often paradoxical" is bound to frustrate anyone who expects neat structures and clear-cut progressions to mark advances in learning, in school or out. Teachers who "move with this movement" must do so within an institutional system inured to short-term, incremental achievement rather than extended organic development. Their art is indeed subtle because it is based on broad conceptions that must be realized within narrow confines. Long-term goals, sequences, and continuities take precedence over lesson plans, units of instruction, and semester-bound courses in guiding their efforts.

Several patterns of development characterize decentering, the primary dimension of human growth. The essential movements are: from simple to complex, from concrete to abstract, from personal orientation to impersonal or "multipersonal" orientation, from activity without thought to thought with less activity, from conception of objects themselves to conception of their properties, from literal to symbolic, from absolute to relative.[6] Such movements are general trends. They occur at varying rates and reach different levels in the developmental hierarchy depending on the particular configuration of hereditary and environmental factors that influence human growth in any instance.

Similar movements can be described for the process of language learning as it represents the larger pattern of human development. Moffett identifies such a series of continuities, calling it a "set of variations on the theme of decentering": from implicitly to explicitly formulated ideas; from addressing a small, known audience to a large, different one; from representing things present to things past and potential; from projecting emotion into the there-then to focusing it in the here-now; from stereotyping to originality of expression; and from lower to higher consciousness of abstracting.[7]

5. James Moffett, *Teaching the Universe of Discourse* (Boston: Houghton Mifflin Co., 1968), p. 59.

6. Sells, "Personality," p. 939.

7. Moffett, *Teaching the Universe of Discourse*, pp. 57-58.

Language learning is an aspect of integrated human learning actualized simultaneously at personal and social levels. It involves psychological as well as social growth. This point can hardly be overemphasized in view of the still prevalent tendency in schools to treat language solely as an object of inspection and study rather than an instrument for learning. The need for young people to use language in ever-widening and increasingly differentiated social contexts remains paramount if the language learning process is to be effectively advanced.

The Process of Language Education

ORGANIZING LANGUAGE LEARNING SITUATIONS

Most textbooks—even those that favor process-oriented learning—treat the elements of the English/language arts curriculum separately. Although organizational demands may require this procedure, its chief effect is probably to suggest that producing and receiving language are separate—and therefore separable—activities. While language-based activities—talking, listening, reading, writing—can be "taught" as individual skills, there is no sound reason to believe that they are best developed separately.[8] The various forms of verbal expression are various forms of the same instrument, language. Process-oriented language education recognizes that "an individual's competence, whether spoken or written, is the product of a single capacity: hence any growth in relation to one mode of using language is likely to have an effect upon the other, even though that effect may be indirect or delayed."[9] The organization of language learning around single activities is superseded by organization that is thought to reflect dominant patterns of human growth and language development.

For the teacher who wishes to organize classroom learning in terms of process, the essential task is twofold: first, to discover the stages of personal and linguistic growth students have attained when they arrive in class; and second, to devise and implement lan-

8. There is even growing support—particularly in Great Britain—for teaching the acquisition of reading and writing skills simultaneously. See Britton, *Language and Learning*, p. 121.

9. Doughty, Pearce, and Thornton, *Exploring Language*, p. 120.

guage learning situations that will advance their natural individual development. The two dimensions of the task are interrelated, since teaching strategies always need to follow from reliable knowledge of what students can already do with language and what they may be expected to do with it as they learn and grow.

General levels of personal growth and linguistic competence cannot often be directly inferred from age and grade in school; learning rates and language styles vary with environmental, social, and cultural conditions. Thus school standards of achievement in language are often misleading because they are "fixed" for ages and grade levels and thereby tend to magnify individual variations in language development, which, after all, occurs not in convenient divisions of time, like semesters, but in a continuum.

Evidence of growth in linguistic competence ought not to be sought in objective achievement tests, which measure knowledge of and about language, but rather in the increasing effectiveness of language usage. Effective writers and speakers, after all, are effective not because they *know* language but because they have developed the ability to *use* it well. And one learns to use language effectively not by imitating, memorizing, or mastering standard forms, but by using it oneself and seeing and learning from the effects of that use. Technical matters like spelling, punctuation, "correct" grammar, and so on, are no more the *basis* of speaking and writing now than they were before they were regularized in the interest of conventionality. The real basics of language usage are the need to communicate, the need to understand, the need to make meanings, the need to interact. Language learning is based on these needs; language education should be as well.

Conceptually, successful language learning situations provide the means whereby students may apprehend for themselves how they are using language and how they could use it more effectively. This should occur at both ends of the languaging process, as students produce language through talk and writing and receive it through reading and listening. But the mere provision of language activities will not insure apprehension, any more than the provision of fishing gear will insure a good catch. Real awareness comes from discovering or being shown the effects of language on others and, conversely, feeling its effects oneself. And since language, as we have seen, is really social behavior, language awareness is best engendered in the context of various social settings.

Strategically, the teacher's task in creating successful language learning situations is to use the relatively restricted but potentially dynamic social setting of the classroom to approximate a broad spectrum of meaningful social contexts. This does not mean just simulating situations, although that will occur occasionally, but developing a learning *community* in which all students are stimulated to extend their language competence and guided to discover their own best ways of doing so. A process of this sort is based on a larger conception of teaching than that typically represented by daily lesson plans and instructional units; it requires time, patience, and understanding as well as a tolerance for difference, both among students and between students and teacher. It requires also the ability to relate, better to integrate, long- and short-term activities: attending to the broad interplay of language production and reception while specifying particular instances of them.

CLASSROOM PROCEDURES AND SEQUENCES

Power and expressiveness in language are developmental matters. They need to be conceptualized and fostered in evolutionary rather than quantitative terms, in terms of progressive expansion rather than incremental gain. Yet many current classroom practices are limited by unduly narrow perceptions of language learning. (At the middle or junior high school level, for example, it is not uncommon for writing to be taught as a series of vertical, "building-block" relationships—clauses becoming sentences becoming paragraphs becoming essays and so on.) A fundamental change in point of view, from language product to language process, encourages the use of teaching strategies aimed at developing language abilities holistically rather than improving them bit by bit. The encouragement of continuous reading of increasing depth and variety, the use of exploratory talk, the relation of writing to talk and to the ongoing work of the class, the provision of realistic situations for using language—these are fundamental strategies for language learning at all stages of development.

As broad operations are selectively refined into specific activities, closer attention must be paid to relationships and sequences that sustain natural cognitive and linguistic growth. Thus, providing situations that call for expanded and deepened thinking (growing ability to be less egocentric and "fixed" in the present, greater capacity for explicitness and objectivity) and thus for increasing clarification and refinement of verbal expression (expanding awareness of different modes of discourse, growing sense of point of view and of audience, increasing ability to discriminate language styles) becomes the central "instructional" task of the teacher. And such manifestations of cognitive and linguistic growth—their frequency and extent—are the chief criteria for evaluating the learning process.

Classroom sequences modeled after cognitive and linguistic growth patterns tend to be longer and more reflexive than much current teaching, which is often organized in terms of the structural characteristics of subject matter and implemented within the perceived constraints of forty-five or fifty minute secondary-school class periods or the thirty minutes a day typically allocated in the elementary school. Covering material and completing assignments give way to exploring and responding to language through language. Development of competence, not mastery of detail, is sought. Greater emphasis is placed on initiating and sustaining learning experiences of increasing scope and depth and less on completing shorter, more directed tasks. And, significantly, there is recurrent examination, usually in discussion, of the learning process itself, so that students may become consciously aware of the ways in which they learn. Evaluating classroom procedures is as much a part of the learning process as language activities themselves; it is, in fact, another kind of language learning experience.

Certain developmental sequences are fundamental to sound process-oriented teaching. In the early elementary years, when psychological barriers to personal response are low, the best language learning activities are often those that focus attention, stimulate interest, and provide a springboard for children's responses to language in modes common to their stage of growth. Such a sequence might involve children *listening* to an oral presentation, such as the reading of a story, and then *responding* to it *orally* and *in play*, or *dramatic action*. They discuss the story they have heard, act it out under the teacher's direction, and then in groups make up and act out a story of their own. Such a pattern tends to encourage children to use their own language in ways that modify and expand it, and provides a suitable linguistic model from which to operate. At this age, when language is at an early stage of development, it is critical for teachers to realize that "we do not learn from the higgledy-piggledy of events as they strike the senses, but from the representation we make of them" [10] and further, that the "fundamental process by which language is used to construct a representation of reality offers by its very nature an invitation to play." [11] The fact that young children more than any other group are naturally playful users of language argues powerfully for the continuation of that activity in the classroom.

In the later elementary years, when children are reading and writing, they need to relate both abilities to their spoken language. Activities at this stage often spring from the exploratory operations of students and the talk arising from them. Reading and writing follow exploration and talk as means of shaping and ordering experience. Advances in reading and writing ability are, at the deepest level, advances in comprehending and composing, which are aspects of mental growth. Thus sequences involving, first, *concrete operations* such as caring for a classroom aquarium or pet; second, *exploratory talk* to accompany such operations; and third, *reading* and *writing* and further *talking* and *listening* about these operations are sequences that assist and extend developmental processes already at work by encouraging children to confront and invent language appropriate to a specific learning situation. At this stage of cognitive growth, which Piaget calls the phase of concrete operations and which extends from age two or three to the onset of adolescence, language works to assist the learner in understanding his world and the operations he can make upon it.

In the junior and senior high school, sequences that interweave language reception and production more pointedly, with the aim of refining various forms of verbal expression, are in order. During this period (roughly the teen years), cognitive growth occurs chiefly at the level of formal operations, in which thought becomes more ab-

10. Britton, *Language and Learning*, p. 72.

11. Ibid., p. 85.

stract and conceptual and language increasingly representational and symbolic. Thus *conscious attempts* to respond to and use language at increasingly higher levels of complexity, abstraction, and explicitness are consistent with natural maturation processes. Sequences may profitably begin with *discussion* of a topic or literary work and then continue with specific activities involving further *thinking, reading,* and *talking,* this time in small groups requiring both individual and collaborative effort. The outcome can be either a *written* or *oral* report that is shared with the whole class. The best learning environment for such a developmental sequence is a language workshop, in which students share their work with others and receive responses to it, constantly expanding and deepening their own verbal expression.

SMALL-GROUP PROCESS

The thrust of process-oriented language learning in school is toward interactive modes of learning and away from presentational ones. Talk is the chief instrument of communication in the classroom and so the most readily available medium for promoting interaction. The suppression of random talk in school in the interest of external order and control represents a confusion of educational and institutional priorities. A sounder strategy is the thoughtful organization of talk in the classroom, with natural communicative impulses being meaningfully directed, and order arising from the common purposes of interaction.

Competence in spoken language is not a matter of form (though some school programs would have it so) but of appropriate articulation of thought and meaning. It is developmental, as are other linguistic capabilities, and so is not properly a matter of study but of practice in relevant social contexts. Again, the teacher's job is to arrange for, promote, and extend a natural learning process.

Children have available much more linguistic competence than usually finds its way into their speech. We need then to create those situations which exert the greatest pressure on them to use their latent resources, to provide those experiences which urge them towards the widest range of language use.[12]

12. Connie Rosen and Harold Rosen, *The Language of Primary School Children* (London: Penguin Education, 1973), p. 64.

Such situations—those that exert the greatest pressure on students to use their language resources—arise most consistently in the purposeful conversation of a handful of learners, or what can be called small-group process.

When a small group, say four or five pupils, is involved in discussion, important processes are at play. A communication system is established that can be examined by teacher and participants alike. There is thus the opportunity to experience its effects firsthand and understand how one's own verbal behavior contributes to it—all without the dubious benefit of a communications "lesson." Furthermore, external social forces are brought to bear on personal cognitive and linguistic resources, with the result that the language and thought of individuals are challenged to meet the collective demands of the group. And if the participants become deeply and personally involved in the discussion, it is likely that the structural complexity of their verbal expression will deepen.[13] At its best, small-group process is a method of exerting pedagogical influence by "open[ing] up the whole range of external, social operations that will lead to internal, cognitive operations." [14]

Group discussion capitalizes on the powerful learning force inherent in verbal interchange, in the convergence of language, experience, and thought that occurs in any meaningful conversation. School talk—class discussion, recitation, teacher-student dialogue—is often organized around subject content and directed toward external, prescribed ends. The *relatively* unstructured mode of group discussion taps deeper, internal forces and is considerably more complex and organized than its deceptively simple and random appearance suggests.

Much more goes on here than appears on the surface, for even the most meagre telling of what has happened demands that some kind of transformation must be imposed on experience. Life does not exist as a vast anthology of unedited narratives. We impose narrative on it; we pluck the tale out of the whirl of experience, and with words marshall it into narrative line and make it something whole and ordered.[15]

13. Ibid., p. 259. Rosen and Rosen attribute this conclusion to Courtney Cazden.

14. Moffett, *Teaching the Universe of Discourse*, p. 93.

15. Rosen and Rosen, *The Language of Primary School Children*, p. 57.

If language and experience are inseparable, as many scholars contend, their growth is interrelated. Experience is made meaningful through linguistic representation as language is made to represent and order an ever-enlarging corpus of experience.

Group discussion affects thought by providing alternatives to individual conceptions and outlooks. In verbal exchange one confronts points of view different from one's own, and one measures personal apprehension and understanding against others'. Or, as one writer puts it, discussion in a group does for thinking what testing on real objects does for seeing:

We become aware of discrepancies between different people's interpretations of the same stimulus and are driven to weigh evidence in favor of alternative interpretations. Certain areas of one's private world are compared and contrasted with other people's, and in seeing differences between them it becomes possible to modify our own world if we wish to. Instead of seeing our own mistakes by contrast with the statements of an unquestioned authority as in the traditional pupil-teacher relationship, we see a variety of interpretations of the same stimulus pattern, and the usefulness of each must be tested in its own right.[16]

The key to implementing group discussion successfully in any class is finding a real motive for talk. Real motivation for talking, as for any human activity, is to be found within people, not within activities themselves or in external forces. Motive implies an emotion or desire operating on the will and causing it to act. The task of the teacher, therefore, is to enlist the emotions and desires of pupils in the support of discussion, not to induce or entice them to talk. Thus, a typical strategy such as assigning an "interesting" topic will succeed only to the extent that something of personal significance is perceived in it. A far more authentically motivating procedure is to pose issues of critical importance for young people in the form of problems for discussion.

At all school levels, significant issues arise most often out of personal experience. For elementary and intermediate school children, discussion at a literal level of various kinds of experiences is natural: vacation trips, hobbies, family life, books, records, films, school, work, play, dreams, and fantasies. For secondary students the same

16. M. L. Abercrombie, *Anatomy of Judgment* (London: Penguin, 1969), p. 62.

is true, but talk based on personal experience tends to evolve more readily into explicit consideration of ideas, concepts, and the *meaning* of experience, that is, into abstractions. Discussion of role-definition and social conduct as well as matters of moral principle is likely: how individuals should respond to peer pressure, why young people must attend school, the effect of authority on individual rights, and so on. Such differences in the levels of abstraction in discussion reflect, of course, different developmental stages in the language learning process.

Teachers need to monitor group process and contribute actively to students' developing conversational abilities. This entails participating in discussions and using discriminative techniques of dialogue —clarifying issues, establishing meanings, probing, relating, extending, summarizing—that can subsequently become part of students' own cognitive and linguistic repertoires. As proficiency in discussion increases, so does the power of the participants to teach each other. By the junior high school years, small group process can be broadened to include "public" forms like panel discussions, in which the presence of an audience urges the language of conversation to grow in formality, complexity, and explicitness. In general, the theory behind group discussion is that "people incorporate into themselves the ideas and arguments they hear, and that their future thinking, even when they are alone, reflects the external dialogues they have internalized." [17] Accordingly, the increasing ability to internalize and subsequently to use new language patterns marks real growth in intellectual development and linguistic power.

DRAMA

Talk and small-group process are central activities in process-oriented language education and give rise to a variety of related learning modes, including drama.[18] It would not in fact be inaccurate

17. James Moffett, *A Student-centered Language Arts Curriculum, Grades K-13: A Handbook for Teachers* (Boston: Houghton Mifflin Co., 1968), p. 292.

18. Conceptually, drama subsumes speech, as Moffett says, and therefore might be expected to precede rather than follow it in educational sequences. Such a pattern is theoretically sound in terms of logic; drama is a larger and more basic construct than language and need not even involve vocal sound, as mime, for example, does not. But pedogogically, talk is both more powerful and more efficient than "raw phenomena" for focusing and directing classroom activities and is, in this sense, the primal medium of education.

to describe process-oriented teaching itself as *dramatic pedagogy*, since its aim is to promote learning through natural action. The use of drama in the classroom is really a conscious effort to magnify elements of everyday life in ways that enable people to understand it—and themselves—better. It is in this sense that one of its major proponents defines drama as "practicing living," and suggests that the same definition hold for education as well;[19] and that, for another practitioner, drama—"what is happening"—is the most immediate, concrete mode of human discourse.[20]

Educational drama—the conscious use of action as an instrument for learning—is significantly different both from theater and from oral reading of dramatic literature. Theater is an art form that endeavors to communicate through the creation of stylized illusion. It requires people of special sophistication and talent to convey meaning through the symbolic world of the stage. Reading dramatic literature aloud or silently is a form of language reception; it is passive rather than active, involving none of the extensive physical movement of drama. Such distinctions underscore the disparate and often conflicting uses of drama—both the activity and the term—in American schools. In planning learning activities, teachers would do well to remember that theater means performing, reading means reading, and drama means doing, and go on from there.

Drama is experiential, a matter of direct participation in real events; it is the primary mode of human conduct. It is both a form of interaction and a means of expression and thus is readily adaptable as a strategy for promoting learning.

The essential components of dramatic action are bodily movement and vocal expression, natural functions of life in and outside the classroom. When a teacher initiates a specific dramatic activity, however, a transformation occurs: some bit of action is extracted, as it were, from the ongoing flow of experience; it is consciously practiced; and it assumes, at least tentatively, a symbolic quality. That is, the action seems to take on meaning beyond the situation in which it occurs. People "discover how to organise the material of their own experience into a model—or image—which will have

19. Brian Way, *Development through Drama* (New York: Humanities Press, 1967), p. 6.

20. Moffett, *Teaching the Universe of Discourse*, p. 47.

validity in organising diverse and distant experiences." [21] This is essentially the same process by which young children use play to test, order, and assimilate their phenomenal and social worlds. Drama is, in fact, a form of play, executed along a spectrum stretching from practicality at one end to art at the other.

The chief forms of dramatic activity are free movement, mime, improvisation, and enactment. Movement and mime are nonverbal action, while improvisation and enactment involve speech and movement in natural, integrated ways. From these fundamental forms derive a number of related activities: charades, role-playing, simulations, games, and various kinds of interpretive work with dramatic scripts.

At the elementary level, the purposes of drama involve promoting personal and social growth through developing and sharpening language skills, fostering creative expression, broadening children's vocal and experiential repertoires, and initiating engagement with literature. Appropriate content for dramatic work is drawn from myth, fairy stories, children's books and television programs, and from personal experiences. [22]

Dramatic activities for primary children arise out of their natural inclination toward physical action and play, the chief form of learning in early childhood. Movement precedes speech in human development, and although the two realms "blend without a seam" and complement each other, the school's predilection for verbal behavior shunts nonverbal modes of expression unnaturally into the background and needs to be offset by deliberate classroom action.

Too often schools attempt to make speech abruptly supplant these [nonverbal] modes, forcing the child off native ground onto strange territory. The fact is that . . . nonverbal expression can provide the best pathway to speech development. The sheer socialization of school helps to promote speech—or can, if the activities permit socializing. The teacher can insure that speech grows out of physical play and bodily movement by extending nonverbal expression into the verbal. More concretely, the teacher orchestrates play with objects, movement to sound, and pantomime into full-blown improvisation, which . . . will be a major method of learning to use language. [23]

21. Douglas Barnes, ed., *Drama in the English Classroom* (Champaign, Ill.: National Council of Teachers of English, 1968), p. 8.

22. Ibid., p. 59.

23. Moffett, *A Student-centered Language Arts Curriculum*, p. 41.

With older students, who tend to be more self-conscious, dramatic activities emerge more readily from talk than from play. Such activities will be mostly improvisational, and ideas for them will come from discussion of issues that can be situationally explored through dramatization. A class, for example, may be discussing vacation trips and come to focus on the difficulties of modern travel. A story is told, and a situation develops from it: a plane is an hour late for departure, and the passengers are forced to remain in the terminal. What do they do? The teacher suggests that the students put themselves imaginatively into the situation (a time perhaps for some brief concentration exercises) and improvise the whole scene. From time to time a new element is injected into the situation—an announcement concerning the flight or an incident in the terminal. Finally the scene is played out, and the class is free to discuss it (from the standpoint of active participants), reenact it in light of the discussion, or write the script for a related scene or story; the possibilities are varied and numerous.

Ideas for improvisation, or "minimal situations,"[24] can also come from sources other than class discussion. Many works of literature —typically poems and short stories—lend themselves to dramatic exploration and interpretation. Here the teacher can reverse the sequence and introduce the reading of a literary work by having students improvise a situation taken from it. (This procedure has the advantage—as does all well-conceived dramatic teaching strategy—of beginning a learning sequence with the personal experiences of students rather than with an object of potential interest, like a book.) And, of course, ideas can be suggested by students themselves as a result of experience, real or imagined.

Drama work in the intermediate and secondary schools can introduce audiences and scripts, two factors seldom stressed in the primary grades. Their use moves drama closer to its formal, public modes, the full realization of which is theater. But play production and performance are not the goals of classroom drama; rather, play before an audience and work with scripts are refinements of dramatic action and follow developmentally from free improvisation.

Classes themselves are the best audiences. Doubling as dramatic participants and spectators, students experience and contribute to

24. Ibid., p. 289.

an integrated process in which they learn from and help teach others. Other, more distant audiences (for example, other classes) can be used when desired but are not necessary for developmental progression.

Scripts are matters for interpretation and re-creation, not oral reading. Scripts can help students advance their intuitive under-standing of dramatic situations by forcing them to improvise from tighter, more structured formats. Instead of the unfettered dialogue of everyday life and of improvisation, there is an established pattern of discourse that must be taken from the printed page and recast in action. Doing so involves a process common to all three but in need of special classroom treatment.

In everyday living, awareness of the verbal and nonverbal context allows us to choose intuitively the patterns of intonation, emphasis, and gesture by which we convey meaning; similarly in improvised drama we make these choices intuitively. When faced with a script, however, the child is likely to "read" it, that is, make relatively neutral choices which demonstrate his uncertainty of the role and of the situation which gives it meaning. This is not a mere technical failure, but a failure to imagine himself inside the dramatic situation, *a failure to recreate it as a work of literature.* What the teacher must do, therefore, is to set up a situation in which the pupils' insight into the nature of the dramatic situation enables them to make intuitively the appropriate choices of voice and movement. This is exactly analogous to the provision of a context of talk for a poem or a prose work. The required insight will arise from classroom talk and improvisation about a situation related to that of the scene to be acted: once the class has begun to act out the situation in an inward way—once it has become a joint symbol for them —it is possible for the teacher to introduce the scripts so that existing insight will enable the pupils to recreate the printed words intuitively.[25]

Developmental sequences in drama are similar in both extended and short-term applications. The basic movements are nonverbal to verbal to integrated expression; free play to situational dialogue and action; and improvisation to re-creation of scripted drama. Like the maturation process itself, dramatic activity develops in a natural progression from self-awareness to successively larger and more complex social orientations—from private to shared experience.

Ultimately, drama stimulates total human development. Growth in linguistic competence is closely allied to growth in thought and

25. Barnes, *Drama in the English Classroom,* p. 59.

personality, and all require social contexts to be actualized. Dramatic pedagogy is the educational counterpart of broad life experience, providing in school a variform learning environment that transcends the social backgrounds of many students. Indeed, "for those [students] who are deprived of a wide range of social experience, dramatic re-creation of realistic situations may be an important way of developing control of a range of registers."[26] A similar condition holds for socially advantaged students, who need alternatives to the language of home and neighborhood. Ultimately, the effects of educational drama must be drawn to larger scale than sheer linguistic competence allows; ultimately, the "consistent intention of all . . . drama work [is] that of helping the natural, organic development of each individual, exploring, discovering and mastering his own resources, and attaining a sensitive, confident relationship with his environment."[27]

RESPONDING TO LITERATURE

Responding is central to interactive learning and process-oriented education. Response to literature is a complex, subjective phenomenon grounded in internal configurations of meaning. It begins in the transaction of literary work and reader. Before it is anything else, it is felt experience: one "enjoys" the work or does not—possibly to the extent that one comprehends it. In a sense, a poem, a short story, or a novel is a "voice" speaking to us and engaging our attention and interest more or less as we derive meaning from it. Subsequently, if our interest has been held, the impact of the work reverberates in us and causes some inner reorganization in our feelings, attitudes, and dispositions. *Formulating* our response involves describing this impact and expressing it to others.

Responses to literary works are unique to individual readers, and are "conditioned by the dynamic interplay of a constellation of factors rather than by single causes."[28] Perhaps more than any other, this principle ought to underlie the teaching of literature.

---

26. Ibid., p. 18.

27. Way, *Development through Drama*, p. 268.

28. James R. Squire, *The Responses of Adolescents While Reading Four Short Stories* (Champaign, Ill.: National Council of Teachers of English, 1964), p. 51.

Attempts to prescribe or condition literary response deny the very foundation and value of literary experience—the unalloyed transaction between the unique individual reader and the unique literary work. In the broadest sense,

the teacher is seen as one who directs, or at least leads a process by which students achieve, within the limits set by their different abilities and funded experience, feeling comprehensions of various works of literary art. This process should be seen as a continuing one (only part of which can occur in the classroom). . . . Response is a word that reminds the teacher that the experience of art is a thing of our making, an activity in which we are our own interpretive artist.[29]

Classroom work with literature needs to be an integral part of the language learning process. Children at all stages of personal development need easy access to a wide variety of reading material, frequent and continuing opportunities to read, and encouragement to increase their capacities for literary response.

In the primary years, children need immediate experiences with literature—experiences that are satisfying to them and so lay the groundwork for deeper, more discriminating responses in later years. The main thrust of elementary work in literature is toward personal enjoyment of literary experience and the expression of that experience through talking, acting out, drawing, painting, writing, and the like—modes appropriate to the "concrete operations" stage of cognitive growth. Independent reading will be widely supplemented by group sharing of literature through oral readings by the teacher and by the use of records, tapes, films, filmstrips, and other media. The literature of the classroom will include stories, poems, and accounts created by the children themselves as well as standard literary sources.

Intermediate-level and secondary-school work in literature should nurture personal response and assist its formulation as well. In general, this means that closer reading of some literary works will occur as well as more talking and writing about literature. It does not mean that reading and writing will necessarily become more analytical, an unhappy yet altogether too common condition in which a work of literature becomes a kind of intellectual puzzle

29. James R. Squire, ed., *Response to Literature* (Champaign, Ill.: National Council of Teachers of English, 1968), pp. 24, 26.

to be solved according to precepts of judgment established in realms distant from personal experience and life in the classroom. Nor does it mean emphasizing the study of the structural and rhetorical elements of literature, an act that enhances neither appreciation nor understanding. Rather, teaching literature should be geared to helping students make sense of what they read in personal terms—whether impressionistic or analytic—and formulate that sense in intelligible ways. In literature as in every phase of the language education process, successful teaching depends on the primary consideration of individual people and the ways in which they *do*, in fact, respond.

The possibilities for both critics and teachers to change a reader's pattern of responses are quite limited. Much the greater part of response depends on the reader's own character. . . . One's whole ability to become engrossed, for example, depends on the capacity to regress and be passively receptive; one of the deepest of human traits, no pedagogy can touch it. . . . What a teacher may be able to do is get his student to accept more complex or exotic works within his established pattern of preferences. It seems very doubtful that he can change a characterological preference for one kind . . . over another. Ultimately . . . response depends on us, not our critics or teachers.[30]

One authoritative study of response to literature has clarified the process by identifying four categories of response: engagement-involvement, perception, interpretation, and evaluation.[31] The authors suggest these modes are latent in all students and occur at whatever level of sophistication is appropriate to an individual's sensibility. No one mode of response is itself more significant than any other. Educational progress is marked by the deepening of response and by the power of its verbal expression.

The value of any one order lies primarily in the way in which it is presented, in the accuracy of the perception, in the cogency of the interpretation, in the persuasiveness of the evaluative position, in the intensity of the testament of engagement.[32]

30. Norman Holland, *The Dynamics of Literary Response* (New York: Oxford University Press, 1968), p. 332.

31. Alan C. Purves with Virginia Rippere, *Elements of Writing about a Literary Work: A Study of Response to Literature* (Champaign, Ill.: National Council of Teachers of English, 1968).

32. Ibid., p. 59.

The central aim of the teacher, then, is to foster reading and responding to literature and to stimulate the expression of personal
response in increasingly powerful ways.

Literary preferences, to the extent they are shaped in school,
develop best from broad experience with various kinds of literature,
classical and popular. The intent is not to train literary taste, but
to provide the means for personal apprehension and discrimination
of literary quality. Response to popular literature is, after all, no
less valid than response to classical literature, and juxtaposing the
two may bring a firsthand realization of their differences. In any
case, the choice of reading material is secondary in importance to
the transaction between book and reader.

Ultimately, response to literature is subjective and is shaped by
both emotion and intellect.[33] To teach literature in ways that deny
this confluence is to misconceive the nature of literary response,
and of the teaching task. For teachers the best conception of the
connective interplay between literature and its audience is one
which recognizes that "the essence of a symbolic work is not in
its visible sensory structure or in its manifest semantic load but in
its subjective re-creation by a reader and in his public presentation
of that re-creation."[34]

WRITING

The schools' typically fruitless attempts to teach writing are
regrettable but hardly surprising in view of the singularly rigid,
narrow, and unrealistic approaches traditionally taken in them.
One recent study of the composing processes of high school seniors
makes this statement about the influence of composition teachers on
their students' writing:

The first teachers of composition—by giving certain descriptions of
the composing process and by evaluating the products of student writ-

33. Recent psychological research has lent greater weight to the contention that human consciousness is organized in two major modes—one analytic,
rational, and verbal, and the other holistic, intuitive, and mystic—each of
which is "controlled" by one side of the brain. See, for example, Robert
Ornstein, *The Psychology of Consciousness* (New York: Viking Press, 1973).

34. David Bleich, *Readings and Feelings: An Introduction to Subjective
Criticism* (Urbana, Ill.: National Council of Teachers of English, 1975), p. 21.

ing by highly selective criteria—set rigid parameters to students' writing behaviors in school-sponsored writing that the students find difficult to make more supple.

These descriptions of the composing process differ markedly from descriptions by established writers and with the students' own accounts, conceptualizations, and practices. Students' awareness of these discrepancies leads to certain behaviors and attitudes: outward conformity but inward cynicism and hostility.[35]

The failure to teach effective writing is often a result of the failure to relate verbal expression to its deeper roots in feeling and thought. Rigid compositional demands often inhibit the internal processes—perceiving, experiencing, feeling, thinking—that naturally precede verbal expression. The representation of personal reality occurs first at the level of intuition and internal formulation and then at successively higher levels of organized verbalization, from ordinary speech and writing to expressions approaching the quality of verbal art. The *act* of writing is really one step in a process of elaboration and refinement of verbal expression rather than a specialized, discrete verbal activity. The best approaches to teaching writing are predicated on the relation of written expression to mental activity and to speech.

Language as it is actually used is a better guide for teaching writing than is "standard usage," which leads almost inevitably—as most current school practice amply demonstrates—to an unduly narrow concern for form and structure, prefiguring the degeneration of the writing process into a series of linguistic do's and don't's. Teaching from an experiential language base preconceives nothing except development of linguistic competence, of which form and structure are but elements. And linguistic competence, as we have seen, is more than the ability to manipulate language; it is an integral part of reality-processing, meaning-making, and self-actualization—of human development. In the same way, teaching linguistic competence in writing goes beyond—rather beneath—mere verbal behavior to tap the primal, preverbal sources of expression—imagination and perception, intuition and feeling, and thought. This is one of the main reasons for the recent (and welcome) advocacy of free

35. Janet Emig, *The Composing Processes of Twelfth Graders* (Champaign, Ill.: National Council of Teachers of English, 1971), p. 93.

writing activities in the classroom.[36]

Teaching based on a broad conception of language usage avoids the pitfalls of teaching based on a limited (and limiting) view of language outcomes and forms. Thus it avoids unwarranted categorizations of writing (such as the infelicitous distinction between "practical" and "creative"), seeking instead to quicken the internal processes that sustain written expression. As in drama, a good writing assignment gives writers the chance to organize and express some of their experience so that they may understand it and themselves better—to make discoveries for themselves about themselves. Growth in written expression, like oral language growth, is a matter of developing appropriate linguistic means to express thoughts and feelings explicitly. And developing appropriate linguistic means of expression, as herein maintained, is a matter of using and responding to language, not merely mastering its standard forms.

Early work in writing needs to capitalize on the playful, metaphoric quality of children's language and should stress storytelling, jokes and riddles, games and puzzles, writing song lyrics, picture captions, diaries, and poetry, as well as describing sensory experiences, observing, recording, and explaining objects and events, giving directions and instructions, transcribing speech, and writing letters. Personal experience, together with its representation in language, is the unifying element in the learning process.

When children . . . are not only concerned with the world out there but also their felt responses, then writing can in the first place seem worthwhile to them and in the second place serve a continuing function for them. . . . For writing permits them at one and the same time to record their observations and their "results," and also to work out in the very process of expressing themselves the uniqueness of the event. . . . It is only in the careful telling that it can be elaborated into this unique event. The re-excitement made possible by the fully formulated expression of the experience raises the value of it, makes it a more durable possession and in the end makes returning to such experience and such exploratory encounters with the world seem the more inviting.[37]

36. See, for example, Ken Macrorie, *Uptaught* (New York: Hayden Book Co., 1970), and Peter Elbow, *Writing without Teachers* (New York: Oxford University Press, 1973). The latter describes the organic, developmental process of writing especially well.

37. Rosen and Rosen, *The Language of Primary School Children*, p. 135.

Continuing work in the junior and senior high school should extend the increasing ability for abstracting, distancing, generalizing, and theorizing. A good deal of revision by expansion will occur—writing based on or proceeding from other writing. More formal kinds of poetry need to be included, as do diaries and autobiographical journals, dramatic scripts, and stories; and writing assignments need to be broadened and lengthened to involve summaries and reports, accounts of investigative actions (exploratory research rather than reference work), and statements of theory. Questions of audience, point of view, and speaking voice take on increasing significance as the teacher seeks to make students more conscious of their own verbal power. Student writing is often aimed, in practice as well as in theory, at audiences outside the classroom and is sometimes "published" in class and group magazines, newspapers, reports, and bulletins.

The recent work of some linguistic researchers—Bateman and Zidonis, Mellon, Hunt, and O'Hare, among others—has strengthened the case for transformational sentence-combining as a means of promoting syntactic versatility in writing. But the effect of such nonrhetorical and specially structured writing activities argues neither for a new brand of grammar instruction in the classroom nor for more than supplementary use in language learning programs. (Embedding and sentence-combining occur in the course of revising real discourse anyway.) As Mellon's study concludes, reading, writing, and discussing must necessarily remain the staple activities of the English class.[38]

Beyond sentence-combining and embedding exercises, the field of linguistics has contributed to a new concern for the relation between cognitive processes and verbal expression. There are recurrent signs in professional literature of the growing recognition that thought and verbalization are stages of a single process and that talk and writing should not be conceived apart from internal operations of cognition and emotion. In the classroom this recognition is reflected to some extent in teaching strategies that stress cognitive stimulation through inquiry and discussion as a prelude

38. John Mellon, *Transformational Sentence-combining: A Method of Enhancing the Development of Syntactic Fluency in English Composition* (Champaign, Ill.: National Council of Teachers of English, 1969).

to writing. The teacher's job here involves helping students to conceptualize and order their writing, a considerably more profound enterprise than merely assigning papers.

At its root, the teaching of written composition serves both personal and social ends. All languaging activities are ultimately affirmations of selfhood and humanness—from the first imitative babblings of an infant to the highest symbolic creations of the literary artist. Our attempts to extend and refine language learning in school should be colored by this recognition.

CHAPTER III

Language Competencies Essential for Coping in Our Society

WALTER T. PETTY, DOROTHY C. PETTY, ANABEL P. NEWMAN,
ELOISE M. SKEEN*

Introduction

The curriculum in English at any schooling level is difficult to describe. In every setting it is based on the interactions of various elements of knowledge and information, numerous ideas and practices, and the personal involvement and personalities of teachers, publishers and test makers, administrators, parents, and students. What happens at a given time in any classroom depends on the interaction of these factors, an interaction that reflects the ascendancy or descendancy in importance at that time of any one or of several of these. Thus, there frequently is a lack of a continuing focus, a fact that too often results in the neglect of the heart of the English curriculum: the development of competency in each individual to use language to meet his or her communication needs.

Just what language abilities does an individual need? Are there different levels of language competency an individual needs for various tasks and at different stages of maturity? Are the competencies needed by the elementary school child different from those of the high school student? Most importantly, what are the competencies needed by the individual who is no longer a student in the school-attending sense? Can these competencies be described? Are some more essential than others? A former Oregon state superintendent put the issue bluntly and in context with these questions: "What competencies are required for America's young people to survive during the last quarter of this century? What survival skills

* The consultant reader for this chapter was Kenneth Johnson, Professor of Education, University of California, Berkeley.

are needed to cope successfully with life as a citizen, wage earner, consumer, and learner?"[1]

The purpose of this chapter is to respond to these questions, to attempt to list and define the language competencies essential for coping in our society. Of necessity, these are broadly stated, since they must encompass the needs of both children and adults in a wide range of societal and economic settings and with a wide range of individual needs and abilities. It is hoped that they will serve as bases for further examination of programs and objectives, and possibly as criteria against which both teaching decisions and student achievement may be measured. It is the task of the reader to make thoughtful application of the statement of competencies to the specific needs of a given set of learners.

A Historical Glimpse

Concern about what the schools will be teaching, about whether students are attaining the competencies considered essential, has long been with us. In his 1873 report to the Quincy (Massachusetts) school board, Francis W. Parker expressed concern about what students could and could not do:

The pupils could parse and construe sentences and point out the various parts of speech with great facility, repeating the rules of grammar in each case, yet were utterly unable to put this theoretical knowledge to any practical use, as they showed when called upon to write an ordinary English letter.[2]

While Parker suggested only one instance of the need to teach for practical application—although he possibly implied others— there were later attempts to respond more specifically to the identification of essential competencies. For instance, in 1926 the Committee on the Place and Function of English in American Life expressed a point of view about what is essential:

The schools might well devote more attention to a number of the language activities which according to the returns [of a survey] are widely used by persons of the many callings and social groups report-

1. Dale Parnell, "The Oregon Walkabout," *Phi Delta Kappan* 56 (November 1974): 205.

2. Francis W. Parker, *Talks on Pedagogies* (New York: E. L. Kellogg, 1894).

ing, and which are reported as giving much difficulty. These activities in particular are: Interviews: word of mouth inquiries; reports to a superior; instructions for subordinates; conferences. Conversation: with casual acquaintances; at social gatherings; over the telephone. Public Speaking: informal discussion; preparing addresses. Writing: informal notes and memos for one's self; formal notes of invitation, introduction, etc. Reading: legal documents. Listening: to an interview, a conference, or a public meeting.[3]

While the citizen of the 1920s—and likely most of us today— would agree with the committee that people converse, write notes, and read legal documents, there would be less agreement about the importance of being able to instruct subordinates, prepare addresses, or write social notes. Yet, as is discussed later, specific behaviors or manifestations of essential competencies may differ according to individual needs, levels of maturity, or variations in setting. For example, each person needs at some time to give directions, whether to someone for getting to a particular destination, to a child for accomplishing a given task, or to a subordinate for performing a specific job. In other words, this ability to instruct subordinates is a manifestation of an essential competency.

The Failure to Develop Essential Confidence

In recent years, opinion has continued to be voiced about the failure of many persons to learn essential skills and abilities. Moreover, this opinion is beginning to be substantiated by an accumulation of evidence gathered by both governmental agencies and private organizations. Some of this evidence is based on the extent of illiteracy reported in census data. For example, a report of 1969 data states that 1.5 million persons born before 1955 are illiterate.[4] For the purposes of this report, an illiterate person was defined as one who is unable to read and write in any language, and who has completed no more than six years of schooling. However, one might ask, "What does it mean to say that a person is 'able to

3. John Mantle Clapp, ed., *The Place of English in American Life*, Report of an Investigation by a Committee of the National Council of Teachers of English (Chicago, Ill.: National Council of Teachers of English, 1926), p. 46.

4. Bureau of the Census, U.S. Department of Commerce, *Statistical Abstract of the United States, 1974* (Washington, D.C.: U.S. Government Printing Office, 1974), p. 115.

read'?"[5]

Literacy is not something that is either present or absent. Ability to read and ability to write are possessed in varying degrees or at varying levels by nearly everyone—including, one suspects, those reported in census data as being unable to read or write in any language.

"Illiteracy" does not necessarily mean the complete absence of ability to read, and "literacy" covers a wide spectrum of capabilities—all the way from, say, being able to decipher a want ad in a newspaper to being able to enjoy a novel by Thomas Mann or read a scientific treatise with understanding.[6]

The issue, however, is not to limit the definition of literacy but to recognize "that something is amiss in literacy training—that large numbers of people probably never reach a level of reading ability sufficient to cope with even the common reading tasks confronting them daily."[7] To this we would add that many people also cannot adequately cope with other communication tasks they are faced with in the real world, including those involving nonprint media (see chapter 4).

Perhaps more meaningful are the data supplied by the U.S. Department of Health, Education, and Welfare, which indicate that approximately one million teenagers cannot read at the beginning fourth-grade level. This figure is based on evidence from reading tests given between 1966 and 1970 to a sampling of 6,768 youths between the ages of twelve and seventeen. Of this group, 4.8 percent could not read at the prescribed level, a percentage which, projected nationwide, gives the one million figure and suggests that an alarming number of young people of these ages—in school and out—cannot read most of the material that they meet in newspapers, job application forms, and directions for performing various tasks.[8]

5. John B. Carroll and Jeanne S. Chall, *Toward a Literate Society*, Report of the Committee on Reading of the National Academy of Education (New York: McGraw-Hill Book Co., 1975), p. 6.

6. Ibid.

7. John R. Bormuth, "Reading Literacy: Its Definition and Assessment," in Carroll and Chall, *Toward a Literate Society*, p. 64.

8. *Literacy among Youth 12-17 Years* (Washington, D.C.: U.S. Government Printing Office, 1973).

It should surprise no one that illiteracy was found to be most prevalent among boys, especially blacks from low-income families. Further, the relationship of illiteracy to both race and income level is marked. Among black males the illiteracy was 20.5 percent. In families with less than $3000 annual income, 9.8 percent of white and 22.1 percent of black youths were found to be illiterate by this measure. Of course, one might question the adequacy of the tests, whether some youths simply rejected them, the influence of chance scores, and the like, but the fact remains that a large number of young people appear to be functionally illiterate.

In the early years of the present decade, as a part of the U.S. Office of Education's Targeted Research and Development Program on Reading, the Educational Testing Service investigated the reading activities engaged in by over 5000 adults. The sample of adults was selected by a stratification procedure that took into account geographic regions, sizes of communities, and types of housing units. The intent was to choose a representative sample of United States households and to interview the adult residents of these households. Following the interviews and the determination of what people said they read and for what purposes, tests were developed dealing with 269 reading tasks. These tasks included reading traffic signs, product instructions, recipes, correspondence, legal forms, periodicals, newspapers, and advertisements. The next step was to administer these tests to various adults. One administration was to adults in various group settings, such as learning centers and manpower training centers, a correctional institution, a community college, and a senior citizen center. The tests were also attempted by adults in individual settings, approximately 750 persons attempting each task.

Such tasks as reading signs and advertisements were most frequently accomplished correctly, while a tuberculin test card was read correctly by only 52 percent of the adults tested individually and 37 percent of those in the group testing centers. The percentages for other reading tasks, given respectively for the individual and center testing, include: election ballot, 74 percent and 15 percent; information on recreation areas, 32 percent and 33 percent; school report card, 37 percent and 40 percent; traffic ticket, 44 percent and 17 percent; employment benefits, 35 percent and

27 percent; and postal insurance information, 45 percent and 23 percent.[9]

Another attempt to determine the language competencies of American citizens was a study made by Louis Harris and Associates for the National Reading Council. This study sought to measure what was labeled a "survival" literacy rate by assessing people's ability to fill out application forms for such things as a social security number, a personal bank loan, public assistance, Medicaid, and a driver's license. The results of the survey indicated "that the extent of functional illiteracy in the nation is much greater than had been previously suspected."[10] For example, it was found that 34 percent of those surveyed could not complete a Medicaid application and 8 percent could not adequately complete a driver's license application. The study also found that "many U.S. Government public forms were too difficult for 18.5 million American adults."[11]

Similar in overall findings, although more complex in its definition of functional literacy as the ability to apply skills to several major knowledge areas important to adult success, is the Adult Performance Level study (APL) conducted from 1971 to 1975 at the University of Texas. APL research reported a greater proportion of adult Americans unable to perform basic skills in computation areas than in writing, but even so found that "16 percent of the adults in the United States, or some 18.9 million persons, are unable to cope successfully" on tasks requiring writing skills.[12]

A continuing effort to determine competence in a number of learning areas is that undertaken by the National Assessment of

9. Richard T. Murphy, *Adult Functional Reading Study*, Final Report, Project No. 0-9004, Grant No. OEC-0-70-4791-508 (Washington, D.C.: U.S. Department of Health, Education, and Welfare; National Institute of Education, December 1973).

10. Amiel T. Sharon, "What Do Adults Read?" *Reading Research Quarterly* 9, no. 2 (1973-1974): 152.

11. Thomas G. Sticht, ed., *Reading for Working: A Functional Literacy Anthology* (Washington, D.C.: Human Resources Research Organization, 1975), p. 184.

12. From a statement of Adult Performance Level study results released by Terrel H. Bell, U.S. Commissioner of Education, October 22, 1975. See also *Adult Functional Competence: A Summary* (Austin, Tex.: University of Texas, March 1975).

Educational Progress, a project of the Education Commission of the States. The Assessment program will periodically report on the knowledge, skills, concepts, understandings, and attitudes possessed by selected American subpopulations. The subpopulations that formed the basis for the first reports were students of ages nine, thirteen, and seventeen and adults between the ages of twenty-six and thirty-five. Findings included the following:

1. Relatively few young Americans could read and interpret graphs, maps, or tables.
2. Less than half of the nation's seventeen-year-olds and young adults could accurately read all parts of a ballot.
3. Only 14 percent of the adults could write letters with no punctuation errors.
4. Only 57 percent of the adults wrote adequate directions for making or doing something.
5. Only 49 percent of the adults composed acceptable letters for the purpose of ordering a product.[13]

As these data are further analyzed, and as further data are collected and studied by the Assessment, we should have additional evidence of what those who have experienced or are experiencing American schooling can do. Though critics of the assessment procedure may speculate about what the individuals tested know that the tests do not measure, a fair-minded interpretation of the data surely should give teachers of English (as well as those in other areas) reason to be concerned about what they have been teaching.

In another vein, the open admissions policies adopted by many colleges and universities in the late 1960s and early 1970s have provided evidence of the failure of many graduates of secondary schools to cope satisfactorily with the language skills needed for successful college work. A corollary to this is that publishers assert that the language in college textbooks has been simplified to adjust for students who cannot read material written at the traditional level. In fact, a pamphlet, "How to Get the Most Out of Your Textbooks," which is distributed by the Association of American

13. J. Stanley Ahmann, "A Report on National Assessment in Seven Learning Areas," *Today's Education* 64 (January-February 1975): 63-64; Sticht, *Reading for Working*, p. 184.

Publishers and is intended for college freshmen, has been revised downward in its readability level.[14] However, open admissions students are not the only ones who are deficient in needed skills. For example, the *Wall Street Journal* reported in 1974 that one-third of the applicants to the School of Journalism at the University of Wisconsin could not meet the minimum requirements in spelling, grammar, word usage, and punctuation, and that at the University of North Carolina, 47 percent of the journalism applicants, mostly at the junior level in college, failed a simple high school level spelling and word usage test.[15] And one might hypothesize that students interested in pursuing a career in journalism could be expected, on the average, to have greater competence in using language than the overall student population.

While the level of writing ability held to be desirable for students in college is not that of "survival" or minimal competence, there is increasing evidence that larger numbers of college freshmen are being required to enroll in remedial English courses. In fact, it is not at all uncommon to find college and university faculty stating that "students are coming from high school with a far less firm grasp on fundamentals than before—middle-class as well as disadvantaged students."[16]

Expressions of Concern

Concurrent with the mounting evidence that too many children and adults have not achieved the language competencies required to cope successfully with life needs has been a growing movement toward accountability. Both educators and the general public are concerned about whether the schools—and other institutions for which they are paying their tax dollars—are doing what they believe should be done. A considerable amount of this concern—though not all—is voiced by minority-group parents who are particularly upset with the failure of many schools to teach their chil-

14. *New York Times*, 10 November 1974.

15. "Publishers Simplify Texts for College Students Who Can't Read," *Phi Delta Kappan* 46 (February 1975): 439.

16. " 'Functional Illiteracy' Rate Is Rising among All Classes," *The Spectrum* (State University of New York at Buffalo), 12 February 1975.

dren the language skills needed for effective reading, writing, and speaking.[17]

This increasing concern has led to demands that schools and individual teachers be held responsible for seeing that students learn the skills and abilities needed for coping with the challenges of life and to the institution of special and broad-scaled efforts directed at helping students to learn those skills and abilities. Perhaps the best known of these are the Great Cities Improvement Program, the Title I Programs of the Elementary and Secondary School Education Acts, and the Head Start Programs. All of these programs were designed to increase the likelihood that children would remain in school for a greater number of years than they might otherwise have done. However, long term results are difficult to assess and the evidence is not at all clear that the retention of some students in school necessarily results in their gaining the competencies thought to be essential.

Another program developed out of the concern for teaching basic competencies was the Job Corps, first established in 1964 under the Economic Opportunity Act. The avowed purpose of the Corps was to increase employability for disadvantaged youth (of those in the Corps 90 percent were male), with a major focus on teaching basic skills, in order "to equip trainees with the fundamental communication and computational skills needed in order to profit from vocational training and to get and keep a job."[18] This goal, as well as the lack of competency of these youth in coping with their communication needs, is reflected in the instructional program, which included handwriting (both manuscript and cursive); spelling (with an emphasis on correcting common spelling errors); letter writing (business and personal); composition (use of topic sentences and paragraph organization); grammar and punctuation; vocabulary improvement and word usage; use of reference materials. A similar program, Project 100,000, was initiated in 1966

17. Opinions differ as to the views of the parents of black children about the need for their children to learn standard English. However, we agree with Baratz that ". . . most black parents insist that they want their children to learn to read and write and talk proper." Joan C. Baratz, "Should Black Children Learn White Dialect?" *Journal of Speech and Hearing Research* 12 (September 1970): 416.

18. B. J. Argento, "The Job Corps Literacy Program," in *Strategies for Adult Education*, ed. Joseph Mangano (Newark, Del.: International Reading Association, 1969), p. 24.

by the Department of Defense because of the influx into the Armed Services of many men "with lower-level language and reading skills."[19] The program resulted from concern among manpower specialists that the services' demands for literacy skills might exceed the ability of the men, and possibly lead to job failure.

A more pervasive effort has been the establishment of the "Right to Read" program by the U.S. Office of Education. The ambitious goal of this program is to achieve 99 percent literacy for people aged sixteen and under and 90 percent literacy for people over age sixteen—and to do so by 1980. The program was founded because of a national recognition that more children were having difficulty learning to read than was desirable and that many of these children were from the lower socioeconomic classes and minority groups. The program is implemented through state and local school boards with the federal government providing funds for instructional assistance in schools. The assistance has taken the form of staff development, program analysis, and information dissemination; the establishment of pilot programs; and the establishment of regional "Right to Read" sites.[20]

Perhaps the most recent development in expressing concern over the failure to teach minimum competencies is shown in the acknowledgment by some State Boards of Education that there are certain abilities students should have acquired before they are awarded a diploma certifying that they have graduated from high school. The state of Maryland, for example, developed pilot programs to test reading guidelines they wished to establish for students at varying grade levels. The guidelines include such statements as these:

All sixth graders in Maryland should be able to read road signs, telephone books, cash register slips, and directions on medicine bottles.

All tenth grade students should be able to read first-aid directions, want ads, hotel reservations, and application forms.

All high school graduates should be able to use indices and read directions on voting machines, income tax forms, bank statements.[21]

19. Sticht, Reading for Working, p. 11.

20. "Beyond the Ringing Phrase: An Interview with Ruth Love Holloway," The Reading Teacher 25 (November 1971): 118-28.

21. Reading in Maryland (Baltimore, Md.: Maryland State Department of Education, 1974-75), p. 11.

California and Oregon have also published minimum requirements for graduation. These are written in the form of behavioral objectives with sample performance indicators that focus upon application of particular skills rather than upon activities or situations of a "practical" nature in which language is used. For example, one performance indicator reads: "Given a sample of writing without punctuation, the student will provide commas, periods, question marks, apostrophes in contractions, and simple quotation marks." [22] Evaluation of the attainment of these requirements, however, is still a major concern. Decisions about how this evaluation will be accomplished—along with what will be done if students fail to attain the requirements—are still forthcoming.

Basic Literacy: Some Definitions

Adult basic education programs, as well as continuing education programs generally, are a further reflection of the failure of many persons to have achieved the competencies essential for coping with crucial language communication activities. Undoubtedly the development of these programs has led to the most realistic and specific definitions of literacy available and to describing the levels of competence that are crucial in the lives of many people. While definitions of literacy tend to be too narrow in terms of describing the competencies needed in all aspects of language use, they are fundamental to extending consideration beyond reading and writing alone and to developing definitions that are broader in scope.

Historically, concern with defining literacy occurred because of interest in comparing data from various countries, since literacy has been and is a major concern throughout the world. In the United States the concept of functional literacy was introduced in 1940, at which time the attainment of competency was equated with the number of years spent in school. Possibly this definition was a matter of expediency, but whatever the reason, a person who had completed four years of school was considered to be functionally literate.

In some views, amount of education has continued to be the

22. *Oregon Graduation Requirements, Models and Guidelines for Personal Development Education* (Salem, Ore.: Oregon State Department of Education, September 1973), p. 3.

principal criterion for determining literacy. As late as 1971, literacy experts such as Laubach suggested that six or even eight years of school are a more realistic measure in terms of present-day society than the lesser number prescribed earlier.[23] However, such a definition fails to recognize that even minimum competence in reading and writing does not necessarily correspond with the years of schooling—a fact clearly evinced by the case of "Peter Doe" in San Francisco, which demonstrated that a student could graduate from high school and still not have the reading skills normally expected at the primary level.

Other definitions, however, recognize that levels of achievement are more important than grade levels in determining literacy. For example, New York State for years described the literate person as one who could read English at the fourth grade level; this has now been changed to the sixth grade level, with material written in either English or Spanish.[24]

Attempts to define literacy have also reflected concern for recognizing differences as to societal complexities and emphases. Gray described a functional level of literacy in a UNESCO monograph which recognized these differences:

A person is functionally literate when he has acquired the knowledge and skills in reading and writing which enable him to engage effectively in all those activities in which literacy is normally assumed in his culture or group.[25]

Certainly what is a functional level of literacy in one society or culture may not be functional literacy in another. Psychological, sociological, and cultural complexities, to say nothing of complexity as it is now reflected in education and technology, may demand a very high level of literacy indeed to be fully functional in some societies or groups. Thus definitions need to be broad and flexible.

23. William D. Sheldon, "Literacy: A World Problem," in *Reading Goals for the Disadvantaged*, ed. J. Allen Figurel (Newark, Del.: International Reading Association, 1970), p. 293.

24. Robert S. Laubach and Sharif Al Mujahid, "Illiteracy," in *Encyclopedia of Education*, ed. Lee C. Deighton (New York: Macmillan Co., 1971), 4:536.

25. William S. Gray, *The Teaching of Reading and Writing: An International Study*, Monographs on Fundamental Education, No. 1 (Paris: UNESCO, 1956), p. 24.

The recognition of this fact by Gray has been extended and stated by the UNESCO committee on the standardization of education statistics as follows:

A person is literate when he has acquired the essential knowledges and skills which enable him to engage in all those activities in which literacy is required for effective functioning in his group and community.[26]

In a report made to the National Institute of Education, the Study Group on Linguistic Communication drew a distinction between basic literacy, comprehension, and functional or practical literacy as follows:

Basic literacy means ability to use correspondence of visual shapes to spoken sounds in order to decode written materials and to translate them into oral language.
Comprehension means ability to understand the meaning of verbal materials.
Functional or practical literacy means ability to read (decode and comprehend) materials needed to perform everyday and vocational tasks.[27]

Recent efforts to assess the levels of competency achieved by children and adults in language and other areas suggest that there is continuing rethinking as to how functional literacy should be defined. Bormuth says that to define the term, detailed specifications need to be given to four parameters: "(a) the skills we wish to observe and the way in which we measure them; (b) the criterion level of performance we expect a literate person to demonstrate on tests of those skills; (c) the kinds of materials on which we test the skills; and finally (d) any characteristics of the person tested, such as his age, his aptitude, and his practical needs (goals), that may be relevant to an evaluation of his level of attainment in literacy."[28] But, however difficult are the tasks of definition and assessment, there lies beyond the much more demanding task of developing a society in which all citizens with the mental capability to become

26. Sheldon, "Literacy," p. 292.

27. George A. Miller, ed., *Linguistic Communication: Perspectives for Research* (Newark, Del.: International Reading Association, 1974), p. 3. (Report of the Study Group on Linguistic Communication, George A. Miller, chairman.)

28. Bormuth, "Reading Literacy," p. 56.

functionally literate will have the opportunity to do so. A further task is to devise the strategies that will enable these citizens to develop the competencies essential for coping with our society.

Dialects and Literacy

The issue of literacy has been affected most recently by an increasing recognition of dialect differences and how these differences may or may not influence an individual's capability for achieving literacy. Attention to the concern about dialect differences has mainly focused on teaching reading, again too narrowly defining literacy and failing to equate it with demonstration of essential competency in all communicative activities.

Major attention has been upon the language of many black children, although more recently there has been a broadening of concern to include dialects generally and the idiolects of individuals. There is evidence of several facts: (a) the percentage of black children learning to read is less than that of children generally, (b) black dialect differs from the dialect of English generally used in schools, (c) the earlier belief that black language or dialect is unstructured and irregular—an immature form of English—has been firmly discounted, and (d) every dialect is systematic and complete and is effectively used in many communication situations.

Recognition of the grammaticality of all dialects, plus an emerging concern for the self-esteem of students, was expressed in the resolution of the Conference on College Composition and Communication (CCCC) in 1972:

We affirm the students' right to their own patterns and varieties of language—the dialects of their nurture or whatever dialects in which they find their own identity and style. Language scholars long ago denied that the myth of a standard American dialect has any validity. The claim that any one dialect is unacceptable amounts to an attempt of one social group to exert its dominance over another. Such a claim leads to false advice for speakers and writers, and immoral advice for humans. A nation proud of its diverse heritage and its cultural and racial variety will preserve its heritage of dialects. We affirm strongly that teachers must have the experiences and training that will enable them to respect diversity and uphold the right of students to their own language.[29]

29. "Students' Right to Their Own Language," *College Composition and Communication* 25 (Special Issue, Fall 1974): 2-3.

In explaining the resolution, this group suggested that

many of us have taught as though the function of schools and colleges were to erase differences. Should we, on the one hand, urge creativity and individuality in the arts and sciences, take pride in the diversity of our historical development, and, on the other hand, try to obliterate all the differences in the way Americans speak and write? Our major emphasis has been on uniformity, in both speech and writing; would we accomplish more, both educationally and ethically, if we shifted that emphasis to precise, effective, and appropriate communication in diverse ways, whatever the dialect?[30]

At its 1974 annual meeting, the parent organization of the Conference, the National Council of Teachers of English, modified the position by making a distinction between spoken and written English, pointing to the need for students to learn the conventions of "what has been called written edited American English."

As suggested earlier, the question of the efficacy of a non-standard dialect for meeting the objectives implied in "essential competencies" is clouded by the reading instruction issue. Fundamentally, this issue is whether the speaker of a dialect that is different from the school dialect should be taught to speak the school dialect either before or while he is being taught to read or whether he should be permitted "to read the materials in his own dialect."[31] This really should not be an issue and remains one only because reading has traditionally been equated with "word calling" by some teachers and more recently with "decoding" by some linguists. Correctly defining reading assures the fact that the reader reacts to what he has read in his own way, which means that in some instances this reaction may require expression through language, either written or oral. In either case the expression may not be in standard English, but that does not mean that reading has not occurred.

While some may consider the above a casual dismissal of what they see as an issue, it is nevertheless true that problems in learning to read have been encountered by speakers of all dialects—whether

---

30. Ibid., p. 2.

31. Herbert D. Simons, "Black Dialect and Learning to Read," in *Literacy for Diverse Learners*, ed. Jerry L. Johns (Newark, Del.: International Reading Association, 1974), p. 7.

these have been labeled "standard," "nonstandard," "edited," or something else. The converse of this is also true: most speakers of all dialects, including those speaking a so-called black dialect, have over the years learned to read. Of course, poor instruction, or lack of instruction, has prevented some students from attaining this learning—and the percentage of black children who have encountered these conditions has been disproportionately high.

The question of reading instruction aside, however, the transmittal of information essential to meeting most citizen needs in America is communicated in standard English.[32] The statement of the National Council of Teachers of English takes into account the need for students to be able to respond to the conventions of "edited American English" in reading and writing, while at the same time respecting the primacy, individuality, and desirable fluidity of an individual's dialectical characteristics. Further, the CCCC "background" material indicates the need for an awareness of the "relationship between linguistic performance and job competence" and suggests that students who learn to write "edited American English" will need "to learn the forms identified with that dialect as additional options to the forms they already control."[33]

Labov, who has studied urban American dialects extensively, wrote in 1972 of the complexity of the task of teaching standard English as follows:

Many skills have to be acquired before we can say that a person has learned standard English. The following list is a scale of priority that I would suggest as helpful in concentrating our attention on the most important problems:

a. Ability to understand spoken English (of the teacher)
b. Ability to read and comprehend
c. Ability to communicate (to the teacher) in spoken English
d. Ability to communicate in writing
e. Ability to write in standard English grammar
f. Ability to spell correctly
g. Ability to use standard English grammar in speaking
h. Ability to speak with a prestige pattern of pronunciation (and avoid stigmatized forms).[34]

32. Miller, *Linguistic Communication*, p. 11.
33. "Students' Right to Their Own Language," p. 15.
34. William Labov, *Language in the Inner City: Studies in the Black English Vernacular* (Philadelphia: University of Pennsylvania Press, 1972), p. 5.

Labov's listing of these abilities does not suggest that all of them are necessary for an individual to learn in school, although some certainly are needed. Nor is there any implication that all are needed for communication activities outside of school—either as a child or as an adult. Furthermore, none of these abilities has been described so definitively by Labov or anyone else that the definition would not be challenged; indeed there is ample evidence that many speakers of standard English may have more than a little difficulty with several of them. Thus, although the Labov list need not be taken as a list of essential competencies, it is indicative of one direction of professional thought in the early 1970s.

We would hope that society may come to recognize that some of these abilities should be replaced by others: the ability to communicate an idea clearly in diverse linguistic settings; the ability to synthesize a large amount of information quickly—including that received by television and other nonprint media; and the ability to operate creatively and flexibly in several languages or a variety of dialects. However, at this time the high-mindedness of a "student's right to his own language" must be looked at straightforwardly. We agree with Johnson that "persons who speak nonstandard varieties of English are socially handicapped."[35] Furthermore, there is a danger that the issue may be perpetuated by mixing linguistic statements with the current humanistic social rhetoric. Problems are not solved by ignoring reality, but the reality need not mean what Jimmy Breslin has characterized as "antiseptic Scarsdale prose."

Determining the Competencies That are Essential

The difficulty in defining literacy or in describing the competencies one needs to communicate effectively is surely evident to the reader. Earlier we reported evidence of efforts to utilize functional criteria rather than norm-referenced standards in judging levels of achievement in several communication skills areas. Miller, focusing upon reading, suggests that "one line of attack would be to ask the educational system to give everyone the ability to read

---

35. Kenneth R. Johnson, "Should Black Children Learn Standard English?" in *Viewpoints: Bulletin of the School of Education, Indiana University* 47 (March 1971): 90.

up to the level required of him by his occupation."[36] In developing this line of reasoning, he arrives at two recommendations: (a) that data be gathered on the level of reading skills required to have access to an occupation; and (b) that data be gathered on the level of reading skills necessary to gain the knowledge to be able to perform adequately in the occupation.[37]

The use of functional criteria in defining essential competencies, of course, is limited in application because of the wide range of any person's communication needs. This limitation is discussed more fully later in this section; however, the point here is that if specific tasks are identified it is possible to determine a functional level of performance. Naturally a job entry level of functioning is adequate neither for continuation and advancement in an occupation nor for functioning in communication activities unrelated to one's occupation.

In 1973 Northcutt reported on research in adult basic education that sought to determine performance levels based on communication tasks wider in scope than those needed for job entry.[38] Northcutt suggested that a definition of functional literacy must consist of four elements: (a) a set of needs or requirements for adult living, the satisfaction of which is necessary for success in adult life; (b) an analysis of the "academic" skills needed to satisfy these requirements or needs; (c) criteria for success in society; and (d) demonstration of the relationship between the behavior and the success criteria. In consideration of these elements, broad goals for adult success were established—goals based upon knowledge, skills, and abilities, which were defined in terms of behavioral descriptions called objectives. These in turn were more closely delimited by a series of specific tasks that served both as criteria of competence and as specific test items in a nationwide survey. For example, in one need area, "occupational knowledge," the broad goal "To be aware of the means by which mobility in an economic environment can be enhanced," was followed by seven specific objectives, one

36. Miller, *Linguistic Communication*, p. 12.

37. Ibid., p. 13.

38. Norvell W. Northcutt, *A Research Project for the Development of Performance Levels from Pragmatic Adult Literacy Objectives* (Austin, Tex.: University of Texas, 1973).

of which is "To know the various sources that may lead to employment." For this "Specific Performance Objective" there were several tasks listed, including (a) to list at least eight sources that may lead to employment; (b) to use newspapers to read employment ads; and (c) to mark employment ads that are sponsored by government agencies, commercial employment agencies, and private employers.

The effort in the study briefly described above reflects the movement in the present decade to specify precisely the components of competence with respect to various curriculum areas as well as to performance in particular life situations. Some success has been achieved in areas and situations that have permitted this specificity. Programs that have reflected this success include those in basic adult education, the armed services, and industry.

Endres, Lamb, and Lazarus speak to the difficulties encountered in stating objectives for attaining essential competencies with this statement: "However indispensable goals may be, . . . selecting a list of them in the English language arts is of course presumptuous and foolhardy unless one stipulates that the purpose of this inventory is to elicit dialogue."[39] Continuing their caution, they observe that "ultimately, objectives are best specified for individual children," which is of course true. But stating goals and being realistic about what people must do are important—and too infrequently done. Further, clarifying goals does not necessarily mean that narrow statements of performance follow nor that individuality is ignored.

What, then, are the basic language competencies each person needs in order to function successfully in our increasingly complex society—not just to exist, but to function as an individual human being and to cope with the situations, opportunities, and problems presented by that society? To make this determination—or even to attempt to do so—requires examining the kinds of communication that are an integral part of virtually every person's life, either daily or in situations where this communication is essential to coping in a societal setting. The settings may vary from the ghettos of

39. Mary Endres, Pose Lamb, and Arnold Lazarus, "Selected Objectives in the English Language Arts (Pre-K through 12)," *Elementary English* 46 (April 1969): 418.

Watts to the Oval Office in the White House; the communication may be a medical textbook, a raised eyebrow, a political cartoon, or the shouted expletive of an angry truck driver; but each of us must and does communicate with others in some fashion, usually many times each day.

Each person listens daily and reacts to this listening. Even the deaf person "listens" in the sense that his interpretation of what is said is influenced by the gestures, manner, and facial expressions of the speaker. We listen to television commercials, news, weather reports, entertainment, and educational programs, to politicians (in person or via media) extolling their own virtues or defending their programs. The motorist listens to get directions for reaching his destination, the baby-sitter listens to instructions for the evening's job, the student listens to a lecturer in the classroom (or to the cassette recording of the lecture), the apprentice listens as the plumber describes the job to be done, and so on. Each needs to comprehend and react to what is heard.

Everyone has a need to read, both language and other symbols, in order to function adequately. We read street signs, precautions and instructions on medicine bottles, advertisements, menus in restaurants. The shopper reads labels describing the fabric content of garments, the student reads assignments, the gardener reads directions for using insecticides or fertilizers, the architect reads blueprints, the traveler reads maps, the electrician reads wiring diagrams, the job-hunter reads want ads, and the voter reads propositions and names of candidates and parties. Unless we read at more than the minimal level of only vocalizing the written symbols, we may arrive at wrong destinations, kill the flowers instead of the insects, buy unwisely, or vote for a party other than that intended.

We must remember, too, that we live in a society that increasingly depends on visual and auditory symbols other than words—symbols that direct their "messages" at us through a variety of media. Since the subtlety and the sensory basis of these messages involve more than words, competency in reacting to them may not require the decoding skills of reading or even those of listening to spoken language. Competency in the essential thought processes, though, is largely the same as that for communication by overt language alone.

For all of the receptive aspects of communication, then, it is necessary to do more than simply hear or see words; one must receive and react with purpose and comprehension. Further, there is a need to be critical and evaluative in receiving communications. Regardless of the life stage of an individual—in school or out—and regardless of that person's occupation, economic condition, ethnic background, or language style, it is necessary to check the authenticity of statements, to be sensitive to propaganda techniques, half-truths, and slanted language.

Each person also speaks daily. We are far from a silent society. Even if one has an occupation in which there is little encounter with other humans, or one in which there is little need or opportunity for talking—such as working on a noisy assembly line—the remainder of the day will likely call for much speaking: ordering a beer, talking about the evening's news, discussing school work with the children, or simply greeting a neighbor. Most individuals actually are not in occupations that restrict speech. The salesman's life is highly dependent upon his ability to put across his product by what he says; a lawyer is equally concerned with having her point of view accepted. The carpenter talks to his helper and to the clerks in the lumber yard, the hotel clerk greets the guests and conveys information to them, the policeman gives directions and answers questions, the social worker questions clients, and so on.

Writing is perhaps less persuasive but is virtually as universal. Writing letters is still an important activity for many persons, as attested to by the volume of mail and regardless of the advertising of telephone companies. For many individuals, writing letters to children away from home or to parents from whose homes they have departed is done regularly—whether this is regarded as a duty, a task, or a cherished opportunity. Much writing that everyone does is of the "complete the form" variety: bank deposit slips and checks, license applications, mortgage applications, income tax forms, mail orders, and so on. One suspects that there are few individuals whose personal lives or occupations do not require writing one or more of the following: records, notes, letters, explanations, directions, summaries, reports. In many occupations the writing may be in several of these forms, and any one may be lengthy and detailed. In other occupations there may be infrequent need and whatever is written may be only a short note. However, active citizens of any socioeconomic group write to editors and congressmen, take minutes at club and lodge meetings, send notes to schools, and prepare reports related to their religious endeavors.

Ability to use locational skills appears to be needed by everyone. The pensioner daily finds his newspapers in the library, the stockholder scans the stock reports or watches the ticker tape, and the child locates another book by his currently favorite author—with no hesitancy in going directly to the fiction shelves. The telephone company advertises that an individual's "fingers should do the walking," implying that the individual knows alphabetical and numerical sequences. Publishers of road maps believe every user will know how to locate specific places using the letter and number codes printed on the borders. The service station attendant checks for correct tire pressures, fan belt types, and spark plug settings for a Chevy, "Beetle," or Eldorado in his service manual—using fairly sophisticated locational skills.

We do not believe it "foolhardy and presumptuous" to state objectives for English teaching or for learning to use the English language, or to attempt to define the "essential competencies" needed by individuals in our society. We believe that the unwillingness of the profession to do so may have brought forth the present concern about the degree of functional illiteracy, the poor expressive ability of college students, the inadequate reading skills of high school graduates, and the failure of a large segment of our population to develop fully their language-using potential. The essential competencies must be the basis of English programs; without adequate attention to the development of these competencies, attempts to teach other elements will be ineffective. From this premise it is necessary for the essential competencies to be stated, since their attainment is not likely to occur from a vague consideration of their importance as an "issue." The listing that follows may be regarded by some readers as incomplete or insufficiently specific, by others as too all-encompassing or perhaps too trivial, and by still others as improperly stated or organized. However, these are the essential competencies as we see them.

Essential Competencies for English Programs

I. Competencies Essential for Receiving Communication from Others

  A. Basic Understandings and Attitudes

    1. To understand that reading and listening skills are needed for learning in school, for most occupations, and for daily living.

    2. To understand that symbols and signs other than those which either graphically or auditorily represent words may transmit meaning.

    3. To understand that the purpose and the degree of involvement of the receiver affect communication.

    4. To understand that reading and listening are means for gaining pleasure directly as well as indirectly in terms of finding avocational and recreational information.

    5. To understand and appreciate various types of language: dialects, levels of usage, jargon, figurative language, and so forth.

  B. Receptive Comprehension Abilities

    1. To follow directions, determine main ideas, recognize important supporting information, and perceive relationships.

    2. To use language structure, context clues, dictionaries, and other aids in gaining meaning.

    3. To relate information received to previous experiences and present knowledge and to draw inferences.

    4. To distinguish between fact and opinion and between the relevant and the irrelevant.

    5. To recognize bias, prejudice, and propaganda and avoid judgments based upon inadequate evidence.

    6. To gain pleasure and self-development from receptive communication acts.

  C. Abilities Needed for Aural Decoding

    1. To identify and discriminate among common speech sounds.

    2. To recognize words, phrases, and larger units of aural communication.

    3. To use the pitch, stress, juncture, and tone of speech in gaining meaning.

  D. Abilities Needed for Visual Decoding

    1. To distinguish and identify individual letters and letter groups in a wide variety of type and script styles.

2. To recognize by sight a core of words and to be able to use structural and phonemic-graphemic knowledge to determine others.

3. To use punctuation marks and other nonword symbols as aids to reading.

4. To make use of facial expressions, physical movements, and graphic and picture symbols as aids in gaining meaning from nonreading communication acts.

II. Competencies Needed for Expression to Others

A. Understandings and Attitudes

1. To recognize that the content of what is said is more important than the mechanics of saying it.

2. To understand that the mechanics of writing and the manner of speaking are aids to communication rather than ends in themselves.

3. To understand that, to communicate effectively, one must be willing to acquire the specific skills or learnings needed for the performance of particular speaking or writing tasks.

4. To recognize that there are levels of usage appropriate to varying occasions.

5. To recognize that one's own personal language or dialect is worthy of respect and is suitable for many situations.

6. To recognize that standard English is needed for certain kinds of oral and written communication.

7. To be sensitive to the opinions and feelings of one's reader(s) or listener(s).

B. Abilities Needed for Organization and Composition

1. To speak or write for particular purposes:
   a. to seek information
   b. to give directions
   c. to make explanations
   d. to give information
   e. to express feelings and/or opinions
   f. to persuade
   g. to make requests
   h. to comply with social amenities
   i. to provide entertainment, pleasure, or comfort

2. To choose content appropriate to the intended audience— that is, the reader or listener.

3. To use varied structures in accord with the purpose, the audience, and the situation.

4. To use language—one's own personal language or dialect or standard English—that is suitable to the occasion, the content, and the audience.
5. To organize ideas and information in ways such as:
   a. using sequential development
   b. using supporting details
   c. giving examples or illustrations
   d. showing cause and effect
6. To use accurate facts and valid sources of information to support ideas.

C. Abilities Needed for Oral Communication

1. To participate in informal as well as formal speaking situations that involve exchange with others without being either overly dominant or reticent.
2. To speak distinctly and to articulate sounds clearly.
3. To use volume, pitch, rate, and tone appropriate to the audience and the occasion.
4. To use suitable gestures and facial expressions.

D. Abilities Needed for Written Communication

1. To write legibly and neatly.
2. To spell correctly the words that are needed.
3. To use accepted punctuation and capitalization.
4. To use accepted form and appropriate language in varying types of written communication.

III. Competencies Needed for Locating Information

A. Understandings and Attitudes

1. To have the desire to acquire knowledge and pleasure from sources outside one's immediate environment.
2. To understand that most sources of information—from the telephone directory to the card catalog in the library—list items alphabetically.
3. To understand that the ability to locate information aids in achieving self-determination and acquiring knowledge.
4. To be aware that it is sometimes desirable and necessary to ask for assistance in locating information.

B. Locational Abilities

1. To know the sequence of the letters of the alphabet.
2. To use alphabetical order to locate information of varying kinds.
3. To give specific information desired when requesting aid in locating someone or something.

4. To use various aids for finding information in books, such as tables of contents, indexes, and format clues.
5. To use such aids as card catalogs, computer searches, building directories, diagrams, maps, and the like to locate facts, materials, places, or people.

While these objectives may be regarded as focusing primarily upon the competencies needed by the school-leaving student or the adult, this narrowness of viewpoint is not intended. These are the communication competencies that require sustained attention in the primary grades of every school as well as at every teaching level that follows. They are competencies that must be functional for every person in our society—regardless of the tasks he or she is called upon to perform. Without them every individual who is in school beyond the primary level, every individual engaged in the most menial of tasks, and every sophisticated and learned scholar cannot communicate at the level of his potential. For many the absence of these competencies means a failure to develop the quality of life that should be their heritage.

The essence of these competencies lies in the processes, not in their specific manifestations. There are obvious differences in their use by particular individuals. The locational needs of the physician are not those of the banker, the plumber, or the bus boy; nor are their reading, writing, listening, and speaking requirements the same. The lawyer's speaking tasks are not the same as those of the carpenter, but both need to speak distinctly and to articulate sounds clearly; both must use volume, pitch, rate, and tone appropriate to their respective audiences and occasions; both have the need to participate in speaking situations that involve exchange with others without either unduly dominating or being overly reticent. By the same token, the college freshman does writing that is different from that done by a file clerk. However, both need the writing skills listed, both need to organize ideas and information in what they write, and both must choose language that is appropriate to the occasion, the content, and the audience.

Implications for Teaching

What are the implications of these objectives for schools and for individual teachers at every level? What responsibilities does the teacher of English have for developing these competencies? May a teacher assume, because a student can read a literary selection at a literal level, that he can respond orally at a comparable level? That he can read directions satisfactorily? Or that he can write about what he has read? We think not. Many teachers have assumed for too long that transfer of learning automatically takes place. Too many teachers of English assume that responding orally to questions in class means that the student can say what he needs to say in initiating a job interview, that writing an essay means he can write a communicative letter or a set of directions, or that the ability to read a story means he will recognize a misleading advertisement. Of course, the essay writer may be able to write a business letter, the story reader may be able to read the encyclopedia entry with understanding, and the student who is orally verbal in class may function effectively in other speech settings, but the English program must determine whether the competencies actually have been attained. At each schooling level there must be provision for teaching them at the appropriate functional level.

In terms of teaching methodology, we believe that the fundamental implication of this listing of competencies is that the teacher must recognize that the major purpose of instruction is not to teach the student to spell, to write a grammatically correct sentence, or to analyze a literary selection, but to teach him to think, to communicate his thoughts to others, to understand and evaluate the communication of others. It is only as the student does these things that the need and the desire to learn the specific skills of effective listening, speaking, reading, writing, and locating information will be attained.

At every educational level—elementary, secondary, and beyond —students must be surrounded with experiences that lead to questions, must be helped to find answers, and then be encouraged to talk about these answers, weigh them, even question them. A variety of materials, presented through a variety of media, can be geared to the interests, abilities, and maturity levels of the students. Both ideas and methods of presentation can be examined and evaluated, not in a prescriptive manner but in a spirit of inquiry and discovery. This procedure should lead to the seeking of additional information, other opinions, other ways of expressing ideas, and should result in many opportunities for students to exchange knowledge as well as to express their own reactions, emotions, ideas, and beliefs, both orally and in writing, and in a variety of forms.

When communication—both intake and output—is truly the the heart of the English program, the skills of communication are natural ingredients. These skills will be learned as the students are ready for them and as they are needed. For example, if a child has examined many books, has had many stories read to him, has talked about their events and characters, has participated in dramatization of stories and poems, has had much experience with language as it is encountered in books—and this experience has been pleasant and fulfilling for him—he will want to learn to read for himself. With rare exceptions, such a child *will* learn to read. Equally, the sixth-grader who has become interested in a topic and wants to share his knowledge with classmates will wish to develop the competencies in oral expression essential for conveying that knowledge in a way that will interest his listeners. He may even use the library and other resources to gain additional information, interview someone who is knowledgeable about the subject, design visual aids or seek out suitable ones. With encouragement and help, he will find the need and desire to use locational skills. In a similar manner the skills of spelling, handwriting, punctuation, and so on will be acquired as students have a genuine need and desire to share ideas through writing. Careful choice of words, correct structuring of sentences, and effective organizing of the content—all are needed for truly functional expression, both oral and written. Students who have something to say can be encouraged to want to say it in the best way possible, particularly if they have had much experience with language that is vivid and apt. When particular forms are needed, whether for writing a thank-you note or a doctoral dissertation, there is purpose for learning them. In addition, students should be helped to examine their competency in all of their communication activities in order to discover those skills and abilities that need development, followed by opportunities to practice them in meaningful ways.

Such a program can be successful, of course, only when each student feels the confidence and the desire to express himself. It is essential, then, to build each student's self-concept so that he will believe his ideas are worth expressing. In "Letter to a Dead Teacher" Bel Kaufman pays tribute to the one teacher who emphasized her worth, not her defects:

Somehow, you made everyone feel special. Once you quoted from Shakespeare: ". . . who can say more than this rich praise—that you alone are you?" I knew you meant me. And so did each of the thirty-four others in the room.[40]

The fact that she is speaking of a high school English teacher leads one suddenly to realize how many other teachers must have failed to give individual attention to this immigrant girl for whom English was a new language—and probably to the others in their classes as well. Certainly this was an earlier day, but individualization is not a new concept nor is the need for language competence for essential tasks. And unfortunately too many teachers are still teaching subject matter, not students, as well as giving too little attention to the skills and understandings these students need most.

We hope the concern about essential competencies will not lead to even greater emphasis upon subject matter, in the belief that this will lead to mastery of those essentials. Rather, the concern should result in emphasis on giving attention to each individual's needs and abilities as well as on diagnostic teaching to discover more exactly what those needs and abilities are. This, in turn, means that input must be selected according to individual abilities and experiential backgrounds so that each student can be successful in understanding and reacting to that input and be challenged to learn skills needed for expressing that reaction, as well as for gaining more information and experience.

A Final Word

The evidence that large numbers of students fail to develop the competencies in using language that are essential for their survival in many school settings, as well as most certainly essential for achieving the vocational and avocational levels to which they may aspire and for which they have the potential, has made the consideration of essential competencies crucial in a yearbook on the teaching of English. This evidence has received public attention and

40. Bel Kaufman, "Letter to a Dead Teacher," *Today's Education* 64 (March-April 1975): 20.

a widespread acceptance of its validity. Parents and other citizens are disturbed, with remediation of this disturbance being sought in the schools. Since the school—and particularly the English program—does have at least the major responsibility for teaching the communication skills and for developing the related understandings, the focus of public concern seems properly placed.

We earlier indicated a recognition that attempts to identify essential language competencies are considered by some to be "presumptuous and foolhardy." Yet a consideration of English programs—at whatever level—in the schools of America surely requires that attention be given to the identification of the essential elements of communication and to their teaching. We have sought to give a focus to these elements by naming them as essential competencies and stressing that professional concern about them should go beyond the concerns about functional literacy, nonstandard English and "the disadvantaged," and the nonachiever in the classroom. The language competencies essential for individuals in these categories are equally essential to all other citizens. The development of these competencies must be the heart of the English program.

CHAPTER IV

The Next Language Art: Views of Nonprint Media

DEBORAH DASHOW RUTH*

*"When you consider television's awesome power
to educate, aren't you thankful it doesn't?"*

Drawing by Donald Reilly; © 1965 The New Yorker Magazine, Inc.

How can we be so sure that television does not do more educating than we think?

Persons who grew up in an earlier generation may be shocked by the small amount of time students of today spend on reading. And, judging from the information obtained from high school juniors and seniors, the years spent in school have little apparent effect in encouraging greater time spent in reading.

High school juniors and seniors in the upper half of their classes spent only seventeen minutes, the median, on a given day reading for pleasure. Those in the lower half spent only five minutes. A total of 30

* Consultant readers for this chapter were Audrey J. Roth, Associate Professor of English, Miami-Dade Community College, North, Miami, Florida; and Frank McLaughlin, editor of *Media and Methods*.

percent of those in the upper half read nothing not required; more than half (53) percent of those in the lower half read nothing.[1]

The Gallup Poll quoted above also showed that those in the upper half of their classes spent fifty minutes a day watching television, while those in the lower half spent one hundred minutes.

The Need for Visual Education

While teachers of the English language arts spend much of their class time on books and other forms of written expression, their students choose to spend much more of their own time outside class on television and other nonprint media. It is this condition that leads George Gerbner to observe:

Teachers and schools no longer enjoy much autonomy, let alone their former monopoly, as the public dispensers of knowledge. The formal educational enterprise exists in a cultural climate largely dominated by the informal "curriculum" of the mass media.[2]

English teachers are rightly worried about the rejection of "literacy" in face of insistent demands for "relevance." But perhaps English teachers can revive interest in literacy and attain relevance at the same time by refocusing their perspective to concentrate on developing "dual literacy" in the visual and verbal modes of expression. This chapter discusses potential effects of new technological developments on the lives of our students. And it shows ways teachers and schools can prepare to meet requirements for developing a dual literacy through wise use of both print and nonprint media.

The twentieth century revolution in communications technology manifests itself most dramatically in "the new media"—the nonprint media—of film, television, videotape, photography, filmstrips, records, audio tapes, radio, and any combination of these used for multimedia presentations. These nonprint media, as a means of communication, both individual and mass, offer new ways of learning

1. George H. Gallup, "Sixth Annual Gallup Poll of Public Attitudes toward Education," *Phi Delta Kappan* 56 (September 1974): 27, 32.

2. George Gerbner, "Teacher Image in Mass Culture: Symbolic Functions of the Hidden Curriculum," in *Media and Symbols: The Forms of Expression, Communication, and Education,* Seventy-third Yearbook of the National Society for the Study of Education, Part I, ed. David R. Olson (Chicago: University of Chicago Press, 1974), p. 471.

and knowing, new avenues for creativity and self-expression; new means to reach and touch feelings. They bring experiences to the classroom that stimulate growth of the whole child, not just of the cognitive functions. The potential of nonprint media for reunifying the cognitive and affective aspects of learning can lead not only to the recognition of the legitimacy of feelings in education, but to a more holistic approach to the education of children and adolescents.

Visual and Verbal Literacy: Complementary, not Competitive

English and language arts courses aim at making students literate through reading and writing. Becoming literate usually means exploring the world of letters to understand one's relation to self, to others, and to the social environments that one inhabits or perceives. Such probing of book worlds develops ability to comprehend and organize literary experiences into meaningful, personal observations, attitudes, and judgments. Our present conception of literacy also includes developing the ability to communicate through speaking and writing. Traditionally, then, English courses have taught literacy by having students *read about* how others organize and communicate their experiences via the written word, and by having students *write about* their own experiences. But students also can achieve a greater literacy by *seeing* how others organize and communicate their experiences via the visual image, alone or in combination with written words. Students thus may come to possess a dual literacy that combines images and words. The "new media" expand the limits of the world of printed words, adding visual and nonverbal aspects to experience. And "seeing" comes fully into its own as an important sense to educate.

Historically, the invention of the printing press made the acquisition of reading and writing skills more accessible to more people. "Literacy" meant exclusively "verbal literacy." With the invention of the camera and related technological developments, another dimension to literacy emerged. The electronic revolution has given us videotape, motion pictures, instant photographs, audio cassettes, and other new modes of communication. Just as our professional predecessors once had to concern themselves with the educational implications of the printing press, so must we now involve ourselves with determining the significance of this new nonprint media technology for contemporary education.

If we agree that an expanded literacy is what we want our students to develop, and that we now have two different but complementary ways to foster its growth, then we must begin to explore how films and other nonprint media can be integrated into English and language arts programs. This is not to suggest that the visual mode replace the verbal mode; rather, we should take full advantage of what both have to offer. The predictions of Marshall McLuhan notwithstanding, the birth and growth of the "new" media will not cause the death of the "old" media. Sol Worth reminds us that "giving up the dependence on words alone does not necessitate throwing out either verbal language or the cognitive skills associated with the ability to speak, read, and write."[3] Clearly, many educators unnecessarily have created what James Morrow and Murray Suid call a false dichotomy between "word media" and "image media." Not only is there no need to make the choice, but it is also important to understand that the various media use both words and images to reinforce each other. For example, most television shows actually are more reliant on words than images to communicate knowledge (television stations report more complaints with a sound loss than with a picture loss); conversely, literature and radio drama often are praised for their appeal to the visual dimensions of imagination.[4] Donis Dondis concludes that the same purposes underlie both visual forms of expression and written language: "to construct a basic system for learning, recognizing, making, and understanding visual [and verbal] messages that are negotiable by all people, not just those specially trained, like the designer, the artist, the craftsman, and the aesthetician."[5]

Nonprint Media in Society: Negative and Positive Potential

Nonprint media actively both reflect and shape the values of

3. Sol Worth, "The Uses of Film in Education and Communication," in *Media and Symbols*, p. 292.

4. James Morrow and Murray Suid, "Media in the Classroom: Some Pedagogical Issues," *English Journal* 63 (October 1974): 38.

5. Donis Dondis, *A Primer of Visual Literacy* (Cambridge, Mass.: M.I.T. Press, 1973), p. x.

contemporary culture and society. Much has been said and written about the effect of Madison Avenue ad agencies and their pervasive and persuasive images of "the good life," romantic love, the roles of men and women, aspirations toward success and security, and the need to be fashionable and up-to-date. Whether or not we "buy" these images along with the products they are designed to sell, we are continually confronted by and immersed in a form of "unreal reality" that is so persuasively projected by the mass media. As adults, we like to believe we are discriminating viewers, aware of the sales pitch behind the attractive visual image. Because we grew up in a largely verbal culture, we learned to have more faith in the printed word and to be more wary of the seductive, manipulative visual image. But what about our children who are caught now between a verbal culture that seems to them increasingly dishonest, irrelevant, or simply inaccessible and a visual culture that seems direct, attractive, and readily accessible?

Where do today's children learn their values? Not from books, according to the Gallup Poll report mentioned above.

By the time most American students are eighteen years old they have viewed approximately 15,000 hours of television—5,000 hours more than they have spent in school. . . . We are in the process of breeding a country of . . . "visual illiterates." The reason is that there is little in present school curricula which helps students make sense out of the visual and aural media that surround them. The school curriculum is, on the other hand, heavily weighted toward helping them understand the print media.[6]

These are indeed worrisome statistics to ponder. The visually illiterate may watch, but does not see; may see but does not understand; and accepts unquestioningly the authority of both the medium and the message. Such is the danger inherent in our rapidly growing nonprint culture that even if our children do learn to read and write inside of school, their inability to respond with the same understanding and judgment to the visual/nonprint media outside of school may effectively neutralize or counteract the growth of sound values acquired through school-monitored print media.

The medium most often blamed for both social and educational

6. Patricia MacKay, "Bridging the Visual Illiteracy Gap," *Theatre Crafts* 6 (October 1972): 6-9.

problems is television. Susan Koch calls attention to the remarks of University of Michigan psychiatrist Derek Miller on possible relations between television viewing and social behavior:

There is a remarkable similarity between those adolescents who take drugs for their vivid visual impressions, which they inertly and passively sit and watch within the picture figures of their own minds, and those who sit as small children in equivalent positions watching a television screen.[7]

And what are the pictures of humanity that cross the television screen? First, there are television commercials with their endlessly repetitive, limited range of stereotyped role models that children pick up quickly and at a very early age: mommies in commercials wearing aprons while they stand in the kitchen talking about detergents, furniture polishes, and cake mixes; wearing slinky dresses while they stand among luxurious surroundings talking about mascara, perfume, and "feminine hygiene sprays." Daddies in commercials are usually in the yard or the driveway talking about shock absorbers, the latest model car, or beer; or they stand in a wood-paneled office talking about life insurance, bank loans, or mortgages. (Of course, these days, men, too, are not without their grave problems of choosing the right deodorant or hair spray.) The values communicated are as superficial and limiting as the models who present them.

Additionally, television programs provide a limited range of stereotyped human behavior, giving insidious, tacit approval to anti-social responses such as hostility, aggression, and violence in dealing with interpersonal problems. "When you consider television's awesome power to educate, aren't you thankful it doesn't?" The caption of the cartoon at the beginning of this chapter reads ominously in this context. A new concentration on developing visual literacy in school may help children respond more wisely to the "television-as-tutor."

Any evaluation of the role of nonprint media in education must include consideration of their power—both positive and negative—to govern perception of what is happening in today's mass media world. The taunting chant heard in the late 1960s, "The whole

7. Derek Miller, quoted in Susan Koch, "This World of English: Technology, Television, and Values," *English Journal* 63 (October 1974): 25.

world is watching," still rings true as the news flashes nightly across millions of television screens. But just *what* is there in the news for the world to watch? *Who* is responsible for selecting what is there to be watched? *How* is this power to *make* the news both used and abused? And what does it all matter to education and the teaching of English?

Item: Reuben Frank, formerly executive producer of NBC Evening News, said: "There are events which exist in the American mind and recollection primarily because they were reported on regular television news programs."[8] Conversely, another news executive remarked, "If the people don't see it, they don't miss it."[9]

Item: "The essence of journalism is the editing process," says Elmer Lower, president of ABC News.[10] Except in rare instances, what is seen on network news is *not* the event itself taking place before a live camera; it is not even a filmed record, but rather a story *about* the event, reconstructed on film from selected fragments of the filmed event. Says Edward Jay Epstein, "Despite the hackneyed maxim that television news 'tells it like it is,' presenting events exactly as they occur does not fit in with the requisites of network news."[11] Epstein quotes a leading film editor: "Given at random, say, half a dozen shots of different nature and subject, there are any number of possible combinations of the six that, with the right twist of commentary, could make film sense."[12]

Item: CBS News's Walter Cronkite reports that he himself sees, edits, writes, rewrites, and, in the case of out-of-town films, introduces virtually every word of material on his news show. Cronkite worries over polls showing that two-thirds of the population get their primary news from television: "I never go home without feeling we've done an inadequate job. I guess we can't do everything; but the things that get left on the cutting room floor, on my desk,

---

8. Edward J. Epstein, *News from Nowhere: Television and the News* (New York: Random House, 1973), p. 9.

9. Ibid., p. 149.

10. Ibid., p. 152.

11. Ibid.

12. Ibid., p. 174.

that ought to have been broadcast that day appall me." [13]

Item: Educator Caleb Gattegno says:

> Even when telecasting is live from nature, the way the cameraman uses his tool brings back the artist and his interference upon the subject being presented. In the case of edited documentaries, it is clear that a number of sensitivities, opinions, beliefs have acted upon the content on cellulose to change mere "nature" into "nature plus art." [14]

These items illustrate misconceptions that the general public have about mass/nonprint/visual media. The "objective eye of the camera" is made a fiction by the editing process; the notion of a "real world" caught by the camera is made false by the cameraman's careful manipulation of the images of reality. Network news and even Cronkite—our seemingly most credible sources of information—present restricted, narrow, edited versions of reality.

Misconceptions or misuses of nonprint media could not survive a literate viewer's ability to discern the factors that control and limit news and so-called documentary presentations. There are also positive strengths through informed study and use of these media on their own terms. Reuben Frank once advised the NBC Evening News staff: "The highest power of television journalism is not in the transmission of *information* but in the transmission of *experience* . . . joy, sorrow, shock, fear, these are the stuff of news." [15] "Seeing with feeling" is a condition well understood by Richard Lacey as he shows how the understanding of documentary effects can contribute to a viewer's ability to comprehend the viewing experience:

> By examining the feelings surrounding these films, by recognizing and valuing intuition in discussion, and by relating intuitive comments to specific effects in the film, we can begin to see when and how film language becomes film rhetoric—a device to persuade by suggestion. . . . This approach to studying documentaries sets the stage for helping students become a discerning audience, one which can *feel* as well as know how it sees. . . . The ability to trust our feelings becomes especially important as we try to distinguish between propaganda and art.[16]

13. *San Francisco Sunday Examiner and Chronicle*, 26 January 1975, p. 19.

14. Caleb Gattegno, *Towards a Visual Culture: Educating through Television* (New York: Outerbridge & Dienstfrey, 1969), p. 12.

15. Epstein, *News from Nowhere*, p. 39.

16. Richard A. Lacey, *Seeing with Feeling: Film in the Classroom* (Philadelphia: W. B. Saunders Co., 1972), pp. 74-75, 68.

Edmund Farrell also recognizes the peril and the promise of the newer electronics media as he warns:

> The electronic revolution must have the guidance of humanists if it is to be the instrumentality for releasing the creative potential of each individual, rather than an ingenious means of further degrading human life. The revolution will continue; what direction it takes depends in good part upon the wisdom and participation brought to it by those of us who profess to teach English because we care about men.[17]

Rather than allow students to be disappointed to discover that the camera is as subjective an instrument as pen or paintbrush, we should help them explore the implications of this knowledge. To discover how the camera is an instrument for *creating* reality, not merely *recording* it, we must put students behind all types of cameras, from Instamatics to video portapaks. Through first-hand experience students will learn that "objectivity" in the nonprint media is simply not possible; they will see that merely pushing the camera's shutter button results from an editorial decision.

Nonprint Media: The Next Language Art for English

The nonprint media often surpass books in their capacity to arouse interest and touch the minds and emotions of students. Their power to grip imagination and motivate students toward creative forms of expression makes them uniquely involving of the *whole* person. There is increasing evidence that nonprint media have significant but underutilized potential for English. For example, based on his studies of the effect of certain kinds of films on the cognitive abilities of children, Gavriel Salomon postulates:

> As the number of different communicational coding systems increases, the mental capacity increases. With the acquisition of each coding system, one becomes able to think in a new way, while also being better able to handle more domains of information.[18]

Another important attribute of nonprint media is their capacity to provide enjoyment for their viewers. Yet enjoyment and play in the learning process are too often ignored. If the enjoyable charac-

17. Edmund J. Farrell, *English, Education, and the Electronic Revolution* (Urbana, Ill.: National Council of Teachers of English, 1967), p. 68.

18. Gavriel Salomon, "What Is Learned and How It Is Taught: The Interaction between Media, Message, Task, and Learner," in *Media and Symbols*, p. 405.

teristics of media can be made to serve as motivating forces toward development of important critical skills and humane responses, then we will move closer to the "impossible dream" of making learning both significant and enjoyable for our students.

Another educational benefit to be derived from nonprint media comes through their use in the classroom to provide practice in coping with "stagings" from real life. The classroom offers a "safe" place for students to learn about how people use the power of the media to affect them in their own lives. They can learn about propaganda and manipulation by watching and discussing various films and television news programs and documentaries intended to convey specific "messages" or information; they can learn about the alluring, persuasive powers of the media by sharing their own responses to films with other students; they can learn about the limits of objectivity in the visual media by making films, videotapes, and photoessays of their own.

Just as direct experiences are features in the socializing process, so, too, are films and television as surrogate forms of reality. Thus, through the experience of film or television in the protected environment of the classroom, students may undergo important socializing processes that constitute rehearsals for coping more effectively in real life on their own.

The classroom is no longer a place for the *accumulation* of information. Perpetuation of this narrow conception of function simply puts the classroom in hopeless competition with the more exciting visual sources of information so easily available to today's students outside of school. Rather, the classroom should come to be a place for the *interpretation* of information, for the *examination* of thoughts and feelings stimulated by information, for *expression* and *creation* of students' own versions of reality through various media.

The best use of nonprint media in our classrooms flows from what they are uniquely capable of doing, rather than from how well they can "stand in" for the teacher or replace some verbal aspect of the curriculum. The primary function of nonprint media in English classrooms has traditionally been as an aid to the teaching of the real, more important subject, rather than as valuable means of learning in and of themselves. And the "real, more important" subject being served always required that the nonprint media be "curriculum-related" to the printed word. To stress a need for balanced approaches to media is not to advocate the complete metamorphosis of all English and language arts programs into nonprint media programs. Rather, we need to establish an effective combination of print and nonprint media that serves the purposes of dual—or full—literacy.

Important uses of media in their own right are specified here. But using the media *as* education rather than as a means to other ends does not mean that the more traditional other ends cannot also be simultaneously served. Richard Maynard reports that he has seen films "stimulate more discussion, inspire more creative writing, motivate more reading, and build up better teacher-student rapport than any educational text, device, or gimmick in existence."[19] Adele Stern reports a similar experience when she notes that "all of the forms of writing—exposition, literary criticism, narration, dialog, description, even poetry—can be found in parallels in film and provide stimulation for a composition program."[20]

Nonprint media can also be of particular use in language training. Robert Probst describes how the showing of a film (or videotape) can provide a uniform stimulus for a class writing exercise, and suggests that comparing written descriptions of the same scene by different students can provide valuable language experiences.[21] This kind of exercise also is useful in demonstrating that even though individuals in a given group may *watch* the same film, they actually *see* different films, because each student's own individual background, values, and other personal considerations determine what each sees and how he or she makes meaning out of what is seen.

Nonprint Media as Communicational Coding Systems

In considering the nature of visual and verbal codings of experience, it is interesting to note that we use the words "I see" to

19. Richard A. Maynard, *The Celluloid Curriculum: How to Use Movies in the Classroom* (New York: Hayden Book Co., 1971), p. 3.

20. Adele Stern, "Using Films in Teaching English Composition," in *The Compleat Guide to Film Study*, ed. G. Howard Poteet (Urbana, Ill.: National Council of Teachers of English, 1972), p. 171.

21. Robert E. Probst, "Visual to Verbal," *English Journal* 61 (January 1972): 71-75.

mean "I understand—I have been communicated with." Although "see" has metaphoric import in this context, it should also take on its literal signification as well. We do not need to use one form to the exclusion of the other, for as Dondis says:

> The implications of the universal quality of visual information does not stop at the point of using it as a stand-in for verbal information. The two are not in conflict. Each has unique capabilities, and yet it is the visual mode that has not been wholly utilized. Visual understanding is a natural means that does not have to be learned, but rather, through visual literacy, only refined.[22]

Are many children "afraid of the dark" simply because they cannot use their vision to deal with their environment? How did the saying, "Seeing is believing" come about? Dondis explains that from infancy we organize our needs and pleasures, preferences and fears, with great dependence on what we see; but we accept this automatic physiological mechanism in our nervous system without realizing that it can be improved through observation or extended into "an incomparable tool of human communication. . . ."[23] For example, because of a verbally-based education, adults continue to be verbally oriented, even when visual imagery accompanies the verbal information. Upon encountering a picture with a caption, most people read the words first, and then look at the picture. Watch visitors to art museums and notice the relative amount of time and attention they devote to the visual object itself compared with whatever verbal information about it is available.[24]

Visual images convey different information than do words, and in different ways. For example, it is rare that a film based on a novel or story conveys the same effects as the written version. The differences are not only in the processes of reworking the verbal information and adding visual information; there are also differences in the mental process the viewer goes through in responding to the combined information source provided by words *and* visual images. One of the reasons the extravagantly filmed version of *The Great Gatsby* was considered a failure was not because of what the film

22. Dondis, *A Primer of Visual Literacy*, p. 148.

23. Ibid., p. 1.

24. Gattegno, *Towards a Visual Culture*, p. 5.

version *did* portray, but rather because of what the written version did *not* portray. For example, Fitzgerald did not provide a physical description of Jay Gatsby, using instead other means to characterize him. Thus, each reader formed a unique "mental picture" of Gatsby. As soon as a real live actor was chosen to play the screen role, each reader, except those who already had "pictured" Robert Redford as Gatsby, was bound to be disappointed. If a fairy tale tells of a princess who is "the most beautiful girl in the world," any illustration suffers by comparison with the reader's own imagined vision. Words, as abstract symbols, require readers to make up their own mental "pictures" in order to acquire meaning.

A film should not be judged, then, on the basis of how "true" it is to the book. This kind of comparison of similar but unlike entities is like judging the quality of an orange in terms of how much it resembles an apple: they are both round, they are both fruit, they both may taste sweet, but their other unshared characteristics begin to make all the difference. It might help film directors who make films from novels to characterize their productions as "inspired by" the novel, thereby avoiding misguided comparisons.

Reading and Viewing Compared

Theories vary about the differences between the reading and viewing experience. One position holds that visual messages go directly into the viewer's cognitive structure without the processing delay necessitated by decoding print symbols into concepts and images. Gattegno represents this view when he concludes:

Sight is swift, comprehensive, simultaneously analytic and synthetic. It requires so little energy to function, as it does, at the speed of light, that it permits our minds to receive and hold an infinite number of items of information in a fraction of a second. . . . In contrast to the speed of light, we need *time* to talk and to express what we want to say.[25]

Another position holds that whatever the source of experience— printed words, spoken words, pictures, or other visuals—a person still must undertake mental processing to render the experience verbal, whether in thought or in language. A significant difference

25. Ibid., p. 4.

between reading a book and watching a film is that the film content provides a wider range of visual and auditory cues not available in the reduced cueing system of print. These additional cues make the information conveyed by the visual media more readily accessible. Still, our need to make meaning out of our experiences requires us to sort, classify, and name our experiences; a process leading to an "encoding" of visual experiences into words becomes necessary. While reading requires a *de*coding of words into images and ideas to make meaning, viewing requires an *en*coding of visual pictures into words to complete the communication of meaning.

Even so, the wide popularity of visual media may stem from their very direct impact on affective responses. Visual forms of experience touch directly the emotional or affective responses of viewers. Our feelings are the first to be involved in either a "live" or a filmed experience. If we touch a hot coal, we feel physical pain; if we see a film with sad visual images, we feel emotional anguish. In both cases the cognitive processes that ultimately may label these experiences will be secondary to the immediate feelings stimulated by the experience. Weeping or crying out are noncognitive forms of expressing pain or sadness; a dancer might express these feelings through body movements. However, if we wish to communicate those feelings to persons not present to witness them, a secondary verbal encoding must occur: "Touching that hot coal caused intense pain," or "Watching that film about the starving children evoked deep feelings of sadness."

The reader, on the other hand, must *first* decode printed symbols and then locate corresponding information and feelings in memory before the reading experience can evoke an affective response. Thus, the student with normal vision but lacking reading ability can watch a film and make a meaningful response to it. This same student looking at a page of print encounters a barrier that allows neither cognitive nor affective experiences to occur.

Nonprint Media Compared: Different Information, Different Potential

So far, nonprint media have been considered together largely without individual distinguishing factors. However, as Edmund Carpenter notes, "Each medium, if its bias is properly exploited, reveals and communicates a unique aspect of reality."[26] A comparison of film and television makes their basic differences emerge. Watching a film is a solitary experience, even though the viewer is seated amidst a large group of other viewers. We *go out* to a movie, to a special building or room constructed for that purpose alone. We pay money for admission, and we sit in a large dark room with no other visual or aural stimuli to detract from the larger-than-life reality on the big screen. Watching a television program is a more social experience, even if it involves only the members of one's own family. We *stay in* to watch television, in our own home, in a room where the television set is little more than another piece of furniture. Our price of admission is the purchase of a set, which we then watch "free" (until the picture tube goes). The "theater" is our lighted living room, with its constant visual and aural distractions from the smaller-than-life reality on the little screen. In terms of the quality of the picture, we almost never see television as well as we see films. Even with the best of reception, for various technological reasons, the television picture is not yet as good as the film image. Ironically, this very fact gives television a kind of reality and immediacy (even though videotape makes this a false immediacy), since "real life" is more like television (rough around the edges) than like film (slick and finished). (Some new developments in television technology will eliminate some of these differences—excellent picture quality in ¾-inch videocassettes, feature length films that can be rented and shown through the home television set without interruption for commercials, and the like).[27]

What television in its finest forms offers its viewers is indicated by Jacob Bronowski as he describes the making of his television series, "The Ascent of Man":

TV is not a lantern lecture—it is a conversation, a kind of fireside chat. . . . If you want to engage people, you must do so on a personal level. . . . I call it the medium of presence. Now obviously the

26. Edmund Carpenter, "The New Languages," in *Explorations in Communication*, ed. Edmund Carpenter and Marshall McLuhan (Boston: Beacon Press, 1960), pp. 173-74, quoted in David R. Olson, "Introduction," in *Media and Symbols*, p. 13.

27. Deborah Dashow Ruth, "A Dual Vision of Literacy: Possible and Probable Futures of Nonprint Media," *Arizona English Bulletin* 18 (October 1975): 156-63.

camera can't be present when the great discoveries are made. But we can take the viewer with us while we come upon the place where it all happened and recreate the aura. . . . I call it bicultural history emphasizing man's two abilities—the scientific, side by side with the poetic. TV is perfect for this.[28]

Daniel Boorstin notes that although television seems simply to combine the techniques of the motion picture and the phonograph with those of the radio, it all adds up to something more—a new way of mass-producing the moment for instant consumption. "Whereas films, church services, sports events, parades, and commemorative events are still shared by the many people who actually attend them, television has expanded the scope of this sharing, although, ironically, isolating people in their own homes at the same time."[29] Having a television set in the classroom and using daytime programs as input for class discussions and activities help overcome the isolating nature of television viewing by relating students' school experiences to their own life experiences with television.

Turning to phonographs, tape recorders, and radio, we can observe further unique experiential characteristics. Effective listening requires learning what not to listen to as well as what to listen for. Yet, the aural media have received little attention in their own right, being almost exclusively employed as supplements to print. It is important to consider how they can provide primary experiences as well, since aural media also can reach emotions directly. With small cassette tape recorders and audiocassettes becoming less expensive, students can use this medium to produce and put on "radio shows" and "readers' theater" presentations, to try "audio-journalism" with various kinds of interviews and reports, and other listening adventures that provide immediate—and repeatable—results. Of course, they can also make original soundtracks for their own films, or make a new soundtrack for an old film.

The more static forms of nonprint media—still cameras, slide projectors, and overhead projectors—present endless possibilities for creative expression, either singly or in multimedia combinations. In-

28. Dwight Whitney, "TV Is Not a Lantern Lecture—It Is a Conversation," *TV Guide*, 4 January 1975, pp. 5-6.

29. Daniel Boorstin, *The Americans: The Democratic Experience* (New York: Random House, 1973), p. 393.

expensive pocket cameras take either prints or slides, offering creative possibilities for personal statements through photoessays and
photojournalism. The proliferation of "blow-up" studios where
any slide or print can be enlarged to life-size or bigger for just a
few dollars offers interesting new ways to explore and express self-
image.

Multimedia presentations, combining film, still pictures, videotapes, and/or audiotape, can provide an infinite variety of visual
experiences both for the viewer and for the creator, whether they
be "happenings" or more tightly structured productions. Either the
"happening," which is strongly improvisational with little predetermined structure and no two presentations alike, or the "production," which is carefully sequenced and repeatable, can provide
a means of developing the expressive talents of students.

Such integrative uses of visual and verbal faculties serve to unify
the senses. Harley Parker traces the disintegrative effect of our educational system, as presently constituted, upon the senses of the
child. Schools take the young child, who uses a style of imagery
derived from direct perceptions through *all* his senses, and, by teaching him the alphabet and its related linear skills of reading and
writing, effectually reduce the child's sensory world into a series
of visual abstractions.[30] Unless the educational system integrates
multisensory experiences into the curriculum, youth will continue
to categorize school activities as separate from—and irrelevant to—
their own multisensorily stimulated lives.

Changes in Coding of Information Require Changes in Teaching

The teaching style and attitude associated with use of nonprint
media affect significantly the way school media experiences are received and perceived by students. It makes a difference if, when
students are shown a film, they understand that the experience is
equivalent in educational value to reading a book. Richard Maynard
emphasizes this point: "If a teacher shows a film and then lets it
die by moving on to what the textbook says, he has sabotaged the

30. Harley Parker, "The Beholder's Share and the Problem of Literacy,"
in *Media and Symbols*, p. 89.

experience and the kids will simply think of films as 'teacher's day off.' "[31]

Three general changes in teaching role and instructional behavior are needed to accomplish the new styles in learning offered through the experiences of nonprint media. First, a teacher will need to change or expand his or her own nonschool experiences with these media; second, a teacher must be willing to relinquish the role of authoritative interpreter and to participate in a mutual exploration of media experiences; and third, a teacher must foster development of a classroom environment that brings "I see" and "I feel" responses into important relations with "I think" responses.

Teachers who want to use nonprint media effectively must spend some of their hours outside class watching the television programs and feature films their students watch in order to encourage and participate in open discussions of these shared experiences. As teachers explore television as today's dominant mode of cultural expression and communication for most children and adolescents, they, too, may strengthen their discriminatory, critical response to television, neither accepting it as it is, nor rejecting it out of hand. There is, however, no media equivalent to "master plots" to help the busy teacher take short cuts to preparation for "teaching" nonprint media. Nothing supplants the experience of viewing, just as "master plots" do not really supplant the experience of reading the original.

Teachers who want to use nonprint media effectively need to risk sharing their traditional authority and learn along with their students. The rewards are likely to outweigh the risks. Richard Maynard, a teacher, describes his experience:

I lectured less, the class discussed more, and I discovered that personally I could be a lot more effective by guiding rather than directing. . . . In terms of selecting the films . . . I called the shots. . . . . But once I turned on that projector, things were different. My students and I were on a new, common ground. We were sharing an experience together. We had begun to communicate.[32]

To the question, "How do you teach film?" Charles Grenier, another teacher, answers:

31. Maynard, *The Celluloid Curriculum*, p. 209.
32. Ibid., pp. 13-14.

You don't. You sit in the back of the darkened room and watch. . . . [Then] you talk with the kids, but, more important, you listen to them . . . [as they] discuss their feelings, their thoughts, themselves. Don't worry about your questions. Listen for theirs. Lead them back to the film when they get too far astray; move them, without pushing, toward making connections, toward seeing relationships; but don't belabor the old kinds of relationships: setting to theme, mood to plot, character to language. Explore relationships that are relevant to the kids, to their own lives. Let them freewheel with their imaginations. . . . Above all, don't force them to see the film your way. Don't, in your infinite wisdom, tell them how and what it means. Don't intellectualize it to death.[33]

The excellent handbook, *Doing the Media: A Portfolio of Activities and Resources,* provides a friendly caution: "media making and media perceiving make authority an anachronism."[34]

Teachers who want to use nonprint media effectively must be as willing to express and share their own feelings as they would have students express theirs. Teachers willing to risk the changes in role and instructional behavior described here will discover fresh opportunities to reach and touch students in a way that can bring back the turned off, tuned out student. And in so doing they will raise imagination and feeling to the same level of respect and acceptance in the classroom as that which has traditionally been granted to thoughts and ideas.

A Model for Teaching Media

In classes at any level, the emphasis should be on active participation in the experience of nonprint media through discussion of reactions to and interpretations of media experiences, through hands-on experimentation with making nonprint media, and through other creative responses stimulated or generated by the viewing or listening experience. This instructional model does *not* begin with a historical study of film, nor does it begin with a literary-based study of film "classics." It also puts aside any of the formal procedures used by critics in reviewing and evaluating films. These three im-

33. Charles F. Grenier, "Film Study Hang Ups," *Media and Methods* 5 (January 1969): 33.

34. Robert Geller and Kit Laybourne, "Some Guidelines for Film/Media Programs," in *Doing the Media: A Portfolio of Activities and Resources* (New York: Center for Understanding Media, 1972), p. 36.

portant advanced studies should not be mixed in with the experiential, participatory aspects of beginning media study. History, esthetics, and formal critical studies are all important aspects of a total treatment of nonprint media; but most students are not yet ready for the more advanced "total treatment." Although children may be too young to appreciate the finer points of film esthetics, they are never too young to derive a great deal of value from viewing and making films. Children do not need to know all about the history of cinema or television in order to use film or videotape as expressive forms. All they need are the necessary motor skills to operate a camera.

Similar considerations apply to older students: it is more important for the student's own growth and understanding to experience the medium firsthand through viewing or hands-on through making before turning to more abstract features of media. Those students who become more deeply interested in the art of film, photography, or television will, independently of any curriculum outline or lesson plan, seek out this information.

A simple developmental sequence for encouraging and dealing with responses to films in elementary and secondary English and language arts classes can be effectively adapted to active viewing of all nonprint media. A loosely structured, flexible, open-ended technique, the sequence presented here helps viewers relate to and make meaning out of shared visual experiences. Animated films (cartoons) work best for starting this discussion sequence, because, as abstractions of social reality, they can depict social relationships and processes without rooting them in specific, identifiable objects or people. A short film without narration but with an easily discernible story line, communicated through familiar visual images, has content readily accessible to students of all ages and backgrounds. The details of the following model have been refined through working with such films with hundreds of teachers and students. A four-stage discussion sequence with a pattern of open questioning has emerged which serves to open up cognitive and affective responses to film, and also to enhance the viewer's ability to use language precisely to discover, examine, and create meaning. Stage 1 is "seeing" (telling what happened); stage 2 is "thinking" (interpreting and understanding); stage 3 is "feeling" (reacting emotionally);

stage 4 is "judging" (exercising critical thinking). In all four stages, the emphasis is on the validity of the individual viewer's responses.

At stage 1 we ask, "What did you see?" or "What do you remember seeing on the screen?" We call for a literal narrative or retelling of what the student saw, in straight, objective, noninterpretive, nonjudgmental language. This stage emphasizes the role of perception in remembering and reporting accurately. Although we all may look at the same film, we all actually see and create different films in our "mind's eye," because we bring to the viewing event our own individual contexts, different cultural experiences and backgrounds. Thus, the first stage of discussion intends to focus the viewer's attention on the objective data on the screen so that the class can begin to unify the shared objective experience of the film. Ideally, the film is shown a second time to enable students to check out the accuracy of their perception and visual memory. This is the only point where a viewer can strictly be said to be "right" or "wrong" in accounting for objective data in the film.

We begin at this stage for two reasons. First, many students—and many teachers, too—want to begin immediately looking for *the* meaning, seeking that one single "correct" interpretation before they are even fully aware of all the data available to their minds and senses. Second, many students' initial response to some films (or some books) is, "That's dumb," or "That's stupid." This is not always an inappropriate response; however, it is judgmental, and thus should be withheld until stage 4. It can be an appropriate response if it is based on reasons derived through observations (stage 1) and interpretation (stage 2).

At stage 2 we ask, "What do you think it means?" or, "How would you interpret what you saw?" The discussion opens up here to construction of possible symbolic meanings, messages, morals, and the like. Any interpretation may be justified if it is linked to the film's available stock of information, as perceived in stage 1 of the discussion. This stage encourages exploration into the subjective nature of meaning. In selecting descriptive labels, in assigning motives, in establishing causal sequences, students should be free to make their own decisions of relevance and applicability. This procedure of allowing meaning to unfold through interaction of personal interpretations discourages the "one-right-answer" syndrome, a pattern of behavior too often observed in teachers and students. There is, in this approach, the implication that no one person—the teacher, another student, or even the filmmaker—can assign a single "correct" meaning to a given work. Each viewer constructs personal meanings, but he or she needs to understand the sources of these meanings. This open-ended discussion enables the objective data on the screen to interact with the subjective nature of the viewer's own predispositions to produce individual meanings.

At stage 3 we ask, "What did you feel during that film?" or "What are you feeling now about that experience?" This is not intended as an invasion of the student's privacy; the student always has the option to "pass" this question. But this is an invitation to share personal reactions, and to discover that others were affected similarly, resulting in a better understanding of other people and of what it means to be human. Discussion at this stage can wander in all directions, since the focus is not the film itself but what different reactions the film caused/evoked in different viewers. Teachers should be prepared to share their own feelings, too.

At stage 4 we ask, "Did you like it?" or "Based on what you thought the film meant, how well did you think the film communicated that meaning?" or "Was it worth communicating?" This is where students may exercise critical thinking on questions of value based on specific reasons for their reactions. When discussions begin at this stage, many students are unable to articulate the reasons for their reactions; but as the teacher takes them through stages 1, 2, and/or 3, they not only get in touch with their reasons, but their initial responses may actually change. In short, they are prepared to fulfill the role of responsible critic. Knowledge of the bases for their opinions, of the processes of judging and criticizing, can place them in an intellectually valid position to challenge the teacher, the filmmaker, or anyone else who insists on that "one right answer." This final stage helps students understand that a film (or a story or poem) brought into the classroom by the teacher can be liked or disliked for intellectually valid reasons.

In the free and open exchange of this four-stage discussion, students will learn to identify attempts by nonprint media to manipulate them. But such discoveries must be allowed to come from the students themselves, not from the teacher's predetermined plan to steer them in the direction of that one "right" interpretation.

Teachers also should avoid limiting the potential range of student responses by giving lengthy verbal introductions to films or even by briefly annotating them prior to viewing, or by narrowing the focus of discussion to identified themes. For the most part, acknowledging the director or filmmaker (the film's "author"), and perhaps also the title will suffice. The film—and the students—will do the rest.

As useful and effective as the four-stage discussion sequence is, it is not necessary to go through every stage for every film, nor is it necessary to proceed in linear order. Certain stages and steps will be appropriate for different films. Once this basic sequence is introduced, subsequent discussions can begin with stage 3 or stage 2, as desired. However, when discussions become bogged down by disagreements over "what really happened," the film needs to be reshown and discussion needs to return to stage 1 observations for the clarification essential to more advanced analysis.

Richard Lacey describes the results of conducting this kind of discussion:

> What emerges . . . is a gradually richer set of relationships among images, sounds and implied ideas. In this way the art of film, instead of being killed by excessive analysis, has a fair chance to continue working on the audience.[35]

Open-ended written responses can also be effective alternatives to discussions. One version, for example, is called "image skimming" (Lacey's term). This procedure has the students spend, say, one minute writing down everything that comes into their minds right after seeing a film. Another version is "first three things," a procedure that has the students write down the first three (or four or five) images, thoughts, sounds, feelings, or any combination of these that come to them as the film ends. Or there also is the "fill-a-page" exercise that borrows from Ken Macrorie.[36] Here students simply write everything that comes into their minds at the end of a film

35. Richard A. Lacey, "Whatdaya Do When the Lights Go On?" *Media and Methods* 6 (November 1969): 77.

36. Ken Macrorie, *Writing to Be Read* (New York: Hayden Book Co., 1968), p. 8.

until they have filled up a page. These written responses, when shared, not only demonstrate how differently we all respond to a single event—especially a visual event—but also once again they demonstrate that there is no "one right answer" over which the class whiz kid, or the teacher, has any monopoly.

If it is true that one learns to write by writing, then the same holds true for making films, videotapes, photographs, and the like. Just as reading books makes some students want to write, so watching films and television will make some students want to make films and videotapes. And just as writing begins in the early grades, so should media making begin as early as kindergarten. Piaget describes the function of intelligence as consisting "in understanding and inventing, . . . in building up structures by structuring reality." [37] Filmmaking provides a means of structuring reality, because a filmmaker must collect a set of "image events" on film and then build up a set of structures by ordering and organizing these "image events" into a sequence for communication. Making a film can help a child learn how to manipulate images and how to communicate with them. [38]

As for the teacher's role in media making, it is more common for teachers to underestimate than to overestimate the potential of children and adolescents for understanding and using media tools. [39] This observation modifies the role of the teacher from that of "director" to that of "producer"; the teacher becomes responsible for establishing an atmosphere for creativity, and the students do the creating. [40]

Nonprint media belong in English and language arts programs of today and tomorrow. The model for the study and making of nonprint media can no more be overdone in English classes than can reading and writing be overdone. They are all part of the whole task of developing expanded forms of literacy.

37. Jean Piaget, *Science of Education and the Psychology of the Child* (New York: Grossman Publishers, 1970), p. 28, quoted in Worth, "The Uses of Film," p. 293.

38. Worth, "The Uses of Film," pp. 289, 293.

39. Morrow and Suid, "Media in the Classroom," 41.

40. Paul Carrico, "Student Filmmaking: Why and How," *Media and Methods* 6 (November 1969): 41.

Evaluation: The Inevitable Question

An admirable statement of goals and objectives from a film-making course developed by Lynn Phillips in Miami reads:

My goals (as a teacher) are to provide students with a new mode for communication and self-expression; to give an opportunity to explore and expand creativity (through filmmaking); to work more effectively in a group oriented situation; and to value one another's contributions and talents in a group task.[41]

But how can progress toward such goals be evaluated? By the number or length of student films made? By the number of arguments that do or do not break out in the classroom? Geller and Laybourne provide the beginning of an answer:

No hard research exists yet to prove that students read better . . . or think better after seeing films or making their own. Empirical observations do show that . . . teachers and students thrive in the open environment that film and media create, that high motivational levels are carrying over to all other levels of learning and teaching. Also new skills in arrangement and ordering, selectivity and editing, perceiving and creating become very apparent. . . . A caution is offered . . . to avoid plunging too quickly into rigid measurement approaches and taxonomies. It can kill off the excitement and fun of innovative learning. It can hinge all experiences to desperately anticipated outcomes.[42]

Nonprint media experiences do not lend themselves easily to conventional forms of evaluation; however, it can be observed that in schools where filmmaking is a potential part of every student's experience, there is a marked increase in other forms of creative expression, especially poetry.[43] Teachers who have worked extensively with nonprint media in their classrooms report that previous scholastic ability has little or nothing to do with whether a student can handle media equipment efficiently or express himself or herself through film or videotape.[44] Maynard calls classroom media ex-

41. Lynn Phillips, "Filmmaking Course (Elective)," in *Curriculum Development Workshop—Seminar in Media: Final Report*, ed. Audrey Roth (Miami, Fla.: Miami-Dade Community College, 1974), p. 12.

42. Geller and Laybourne, "Some Guidelines for Film/Media Programs," p. 32.

43. Carrico, "Student Filmmaking," pp. 42-43.

44. Ellie Waterston, "Super 8 Filmmaking," in *Doing the Media*, p. 94.

periences "fantastic intellectual equalizers," putting the academi-
cally "slowest" student on the same plane as the brightest ones.[45]

The report at the end of the first year of "Project Success," a
media studies program at Mamaroneck School in New York, provides an idea of what can be expected:

> Parents as well as teachers learned about the different forms of
> media and their possible application to the classroom. Together we saw
> students who had been bored with school become excited about the
> learning processes through their work in media. . . . This media program
> won't solve all the problems kids have relating to school, but I feel
> very strongly that it is a step in the right direction.[46]

Locating Nonprint Media Resources for English

Getting more nonprint media into the curriculum requires knowing and locating resources. Just as there is no way of getting to know
the television programs or the commercially distributed feature
films that the students know other than by watching them, there
is no way of getting to know which short films or videocassettes
are best for classroom use other than by previewing them. In selecting media for the classroom, it is important to view them in advance
of use mainly to assure quality and determine appropriateness. So
many excellent films and videocassettes are available that use of any
that are less than excellent is inexcusable. Users of media do, of
course, have to concern themselves with what is acceptable by
"community standards." Nevertheless, one needs to be wary of any
well-meaning but misguided attempt to "protect" students from
harsh realities. The prime time television and the evening news programs that students regularly view show just about everything except explicit sex. If students are to learn to deal easily with the
routine information in their daily experiences, this "informal curriculum of the mass media" must be brought into the classroom and
subjected to critical scrutiny.

For media ideas, people, and resources in general, the Center for
Understanding Media in New York City can supply a broad range
of information. For professional literature, the National Council of
Teachers of English has a large and growing list of books and

45. Maynard, *The Celluloid Curriculum*, p. 209.

46. Frank Lifrieri, "Project Success," in *Doing the Media*, p. 136.

pamphlets; a brochure describing all of its media-related publica-
tions is also available. For short films, there are dozens of distribu-
tors, many of which are familiar to district audiovisual or media
personnel. Many of the animated films from studios in Eastern
Europe are excellent, as well as almost any short film made by the
National Film Board of Canada. Also, look for award winners—
Academy Awards, the Ciné Golden Eagle, and awards made at the
Atlanta and Chicago Film Festivals, and at the American Educational
Film Festival. For in-service courses in media, many local university
or college extension divisions offer both summer and year-round
programs designed for teachers.

Contrary to current mythology about expensive hardware and
software, a great expenditure of money is not necessary to introduce
nonprint media activities into the curriculum. The first thing to do
is make an inventory of school and district equipment. Such a search
may yield surprising results, such as cameras and portable videotape
equipment used by many athletic departments to film or tape football games. Virtually every school has a clutch of 16-mm projectors,
overhead, slide, and filmstrip projectors, and phonographs. Students
can make films without cameras by scratching with a pin or doodling
with a felt pen directly on 8-mm or 16-mm film leader available free
from television stations or film processing centers. An amazing
amount of equipment can be scrounged or borrowed from home,
photography stores, and hardware stores. Cost need not be an ob-
stacle to the development of effective media programs. By beginning
with what is available and inexpensive, such programs will surely
grow as their results are noticed.

Forecasts: What's Ahead in Nonprint Media
for English Instruction

On the technological level, television seems to be the medium
with the most far-reaching implications as its development continues. Such innovations as video-discs (you "play" a television program the way you "play" a record), the ¾-inch videocassettes (the
picture quality is excellent and operation is simple), portable videotape equipment (prices have been reduced significantly), large-
screen television projection (television no longer requires the class
to huddle around a single set), are causing television to emerge as

the most flexible and widely usable nonprint medium of them all, combining nearly all of the capabilities of film, television, and even the nonmoving media. The implications for the imaginative English classroom are fascinating; the possibilities are endless.

Two other growing developments in this field will make television the medium of total access and total immediacy: cable television, with its potential for broader audience access to existing broadcasts as well as specialized programming for specialized audiences; and satellite broadcasting, with its potential for broadcasting an event or message for the whole world—McLuhan's "global village"—to watch.[47]

On the educational level, Audrey Roth of the English Department at Miami-Dade Community College North, member of the Committee on Media of the National Council of Teachers of English, suggests that use of small, portable videotape recorders will increase and that the development and dissemination of ¾-inch videocassettes will make possible better uses of videotaped programs. Communities will pool media resources and consultants, as much out of interest as out of the need to meet rising costs of film rentals, and more use will be made of professional media people in the classroom. Frank McLaughlin of the English Department at Fairleigh Dickinson University, editor of *Media and Methods* magazine, bases his predictions on the relative health of the American economy. Assuming improved conditions, McLaughlin foresees more elective courses in nonprint media in English as well as other curricula; less use of feature films (which are still expensive to rent) and more emphasis on short films (which would be greatly helped by development of a "Films in Print" catalogue or periodical of all short films available); a gain in the importance of nonprint media in conjunction with increased interest in affective and process-oriented education; more higher-education emphasis on nonprint mass media communication, including M.A. and Ph.D. programs; and "English as Communication Arts" as a possible new philosophical shift that would enhance the importance of nonprint media. A hope, more than a prediction, expressed by William Strong, is that media study will do more than teach students how to see. He believes that the mid-twentieth century media environment has conditioned people to

47. Ruth, "A Dual Vision of Literacy."

insulate themselves emotionally, and that developing media literacy can be the means to educate all of the senses, to resensitize man's humanness.[48]

On the philosophical and attitudinal level, a single recent finding is significant: In 1959, of the people asked which one of the four media they would most want to keep, supposing they could continue to have only one (radio, television, newspapers, or magazines), 32 percent said newspapers, while 42 percent said television. In 1974, 59 percent said television, while only 19 percent said newspapers.[49] Fortunately, such a choice will probably not be necessary. But changes in attitude and behavior, coupled with rapid advancements in nonprint media technology, are too important for educators to ignore.

Douglass Cater predicts that the next decade or two will radically alter America's system of communications, either for better or for worse, and television will be the key factor. He sees the need for new approaches to television criticism that would enable us to examine systematically the style, technique, and message of the best of television programming rather than continuing to lament over the worst. Such new criticism should extend to elementary and secondary schools, where children could be "stimulated to think about the medium which so dominates their waking hours."[50]

David Littlejohn notes differences in attitude toward television as a kind of "generation gap":

The intellectual born and educated much before 1950 may spend much of his life trying to wish television away, or at least to convert it into something closer to his own past of reading, reason, naive wonder, and private imagination. . . . But . . . the generation after 1950 will think about television in entirely different ways. They will accept its pervasiveness, its slickness and tricks, its limitations and potentials far more freely and guiltlessly than I can. . . . Good things *do* happen on

48. Carole Masley Kirkton, "Media Literacy: Focus on Film," *English Journal* 60 (September 1971): 834.

49. The Roper Organization, Inc./Burns W. Roper, *Trends in Public Attitudes toward Television and Other Mass Media, 1959-1974* (New York: Television Information Office, 1975), pp. 4-5.

50. Douglass Cater, "Introduction: Television and Thinking People," in *Television as a Social Force: New Approaches to TV Criticism*, ed. Douglass Cater and Richard Adler (New York: Praeger Publishers, 1975), pp. 1-7.

television, because good people do get into TV and learn to live with it. . . . The secret is not to ignore or despise the audience-trapping tricks of "Hogan's Heroes" or "The Dating Game," but to use them better, and to better purpose. . . . [Television] is now the dominant mode of communication in this country.[51]

To this, Cater adds: "Television is not to be repealed, but to be lived with, adjusted to, and, most of all, understood and approached creatively." [52]

But how can developing visual literacy through "the next language art" have an effect on this gangling adolescent of our technology? Kit Laybourne, of The Center for Understanding Media, suggests that as we help students make sense out of television and as they develop their own values and expectations, it is possible that we will be helping the television medium improve itself. "Better TV depends on better TV audiences." [53] In fact, the Center has found that student use of videotape led to more discriminating viewing of television. Indeed, the effects of media literacy today on media quality tomorrow can only be beneficial.

To become fully literate in today's world means, as John Culkin bids us:

. . . to acknowledge the existence and influence of this new media culture and enable the child to master its codes and to control its impact. We should want them to be active, intelligent, appreciative and selective consumers of the total media culture, just as in the past we have tried to develop taste and appreciation for the traditional arts and humanities.[54]

As nonprint media technologies continue to develop and have their effects on the lives of our students and on us, the goal of "expanded literacy," visual along with verbal, should be part of every English and language arts curriculum. If we can help our students to live wisely and humanely within this new media culture, as teachers we will have made an important contribution to the elimination of the "relevance gap" without sacrificing education, literacy, or our students in the process.

51. David Littlejohn, "Communicating Ideas by Television," in *Television as a Social Force*, pp. 63-79.

52. Cater, "Introduction: Television and Thinking People," p. 5.

53. Kit Laybourne, "Television Study," in *Doing the Media*, pp. 170-71.

54. John Culkin, "Doing the Truth," in *Doing the Media*, p. 8.

CHAPTER V

√ *Values in the English Classroom*

HELEN C. LODGE*

Introduction

Courses of study, textbooks, and teachers' statements of their instructional goals all assure the reader that concern with building moral values is an important outcome of the study of English. Despite changes that have altered landmarks in English instruction in the last twenty years, the examination of values and the gradual formulation of a coherent code of ethics have remained a desired outcome of instruction in the English language arts.

A theory of teaching explicitly for values, focusing on clarification of values, is receiving increasing attention[1] because it focuses thinking on a central need of the decades ahead—the need to involve students in a study of their values as guides to action through examining dilemmas that all individuals face, making choices, and looking at moral consequences. Students coping with these dilemmas and their consequences must commit themselves, must look at consequences of choices made, and thus must look at themselves.

But complex moral dilemmas, often more complex than those devised by value clarification strategists, are inherent in much of the content taught and literature experienced in the English language arts. Unlike many other areas of study, English succeeds much of the time if it moves students to look at their own ex-

---

* Consultant readers for this chapter were Lawrence Kohlberg, Professor of Education and Social Psychology, Harvard Graduate School of Education, and Dianne L. Monson, Professor of Education, University of Washington.

1. The theory was first set forth in Louis E. Raths, Merrill Harmin, and Sidney B. Simon, *Values and Teaching* (Columbus, Ohio: Charles E. Merrill Publishing Co., 1966), in Sidney B. Simon, Leland W. Howe, and Howard Kirschenbaum, *Values Clarification* (New York: Hart Publishing Co., 1972), and in numerous articles in educational journals.

periences, at the world of experience that they reconstruct through language, and at their values. Good teaching practice in English has always led to the examination of values.

Glimpses of Present Practice

SENIOR HIGH: LITERATURE

The school is a large urban high school in a working class area; the class, an "average" class of about thirty-five tenth graders with reading ability ranging from sixth through ninth grade as measured on standardized tests; the situation, the students have listened to a recording of Robert Frost's "The Death of the Hired Man," while following the printed text of the poem in their books. Students have now divided into their permanent discussion groups to look at questions probing their reactions to the poem and to raise questions of their own. The leader of one group is a boy who knows how to get each member of the group to commit himself. The girl sitting next to him takes notes so that the discussion can be reported back to the class as a whole. The leader reads a two-part question asking which character in the poem seems most real and for which character the reader feels most sympathy. Each member of the seven-member group speaks in turn and gives reasons for his selection. Most members vote for Silas, the hired man, on both counts. Each member cites reasons for his choice—Silas's poverty, his need to save face, to preserve his self-respect even though he is dying. One girl votes for Mary on both counts because Mary is compassionate and is able to help Silas preserve his self-respect. The final member of the group, a Mexican-American male, soft-spoken but insistent, votes for Warren on both counts. Warren, he explains, is the one who must make hard decisions because he is the provider, the head of the family, the one who must look ahead. Thus the decisions Warren makes are sometimes hard but necessary. Nonetheless Warren shows compassion and is allowing himself to be persuaded to rehire Silas when news comes of Silas's death. The leader, surprised that someone has thus justified Warren's actions, polls the group to find whether Rudy has changed anyone's opinion. Each member concedes that Warren may have understandable reasons for not wanting to take Silas back at once. Two people in the group state that Warren reminds them of their fathers. While no one changes his vote within the group, all members concede that perhaps the dilemma in the poem is more complex than they had thought. Rudy lapses into silence, his manner conveying that he feels his contribution has been important.

JUNIOR HIGH: LITERATURE

The next school is a junior high school in a lower-middle-class area of megapolis. The class is a noisy mixture of eighth graders who have just read a short story, "The Dead Dog." The story concerns an old man forced through circumstances to live with his son and daughter-in-law. Part of his daily routine is to take the household pet, a little dog, out of the apartment for a walk. On an impulse the old man, while walking the dog, removes the dog's leash. The dog, unaccustomed to freedom, runs into the street and is killed by a passing motorist. Before the old man returns to the apartment, he carefully reattaches the leash to the dead dog. There the story ends. The classroom is loud with frustration and annoyance over the story. Comments fly that the story is "dumb" and pointless, that the daughter-in-law is put upon and the old man responsible for the death of the family pet. The teacher selects two students from the class, instructs them briefly, and sends them outside. He then informs the class that the two are going to "play out" what happens when the old man returns to the apartment. Meanwhile the other members of the class are to write down what they think will take place at such a meeting. What explanation does the old man make to the daughter-in-law concerning the death of the dog? The two students reenter the class and take their places at the front of the classroom. At first they are a bit self-conscious, but soon they enter into the characters they are depicting. The woman asks, "How did the dog get into the street?" She persists, "How did the dog get away? How could the accident have happened? You said the leash was still on the dog." The old man stalls. He does not tell her that he removed the leash even momentarily. He tells her that he cannot explain the accident, that he does not understand how the accident happened. The improvisation ends with the two staring at each other, the woman hostile, the old man regretful but silent and reserved. Class discussion reopens and veers toward the importance of the old man's freeing the dog and then reattaching the leash to its body. This time the class discusses the man's lack of freedom, his lack of trust in his relationship with his daughter-in-law. Some members even draw parallels between his lack of freedom and the dog's. The class feels some relief at having "understood" the story. One or two members volunteer that old age must be lonely. One boy states that he would not want to live to be as old as the old man in the story. One girl challenges that comment by stating that when old age does come he will want to live, to feel that he counts for something, and to be treated with respect. The class listens thoughtfully. There is a moment of stillness before the students begin their next activity.

ELEMENTARY: LITERATURE

The school is middle class, suburban. The children are fifth and sixth graders who achieve at grade level or above, who know each other well, and who are aware of their own achievement level and of their comfortable middle-class status. Yet even within this apparently cohesive group of children are a number of "fringers": one child who has run away from home, some children who feel a lack of acceptance at home, some who achieve partly to attain parental acceptance. The teacher shares with them a picture story book, introducing it by saying that it is a story she reread recently and liked, one that they may have missed reading earlier. The story is *Crow Boy*, by Taro Yashima, a tale set in Japan. The class, grouped around the teacher, follows with interest each succeeding picture, each episode in the story of Chibi. It is the story of the little isolate within the class who finally emerges in his last year of elementary school as a child uniquely attuned to the rhythms of nature, who can imitate the call of any bird but especially the calls of crows. Chibi comes into his own through the efforts of a new young teacher, Mr. Isobe. The class sighs with satisfaction as the story concludes. The teacher asks a few questions, largely speculative ones: How do you suppose the isolating of Chibi got started? Why do you think Chibi continued to come to school so faithfully? What was there about Mr. Isobe that made him special? Have you ever known someone like Chibi? The discussion gains momentum. As children explain what happened to Chibi, they reveal that they know how the process of victimizing an outsider, someone obviously different from them, begins and continues. Here and there both boys and girls indicate that children they have known in earlier grades had been in the same situation as Chibi. Two children within the group—girls—volunteer, "I know how Chibi felt." The discussion concludes with the teacher attempting to sum up what the children have said: the people we isolate and make fun of are often people we don't understand; often we don't really value the uniqueness of people; we want them to be just like us.

SENIOR HIGH: LANGUAGE

A senior English class designed for general students, most of whom are not college bound, is seeking to understand the obligations of the press in America. At school they are receiving the Los Angeles *Times* for two weeks. These students come from families that receive no newspaper except a "shopper" delivered weekly. Many of them follow the news only on radio and television. Thus they seldom follow the development of important national and international news stories. They express their own frustration and anger in trying to understand what happened to alter petroleum guidelines so that gas and oil prices skyrocketed. Their only comment about the congressional hearing is that "Everybody's lying. Everybody's trying to make a buck." The guarded language of the witnesses called before the congressional committee is, they know, language designed to conceal. Few within the class express any sentiment that government institutions can work for them to protect their interests. The teacher realizes that to get a sense of commitment from these students, he must first cope with their sense of powerlessness.

The Reaffirmation of a Concern for Values

The post–Vietnam War, post–Watergate era in education has begun with changed students, changed teachers. Most teachers are still mindful of their obligations to teach content and traditional skills; the push for goals, performance objectives, and measurable gains sustains pressure for content and skills. But both teachers and students are looking for something more in an era when the viability of our institutions has been called into question, indeed when

the capability of our political institutions has so recently seemed
to depend on the insights, the integrity, and the willingness of a
few men and women to act. Teachers are looking again at their
subject primarily for those aspects of it that are humane, that extend human experience and human sympathies. These aspects nurture thoughtful assessment of oneself and one's values in relation to
the larger society and its values as reflected in its literature and its
language, particularly its public language. Both students and teachers in the last decade have become more accustomed to small-group
work, to role playing and improvisation. Within these groups and
within improvised situations students listen to each other as they
respond to dilemmas encountered in literature, weigh the actions
of characters, seek to extend their experience and understanding,
and examine public language to determine its purpose and credibil-
ity. These students are mindful that they represent a generation
that must live out its span of years on this earth in a world it never
made but must somehow change, if change is possible. Teachers,
on the other hand, they see as representing the older generation,
the establishment, which must somehow rationalize the past and
protect itself. A good teacher they regard as an adult with some
warmth, an awareness of them as human beings, some knowledge
of the patterns of their lives, one who directs learning, who keeps
things organized and orderly. But a teacher's view of the world
and of reality is, as they see it, bound to be influenced by his membership in an older social order.

Teachers' awareness of the value of literature as a means of
enabling students to grapple with human problems is not new.
Concern with personal involvement, with literature as experience,
and with awareness of values built and clarified by both real experience and vicarious experience goes back to earlier decades, to
a pre-World War II era when curriculum builders sought to construct a curriculum for English where stories, poetry, plays, and
novels were clearly within the intellectual and emotional range of
the readers and much of the reading done outside class was individual. Louise Rosenblatt's *Literature as Exploration*, first published
in 1937 and republished in 1968, has proved a beacon for two
generations of English teachers in its clear insistence that well-
selected literature is an experience for the reader because it uses his

uniquely human capacity to sympathize, to identify with the experiences of others. The vicarious experience of reading can offer escape from the narrow confines and demands of real life and can compensate for its failures and shortcomings. For the adolescent, reading is thus a means of understanding certain stirrings and impulses within himself and of seeing, perhaps, a pattern within life that has meaning.[2]

Literature as Experience, Personal and Aesthetic

BROAD READING: THE FIRST ELEMENT

But how does literature become experience for the reader? Charting the process is uncertain, even hazardous in research. The beginning stage, one that cannot be bypassed, is undoubtedly unconscious enjoyment. Children's—and sometimes adolescents'—experiences with literature begin with hearing it read by parent, teacher, or recording artist; or by being able independently to render print into speaking voice and to follow plot or description with trepidation or wonder or delight in the humorous. Broad reading is basic to attaining this sense of pleasure; encouragement of broad reading is the beginning of wisdom in building the base for the discriminating reader, who emerges, if he emerges at all, later on.[3] Room libraries representing a wide assortment of books, membership in book clubs at elementary, intermediate, and high school level, and well-stocked school libraries are testimonies to the effort to provide the broad base. Realistic stories for children and junior novels also foster the process of imaginative entry into the literature, the first essential element in the aesthetic experience.[4] This process of imaginative entry may be relatively easy in such children's stories as *Little House in the Big Woods, The Bully of Barkham Street* or *Old Yeller* or in such junior novels as *That Was*

2. Louise M. Rosenblatt, *Literature as Exploration* (New York: Noble & Noble, 1968).

3. Margaret J. Early, "Stages of Growth in Literary Appreciation," *English Journal* 49 (March 1960): 161-67.

4. Dwight Burton, "Teaching Students to Read Imaginative Literature," in *Teaching English in Today's High School,* ed. Dwight L. Burton and John S. Simmons (New York: Holt, Rinehart & Winston, 1970), pp. 90-105.

Then; This Is Now, which seem almost literally true to young readers. Teachers at the intermediate and high school level have tried to foster, even to "steer" the process of imaginative entry into more difficult literature by encouraging students to examine elements in their own experiences that have some of the elements of the central experience of the literature they are about to read.

GUIDED READING: THE SECOND ELEMENT

Reading literature as a means of deepening one's knowledge of human character, of human dilemmas and their resolution, and of increasing one's capacity for critical thought or awareness of major currents of thought, calls for more complex, more sophisticated responses to literature. These responses are bound up with more than imaginative entry into a work; they are dependent upon abilities to perceive meaning, artistic unity, and significance. These responses, research indicates, seem to depend upon the reader's willingness to react with genuineness, to suspend judgment, to search for meaning, to weigh evidence, to judge details objectively, and on his ability to respond emotionally at the same time that he responds to literary structure. This kind of reading is reflective and thoughtful rather than unreflective and uncritical.[5] Traditionally, teachers have tried to guide this kind of reading through questioning. Perhaps question asking, as one researcher has suggested, is the process student readers themselves must learn; and readers must become increasingly adept at asking their own questions and at seeking out and testing their own answers as they read.[6]

AESTHETIC AWARENESS: THE THIRD ELEMENT

The search continues for methods of teaching literature that will engage students and will permit them to examine and evaluate their own responses to literature without responding in purely egocentric terms. Engagement with literature, a private experience for many readers, may lead to thinking about questions of right

5. James Squire, *The Responses of Adolescents while Reading Four Short Stories* (Champaign, Ill.: National Council of Teachers of English, 1964).

6. Jerry Ward Ring, "A Study of the Interpretive Processes Employed by Selected Adolescent Readers of Three Short Stories" (Ph.D. diss., The Ohio State University, 1968), p. 55.

and wrong, of whether an action is justified, of admirable and less than admirable qualities.[7] This engagement, as best we can chart it in research, takes place in classrooms where the formal study of literature is not allowed to become the prime focus, where the teacher succeeds in creating an atmosphere in which students feel free to discuss spontaneously their reactions to the literature. Here the teacher functions as facilitator and guide who can help students identify their own assumptions, stock responses, and prejudices, can make areas of agreement and disagreement clear, can clarify their intellectual and emotional experiences with the literature, can even use such responses in day-to-day planning.[8]

Evidence as to how the reader gains insight into himself, into his own feelings about such values as justice and love, perhaps how he incorporates some character traits from real people and from literary characters into his ideal self has come from adults looking back on their childhood and adolescence.[9] Often such evidence comes inadvertently rather than through planned research. The late James Agee, at the age of eighteen, wrote to Father Flye, the teacher of his early years, who became his lifelong friend and confidante:

> I've been reading *Leaves of Grass* since I came back. You know, since last winter or so I've been feeling something—a sort of universal —oh, I don't know, feeling the beauty of everything, not excluding slop jars and foetuses—and a feeling of love for everything—and it seems as if I'd dived into a sort of infinitude of beautiful stuff—all the better (for me) because it was just what has been knocking at me unawares . . .
>
> Have you read *Sorrell and Son?* I haven't, but I saw (don't laugh) an excellent movie made of it. Filmed in England, Dorothy was with me, and (she's read it) says it follows the book word for word. So I do feel I've license to say it's a very beautiful and moving story—a

7. Rosenblatt, *Literature as Exploration*, pp. 86-87.

8. Nathan S. Blount, "The Effect of Selected Junior Novels and Selected Adult Novels on Student Attitudes toward the 'Ideal Novel'," *Journal of Educational Research* 59 (December 1965): 179-82; Faye Louise Grindstaff, "The Responses of Tenth Grade Students to Four Novels" (Ed.D. diss., Colorado State College, 1968).

9. Katharine Lind, "Social Psychology of Children's Reading," *American Journal of Soociology* 41 (January 1936): 454-69.

real tragedy (in a way) with no dirty slush. And not overdone. Perhaps
the best thing about it is that, while Sorrell had a terrible lot to stand,
he had at least an equal number of lucky breaks. It's the most perfect
thing on the theme that I can imagine. And its theme isn't to be
sneezed at. I hope you'll read it if you haven't.[10]

The young Agee's statements also demonstrate another important insight made explicit in *Literature as Exploration:* that the response of a particular reader has its roots in his capacities and his
experiences—his concerns, all of which operate as factors to determine what he selects from the work, the whole nature of the
transaction between author and reader.

The study of literature, at any level, attempts to develop imagination, to refine the perception and discrimination of human qualities,
to clarify and refine feeling, and to increase the capacity for new
and original types of response. The child reader of *Charlotte's Web*
or of William Armstrong's *Sounder* may respond to feelings of
loneliness, to injustice in the social order, to the paradox of the
finality of death but the continuity of the life cycle and the possibilities for change within it. The adolescent reader of *My Antonia*
may respond to the openness and the generosity of Antonia and
feel that her capacity for love, for hard labor, and for endurance of
injustice and pain render her in her later years triumphant and ful-
filled far more than is the narrator, Jim Burden, whose life out-
wardly seems placid and successful.

Both children and adolescents respond to the reading of biography. Curiosity about the lives of real people and a search for
models of desired qualities can lead readers to this genre. The reading of biography or fictionalized biography at any level can prove
rewarding when the work is complex enough to permit glimpses of
a human being who has experienced failure and rebuff as well as
success, who has felt inadequate and unworthy at times and may
even have committed acts he lived to regret as well as acts that
made him live on as one who achieved greatly. Jean Lee Latham's
Carry On, Mr. Bowditch, James Daugherty's *Marcus and Narcissa
Whitman*, Mari Sandoz's *Crazy Horse*, and Stanley Vestal's *Kit
Carson* are such biographies. Many adolescents have sought out

10. James H. Flye, ed., *Letters of James Agee to Father Flye* (New York:
George Braziller, 1962), p. 34.

Helen Keller's autobiography or a biography of Annie Sullivan, Helen Keller's teacher, after in-class reading of *The Miracle Worker*.

Literature as aesthetic experience affects some readers powerfully. Because literature affords the reader privacy in coming to know himself and his values as he lives vicariously, teachers prize it highly. Much research of the last decade has attempted to find out under what circumstances the kind of response to literature involving aesthetic awareness along with personal involvement takes place. The circumstances seem to be these: (a) that the reading is of the reader's own choosing;[11] (b) that literature has first been selected so that it is at a level that the child or adolescent reader can read as experience;[12] and (c) that such literature is then taught so that the reader's intellectual and emotional responses are accepted, clarified, and used by teachers to help students respond to it fully as aesthetic and personal experience.[13] The International Study of Achievement in Literature, a study of student literary response in ten countries, indicates that in England an affective-interpretive pattern of response rather than simply an objective-formalistic pattern of response correlates best with cognitive achievement.[14] This finding is consistent with the above studies. A significant finding of the same study was that there is a closer similarity of teacher and student in their approach to literature than of national specialist and student—a tribute to the power of the teacher that will gratify literature teachers everywhere.[15]

Language and Values

LANGUAGE AS A REFLECTION OF VALUES

Both children and adults reveal themselves and confront their values in their own uses of language, oral and written. Concerns for

11. Fehl Shirley, "The Influence of Reading on Concepts, Attitudes, and Behavior," *Journal of Reading* 12 (February 1969): 369-72.

12. Blount, "The Effect of Selected Junior Novels and Selected Adult Novels."

13. Grindstaff, "The Responses of Tenth Grade Students to Four Novels."

14. Alan C. Purves, *Literature Education in Ten Countries* (New York: John Wiley & Sons, 1973), p. 243.

15. Ibid., p. 306.

freedom from racial and ethnic stereotypes and for equality between the sexes have bred awareness in student and teacher that stereotypical depictions of minorities and of girls and women in the readers used in elementary school, in history books, and in the anthologies used in elementary and secondary schools have resulted in a society repressive of racial minorities and of women. To achieve a more balanced perspective, publishers are changing the picture of society presented in textbooks to reflect cultural pluralism and equality of the sexes. Seemingly society has shifted its sights to focus deliberately on cultural pluralism and on flexibility in occupational roles. We are even attempting to change language that seems to define the masculine role as one of dominance and leadership.

LANGUAGE AND SELF-DEFINITION

Reflecting on one's own uses of language in reconstructing experience is a means of working toward self-definition. Keeping a daily written journal can help the writer sort out the personally significant within the commonplace, an activity that moves the writer toward self-knowledge and understanding. To get students to say what they mean instead of "Like, man, it was great," or "Wow, but I can't explain it!" is to move them toward a commitment to share an experience or a statement of reasoning for or against something rather than an expression of feeling so vague that it can be said to have only positive or negative valence. In composing dialogues and scripts, writers can construct an image of the larger society of which they are a part as they devise situations involving language to conceal or to distort meaning as well as to communicate. In dramatic improvisation, as in the extension of the short story "The Dead Dog," students confront the larger dilemmas of our time.

LANGUAGE AND CRITICAL AWARENESS

Walker Gibson reminds us that the whole basis for man's knowledge of his own past and his speculations regarding his future lies in man-made tools for thinking and valuing. Becoming an adult means that man achieves critical awareness of these very tools.

For the child, then, the Renaissance is a "movement" that "happened" in history. It is names and works of literature, pictures and buildings. For the adult it is all that, of course, but something more. It is a *word—*

reputed to be largely the invention of 19th-century historians. This is a profound and disquieting piece of learning, but a necessary one for *adult* education.

The question arises, at what point in the educational treadmill does one pass from child learning to adult learning. At what point does one stop learning the vocabulary, more or less as absolutes, and begin to see the vocabulary as *words*, created by human beings in the presses of their complicated circumstances? When does "the Renaissance" cease to be a Thing and become a historian's Term? Everyone's answer to this will differ, and it will depend of course on all sorts of questions about student readiness and sophistication. But I should hazard that the "moment" might be somewhat between the 10th and 14th grades. It is the primary responsibility of undergraduate liberal education. Is it too much to add that it is absolutely necessary for the preservation of man and society?

It follows that no talk of "clarifying values" should disregard the crucial importance of *un*-clarifying those values at some point in the educational process. Let us teach children to name things, to believe things—"be neat in everything," as Yeats said. Then let us teach adults the pitfalls of naming, to believe and disbelieve simultaneously, and to act in the knowledge of man's limitations. All the great artists have known this, which is one more reason to argue for the English teacher's central role in education. How can we know the dancer from the dance?[16]

Teaching for Values

NURTURING THE ETHICAL ADULT

The search for a new pattern of teaching-learning that will be humane, flexible, supportive of the learner, concerned with total growth goes on in this decade. Teachers are reading anew such volumes as *Values and Teaching* and *Values Clarification*. These explications of procedures for teaching values offer teachers hope of coming to know their students better and of involving the apathetic, who may now constitute a majority of students at intermediate and high school levels, as teachers see them. These procedures may help students who are uncommitted, inconsistent in their value systems, or confused by the multiplicity of life styles to which they are daily exposed in the mass media. They may also allow for a balance of affective and intellectual experiences in the classroom.

16. Walker Gibson, letter to James Squire, August 26, 1974.

Thus a study sheet for Steinbeck's *The Pearl* might include these questions:

What did the pearl represent to Kino? To Juana? To the pearl dealers? To you as a reader?
If you were Kino, would you have flung the pearl back into the sea? How might you have sought to overcome the problems that Kino faced? [17]

These questions seem to foster both identification and literary analysis.

Less acceptable to many teachers are the values sheets that teachers sometimes use early in the semester. These sheets raise an issue through a provocative statement, for example, a newspaper account of citizens who shortchange the automatic tollbooth on a thruway. They confront students with a number of alternative responses among which students must choose. These sheets, designed to force students to examine one aspect of their value systems, may ask students to reveal more than they wish, may ask them to make decisions on the basis of minimal data, may seek consistent answers before such answers are genuinely possible for students. In using values clarification materials, the English teacher must choose carefully materials that do not oversimplify human problems, do not distort literature, do permit judicious thinking and student privacy.

The strategies suggested in these publications force students to think about their values, to make choices, to examine their decisions, to reveal themselves to themselves. Using this approach, as Raths pointed out in 1966, requires teacher commitment to a role as inquirer, as clarifier of student response in an atmosphere of free choice rather than as judge or evaluator of the response.[18] Students generally know a teacher's values; what matters is that the teacher does not force these values on students. One study involving the training of teachers to use this approach indicates that high school teachers, traditionally oriented to subject matter, were less successful in learning and using the theory than elementary teachers. Research in support of these procedures in changing student attitudes

17. R. Baird Shuman, "Values and the Teaching of Literature," *Clearing House* 48 (December 1973): 235.

18. Raths, Harmin, and Simon, *Values and Teaching*, p. 213.

toward academic achievement and toward themselves is slender. One study indicates some positive growth in academic achievement for elementary school children.[19] Much of the research is unpublished; much of it was inadequately controlled and dealt with small numbers of subjects. The procedures failed to effect changes in children "with unmet emotional needs." [20] (How these children were differentiated from others is not revealed.) Apparently these children had difficulty in academic learning as well as in learning values.[21]

Whether to use value clarification strategies and to adopt the role advocated by Raths, Harmin, and Simon are matters that the individual teacher will decide. Some teachers will certainly choose to analyze literary characters through the more complex and more subtle moral dilemmas posed in literature. For these teachers it will be an easier and perhaps better way of confronting students (some of whom want their views kept private) with the nature of moral choices. Other teachers will continue to work with language as a vehicle for the analysis of our society—the language of advertising, of public figures in the news, of public address—and student examination of his own language as a vehicle for self-analysis. Many teachers will adapt values clarification materials to suit their teaching styles. For example, one young teacher chose to use literature for value clarification in this way. At the end of a unit she used a questionnaire: "Of the characters we have met in short stories, novels, and poetry in this unit, which character would you like to have run for public office? Which one would you like to counsel? Which one resembles closely someone you already know? Which one would you want for a friend? Please comment on *one* of your choices."

Whatever decision a teacher makes, teaching for values in the decade ahead can be more informed by research that illuminates the development of ethical maturity than at any earlier time. Man is "a social creature highly influenced in the most subtle ways by his fellow men," researchers tell us.[22] He "cannot even run rats through

19. Ibid., pp. 207-19.

20. Ibid., p. 214.

21. Ibid.

22. Richard L. Gorsuch, "Moral Education from a Psychological View of Man as an Ethical Being," *Educational Forum* 37 (January 1973): 169-78.

mazes without unintentionally influencing them to run in accordance with his expectations." [23] So even when the teacher attempts to help students freely to choose their own values it cannot be assumed that students are completely uninfluenced by the teacher at the time of choice, although the attempt itself may be worthwhile.

SENSING LEVELS OF THINKING ABOUT MORAL VALUES; WORKING TOWARD HIGHER LEVELS

Researchers attempting to clarify the growth of moral judgment have focused on the act of thinking and have attempted to identify and describe systematic shifts in styles of thinking about moral problems, about human dilemmas. The numbers of categories employed in these studies have been small. Piaget used four; Peck and Havighurst, five; Williams (in England), five; Kohlberg, three, each divided into substages, giving a total of six levels.[24]

While these researchers agree, in major outline, on the ethically mature person and on the general nature of the sequence from childhood to mature adulthood, they are not in total agreement as to whether the stages represent developmental levels of thinking with the sequences culturally universal, as Kohlberg maintains; or a typology of individuals, as Peck and Havighurst suggest; or a pattern of response through which an individual's preferred mode of moral thought may be inferred, as Williams hypothesizes. But the direction of growth of the moral individual proceeds as in Kohlberg's typology, which is given in table 1, as summarized by Gorsuch.

Kohlberg and other researchers remind us of how great a convergence we have on basic values within our culture and indeed share with other cultures. Tentative data from an examination of stage 6 indicate that thinking here is guided by concern for justice. The meager data concerning the highest stage are the direct result of finding so few people who have attained this level.

While the results of this research are tentative, teachers would do

---

23. Ibid.

24. Jean Piaget, *The Moral Judgment of the Child* (London: Routledge & Kegan Paul, 1932); Robert L. Peck and Robert J. Havighurst, *The Psychology of Character Development* (New York: John Wiley & Sons, 1960); Norman Williams, "Children's Moral Thought," *Moral Education* 1 (May 1969): 3-12; Lawrence Kohlberg, "A Cognitive Developmental Approach to Socialization," in *Handbook of Socialization Theory and Research*, ed. D. A. Goslin (Chicago: Rand McNally Co., 1969), pp. 376-77.

TABLE 1

KOHLBERG'S STAGE SEQUENCE

I. Preschool Level

Stage 0:   *Amoral.* Child responds in terms of specific situations. He does not appear to comprehend the ethical question.

II. Preconventional Level

Stage 1:   *Fearful-Dependent.* The child's major concern is with the possible punishment following any transgression. He considers issues only from his point of view and defers to superior power or prestige.

Stage 2:   *Opportunistic.* This is the naively egotistic orientation of the unenlightened hedonist. Right action is that which benefits the actor. He responds to sanctions in situations but not to moral principles.

III. Conventional Level

Stage 3:   *Conformist: Person Oriented.* The person's concern is with approval, and with pleasing others. The concern is often generalized so that conformity to stereotypical images of the majority's opinion occurs.

Stage 4:   *Conformist: Rule Oriented.* Essentially, the "other person" of Stage 3 is replaced by an authoritative source of rules and regulations. These are often interpreted legalistically.

IV. Postconventional Level (Mature young adult)

Stages 5, 6: *Principled Autonomy.* Recognizing the relativity of authority systems, the Stage 5 person has a social contract/social utility approach to ethical issues. The Stage 6 person appeals to principles of choice stressing logical universality and consistency, with values of justice, mutual respect, and trust dominating his decisions.

SOURCE: Richard L. Gorsuch, "Moral Education from a Psychological View of Man as an Ethical Being," *Educational Forum* 37 (January 1973): 173. Table 1 is a summary of data in Lawrence Kohlberg, "A Cognitive Developmental Approach to Socialization," in *Handbook of Socialization Theory and Research*, ed. D. A. Goslin (Chicago: Rand McNally, 1969), pp. 376-77.

well to ask themselves these questions:

1. Do I identify occasions (events, literary scenes, analyses of public language) and use them for discussion of ethical issues?
2. Do I know my students well enough to know the level at which advocacy of courses of action as solutions to a moral dilemma can be used? (Evidence exists that the outcome of discussion of these concerns depends on the level of the reasoning. If the level is slightly

more mature than the levels the child or adolescent normally uses, he is more likely to accept a line of reasoning than if it is slightly less mature than his level.)

3. Is the level of discussion I am using with students—for example, a discussion of man's tendency to isolate and ridicule those he doesn't understand as in *Crow Boy* or a discussion of the need for autonomy and respect in old age as illuminated in "The Dead Dog"—appropriate to the level of the students?

Kohlberg helps us organize our thinking about development of moral values by giving us perspective. We see that a response is not an indicator of moral worth but part and parcel of the developmental nature of human thinking. Thus the classroom dialogue between teacher and student, between student and student must have as its goal to stimulate the minds of participants and listeners to work toward higher levels of thinking.

In the post-Watergate, post-Vietnam classroom it is difficult for the teacher to feel the satisfactions traditionally associated with teaching. Ties between teacher and home, teacher and student often seem weaker. Old family patterns seem to be breaking up; no new pattern is yet emerging. Peck and Havighurst indicated that a child's home is so important in the formation of character that it is difficult to find later forces that have much effect in changing character.[25] The models that children and adolescents take for themselves often come now from the peer group and from the peer culture rather than from adult society. These models used to come from parents, teachers, and other significant young adults within the community. One effect of affluence and technology in our society may have been to decrease the need of our adult society for its adolescents. Hence a youth culture exists that is little related to adult society and adult roles. Trust in the larger institutions of society is at low ebb. Reestablishment of ties with the generation coming of age depends on a revitalization of our institutions—political, social, business—so that they are truly responsive to social needs and can provide economic opportunities and responsibilities for the young.

A new willingness to grant that these responsibilities do exist is being voiced in our society and acknowledged by spokesmen within these institutions. Whether desired change can come, the next

25. Peck and Havighurst, *The Psychology of Character Development*, pp. 156-57.

decade will see. Teachers need to reestablish and strengthen ties with those they teach. Opening the channels of communication with them on the moral decisions they are making and will make is a start. Literature and a study of the uses of language are natural means for opening these channels and for illuminating these moral decisions. Seeing students as individuals at varying points in the maturing process, in a society in which it may be more difficult than at any previous time to know oneself and to achieve moral maturity, may help teachers in working for the attainment of the better society that man is capable of making. The attainment of such a society is the task teachers share with those they teach.

CHAPTER VI

Changing Content in the English Curriculum

The what of teaching cannot easily be distinguished from the how of teaching as the contributions to the Yearbook readily indicate. Yet the content parameters of English have so expanded over the past two decades that any review of current developments would seem incomplete without direct consideration of the changing nature of the discipline. In selecting five areas for special consideration in this chapter, the authors illustrate the gradual broadening of subject matter that has occurred both as a result of scholarly and professional developments and as a response to new instructional requirements. That many of these changes have precipitated controversies in individual communities is perhaps less significant than their demonstration of the vitality of English studies in a changing social and educational setting.

THE EDITOR

A. Humanities in the Schools

EVELYN M. COPELAND*

The Humanities Course

The late 1950s spawned the "humanities course." At first it was just that, a course. Although an occasional pioneer did develop some humanities lessons for the elementary grades, the first courses appeared almost exclusively in secondary schools. Although occasionally a teacher did create a course for students who were not going to college,[1] the first humanities courses were generally designed for

---

* Consultant reader for this chapter was Jewel J. Bindrup, English Education Specialist, Utah State Board of Education.

1. Springfield (Vermont) High School was such an exception, where a senior course replaced English and social studies for students who were not

academic seniors. They often started with Greek literature, supplemented by classical art and music. They commonly combined English and social studies. They were full-year courses and, though content-centered, invariably crossed conventional content boundaries, eschewed a basic text, and more often than not were team-taught. With rare exceptions the first humanities courses were organized in one of three ways: by chronology, by great themes, or by great epochs. Beyond that each was refreshingly individual.[2]

Their individuality was due in large part to their grassroots origins. Virtually the only school materials commercially available and specifically carrying a humanities label in the 1950s were three sets of four films produced by Floyd Rinker and the Massachusetts Council for Television in the Humanities, whose original idea was to bring outstanding professors, professional actors, and other artists into the English classroom via film.[3] In the first set Clifton Fadiman raised and answered the questions "What are the humanities?" and "What is drama?" In the second and third groups Maynard Mack and Bernard Knox respectively discussed *Hamlet* and *Oedipus Rex* with scenes by professional actors interspersed throughout the discussions. The films, the first of a much longer projected series, bore the general title of *The Humanities*. Their production was largely coincidental with the humanities course, but they nourished each other.[4]

A prime mover of the early humanities courses was the John Hay

---

going to college. This and many other early courses are annotated in Robert W. Horne and Socrates A. Lagios, "An Overview of Humanistic Programs throughout the Country," *English Leaflet* 63 (Fall 1964): 39-57.

2. Ibid.

3. Floyd Rinker, on leave from his position as Head of the English Department, Newton (Massachusetts) High School, was the original architect and general editor of the projected series. Encyclopaedia Britannica Educational Corporation later took over the program and added many more films in literature, art, and philosophy.

4. These films, still distributed by Encyclopedia Britannica Films, are entitled *The Humanities: What They Are and What They Do*; *The Theatre: One of the Humanities*; "*Our Town*" *and Our Universe*; "*Our Town*" *and Ourselves*; "*Hamlet*": *The Age of Elizabeth*; *What Happens in* "*Hamlet*"; "*Hamlet*": *The Poisoned Kingdom*; "*Hamlet*": *The Readiness Is All*; "*Oedipus Rex*": *The Age of Sophocles*; "*Oedipus Rex*": *The Character of Oedipus*; "*Oedipus Rex*": *Man and God*; and "*Oedipus Rex*": *The Recovery of Oedipus*.

Fellows Program, which supported more than two thousand women and men from the nation's schools in the studies of the humanities between 1952 and 1966.[5] Several unique features contributed to the long-range effect of that program. First, it brought together in comparatively small numbers in any one place teachers of varied disciplines plus administrators. Then, over a period of time, matching fellowships by school districts and a remarkable amount of follow-through by the program itself built up a nucleus of committed teachers and administrators within school districts. In addition, both the one-year fellowships and the summer institutes themselves were examples of what a humanities course in the schools could be. Participants experienced firsthand the stimulation of genuine intellectual pursuits unhampered by tests, term papers, and grades. All this did much to "pierce the sheepskin curtain" [6] and to send teachers home saying, "My students would find this way of learning exciting." The John Hay summer, or year, was a translatable experience.

Humanities Programs

Whereas in the early 1960s a good conversation starter at any English or social studies conference was "Do you have a humanities course in your school?" by the mid-1960s the question among humanities teachers was as likely to be "Is one course really enough? Don't we need a humanities program?" The interest in developing a "humanities program" ranged from expanding an existing course, as Morris R. Buske did at Oak Park-River Forest High School in Illinois,[7] to developing completely new programs. By 1964 Richmond, Virginia, had developed several approaches to the humanities, giving students options in both content and time schedules. In Baton Rouge, Louisiana, Helen Brown had initiated the American Studies

5. For a history of the John Hay Fellows Program and the climate that spawned the humanities in the schools, see Daniel Powell, *John Hay Whitney Foundation*, (New York: John Hay Whitney Foundation, 1972), vol. 2, *The John Hay Fellows*.

6. The expression was coined by Charles R. Keller. See his "Piercing the 'Sheepskin Curtain,'" *College Board Review*, no. 30 (Fall 1956): 19-23. Keller was director of the John Hay Program from 1958 to 1966.

7. Morris R. Buske, "Evolution of a Humanities Course," *Humanities Journal* 3 (Fall 1969): 22-28. In this article, Buske summarizes his method for organizing a humanities course.

Humanities Program, which today enrolls eleventh graders in almost every high school in East Baton Rouge Parish. At the same time Henry Ray, Director of Learning and Teaching Resources in Southampton, Pennsylvania, was developing a humanities program expressly for elementary schools.[8]

As education in the humanities grew to include more students at more grade levels and as people tried to define what the humanities in the schools really were, definitions shifted from the statement that the humanities are those subjects like art, music, literature, history, drama, and philosophy that deal with our humanness to statements about what the humanities do for students. "The humanities provide the strength to cope with the contemporary scene," Miller said. "They offer meaning to existence; they offer alternatives in thought and action." [9] Keller, who had always stressed the importance of content in the humanities, was not relinquishing that position in the least when he reminded teachers in a talk called "Dear Nancy" that in the selection and use of that content they must also be alert to what students want. First, he said, students want time. They want opportunities to see relationships and time to make choices. They want relevance and chances for involvement; they want to be listened to and to be treated as individuals by people who care.[10] Humanities courses and humanities programs were expanding to embrace the more encompassing concept of humanized education.

Humanized Education

One session of the National Council of Teachers of English Humanities Conference in New Orleans in 1972 was called "Humanizing Administrators." The double entendre was intended: Hu-

8. *mssc/dellwood,* annual report of the Metropolitan School Study Council (New York: Metropolitan School Study Council, 1965), pp. 8-9.

9. Bernard S. Miller, *The Humanities Approach to the Modern Secondary School Curriculum* (New York: Center for Applied Research in Education, 1972), p. 23.

10. Charles R. Keller, "Dear Nancy," Comments at the preconvention workshop in the Humanities, New York State English Council convention, Syracuse, New York, April 23, 1970. Keller's comments were reprinted in *Humanities Horizon,* newsletter of the Encyclopaedia Britannica Educational Corporation (Chicago), May 1971.

manizing administrators *are* a boon to any school, but humanizing administrators *is* not always an easy task. The same applies to humanizing teachers, or education or, for that matter, students.

Teaching the humanities tended to humanize teachers, and when teachers did become humanized, several things happened. Courses, for instance, became less crowded with content. As Charles Bart of Arrowhead High School in Hartland, Wisconsin, observed, "A few selected ideas, moments in history, concepts—'postholes' as Charlie Keller would call them—open up just as many ideas as trying to cover masses of material." [11] Further, once aware of what students were thinking and wondering, teachers guided them to materials that helped them find answers to things that mattered to them. Teachers listened to the language of young people for what it was trying to say rather than for its deviations from standard middle-class conventions. Teachers encouraged students to express themselves creatively and imaginatively. They did not insist that all students learn the same things or arrive at the same answers. When teachers found the time and heart to bring these all together so that students found relevance and joy in their learning, then a school—or a part of a school—might be said to have moved from a humanities program to humanized education.

Of course humanized teachers existed before humanities courses, and not all humanities courses produced humanized teachers. Of course, in uncrowding the content, some teachers went farther from content than others. Sensitivity training and life experiences sometimes crowded out the books. In general, though, the humanities probably more than any other one influence led to humanizing education where humanizing did take place and contributed to such changes as phase/elective programs. But while electives in a given subject were a liberating step, most phase/elective programs were not interdisciplinary, and the inevitable consequence of humanizing education was that it became even more interdisciplinary—more integrated—than the first humanities courses were. Conventional and artificial boundaries gave way, not only between disciplines but

11. Charles Bart, "Our Program after Six Years," mimeographed (Hartland, Wisc.: Arrowhead High School, 1971), p. 1.

between school and the larger community, between intellectual pursuits and social needs.

Interdisciplinary Studies

Interdisciplinary studies did not by any means spell the demise of the humanities course, but the humanities course of the mid-1970s is likely to be much more active—more involving—than the humanities course of the mid-1960s. Here Mark Wendland describes part of his humanities course at Ord (Nebraska) High School:

"Our current interests are in Judaism. We are producing *Fiddler on the Roof* in April and the humanities class is researching Jewish life. Our latest field trip included eating a Jewish Sabbath meal, visiting the synagogue in Omaha, and speaking with a rabbi. Much energy has been focused on art, literature, traditions, religion, music, history, and current events. . . . Last week we experienced Jewish cooking and kosher traditions. Next week we talk about concentration camps and *The Exodus*. . . . Young people learn much about themselves and *their* culture as they study another culture.[12]

Keller proposes other interdisciplinary studies in a variety of minicourses. What happens, he wonders, if students start investigating the spirit of '76—1676, 1776, 1876, 1976? Where will their probings take them? What relationships may they discover? What might they predict for the year 2076? Another minicourse would start with Benjamin Britten's *War Requiem* and let the words and text take students back to Ralph Vaughan Williams's "Dona Nobis Pacem" and Wilfred Owen's poetry. Add Picasso's *Guernica*, Hemingway's *Farewell to Arms*, Willa Cather's *One of Ours*, and selections from Pablo Casals's *Joys and Sorrows*. Let probing, seeing relationships, and discovering become habit forming. And let a good minicourse grow into a maxicourse.

Interdisciplinary studies are currently being developed in New York state through Project SEARCH,[13] the proponents of which believe that "school learning should be an integrated experience of the emotional, the intellectual, the perceptual, and the aesthetic. It is, therefore, necessary that the arts become an integral part of the

12. Mark Wendland, letter to this writer, March 4, 1975.

13. Project SEARCH is a consortium of five school districts representing rural, suburban, and urban areas; public and private schools; and elementary and secondary students.

basic curriculum. Learning becomes a synthesis of the whole life of the student." [14] Elaborating upon this philosophy, Jerrilee Bunce, Coordinator of Arts for Project SEARCH, says ". . . an integrated experience includes the student/school/community. The arts and humanities as equal components in acquiring cognitive skills in math, science, English, reading, social studies are the vehicles through which the integration can take place." [15]

Four things are noteworthy here: first, the involvement of the whole person in active learning; second, that integrated learning must reach beyond the school walls to the community in the largest possible sense—parents, artisans, libraries, universities, museums, theaters, the performing arts and artists; third, that the arts, humanities, and sciences are brought inextricably together; and fourth, that projects on the scale of Project SEARCH need professional and financial help beyond that of the local school district.

Trends

ACTIVE LEARNING

"A humanities program will succeed," Bernard Miller predicts, "when the appeal is visceral as well as cerebral. . . ." [16] Active learning is one way to make it visceral. Eliot Wigginton's experience in helping students to record the local culture with *Foxfire* in Rabun Gap, Georgia, is being repeated with variations in other communities.[17] Students in rural northern New York are recording and photographing their conversations with elderly citizens as they try to perceive their traditions, their culture. Then the students extend the oral stories with drama, dance, and sound and visual art, exploring the oral stories for values, isolating those values that are inherent in their own community, and making decisions about whether those values will work for them today.[18]

14. "Integrated Arts Project SEARCH" (Albany, N.Y.: New York State Education Department, Division of Humanities and Arts. n.d.), p. 18.

15. Jerrilee Bunce, letter to this writer, February 11, 1975.

16. Miller, *The Humanities Approach*, p. 27.

17. Ford Foundation is supporting several similar projects in Indian and Chicano communities.

18. This program is funded by Project SEARCH.

Wanting to offer students learning outside the conventional curriculum and to increase their awareness and sensitivity to the many
opportunities for self-education outside the classroom, the Mt.
Diablo (California) Unified School District has a summer program
for advanced sixth graders in which they explore, through independent study, field trips, and group work, both arts and sciences in
an attempt to better understand their relationships to each other and
to their environment.[19]

In Fairfield, Connecticut, students in "Whole Earth Learning:
An Experience in Democracy" meet for three hours a day with one
teacher.[20] They elect the course knowing that they will receive
credit for English, social studies, and physical education if they keep
reading and thinking and biking and back-packing and forest-clean-
ing with reasonable competence. They elect the course knowing
that it will be physically, intellectually, and emotionally challenging.
What they do not know when they elect the course is how demanding are the skills of human relationships that will be involved or how
enriching are the frustrations of group decision making.

SCHOOL AND COMMUNITY COOPERATION

Increasingly learning is coming out of the schools and into the
community, and conversely the community is going into the schools.
But *increasingly* does not mean that the practice is yet widespread.
Although not typical, the following incident does show promise. In
June, 1972, Julia Gump, principal of Stockbridge Elementary School
near Columbus, Ohio, applied to the National Humanities Faculty
(NHF) for help: "Our community is 80 percent Appalachian. Most
of the adults are high school dropouts. . . . We want to work on
something that includes pride in Appalachian culture as well as a
better understanding of the whole American way of life." [21]

NHF accepted the application, and during the following year six

19. Richard R. Adler, ed., *Humanities Programs Today* (New York:
Citation Press, 1970), pp. 32-41.

20. The course is taught by Peter Meyer, Roger Ludlowe High School,
Fairfield, Conn.

21. The National Humanities Faculty is the only national corporation
whose sole purpose is to help teachers improve the teaching of the humanities
in the schools.

faculty members of NHF worked with the Stockbridge Elementary School. In addition to a Canadian author and Eliot Wigginton with his *Foxfire* experience in rural Georgia, the faculty came from the Folklore Institute at the University of Indiana, the Archive of Folksong at the Library of Congress, the Appalachian South Folk Life Center in Pipestem, West Virginia, and the Save the Children Federation in Berea, Kentucky.

A year later Principal Gump reported favorably on the school's progress. A number of young teachers who were working for their master's degrees had turned their courses into something related to what Stockbridge was doing. Literature courses at the university developed bibliographies with annotations, questions, and suggested activities. Parents were starting to volunteer to help in the school, and for the first time parents had asked the school to offer a program for them. Here, with the aid of a national humanities organization, schools, parents, and university worked together to make learning more pertinent, more joyous, and more rewarding for everyone involved.[22]

THE PERFORMING ARTS

Because of increasing support from local, state, and federal sources, what was once only a matter of field trips to plays and museums has become in the mid-1970s an active involvement of students in the visual and performing arts. One means of this involvement is the Artists-in-the-Schools (AIS) program, which was first tested by the National Endowment for the Arts in six states in 1969-70. By 1974-75 Maine alone had twenty-one professional artists in its classrooms, provided partially by the National Endowment for the Arts and partially by state funds. The artists represented a wide range of arts—poetry, filmmaking, dance, painting, pottery, printmaking, photography, mime, music, and theater.[23] Currently Tucson, Arizona, working with AIS, has six-week programs at both

22. A full report of the Stockbridge cooperative project is on file at the headquarters of the National Humanities Faculty, 1266 Main Street, Concord, Mass. 01742.

23. *Perspective* 8 (January-February 1975): 1. *Perspective* is the newsletter of the Maine State Commission on the Arts and Humanities, published in Augusta, Me.

Catalina High School and Division Elementary School that bring movement specialists and a dance company into the schools to teach movement as an art form and as a way of learning. This means that today's students not only watch professionals perform but also talk with them, work with them, and are instructed by them.

Given a chance to be creative themselves, students do remarkable things. At E. O. Smith High School in Storrs, Connecticut, students wrote, cast, directed, and performed "Oedipus—A Rock Opera." Bernard Marlin, history and humanities teacher, described it as

> . . . one of the very best evenings in the history of our school. Oedipus was absolutely fantastic. How about the ending of Act One, with Oedipus just being crowned, a soft light on him, and the chorus singing "I want a girl just like the girl that married dear old Dad." Just enough levity to keep the audience involved, but never getting too far from the genuine questions posed.[24]

PROFESSIONAL AND FINANCIAL ASSISTANCE

The National Council of Teachers of English organized the first national humanities conference for teachers in 1966 and continued to sponsor annual meetings through 1972, at which time the National Association for Humanities Education (NAHE), founded in 1968, assumed responsibility for the national conferences.[25] But the trend almost from the first has been toward state and regional meetings. Usually they are cosponsored by two or more groups who pool their resources, as did the South Dakota Division of Secondary and Elementary Education, the U.S. Office of Education, Region VIII, in Denver, and Black Hills State College in a conference on humanizing education in the fall of 1974. More and more, state departments of education are contributing leadership in humanizing education.

---

24. Bernard Marlin, letter to Charles R. Keller, May 1975.

25. The last humanities conference sponsored by the National Council of Teachers of English was held in New Orleans and is memorable for the fact that as many students as adults appeared on the program. The first national conference sponsored by the National Association for Humanities Education was held in 1970 at Baldwin-Wallace College, Berea, Ohio. Since then NAHE has sponsored national conferences in even-numbered years and regional conferences in alternate years. Leon C. Karel is Executive Secretary of the National Association for Humanities Education, Box 628, Kirksville, Mo. 63501.

The State Board of Education in Utah, for one, has initiated a state-wide program for developing gifted and talented students through the arts.[26]

The mid-1970s also find many colleges and universities contributing to the humanities in the schools in a variety of ways. A unique position at the University of Nebraska is the Special Assistant to the President in the Arts. One of the charges to Vaughn Jaenike, the first to hold the position, was "to coordinate the sharing with schools and communities throughout the State those art groups and individuals already on campus." [27] NAHE cosponsored five humanities workshops with universities across the country during the summer of 1975. Barry College in Florida ran a five-day workshop for secondary-school teachers, for which the National Humanities Faculty provided the professional services. NHF has a vast variety of scholars and artists ready to help in its school projects.[28] People power is clearly available.

But financial assistance is another matter. Private foundations and trusts, notably Ford and the John D. Rockefeller III Fund, have from the first given some support to the humanities in the schools. However, the National Endowment for the Arts and Humanities has to date given schools a very low priority.[29] Some years have been better than others, but the total available to elementary and secondary schools in 1975 was approximately $2 million divided among some twenty to twenty-five projects.[30] Concurrently the National

26. Jewel Bindrup, a member of the State Leadership Training Team for Gifted and Talented in Utah, is State Consultant for Gifted and Talented.

27. *Curriculum Report* 3 (February 1974): 5. Jo Ann Kimball succeeded Jaenike when he became Dean of the School of Fine Arts at Eastern Illinois University. *Curriculum Report* is published in Washington, D.C., by the National Association of Secondary School Principals; the February 1974 issue is a twelve-page review of the state of the humanities in the schools.

28. The National Humanities Faculty was established in 1968 and was initially sponsored by Phi Beta Kappa, the American Council of Learned Societies, and the American Council on Education. It became an independent nonprofit educational corporation on September 1, 1973.

29. The National Endowment for Arts and the Humanities, created by the Congress in 1965, consists of separate endowments for the arts and for the humanities. It is supported by federal funds.

30. These grants ranged from $4,000 to $740,000.

Endowment for the Humanities awarded $2.7 million to the National Humanities Institute at Yale.[31]

A recent three-year school grant from NEH went to the Indiana Humanities Project, which held its first institute in August, 1975. The institute was jointly supported by NEH, the Indiana Department of Public Instruction, and the school districts participating in the pilot project (1975-76), "Teaching Humanities in Secondary Schools." The Project's director is Ardis Sanders; and at this writing the Project's impact on humanities education is a dream that is only beginning to materialize. The reality still lies ahead. But at least the dream is funded and peopled.[32]

Conclusion

Though the world's problems—war, pollution, energy, hunger, population control—cry out for solution, traditional education has had virtually no effect on any of them. Nor are solutions likely to be found in an educational system that separates the world of fact from the world of value, that separates learning from doing, that separates thought, feeling, and action. Something does happen to those who experience the humanities way of learning. Joanna Klick, who has been teaching humanities for fifteen years at David Douglas High School, Portland, Oregon, wrote on the brink of the sixteenth year, "I don't know what to expect in Humanities. . . . The students last spring said, 'We're lining up a wild group for you next year.' That's usually the best kind."

"This is the first time a course ever had anything to do with me," one senior said after three months in a humanities class. A young lady wrote from a big university early in her freshman year:

As I look back on high school, I realize how much I learned in my humanities class about myself and about life. If I had not learned many of the things I think are essential, I should be totally lost here. But I

31. The University of Chicago received a similar grant. For the programs of the National Endowment for the Humanities for fiscal year 1975, see *Humanities* 4 (October 1974): 6-7. *Humanities* is the newsletter of the National Endowment for the Humanities, published in Washington, D.C.

32. Ardis Sanders had devoted a year of preparation to the project before the first institute was held. Her address is Foundation Grants, 600 Cumberland Avenue, West Lafayette, Ind. 47906.

must admit (rather proudly) that I am not lost at all. I know where I'm at—and more importantly—where I'm going.[33]

She was better off than Alice in Wonderland, who inquired of the Cheshire Cat, "Would you tell me, please, which way I ought to go from here?" What about American education? Do the world's problems cry out loudly enough and the student responses clearly enough so that it knows which way it ought to go from here?

33. A graduate of Elkhart (Ind.) Central High School in a letter to Charles Keller, September 1973.

B. Literature

KENNETH L. DONELSON*

General Influences on the Changing Literature Curriculum

At least five general trends or movements have influenced the literature curriculum in the past fifteen years, four positively, one potentially negatively.

THE DARTMOUTH CONFERENCE

While the 1966 Anglo-American Seminar on the Teaching of English at Dartmouth probably had little direct effect on classroom teachers, it produced a number of documents that have affected curriculum planners. Notable were Herbert J. Muller's *The Uses of English*, John Dixon's *Growth through English*, Paul A. Olson's *The Uses of Myth*, and Douglas Barnes's *Drama in the English Classroom*.[1] Several characteristics of British teachers that were apparent at the Conference, including their obvious concern for their students, their use of improvisational drama and modern literature, and their evident dislike of rote learning and literary history, have had some effect on the modern literature curriculum.

FEDERALLY SPONSORED PROJECTS

The high hopes of the Project English Curriculum Centers for curriculum reform in English were never realized despite the money and effort that went into the Centers. Their impact on the literature

---

* Consultant readers for this chapter were Norine Odland, Professor of Children's Literature, University of Minnesota; and Gladys Veidemanis, Chairman, Department of English, Oshkosh North High School, Oshkosh, Wisconsin.

1. Herbert J. Muller, *The Uses of English* (New York: Holt, Rinehart & Winston, 1967); John Dixon, *Growth through English* (Reading, England: National Association for the Teaching of English, 1967); Paul A. Olson, ed., *The Uses of Myth* (Champaign, Ill.: National Council of Teachers of English, 1968); Douglas Barnes, ed., *Drama in the English Classroom* (Champaign, Ill.: National Council of Teachers of English, 1968).

curriculum was slight even though they produced many documents and several Centers had their materials published commercially.[2] Much more influential were the English institutes of the middle 1960s under the National Defense Education Act and the Education Professions Development Act. Whether they were innovative in structure or whether they followed the usual pattern of sections devoted to language, composition, and literature, these institutes exposed an incredible number of English teachers to new ideas and trends in the teaching of literature, many of which they tried in their classrooms.

ROMANTIC CRITICS OF AMERICAN EDUCATION

Though critical of both the content of the curriculum and the teachers, the romantic educational critics of the 1960s and 1970s have proved highly influential with some classroom teachers and many curriculum coordinators. John Holt's *How Children Fail*, *How Children Learn*, and *What Do I Do Monday?*, George Dennison's *The Lives of Children*, Jonathan Kozol's *Death at an Early Age*, Charles E. Silberman's *Crisis in the Classroom*, Satu Repo's *This Book Is about Schools*, and Daniel Fader's *The Naked Children* have led teachers to reexamine the purposes and aims of the literature curriculum.[3] The most influential critics have been Neil Postman and Charles Weingartner whose *Teaching as a Subversive Activity* and *The Soft Revolution* have disturbed and intrigued teachers and have changed many aspects of the curriculum in many schools.[4] This change has tended to be in the direction of the student-centered, response-oriented teaching recommended by the Dartmouth Con-

2. See G. Robert Carlsen and James Crow, "Project English Curriculum Centers," *English Journal* 56 (October 1967): 986-93.

3. John Holt, *How Children Fail* (New York: Pitman Publishing Corporation, 1964); idem, *How Children Learn* (New York: Pitman Publishing Corporation, 1967); idem, *What Do I Do Monday?* (New York: E. P. Dutton & Co., 1970); George Dennison, *The Lives of Children* (New York: Random House, 1969); Jonathan Kozol, *Death at an Early Age* (Boston: Houghton Mifflin Co., 1967); Charles E. Silberman, *Crisis in the Classroom* (New York: Random House, 1970); Satu Repo, ed., *This Book Is about Schools* (New York: Pantheon Books, 1970); Daniel Fader, *The Naked Children* (New York: Macmillan Co., 1971).

4. Neil Postman and Charles Weingartner, *Teaching as a Subversive Activity* (New York: Delacorte Press, 1969); idem, *The Soft Revolution* (New York: Dell Publishing Co., 1971).

ference. Thus, insofar as literary education is concerned, the recommendations of the romantic critics and the Dartmouth participants have tended to reinforce one another.

STUDENTS

As critics have pointed to the need for change, students have become more forceful in demanding some voice in developing the curriculum to fit their own tastes and needs. Too often, individualizing instruction has been an educational cliché much mouthed, little followed. To attract young people to literature, teachers have learned that they must select works and develop a literature curriculum that supports the following principles:

1. Literature exists to be enjoyed, to entertain humanity.
2. Literature allows young people to see themselves and their problems.
3. Literature provides vicarious experiences beyond the possibilities of any one person's life.
4. Literature exposes young people to many values and many value systems and ideas and practices, often at sharp variance with their own.
5. Literature gives young people a chance to see their language at work, and an opportunity to perceive how different authors can shape the lives of characters and affect the feelings and beliefs of their readers.
6. Literature encourages young people to see the world as it is, neither all good nor all bad, but all human.
7. Literature promotes the recognition of ideas and emotions that lead to action, and actions have consequences.

In Wallace Stevens's words, "Literature is the better part of life. To this it seems inevitably necessary to add, provided life is the better part of literature." [5]

PARENTS AND COMMUNITY MORES

An influence that is worrisome and potentially negative is the growing militancy of parents. Communities that once left teaching to teachers have increasingly demanded knowledge about the con-

---

5. Wallace Stevens, "Adagia," in Wallace Stevens, *Opus Posthumous*, ed. Samuel French Morse (New York: Alfred A. Knopf, 1957), p. 158.

tent and aims of the literature curriculum and how it can be justified. In part, this interest or demand may stem from heightened ethnic awareness, a fear of permissiveness, a desire to return to the basics, the reputed filth or unpatriotic or antireligious content of some material, a worry about rising school taxes, or many other factors. While the urge to become involved in curriculum decisions may in some cases arise more out of ignorance or misinformation than anger or discontent, literature teachers can no longer ignore or give mere lip service to parents or community mores in planning the curriculum.

Specific Influences on the Changing Literature Curriculum

Specific influences that have stemmed from the Dartmouth Conference, federally sponsored projects, romantic critics, students, parents, and other sources include the following.

PAPERBACKS, TELEVISION, AND MOTION PICTURES

Although early attacked for garish cover or content, paperbacks had become a basic part of many schools' literature curricula by the 1960s. Popular with students and teachers alike because they were widely available and inexpensive, paperbacks greatly expanded literature programs, sometimes supplementing and often supplanting the basic anthology or textbook. The several school paperback book clubs and increasing publication of a large number of titles by paperback publishers did much to vitalize and broaden the possibilities in teaching literature, especially in titles of children's, adolescent, ethnic, sports, and science fiction literature.

Television or motion picture productions of books like Neufeld's *Lisa, Bright and Dark*, Gaines's *The Autobiography of Miss Jane Pittman*, Shakespeare's *Romeo and Juliet*, Fitzgerald's *The Great Gatsby*, or Seuss's *Horton Hatches an Egg* have attracted students; and the ready availability of these works, often in paperback, has allowed discussion and comparison of television or film versions with original form.

RESPONSE TO LITERATURE

Richard Adler wrote, "A recent trend in the teaching of literature is an emphasis in the classroom upon *exploring* literature with students rather than *teaching* about literature."[6] Encouraging students to explore and respond openly and honestly, rather than merely to parrot back what the teacher has said, is the aim of the response-centered approach. Ideally, the outcomes of the response-centered curriculum will be:

1. An individual will feel secure in his response to a poem and not be dependent on somebody else's response. An individual will trust himself.
2. An individual will know why he responds the way he does to a poem —what in him causes that response and what in the poem causes that response. He will get to know himself.
3. An individual will respect the responses of others as being as valid for them as his response is for him. He will recognize his differences from other people.
4. An individual will recognize that there are common elements in people's responses. He will recognize his similarity to other people.[7]

Starting with I. A. Richards's *Practical Criticism* and Rosenblatt's *Literature as Exploration*, the response-centered approach has stressed both literary work and student, not one but *both*.[8] A sizable bibliography and many enthusiastic teachers testify to its wide use, and this approach promises to become the basis of the literature curriculum in many schools.[9]

THEMATIC UNITS AND ELECTIVES

While thematic units or literary course electives are not new, both have had a recent resurgence of attention. Thematic units on animals or families or courage or man's inhumanity to man are common in both elementary and secondary literature programs, but

6. Richard Adler, "Answering the Unanswered Question," in *Classroom Practices in Teaching English, 1974-1975, Re-Vision*, ed. Allen Berger and Blanche Hope Smith (Urbana, Ill.: National Council of Teachers of English, 1974), p. 72.

7. Alan C. Purves, ed., *How Porcupines Make Love: Notes on a Response-Centered Curriculum* (Lexington, Mass.: Xerox College Publishing, 1973), p. 31.

8. I. A. Richards, *Practical Criticism* (New York: Harcourt, Brace & Co., 1929); Louise L. Rosenblatt, *Literature as Exploration*, rev. ed. (New York: Noble & Noble, 1968), first published in 1938.

9. Alan C. Purves and Richard Beach, *Literature and the Reader: Research in Response to Literature, Reading Interests, and the Teaching of Literature* (Urbana, Ill.: National Council of Teachers of English, 1972), pp. 1-60.

paperbacks have allowed, even encouraged, teachers to develop units on death, myth and humanity, man and superman, the fractured family, and many others.

Electives owe much of their contemporary popularity to the work of the Trenton (Michigan) Public Schools as published in *APEX: A Nongraded Phase-Elective English Curriculum*.[10] Elective courses have fallen into several general classes: genre electives such as "The Modern American Novel," literary history electives ("English Literature" or "American Literature"); thematic electives ("The World of Tomorrow" or "Adolescence and the Loss of Innocence"); humanities electives ("Art and Man Today" or "Love and the Arts"); masterpiece electives ("The Great Books" or "World Masterpieces"); skill or individualizing electives ("Reading and Literary Skills for College" or "Paperback Power"); and single author electives ("Shakespeare's Plays" or "Mark Twain"). Sometimes freely elected by students, sometimes a certain number required for each student, electives are aimed at arousing or capitalizing on student interests.

READING INTERESTS AND FREE READING

Studies of the reading interests of students over the years have pointed up the discrepancy between the kinds of literature preferred by students and the literature used in schools. Teachers concerned about student involvement with literature begin with student interests, and one way of capitalizing on student interest is a literature curriculum that includes free reading, sometimes called individualized reading. Free reading allows class time, ranging from an hour or two a week up to an entire semester, when students read what they wish. A variation on free reading that proved popular and influential with literature teachers was Fader and McNeil's *Hooked on Books: Program & Proof*.[11] A large body of research has developed about reading interests and free reading.[12]

---

10. Project APEX, *Project APEX: A Nongraded Phase-Elective English Curriculum*, 4th ed. (Trenton, Mich.: Project APEX, Trenton Public Schools, 1970).

11. Daniel N. Fader and Elton B. McNeil, *Hooked on Books: Program & Proof* (New York: Berkley Publishing Corporation, 1968).

12. Purves and Beach, *Literature and the Reader*.

ETHNICITY

Multiethnic literature entered the literature curriculum when black students pushed for recognition and acceptance. Their arguments that American literature and literature anthologies were lily-white and irrelevant to their lives may have overstated the case, but there was truth in the charges. Black literature courses soon followed. Unhappily, these electives sometimes had the effect of effectively segregating black literature from the mainstream of modern literature. The electives having been established, too many teachers assumed the problem had been neatly disposed of, and the bulk of many literature courses remained lily-white. Black authors worth reading for ideas and emotions deserve a place in all literature classes, as do writers from other ethnic groups like American Indians, Chicanos, and Puerto Ricans. Recent Caldecott and Newbery award winners, the inclusion of more minority writers in anthologies, monographs published by the National Council of Teachers of English,[13] and many paperbacks from commercial publishers indicate that even if the impact is less than it should be, students in literature classes are still more and more likely to become aware of minorities and minority writers.

SEXISM

Teachers have become increasingly concerned about sexist language and stereotypes perpetuated in elementary-school readers and secondary anthologies and literature programs. Additionally, women writers have seldom received much serious attention in secondary school. A growing number of paperbacks devoted to women's writing, many articles in *English Journal* and *Media and Methods* about sexism and literature by and about women, and a developing militancy among women attest to the seriousness of the concern and indicate likely changes in store for the literature curriculum.

SCIENCE FICTION

Science fiction has been the favorite reading of many students for years, and English teachers have increasingly used it to develop

13. Barbara Dodds, *Negro Literature for High School Students* (Champaign, Ill.: National Council of Teachers of English, 1968); Anna Lee Stens-

units or electives like "Man's Tomorrows" or "Utopian Literature."
Part of the popularity may stem from the growing literary respectability of authors like Ray Bradbury, Robert Heinlein, Isaac
Asimov, and Arthur Clarke, part from the feeling that science fiction
is becoming reality. In any case, a form of literature once consigned
to leisure reading is becoming a staple in the literature curriculum.

ADOLESCENT LITERATURE

While children's literature has been honored and used in elementary schools for years, literature written specifically for adolescents has only recently achieved a limited respectability and use
in secondary literature programs. To argue, as critics have, that
adolescent literature is more timely than timeless, or that it is
simple-minded, simplistic, and insulting to the reading levels and
intelligence of young people is to miss the point of adolescent
literature. Young people recognize and resent the inherent fatuity
and condescension of these arguments since many students read,
empathize with, respect, and enjoy the works of authors like John
Donovan, Robert Cormier, Robert Newton Peck, Mary Stolz, Vera
and Bill Cleaver, Robert Lawson, M. E. Kerr, and Paul Zindel. These
authors, among others, have much to offer young people who
worry about survival in their own personal worlds.

CONTEMPORARY LITERATURE

Classic literature or literature out of the past may once have
been the content of the literature curriculum, but contemporary
literature is now firmly entrenched alongside older material. In
selecting either paperbacks or anthologies, teachers are concerned
that a balance of the old and the new be presented to young people.
If the old is needed to establish the richness of our heritage and our
continuity with the past, the contemporary is needed to establish
students' relationships with their world today and tomorrow and
the joys and sorrows and stresses that are a part of contemporary
literature and life. Contemporary literature may have been introduced in part as a reaction to anthologies primarily containing

---

land, *Literature by and about the American Indian* (Urbana, Ill.: National
Council of Teachers of English, 1973).

material with publication dates prior to 1900, and in part to placate students who demanded something more immediately relevant to their lives. For whatever the original reasons, contemporary literature is now evident in the curriculum and in new anthologies.

Selection and Censorship

Selecting materials for specific students to accomplish specific objectives has always been a major problem for teachers. As the wealth of material increased, the problem grew larger. As the response-centered curriculum, thematic units and electives, and free reading became more pervasive, the problem grew more complex. As the need for presenting newer and different kinds of literature became more obvious and no more time in the day was available, the problem grew more desperate.

Selection has always implied a careful examination of possible materials by professionally competent teachers who attempt to choose the best and most intriguing literature the community will accept or tolerate. Compounding the normal difficulty of an already complex process was the growing demand by parents, lay people, and community leaders that they too be involved. In effect, the expertise of English teachers to choose appropriate materials and objectives had come under attack.

Sometimes, the parents, lay people, and community leaders urged that more attention be given to older, more conventional literature. Sometimes, they urged that more attention be paid to ethnic literature. But more and more, they urged or demanded that certain works or movements or ideas be removed from the literature curriculum.

Censorship has always been a part of the lives of literature teachers, but the frequency and seriousness of incidents have intensified. Even traditional standards like *The Adventures of Huckleberry Finn, Romeo and Juliet,* and *The Spoon River Anthology* have been attacked. Ethnic literature, women's literature, science fiction, adolescent and children's literature, and contemporary literature have seldom been exempt from adverse comments or out-and-out bannings. Books as varied as Cleaver's *Soul on Ice,* Joseph's *The Me Nobody Knows,* Kesey's *One Flew Over the Cuckoo's Nest,* Steig's *Sylvester and the Magic Pebble,* Kerr's *Dinky Hocker Shoots*

Smack, Asimov's *Fantastic Voyage*, Ehrlich's *The Population Bomb*, Vasquez's *Chicano*, and Sendak's *In the Night Kitchen* have been banned, hidden, conveniently lost, or temporarily removed from libraries and classrooms.

No single or easy explanation for the rising number of censorship incidents is possible, but some reasons may be hypothesized. United States Supreme Court decisions in 1973 (especially *Miller* v. *California* and *Paris Adult Theatre I* v. *Slaton*) and 1974 (especially *Jenkins* v. *Georgia*) created a climate encouraging to some would-be censors. Though these decisions were clearly aimed at hard-core pornography, they argued against a continued use of national standards in determining obscenity and for the use of local or community standards. Prosecuting attorneys proved generally ineffectual in getting convictions even after the 1973 and 1974 decisions, and, angered by the seeming indifference of attorneys, judges, and juries, censors turned to something else they could attack with far greater likelihood of success: anthologies and contemporary literature and ethnic material used in schools.

Almost invariably, the major cause of censorship has been the unwillingness of many people to accept the school's responsibility to educate, to free, to allow students to read and pursue anyone's vision of the truth no matter where that may take them. Censors would doubtless prefer that schooling become an indoctrination into the community's status quo. Teachers faced with censors where there is no possibility of discussion or reasonable compromise must fall back on policy statements like the National Council of Teachers of English pamphlet, *The Students' Right to Read*.[14]

Teachers of literature are aware that local community mores can never be ignored in choosing curriculum materials, just as they are aware that students are a part of an even greater community, the community of humanity, yesterday, today, and tomorrow. For that reason, the problems of selection and censorship are not likely to lessen in the near future.

14. Kenneth Donelson, ed., *The Students' Right to Read* (Urbana, Ill.: National Council of Teachers of English, 1972).

C. Language

MARY M. GALVAN*

Introduction

The purpose for which language is studied at school largely determines not only the amount of emphasis placed on the subject but the theoretical model of language that is followed. Current emphasis in language study focuses on enabling students to gain control over all four language skills: listening, speaking, reading, and writing. Not only are all four skills important; each is directly related to another.

A second current goal for language instruction provides for each student to learn whatever kind of language will help him achieve his own goals as well as society's. The single model of excellence that was reflected in grammars of past centuries is not acceptable in a society that prizes communicating effectively with people, achieving a variety of purposes, and employing a repertoire of communication skills. Language texts for school programs now recognize that the complex communication needs in today's world call for the development of a wider range of language skills than ever before.

Curriculum planners today incorporate into their programs those aspects of language learning that result in the development of useful communication skills. Once teachers defended rigorous training in parsing or diagramming sentences as assisting students to understand the nature of sentences so they could write better ones. No significant study, however, has demonstrated much relationship between the study of formal grammar (particularly parsing or diagramming) and improved writing. Mellon, for example, demonstrated that the study of grammar resulted in improved writing only when directly tied to the production of certain types of de-

* Consultant readers for this chapter were Marianna W. Davis, Professor of English and Chairperson, Division of Information and Culture, Benedict College, Columbia, South Carolina; and Owen Thomas, Professor of Linguistics and Education, University of California, Irvine.

sired sentences.[1] An unfortunately large number of current language textbooks are still meeting the market demand of less well-informed teachers who, in spite of logic or evidence, insist on teaching formal rules and structures of language unrelated to any practical purpose.

If it is true that students can learn to communicate with less formal study of language than provided in the past, it is equally true that teachers must know a great deal about language, including the varieties within a given language, in order to provide students from a variety of linguistic backgrounds with equal opportunity for education. Planners of language programs would do well, then, to separate in their thinking and planning what the *student* needs to know about language and what the *teacher* needs to know in order to assist the student toward his own and society's goals.

Effective teachers must understand on the one hand the organization of the language system a student brings with him to the classroom, and on the other hand the nature of communication forms that elicit the best response in a given social situation, that is, what is currently correct within a social group. The teacher's repertoire of pedagogical skills, then, would include strategies for increasing the student's language ability by building on the foundation of what is already known toward some reasonable and socially approved goal. Such teaching requires a deep understanding of language organization as well as the skills of teaching (or promoting) language development.

There are several reasons for students to study language. In the first place, such study is interesting for its own sake. Second, since a school-age student has already acquired a system of language, further development of his ability involves an understanding both of his own system and of his communication goals. Third, in a world where the student's mind is constantly bombarded by verbal stimuli (propaganda, literature, mass media, interpersonal encounters), his very psychological survival may well depend upon his ability to understand the nature of the language incorporated in the stimuli and to make an effective response to the stimuli.

In shaping the language curriculum, schools are making increas-

1. John C. Mellon, *Transformational Science-combining* (Champaign, Ill.: National Council of Teachers of English, 1969).

ing use of the work of linguists, scholars who systematically observe and record what goes on in language. In the last decade, many linguists have become increasingly concerned about the role of language in society, the power of language to oppress or emancipate, the function of language in shaping social attitudes. The emerging field of sociolinguistics is deeply concerned with describing language phenomena in such a way that students from all linguistic groups may both profit from education and be prepared to share more fully in the benefits of a multicultural, multilingual society.

Fundamental Principles

Certain fundamental statements underlie the work of modern linguists as well as planners of language instruction. Although linguists may differ with each other on methods of organizing and describing language data, they will agree with the following principles that have great impact on school programs.

1. All living languages change; each language has a history that partially explains any development in the language. Wisely, few teachers today seriously try to prevent changes in the English language as if to stem the tide of corrupting influences. Most teachers and their students now view language change and language history as interesting developments to be studied and appreciated. Dictionaries are frequently used as textbooks to reveal the chronicle of the language. Students are encouraged to watch news accounts about historical events for changes in the language that accompanied the event. Attitudes about such rules as "never ending sentences with prepositions" are taken much less seriously now than they were when Winston Churchill denounced the rule as "foolishness up with which I will not put."

2. Language is a product of humans, created and maintained by humans. Hence, language rules are arbitrary. Once earlier grammarians forbade the use of the double negative in English on the grounds that two negatives make a positive. The statement, highly logical in parts of mathematics, had little relevance for language. Speakers of many languages—French and Russian

among them—use two or even more negatives together. In English, however, conventions of correctness forbade the use of the double negative.

All human languages are made up of an intricate system involving sounds, vocabulary items, grammatical structures, stylistic devices, and even gestures. Yet individuals are able to learn much of their language before they reach school age. The reason for such achievement is that the *system* that underlies each language makes it learnable. Teachers have often held the view that there was neither rhyme nor reason to the English spelling system and that English spelling was harder to learn than that of other languages. Recent studies of the English spelling system have demonstrated it to be systematic, however complex, and spelling instruction based on these findings is proving to be increasingly efficient.

3. All languages have variations called dialects. There is probably no such thing as a dialect-free language. Although some dialects of a language enjoy a greater social prestige than others (because the speakers enjoy such prestige), there is no reason to believe that one dialect is intrinsically more logical or functional than any other. The work of both regional and social dialectologists has demonstrated the systematicity and functionality of a range of dialects. Such information should assist teachers in working tolerantly and intelligently with children whose speech is different from their own.

4. Each language has its own unique structure, which should be described in terms of itself instead of in terms of another language. Any language is capable of describing anything in the culture of the people speaking the language; it has no responsibility, however, for expressing ideas or values that are not part of the culture. Each language has a means of expressing whatever the speakers of the language need to say. Some teachers, without the training to understand the nature of languages and dialects other than their own, have assumed that a student who could not express an idea in the teacher's language was retarded or nonverbal. Many standardized tests, as an example, are still clearly based on teacher language and teacher values.

Educational Applications

Modern linguistic studies have given schools a new base for forming attitudes about language based on the foregoing principles. Sound language arts programs at all grade levels include information about five critical areas of language. Each area makes a contribution to language development as well as an understanding of communication in its cultural milieu.

Language history includes a study of the relationship of English to the family of languages. Questions to be considered would include why the alphabet used by Arabs is so different from our own; why certain verb forms in English are such problems; or why the grammar of English is so similar to German while so many English vocabulary items are similar to French and Latin. The answers lie in the history of the English language. Every major change in the English language has had some impact on our spelling system. Sound changes more rapidly than spelling, and the English-speaking people do not happen to have an authorized body (such as the Royal Academy in Spain) to keep sound and spelling changes moving more nearly at the same pace.

Lexicography is the study of dictionaries and provides a systematic way to study language history. Some can recall the furor with which *Webster's Third International Dictionary* was greeted. How dare, the critics screamed, a dictionary acknowledge the existence of language forms teachers had been trying for years to stamp out, such as the word *ain't!* [2] That dictionary did indeed acknowledge the existence of *ain't* but added that it was not generally accepted in formal, correct speech. Used properly as a reference tool, the dictionary gives rich information about the language and about the conventions that surround it. The lexicographer reserves judgment about his data, electing to record what is there with the greatest accuracy he can muster. Many students are fascinated with a study of how a lexicographer collects and presents his data and with the story of language incorporated in the dictionary. They are less excited about regarding a dictionary as a final judg-

---

2. For an interesting collection of criticisms, pro and con, of *Webster's Third*, see James Sledd and Wilma R. Ebbitt, *Dictionaries and That Dictionary* (Glenview, Ill.: Scott, Foresman & Co., 1962).

ment of their speech (a job few current dictionary makers would accept anyway) and about memorizing definitions.

Semantics is the study of meaning. In a school curriculum it may take a form as simple as studying the denotative and connotative meanings of words. It may also take the complex form of evaluating a message when the sender's intent is to manipulate the thinking or action of the receiver.

General semanticists such as Hayakawa and Korzybski were primarily interested in the meaning of words and how they could be organized for certain effects. More recently semanticists have broadened the field to include the question of how a total message manages to achieve a given effect. Linguists such as Jerry Fodor and Jerrold Katz have called for a linguistic theory that has meaning as the basis of the deep structure of a sentence. Language philosophers and sociolinguists are also broadening their fields to include semantics.

In a time when students are bombarded with verbal stimuli from many sources, the study of how language is used to convey meaning becomes necessary. Such study enables students to be more effective humans at the same time that it protects them from messages intended to manipulate or delude.

Grammar is made up of the form and order of the elements of language as well as the processes humans use in producing speech. Psycholinguists such as Eric Lennenberg have documented the fact that virtually all human beings, excepting only the severely retarded or impaired, have the capacity to learn to talk at an early age. Language development includes learning not only the components of language but the devices that pull the parts together into meaningful and effective speech.

Prescriptive grammar instruction is included in some school curricula when teachers assume that a child does not know grammar and must be taught it. In reality the fact that the child can produce meaningful sentences is evidence that he has already developed a grammar. Descriptive grammar instruction, on the other hand, brings to the child's conscious level of awareness what he already is capable of doing; that is, putting sentences together for the purpose of transmitting messages. It also describes for the student additional devices that he may employ for greater effectiveness.

The role of the linguist is to describe the elements and devices that make up grammar. Owen Thomas has described the models of grammar being used in school curricula and in instructional material.

All grammars . . . are models of the reality of language. And as you might suspect, some models are "better"—more accurate, more useful, more complete—than others. Traditional grammar is a model and a useful one. It contains many accurate explanations of linguistic reality. Structural linguistics is also a model, and as such, it tells us many interesting and important things about language. But only one grammar, the transformational, specifically attempts to define all the elements, all the operations, and all the laws of a language. In other words, a transformational grammar is a model of an ideal speaker's competence, the closest thing we have to an actual definition of competence itself.[3]

Curriculum planners who are not well informed about linguistics should not assume that present grammatical models offer the final word. Scholars are developing additional ways of describing what happens when humans produce and understand language. Of particular interest to schools are recent studies that utilize linguistic information to describe the processes babies and young children go through in learning grammar or the processes an individual uses in mastering a second language, quite different from learning the first one. A significant number of sociolinguists are searching for a model of language that will incorporate information about existing dialect differences into the basic framework. Such a grammar is needed for successful study of language variation.

Teachers would be wise to study something of all the models and choose those aspects that work best in their classrooms with their students. They should also stay abreast of the literature to be advised of new grammars in this fledgling field that will serve the classroom even better.

Usage and dialect study is taking an increasingly important role at school. Language scholars and instructional personnel alike are today aware of the variety of styles and dialects used effectively by members of a multicultural society. As a consequence, organizations such as the National Council of Teachers of English have resolved

---

3. Owen Thomas, "Competence and Performance in Language," in *New Directions in Elementary English*, ed. Alexander Frazier (Champaign, Ill.: National Council of Teachers of English, 1967), p. 90.

to protect the student's right to his own language.[4] Even when a justifiable goal of schools and organizations such as the National Council is to help students achieve all the proficiency possible in using language, two facts about the student's own language must be taken into account. First, the language (or dialect) of his family and social group does function for him. Second, additional language learned at school must be built on the solid foundation of the system already learned.

That most students have a need to produce the more uniform written code is clear; that they will need to read the more uniform code referred to in the National Council's statement as "literary English" is also clear. There is abundant evidence, however, that students speaking many varieties or dialects of English can successfully master reading and writing the more uniform code without significantly altering their own oral code.[5]

The first of two goals for a study of dialects at school is to insure the participation of speakers of various dialects in a multilingual, multicultural society. Such study would probably include factors that produce different dialects: the region of the country in which one lives, and one's age, social class, amount of education, vocational aspiration, sex, and peer group orientation.

Another important goal for the study of dialects involves social attitudes about language variation. As has been pointed out earlier, linguists have repeatedly demonstrated that one language is not *inherently* better than any other language. No qualified linguist would, however, deny that certain languages and dialects of languages enjoy a higher prestige than others.

If better understanding between people is to be achieved in the future, it will probably be through the efforts of a generation taught to respect the differences in people. The more contact children and teachers from various ethnic groups have with each other, the greater the need for a planned program of understanding.

4. "Students' Right to Their Own Language," *College Composition and Communication* 25 (Fall 1974): entire issue.

5. Two collections of readings will be helpful to school personnel preparing reading programs for minority students: Doris V. Gunderson, ed., *Language and Reading* (Washington, D.C.: Center for Applied Linguistics, 1970), and Joan C. Baratz and Roger W. Shuy, eds., *Teaching Black Children to Read* (Washington, D.C.: Center for Applied Linguistics, 1969).

An outstanding black scholar, Lorenzo Dow Turner, has described the richness of the history of black dialect, tracing its origins to African languages.[6] More recently William Labov, a student of social dialects, has written repeatedly that the first step in the successful education of black children is the appreciation of the logic, the systematicity, and the expressive quality of the nonstandard language of black people.[7] Neither teachers nor students are likely to develop genuine tolerance and appreciation for language variety without a thorough understanding of linguistic variation. Other scholars, representing two races (among them Carol Reed, Roger W. Shuy, Geneva Smitherman, James Sledd, Juanita Williamson) are using information about language variation to promote more tolerant and successful practices at school.

The overall goal for the study of English usage today is to develop a sense of appropriateness in language. To this end students are asked to study a wide variety of usage forms and their effectiveness in a given situation. Appropriateness varies with situation, speaker, audience, purpose, and content of the message. Teachers and students should be concerned with getting the best possible response in the widest variety of communication events. The best prepared teacher for this type of situation will be one who understands language deeply, reads widely, observes accurately, and is an active participant in the communication process.

Conclusion

A former president of the National Council of Teachers of English, Harold B. Allen, once remarked that it is possible to study language without studying anything else. It is not possible, however, to study literature without studying language; nor is it possible to study composition without studying language. What Allen meant is that language is the core of the English curriculum and it

6. Lorenzo Dow Turner, *Africanisms in the Gullah Dialect* (Chicago: University of Chicago Press, 1949).

7. William Labov, *Language in the Inner City* (Philadelphia: University of Pennsylvania Press, 1972); idem, "The Logic of Nonstandard English," in *Language and Cultural Diversity in American Education*, ed. Roger D. Abrahams and Rudolph C. Troike (Englewood Cliffs, N.J.: Prentice-Hall, 1972), pp. 225-61.

is inevitable that schools must accept the responsibility for teaching it well.

Focus for the language program must be on language growth, the interrelation of all the language skills, and the development of language performance to the extent of an individual student's ability.

The preparation of every English teacher must encompass a careful study of language, including a general study of linguistics. Teachers of students of all ages need the skills necessary to direct the language development of all children. Teacher preparation should include studies that promote tolerance and appreciation for the richness and variety possible in any language. Also vital are studies that equip teachers to deal with emerging and promising programs.

D. Composition

ELISABETH MC PHERSON*

The Process of Writing

Good writing classes concentrate on communication rather than mere "correctness," on coming to terms with experience. Writing forces form on what has been amorphous, makes precise and permanent experience that has been vague and fleeting. An eight-year-old capturing memorable moments at the city zoo; a thirty-eight-year-old untangling the snarls that led to divorce; a high school junior searching to see why *Catcher in the Rye* still says something other books have not said; a college senior finding order in the chaos of a month in the day care center—all these writers are attempting the same thing. They are trying to define their experiences, and, through those experiences, define themselves. Such self-discoveries can be satisfying, but the process of discovery is seldom easy. Honest writing is hard work. And students of any age will endure the struggle of putting their selves and their lives into words only for teachers who respect both the struggle and the result. Students will write honestly—and effectively—only for teachers who read with sympathy.

Good teachers of writing see the product—often a flawed piece of writing—as part of the process, an attempt to understand and control experience. Such teachers have abandoned the notion that satisfactory products can be achieved through knowledge *about* writing, through drills on usage, rules for punctuation, expeditions in search of topic sentences. The available research on written composition is scanty, but what does exist seems to show that intensive evaluation has little or no effect on writing improvement.[1] Most

---

* Consultant readers for this chapter have been Stephen N. Judy, Associate Professor of English, Michigan State University; and Richard Lloyd-Jones, Professor of English, University of Iowa.

1. Lois V. Arnold, "Writer's Cramp and Eyestrain—Are They Paying Off?" *English Journal* 53 (January 1964): 10-15.

composition teachers continue to believe that people learn to write well by writing, and only by writing. Good teachers of writing are just as interested in skill as their predecessors who circled every misspelled word, red-marked every deviation from approved classroom dialect, cried "awk!" at every clumsy wording. But their definition of skill is different. They see the superficial etiquette of writing as less important than its substance. For them, writing skill is the ability of a writer to share meaningful experience with readers in a meaningful way; to understand the needs of readers and adapt to those needs; to recognize the purpose of the writing and use that purpose as a guide; to adopt a voice or a point of view in each piece of writing and maintain that voice; to be able to shift voice or point of view according to the purpose of the writing; to move from one level of abstraction to another; to play with language, creating metaphor and avoiding clichés; to support general statements with specific details and examples; to present ideas in such a way that the relationship between them is clear; to be able to discard, revise, and rewrite.[2]

The Open Classroom

Skills such as these are achieved not by attacking weaknesses but by recognizing strengths, a method that can truly be called developmental. This method assumes that all writing, no matter how incoherent or how incomplete it appears, does represent an attempt at communication, an attempt that must be treated with respect. One successful way of helping students to move toward completeness and coherence is through strategies associated with the "open classroom." "Open" does not mean simply walking in and saying to students, "OK, it's all yours," or arranging chairs in a circle and waiting for something to occur spontaneously. Rather, an open classroom is a situation of collaborative learning, in which the teacher responds to what students have written not by grading or criticizing but by asking questions that show a genuine desire to understand what the writer is saying. Indirectly the questions lead to clearer or more specific writing. Collaborative learning also in-

2. See Commission on Composition, *Teaching Composition: A Position Statement* (Urbana, Ill.: National Council of Teachers of English, 1974).

volves talk among all the students in the class, talk about what went on before the writer began to write, talk about what has actually been written. In such classes, the teacher becomes not the voice of authority handing down rules, but a participating member of a group all of whose members are engaged in the same enterprise. Such teachers think of all writing as a creative process and believe that the writer's self cannot be separated from the words that appear on paper; to attack the writing is to attack the writer.

Encouraging students to write freely does not end in a long series of inchoate outpourings. Instead, a sense of form develops naturally as students learn to control the way they communicate their selves to the group. As they come to enjoy writing as communication, they want to polish what they have written, to make it "look better." Developmental approaches do not ignore the conventions of edited American English, or the necessity of organizing and supporting ideas, but those aspects of writing are discussed as needed, not as a prior condition to attempting to write. Teachers share with students the knowledge that the final editing of any writing is often a collaborative process, just as professional writers expect, and get, such assistance from their editors.

Other approaches—journal writing, language games, and role playing, for example—help students to feel comfortable with writing. Whatever approach is used, the shift is from criticizing the product to cooperating in the process. This shift in emphasis did not come at once, from a single cause; it resulted from several events in the 1960s, all with their roots farther in the past, events that made several groups ask questions.

The Purpose of Writing

The most significant question teachers asked (greatly simplified) was "What do we teach writing *for?*" and the answer (also simplified) was "To help students grow—in their ability to understand themselves and their experiences, in their ability to share those experiences with other people." The Dartmouth Seminar, held in 1966, focused attention on what writers like Kohl, Kozol, and Leonard, among others, were saying at about the same time.[3] Dixon,

3. Herbert Kohl, *36 Children* (New York: W. W. Norton & Co., 1967); idem, *The Open Classroom* (New York: Random House, 1970); Jonathan

summarizing what went on at the seminar, suggests that English teachers must move from the question, "What is English?" to a consideration of the question, "What is involved in the activity of bringing together and composing the disorder of our experience?"[4] Although most of Dixon's book deals with younger children, the philosophy it embodies fits composition teaching at all levels, from kindergarten through college. When the main purpose of writing is seen as discovery, the job of the teacher shifts from laying down rules and formulas to finding ways that will help those discoveries take place. Using language to explore experience becomes a pleasurable human activity, replacing the pain of never quite doing what was wanted, never quite doing it right. After 1966, as more teachers adopted this objective, mistakes and usage variations moved into the background, because marking errors is a way of criticizing the product, not a way of helping its production. The true content of the course became the students themselves, their vision of the world, their attempts to use language to enlarge that vision. As content shifted toward individualization, standardized tests, which are based on norms rather than variation, and which concentrate on the ability to edit rather than the ability to create, automatically became suspect as a means of labeling and sectioning students.[5]

The question students asked, sometimes in words, sometimes through sit-ins and violence, was "What good it is? What do establishment-oriented, required courses have to do with the real things that matter?" Although the tumult of the 1960s was not directly concerned with the content of composition courses, the protests had a tremendous influence on them. Many high schools stopped requiring the traditional four-year sequence in English and developed minicourses from which students could select what appealed to them. In college, students' demands for relevance produced a

---

Kozol, *Death at an Early Age* (Boston: Houghton Mifflin Co., 1967); idem, *Free Schools* (New York: Bantam Books, 1972); George B. Leonard, *Education and Ecstasy* (New York: Dell Publishing Co., 1968).

4. John Dixon, *Growth through English* (Reading, England: National Association for the Teaching of English, 1967).

5. Task Force on Measurement and Evaluation in the Study of English, *Common Sense and Testing in English* (Urbana, Ill.: National Council of Teachers of English, 1975).

spate of far-out readers; classes, sometimes, became forums for political activity, or "happenings" in which nothing very directly connected to writing actually happened. The tumult died down, but the effects lingered. High schools and colleges that had dropped or reduced composition requirements found it hard to reinstate them. Some courses were lost and the wildly exotic materials disappeared, but the freer, more experimental approaches developed in response to student demand were retained. The cry for relevance was, in its best sense, a plea on the part of students to be shown why what they were doing mattered, how it related to their lives and their understanding of themselves.

The Impact of Political Upheaval

Less obviously connected with composition, and even more influential on it, were the civil rights movements. The insistence that minorities be admitted as full citizens, and full participants in equal education, led to new examination of what "equal" meant. It revived a question the burgeoning community colleges had already struggled with: was "open door"—everybody freely admitted—synonymous with "revolving door"—half the students shoved right out again? Under open admission policies, even four-year colleges admitted more and more students whose economic levels, experiences, cultural values, and dialects were different from those of the students the colleges were accustomed to. The old approaches and the old materials, geared to the expectations of middle-class students, often did not work with the new students. High schools wrestled with homogeneous grouping; they speculated that students might progress faster isolated with other students speaking the same dialect and sharing the same background. When homogeneous grouping sometimes led to drilling "deficient" students into linguistic conformity, while the more traditional groups progressed to "real writing," teachers began to ask whether a diversity of language and experience might help all students to grow. Standardized tests, as a basis for sectioning students into special classes, became increasingly suspect. As a recent report points out, such tests sometimes "discriminate against a student because that student uses a dialect different from that of the test or comes from a culture whose values, understandings, and perceptions are different from those expected on a test."[6]

To counter these inequities, the National Council of Teachers of English appointed a Task Force on Racism and Bias in the Teaching of English, and its members worked to ensure that text materials represented more than the ruling white culture.[7] Partly from a wish to make composition teaching less racist, partly from a belief that good writing almost never results from a rigid insistence on a nonexistent "standard language," the Conference on College Composition and Communication adopted a resolution affirming the students' right to their own language—the "dialects of their nurture or whatever dialects in which they find their own identity and style"—and shortly afterward published a background booklet explaining their position.[8] Although the language statement originated with college composition teachers, it came out of awareness that attitudes toward writing, and confidence in the ability to write, are set long before students reach college. Late in 1974 the entire National Council adopted a similar position statement. Both language statements are intended for writing teachers at all levels; both urge teachers to stop asking, "How can we deal with these terrible deficiencies?" and ask instead, "How can we help all our students write better?"

Just as the social movements of the 1960s led to a new kind of student and thus to a new kind of teaching, so the political upheavals of the 1970s led to a fresh examination of what ought to be taught. Shocked reaction to the revelations of Watergate caused thousands of teachers to pull out their old copies of George Orwell and ask again the old questions about politics and the English language. What such semanticists as Korzybski and Hayakawa had been saying for a long time became important,[9] and political utterances and propa-

6. Ibid., p. 20.

7. Ernece B. Kelly, ed., *Searching for America* (Urbana, Ill.: National Council of Teachers of English, 1972).

8. Conference on College Composition and Communication, *Students' Right to Their Own Language* (Urbana, Ill.: National Council of Teachers of English, 1974).

9. Alfred Korzybski, *Science and Sanity*, 4th ed. (Lakeville, Conn.: Institute

ganda returned as lively content in composition courses. Students examined slant in government speeches, in newspapers, in television newscasts; they collected their own examples of deliberate omission and language that obfuscates. Two resolutions passed by the National Council of Teachers of English in 1971, urging that the Council "study dishonest and inhumane uses of language and literature by advertisers" and "study the relation of language to public policy, to keep track of, publicize, and combat distortion by public officials, candidates for office, political commentators, and all those who transmit through the mass media," had led to the formation of a Committee on Public Doublespeak, and the scandals high in the government led to increased demand for the classroom materials the committee was producing.[10]

The televised hearings on prime time made it even clearer that phrasing questions clearly, answering directly and honestly, are more important and more difficult skills than making pronouns agree. Even though one English teacher found the testimony scandalous because "some of the most highly educated participants were guilty of breaking the grammatical rule that the subject of the gerund must be in the possessive case," [11] thousands more were scandalized by the way language was used to distort facts—a question of ethics—and to distort language itself—a question of style. They were disturbed by such bureaucratic maunderings as "indicated" for "said," "at that point in time" for "then," "inoperative" for "lying," and so on. The televised hearings gave new life to vocabulary study already begun when "pacification" meant "bombing" and "body count" was a euphemism for "human beings killed." The publication of the presidential tapes emphasized the contrast between public and private language, and gave new impetus to a consideration of what those differences ought to be. Straightforward student writing, in whatever dialect, took on added value; students who can define their

---

of General Semantics, 1958); S. I. Hayakawa, *Language in Thought and Action*, 3rd ed. (New York: Harcourt Brace Jovanovich, 1972); idem, *Use and Misuse of Language* (New York: Fawcett World Library, 1966).

10. Hugh Rank, ed., *Language and Public Policy* (Urbana, Ill.: National Council of Teachers of English, 1974).

11. This comment was reported by Walker Gibson in his presidential address to the National Council of Teachers of English, Philadelphia, November 1973.

terms, choose their words precisely, and avoid jargon are more resistant to language pollution and less likely to produce it themselves.

Scholarly Influences

Other forces also pushed toward change. McLuhan's widely publicized suggestion that electronic media would dominate the future raised questions of whether teaching reading or writing, beyond the bare demands of minimal literacy—the ability to fill out tax returns, the ability to read traffic signs—was worth the effort spent on it. High schools and colleges began to offer courses in film, where students composed with cameras instead of pencils. In media sections students analyzed the effect of pictures in television ads. But these new ways of composing and criticizing often contributed to writing rather than replacing it. Advertisements could not be examined without an increased consciousness of symbols and connotations, of choices carefully made to get deliberate effects. Producing a film, however simple and short, inevitably led students to consider what they should film; what point of view they should film from; what shots should be kept and what discarded; what order the scenes should be arranged in; what they wanted the film to communicate to the people who saw it. Making films helped students see what composition is.

The tentative findings of the "new rhetoric" have also influenced the way writing is taught. Generative rhetorics, based on the idea that discourse is a succession of hierarchical levels ranging from very abstract and general statements down to very concrete and specific data,[12] imply that students will be helped by manipulating sentences, subordinating, coordinating, rearranging, by moving from generalities to specifics and back again. Another approach is to use the traditional Aristotelian "topics" as ways of problem solving, as questions to be asked in what to say about a subject, somewhat as free modifiers are used to generate sentences. Topics generate ideas and thus become a kind of prewriting.[13]

Another suggestion is that essays can be developed in a series

12. Francis Christensen, *Notes Toward a New Rhetoric* (New York: Harper & Row, 1967).

13. W. Ross Winterowd, " 'Topics' and Levels in the Composing Process," *College English* 34 (February 1973): 701-9.

of moves, deliberately made, to achieve a particular purpose, and that this linear plan—different from outlines in that it tells why, not what—can complement generative rhetoric. In this prewriting, students ask themselves where to start, where they want to get in the end, what they want readers to believe or feel, and how they can get readers to respect their position. The linear plan shows the relationships between the students' ideas.[14]

More influential, probably, have been the ideas of a group who might be called "psycho-rhetoricians"—Piaget, Britton, and Moffett, for instance.[15] They see language as growing directly from human experience, and thus make rhetorical definitions in terms of individual human beings rather than discourse modes. Their ideas contributed to the growth of open classrooms, "free" assignments, and "free" responses.

Most rhetorical studies, in fact, have supported the changes that have occurred in good composition teaching. A series of seminars held in 1970, in which scholars from several disciplines were asked to respond to the question, "What is the essential outline of a conception of rhetoric useful in the second half of the twentieth century?" produced a variety of emphases, none of them in disagreement with the directions composition has taken.[16] One recommended studying the relationship between speaker and listener, between reader and writer. Another saw rhetoric as the study of all the arts of changing men's minds—psychiatry, advertisements overt and covert, motion pictures and television, fiction, protest marches and demonstrations, and all the various nonverbal symbols that induce people to form or change their values. Still another respondent was concerned with mass communications and the contextual clues that accompany them, including the speed at which information is disseminated through electronics. All of them agreed that rhetoric has, and must continue to have, an ethical component, and that rationality

14. Richard L. Larson, "Toward a Linear Rhetoric of the Essay," *College Composition and Communication* 22 (May 1971): 140-46.

15. Jean Piaget, *Language and Thought of the Child* (New York: New American Library, 1955); James Britton, *Language and Learning* (Miami, Fla.: University of Miami Press, 1970); James Moffett, *Teaching the Universe of Discourse* (Boston: Houghton Mifflin Co., 1968).

16. Lloyd F. Bitzer and Edwin Black, eds., *The Prospect of Rhetoric* (Englewood Cliffs, N.J.: Prentice-Hall, 1971).

and reason must be the basis for decision making, whether the decisions are individual or international. The seminar recommended that writing teachers give wide acceptance to new means of composition, letting students dictate rather than write their papers, or present their writings in the form of journals, or act as each other's editors.

Reactions to Change

Composition teaching has changed, but the changes have not occurred without opposition. As the discussion of new attitudes and new approaches became more widespread and more public, people outside the discipline, and a few inside it, misinterpreted what was happening. They saw the emphasis on self-expression and identity as an orgy of self-indulgence, a refusal on the part of some English teachers "to do their job." Instead of realizing that journal writing encourages fluency, develops self-confidence, and lets students play with language unhampered by discouraging grades and structured assignments, critics of the new methods condemned journals as a frivolous waste of time that should have been spent on "marketable skills." Some states legislated accountability and demanded specifically stated objectives that could be measured in quantitative terms. As money becomes scarcer, the pressure for a return to the so-called skills—spelling, punctuation, "correct usage"—becomes greater.

But whether the pressure comes from parents, from other departments, from administrators, or from legislators, good composition teachers continue to resist. They refuse to dehumanize writing, to treat it as impersonalized or standardized. They see "learning laboratories" not as devices for saving money by putting large numbers of students through mechanized drills, but as special services where students with special problems can seek special, individualized help. Whatever approach these teachers take in their own classes, they regard student writing as an attempt to communicate, not as a contest in "correctness."

Such teachers agree that good writing is neither mechanical nor formulaic, and thus there can be no absolute formula for producing it. Good writing *succeeds*, and success implies achieving its purpose (which may or may not have been consciously specified); meeting the needs of its audience (which may or may not have been consciously identified); adhering to a set of values (which may or may

j

not have been consciously recognized). Looking at the product—the finished writing—it is often possible to isolate the elements that make it successful. Looking at the process—what goes on before and during the writing—it is difficult to be sure what teaching method, or combination of methods, has led to success. It is hardly surprising, therefore, that the content of good composition courses varies almost as much as the variety of teachers who teach it, the variety of students who take it.

E. Reading in the Secondary School

MARGARET EARLY*

The Present Scene

By the mid-1970s it was no longer a question of whether reading should be taught in secondary schools. Now the questions turned on how and when, to whom and by whom. English teachers found themselves at the center of the movement to continue reading instruction into the high school and beyond, not stopping at third grade or sixth. The idea was not new.[1] But the implementation, even in the 1970s, was meager and of dubious quality.

In most middle schools and junior high schools, students were pressed into reading classes for at least a semester, but instruction was seldom differentiated, except in pacing, and seldom met the needs of students who had outgrown basal readers but had not yet acquired skills for studying content textbooks or for coming to grips with mature literature. In senior high schools, reading instruction, if admitted at all, was usually confined to "remedial laboratories" or infrequent "developmental" classes in speed reading and study skills.

To improve this situation would require the energies and imagination not only of reading personnel but of all teachers and administrators. But reading specialists at the secondary level were scarce in the 1960s and 1970s. If instruction in reading were to be improved, or in most cases begun, and if such instruction were also to be integrated into all subjects in the curriculum, then responsible leadership was essential. Most people—administrators, teacher educators, publishers, school boards—expected English teachers to take the

---

* Consultant readers for this chapter were Michael F. Graves, Associate Professor, Department of Curriculum and Instruction, University of Minnesota; and Walter R. Hill, Professor, Faculty of Educational Studies, State University of New York at Buffalo.

1. See, for example, *Reading in the High School and College*, Forty-seventh Yearbook of the National Society for the Study of Education, Part II, ed. Nelson B. Henry (Chicago: University of Chicago Press, 1948).

lead. Many responded by themselves becoming reading teachers, remedial specialists, reading consultants, learning disability specialists, and they divorced themselves from the discipline of English. Others resisted demands being made upon them to teach reading/study skills themselves and to take the lead in persuading teachers in other disciplines to share the responsibility.

Changing Attitudes

Changes in these attitudes are appearing. In this decade, reading methods courses are usually included in undergraduate and graduate programs for prospective English teachers and they are required for certification in a growing number of states. School administrators are more often than not looking for English teachers who expect to include reading in their curriculum and know how to teach it. And the pressure to teach reading comes from within the profession as well as from nationwide movements like the "Right to Read" program.[2]

English teachers generally have become concerned with how well and how widely students read, more than with what they read or how they respond to specific works of literature. The result has been to change the content of literature, as noted in the previous section, as well as methods of teaching and organizing the curriculum. Changes can be seen in the choices made by individual teachers in the ways they teach. Changes are even more dramatically visible in the redesign of a department's offerings, which may open up to students a spate of reading electives.

Enthusiasm for elective systems hit secondary English departments at about the same time as demands for reading instruction gathered momentum. In many ways it was a fortunate confluence. With electives in reading, more than in the usual comprehensive full-year courses, one is likely to get well-structured, intentional, differentiated instruction. Typical of the number and variety of electives in a three-year program are these in a Colorado high school: basic reading skills (individualized, repeatable); developmental reading; speed reading; advanced reading I (study of structure and style of different types of writing, requiring six works of fiction and

2. See page 75 for a discussion of the influence of the "Right to Read" program on elementary and secondary schools in the 1970s.

nonfiction); advanced reading II (study of two novels in depth); reading for research; a reading seminar (independent study on topic of student's choice); reading nonfiction; and reading skills for college.[3]

In other schools across the country, in addition to these electives are found various kinds of word study (for example, etymology, semantics, "forty days to a more powerful vocabulary"); individualized reading (guided free reading); psychology of learning (diagnosis and self-evaluation of learning styles); reading and the mass media (a study of public language); children's literature (may include reading to young children); reading newspapers and magazines.

An All-school Program

Electives in reading are no substitute for the ideal all-school developmental program, but they can be an effective interim stage preceding full-scale and adroit integration of skills and content. They may be a necessary interim in schools that are experimenting with independent study, inquiry and discovery methods, and the integration of content fields. The long-espoused "directed reading lesson" and the newer "advance organizers"[4] and "instructional frameworks"[5] are not easily reconciled with a discovery approach. Teachers find it difficult to teach methods of textbook study when students are using a variety of texts. Standard approaches like Robinson's SQ3R, which fit very well the expository style of older information-dispensing textbooks, are much less useful for texts designed to inspire discovery learning.[6] Moreover, new curricular designs, including elective systems, increase the numbers of students that teachers contact during the year. In nine-week English courses,

3. Pauline Hodges, "Reading as an Elective in the English Program," *Journal of Reading* 18 (October 1974): 30-33.

4. David Ausubel, "In Defense of Verbal Learning," *Readings in School Learning*, comp. David Ausubel (New York: Holt, Rinehart & Winston, 1969), pp. 249-65.

5. Harold L. Herber, *Teaching Reading in Content Areas* (Englewood Cliffs, N.J.: Prentice-Hall, 1970), pp. 31-39.

6. Jane H. Catterson, "Problems and Principles in Teaching Middle School Reading," in *Reading in the Middle School*, ed. G. G. Duffy (Newark, Del.: International Reading Association, 1974), p. 96.

for example, teachers complain that they have too little time to diagnose reading and writing skills. But a reading elective based on diagnosis and self-evaluation of learning styles could yield information for many teachers to share. Short-term electives in study skills, especially when prepared in cooperation with content teachers, provide instruction not so surely arranged for in the content subjects themselves when students are working in many texts.

The titles of reading electives given earlier suggest how much reading as a "subject" can overlap with what is traditionally thought of as English. Through experimenting with reading electives, varying the offerings and evaluating thoroughly, a group of teachers can come to practical understandings of the differences between reading as a process and literature as a discipline. Students need both. In elective programs students can be counseled to choose the right balance for their individual needs. In more conventional full-year courses teachers must decide what is a fair balance. For teaching reading/study skills applicable to informational prose in no way substitutes for teaching how to read literature. Conversely, English teachers, when they are solely responsible for the whole reading/ study skills program, are scuttling it if they teach mainly how to read poetry, fiction, and drama, and neglect informational prose.

The Reading of Literature

Teaching how to read literature has certain limited parallels with teaching how to read all other kinds of writing. Obviously, since language is the common element, teachers of all subjects are concerned in varying degrees with phonological, semantic, and syntactic considerations. Readiness is always essential to insure comprehension; English teachers speak of "setting up points of connection"[7] or providing "imaginative entry,"[8] whereas reading teachers talk of "structured overviews" and "conceptual background." But comprehension of a different order results from reading a poem or a novel than from reading a scientific or historical report. Empirically,

7. Louise Rosenblatt, "Literature: The Reader's Role," *English Journal* 49 (May 1960): 304-10, 315.

8. Dwight Burton, "Teaching Students to Read Literature," in *Reading Instruction in Secondary Schools*, ed. M. J. Early (Newark, Del.: International Reading Association, 1964), pp. 87-100.

it is hard to prove these differences,[9] but intuition and experience suggest that some of the skills emphasized by reading teachers (for example, finding the main idea, subordinating details to main ideas, SQ3R, summarizing and outlining) have little pertinence to reading much of literature. More pertinent are the ideas developed by Henry in *Teaching Reading as Concept Development: Emphasis on Affective Thinking*.[10] Henry shows how English teachers can, through their questioning, guide students "to seek out a number of relations and to put this growing set of relations into a tentative structure." [11] Thus he sees reading instruction as helping students to exercise four operations in logic—joining (through comparison and generalization), excluding, selecting, and implying (cause-effect, proof, condition). Chiefly, Henry illustrates the exercising of these logical operations in the analysis of individual works (to find relations) and the synthesizing of relations found in one or more works. Among several applications of his theories he describes an experiment in which eleventh-grade English classes structure the concept of man and nature from their reading of seventeen works of literature.

Henry offers one way of teaching the reading of literature, a way that should encourage experimentation and research and should also, as he hopes, ease the alleged tension between reading and literature. A less direct approach is described by Kahn,[12] who sets up five courses or units of study related to each of five purposes for reading literature and suggests works on several levels of readability.

Henry's study reminds us that the principle of relatedness is essential in evolving a literature curriculum that teaches how to read. Kahn's study says once again that the thematic unit, long familiar to English teachers, is an appropriate vehicle, since it

9. Chester W. Harris, "Measurement of Comprehension of Literature: I. The Nature of Literary Comprehension," *School Review* 56 (May 1948): 280-89; idem, "Measurement of Comprehension of Literature: II. Studies of Measures of Comprehension," *School Review* 56 (June 1948): 332-43; Alan C. Purves, *Literature Education in Ten Countries* (New York: John Wiley & Sons, 1973), p. 34.

10. George Henry, *Teaching Reading as Concept Development: Emphasis on Affective Thinking* (Newark, Del.: International Reading Association, 1974).

11. Ibid., p. 4.

12. Norma Kahn, "A Proposal for Motivating More Students to Lifetime Reading of Literature," *English Journal* 63 (February 1974): 34-43.

provides for differences in students' interests and abilities and adapts well to the exercise of analysis and synthesis, which teachers can handle through small-group discussion techniques and study guides.

Because of the tight integration of the receptive and expressive skills, English teachers can hardly miss (though they often do) teaching how to read in teaching composition and language. In connection with the former, for just one example, they teach ways of organizing ideas that are equally applicable to the analysis of other writers' ideas. In connection with language, again to cite just one example, they teach the detection of "doublespeak," or how to read the language of persuasion and politics.

Staff Development

English teachers today find themselves in schools that are moving from no reading instruction to piecemeal services toward a full-scale developmental program involving the total staff and student body. At one end of this progression English teachers are accountable for *all* reading instruction because there are no reading personnel (other than remedial teachers, perhaps, who reach only a small part of the student body). In schools with reading departments, the English staff may be responsible only for teaching how to read literature, broadly defined to include nonfiction, especially current articles and essays from the mass media. In still more advanced schools reading consultants may be free to help teachers in all subject areas integrate reading skills with content learning.

In any of these situations the full participation of the English department is called for. If reading consultant services are ineffectual or nonexistent, the English department may have to take the first steps in organizing an all-school program. Such a program will not emerge until all teachers, or almost all, are concerned and competent to teach reading. First steps—to be taken simultaneously in many instances—include winning financial and moral support from administrators, school board, and parents; surveying students' and teachers' attitudes and abilities; studying problems and solutions in comparable schools; defining goals and setting up a three- to five-year calendar; defining needs in resources and personnel; and planning for short-term and long-range evaluations.

Staff development, not for English teachers only but for all the faculty, is an immediate and continuing goal. Experiences that will increase all teachers' expertise include team teaching in which one member of the team has had training in reading; intensive released-time workshops in which teachers prepare materials that teach not only content but the reading/study skills that make its comprehension possible; curriculum development in each field with reading consultants participating; employing content teachers as tutors in the remedial laboratory or learning center; and team planning practices.[13]

Staff development is expensive, involving as it must additional personnel to relieve teachers of classroom responsibilities and bringing in expert consultant help. Time and money are well spent on staff development only when it is ongoing. The occasional half-day workshop on reading problems is almost always a waste of time.

Provision for Referral

English teachers have many responsibilities in the secondary reading program. One they do not have is attempting to teach beginning reading skills to nonreaders. For dyslexics and seriously deficient readers, they have the responsibility of referral to specialists. Meanwhile, in continuing to teach English to these students they must substitute nonreading approaches. For less seriously deficient readers, they have the responsibility of knowing books, articles, printed matter of any kind that they can read, even though it is not literary, even though it is written in the vocabulary and sentence structure of second grade readers. English teachers, like teachers in all other subjects, have an obligation to use—and teach—reading at levels below "grade level," not to succumb entirely to nonprint media as a vehicle for all the ideas of their courses.

If a remedial program is underway in their schools, English teachers should know everything about it: how to make referrals, how to evaluate a student's progress, what kind of progress to expect, how to work with students in regular classes while tutoring proceeds, how to differentiate effective remedial techniques from time-serving measures. Perhaps the surest way to develop such in-

13. Olive S. Niles, "School Programs: The Necessary Conditions," in *Reading Process and Programs* (Urbana, Ill.: National Council of Teachers of English, 1970), pp. 41-74.

sights is to spend time in the program as a tutor. If remedial services are lacking, English teachers should know whether or not to recommend them, deciding whether the chances for success are worth the high costs and risks. One risk is that the remedial clinic will short-circuit a full development program.

Obviously, a truly effective secondary reading program cannot be contained in the English curriculum. English teachers should see that it spreads. At the same time, they must recognize that the central responsibility is theirs because growth in and through language is their specialty. And more than other disciplines, the content of English can yield to the needs of adolescents, can offer diversity of ease and challenge, can help them to find real and lasting reasons for reading even in an electronic age.

CHAPTER VII

Creating Learning Environments

ALLAN A. GLATTHORN*

Introduction

Much educational innovation has been concerned with changing
the learning environment—developing new arrangements of time,
staffing, space, resources, and pupil groupings. Despite mounting
evidence that no single set of arrangements seems to be optimal
for all pupils, innovators have continued to propose modifications
and new combinations of those components in an attempt to bring
about improved pupil attitude and performance. Such attempts to
create new learning environments have had a clear impact on how
the English language arts are taught; in fact, it seems to me that
English teachers have always been among the first to experiment
with such changes.

This is not to say that the conventional classroom is passé. In
fact, it seems safe to assume that in many of the elementary and
secondary schools of the nation, English is taught in a way that
deviates very little from the traditional pattern: one teacher explains
or lectures to thirty pupils. And there are those who have argued
that this much-maligned "traditional" teaching is, in fact, quite
effective, at least for those who in Piagetian terms are at the stage
of formal operational thought.[1]

Schoolwide Models

Despite the tenacity of this teacher-centered model, several different learning environments have been promulgated during the past

* Consultant readers for this chapter were Robert A. Bennett, Director of
Program Development, San Diego City Schools; and Vernon H. Smith, Professor of Education, Indiana University.

1. See, for example, David Ausubel, *The Psychology of Meaningful Verbal
Learning* (New York: Grune & Stratton, 1963).

decade as solutions to the problems of pupil nonachievement and boredom. Some models have attempted a comprehensive reorganization of the entire school environment; others have focused on the individual classroom. Since both the schoolwide and the classroom models have implications for English, it seems useful to examine both. Three schoolwide models have been widely implemented: the flexibly scheduled school, Individually Guided Education, and alternative schools. While they have some interesting similarities, there are also important differences among the three; we thus might fruitfully examine each separately.

FLEXIBLY SCHEDULED PROGRAMS

The flexibly scheduled classroom developed out of the attempts of J. Lloyd Trump to find a more effective model for the secondary school.[2] His notions were further developed by Dwight W. Allen and his colleagues, who were able to produce a computer program sophisticated enough to deal with the scheduling complexities of the flexibly scheduled school.[3] As both Trump and Allen agreed, the flexibly scheduled school would be characterized by four related features: a modular schedule; large- and small-group instruction; independent study in resource centers; and a differentiated staff.

The modular schedule is an attempt to gain greater flexibility in the use of time. Instead of classes meeting for a daily forty-five-minute period, the schedule is built from shorter modules of time (fifteen minutes, for example). The modular schedule obviously affords the teacher more choices initially in determining the length of the period; for this reason, it appeals to many secondary English teachers who see it as a way of escaping the rigidity of the forty-five-minute class.[4] The modular schedule, however, has made little impact on elementary language arts classes. Elementary teachers used

---

2. J. Lloyd Trump, *Images of the Future: A New Approach to Secondary Schools* (Washington, D.C.: National Association of Secondary School Principals, 1959).

3. Robert N. Bush and Dwight W. Allen, *A New Design for High School Education: Assuming a Flexible Schedule* (New York: McGraw-Hill Book Co., 1964).

4. For example see the balanced assessment of the flexibly scheduled school from an English teacher's point of view in James J. Backen, "Flexible Scheduling: Facts, Fantasies, and Fads," *English Journal* 60 (March 1971): 363-68, 372.

to having large blocks of time available see no need for programming "flexibility."

There have been almost no systematic attempts to evaluate the impact of this time flexibility on the development of language competency. The only evidence to support the modular scheduling aspect of the flexible classroom comes from several surveys of teacher and student opinion; such surveys, predictably, report that those participating in the innovation feel favorably disposed towards it.[5]

In some respects, however, the complexity of the modular schedule results in a new kind of rigidity; once generated and implemented, the modular schedule is difficult to alter. Teachers who want maximum flexibility on a day-to-day basis often prefer a block-of-time scheduling that gives small teams of teachers two or three hours to divide each day as they choose. The proposals to vary the size of the instructional group are linked to the same concern for flexibility. Teachers traditionally have been assigned five classes of twenty-five to thirty-five pupils; and the efforts of the National Council of Teachers of English to reduce teacher load have historically focused on attempts to reduce class size to a more manageable figure. Proponents of flexible group size have countered that such reductions in class size are not economically feasible and would not affect the nature of the teacher-pupil interaction. Instead of assigning one teacher five classes of thirty pupils that would meet five times a week, they contend we should give that teacher one weekly lecture group of 150 and ten semiweekly seminar groups of fifteen. The intent here, as Bishop points out, is to relate the size of instructional group to the nature of the instructional activity: the large group is used for teacher lecture, films, demonstrations, where interaction is not important; the small groups are used for discussions where a high level of verbal response by pupils is essential.[6]

To begin with, what do the research and our experiences say about large-group instruction in English? Several studies over the

5. See, for example, David W. Beggs, *Decatur-Lakeview High School: A Practical Application of the Trump Plan* (Englewood Cliffs, N.J.: Prentice-Hall, 1964).

6. Lloyd K. Bishop, *Individualizing Educational Systems* (New York: Harper & Row, 1971).

years have provided persuasive evidence that lectures and films are as effective in transmitting information to groups of 150 as they are to groups of thirty.[7] Thus, large-group instruction seems to be an efficient method for didactic instruction. However, my experience and the testimony of other teachers suggest that problems of pupil inattention and disruption increase significantly in such large groups, to the extent that additional teachers and aides are needed for supervision, with a net loss of instructional efficiency. A group of fifty to seventy seems to be a reasonable compromise: it is large enough to increase staff efficiency; it is small enough for an assertive teacher to manage without additional help.

The use of small-group instruction seems to hold much promise for the teaching of English. Teachers, of course, have always argued for smaller classes; administrators have always responded by pointing to the many studies that indicate that class size does not affect pupil achievement. Yet such studies typically have compared standard class groups of twenty with standard class groups of thirty; the absence of any significant difference between such groups is predictable and understandable. However, when researchers have turned to the effects of small groups of six to twelve, they have been able to find some important differences.

Stumpe found that a nongraded group of ten to twelve pupils who used group processes and individualized instruction achieved significant changes on personality measures and significant gains on measures of achievement, as compared with pupils in a standard class program.[8] Rinne reported that he was able to achieve a higher level of pupil participation in small groups that were used as part of his English program than when large-group instruction was used.[9] DeVries and his associates discovered that pupils working in small cooperative groups achieved several important gains:

7. A good summary of the research on methodology and achievement can be found in Robert Dubin and Thomas C. Taveggia, *The Teaching-Learning Paradox* (Eugene, Ore.: Center for the Advanced Study of Educational Administration, 1969).

8. Doris M. Stumpe, "Study of a Nongraded Supplementary Group Communication Skills Program: Rationale, Pupil-Personal-Social Characteristics, and Program Effects" (Doctoral diss., St. Louis University, 1967).

9. Carl H. Rinne, "Teaching in Small Groups," *English Journal* 56 (February 1967): 289-92.

Small groups create an atmosphere in which students can positively reinforce each other for involvement in the academic task, as well as provide sanctions to disruptive or irrelevant behavior. . . . Finally, the data suggest that small group experiences provide an important, and perhaps unique, reality test for a set of interpersonal skills not typically developed in secondary schools.[10]

A third part of the typical flexible-schedule "package" is the use of independent study through unscheduled time. Schools have always expected students to work on their own, either in supervised class study, in a study hall, or at home. The flexibly scheduled schools have expanded this idea and introduced some variations. First, Bush and Allen have argued that the amount of independent study time should be increased to as much as fifty percent of the student's total day.[11] Second, flexibly scheduled schools have typically changed the general study hall into several specialized resource centers. Thus, an English resource center is usually equipped with paperback novels and nonfiction works, word games, filmstrips, disc recordings of poetry and drama, audio cassettes, and self-instructional print materials. Third, students have easy access to such centers. Finally, the independent study time is not intended to be used just for doing "homework" or completing rote exercises, but also for mastering basic content and exploring new areas of interest.

Evaluations of such independent study programs have turned up mixed results. To begin with, it is clear by now that students can acquire much of the basic content of any course through self-directed study.[12] However, pupils do seem to vary considerably in their ability to work on their own and to manage their own behavior; and many schools using independent study now find they must assign additional teachers and aides to the resource centers to direct learning and supervise conduct. Also, I have noticed that both high

10. David L. DeVries et al., *The Effects on Students of Working in Cooperative Groups: An Exploratory Study* (Baltimore, Md.: Johns Hopkins University Center for the Study of Social Organization of Schools, 1971), pp. 21-22.

11. Bush and Allen, *A New Design for High School Education.*

12. See, for example, Dubin and Taveggia, *The Teaching-Learning Paradox*; H. E. Gruber and M. Weitman, *Self-Directed Study: Experiments in Higher Education*, Report No. 19 (Boulder, Col.: University of Colorado Behavior Research Laboratory, 1962).

school and college students often report negative attitudes toward programs that minimize the amount of interaction they have with teachers and peers.

The fourth aspect of the flexibly scheduled program involves a differentiated teaching team. Team teaching, of course, is not a new idea. As early as 1959 Trump advocated a team-teaching model designed to provide time for the team of teachers to plan together, to share the large-group responsibility, and to work flexibly with small groups of pupils.[13] Allen was one of the first to add to the notion of teaming the idea of differentiation of function, responsibility, and salary.[14] In Allen's model, a typical differentiated team might include one highly experienced and competent leader of the English team (earning a salary equivalent to an administrator's), two or more experienced master English teachers charged with the chief instructional responsibility, perhaps one or two probationary teachers who would assist in the teaching, one or more teacher interns, and a teacher aide.

There has been very little systematic evaluation of differentiated teaming. There is no conclusive evidence that a differentiated team of English teachers can produce greater growth or more positive attitudes than several individual teachers working in their own classrooms. There is obviously a compelling logic for capitalizing upon the diverse talents of teachers by helping them plan and teach together and for relating salary to function, responsibility, and experience. There are, however, counterarguments that seem just as persuasive: pupils like to be able to identify with one teacher, not with a team; and the hierarchical nature of the differentiated team seems to run counter to strong cultural and professional pressures for participatory decision making and egalitarian relationships.

The number of flexibly scheduled English classrooms seemed to hit a peak in the late 1960s and then wane, if the number of articles in professional journals is an indicator of popularity. Despite this seeming decline in interest, the flexibly scheduled English classroom is still much in evidence and seems to be a viable model for many

13. Trump, *Images of the Future.*

14. Dwight W. Allen, "Differentiated Teaching Staff," *California Education* 3 (June 1966): 12-15.

teachers and students. Although I now believe that the modular schedule and the differentiated staff are superficial rearrangements of external elements, it seems to me that the other components of the flexible program have a more pervasive impact on the learning process. The small group does seem to change the nature of the human transaction in learning. Independent study can help the pupil assume more responsibility for learning content, thus freeing the teacher to facilitate other types of learning. And the flexibly scheduled classroom seems to make one more contribution: it creates a receptivity for change that makes it easier for other models to gain the attention of administrators and teachers.

INDIVIDUALLY GUIDED INSTRUCTION

Individually Guided Education (IGE) is a more recent attempt to revamp the total school environment. Developed by Herbert J. Klausmeier and his colleagues at the Center for Cognitive Learning of the University of Wisconsin, IGE embraces both an elementary and a secondary model. The two models have the following features in common: the school is organized into small units of 75 to 150 pupils, with multi-age and cross-grade grouping; each unit is taught by a hierarchical team of instructional specialists headed by an appointed team leader; all learning emphasizes behavioral objectives, self-paced instruction, and criterion-referenced testing; a continuous progress placement policy is implemented; variable instructional groupings are used in a block-of-time schedule; and schoolwide leadership responsibilities are shared by an Instructional Improvement Committee. The secondary model proposes more interdisciplinary study in its curriculum units than does the elementary. And, according to one proposal, secondary teams are organized into five divisions (environmental science, applied technology, management science, community studies, and communication arts),[15] whereas elementary teams are not so divided.

In the IGE model, secondary English teachers would work in the communication arts division, responsible for the instruction of perhaps 200 students. The team would be led by a "division leader" and

15. Katherine M. Koritzinsky and Steven J. White, *IGE/MUSS: An Instructional Management System for Secondary Schools* (Madison, Wis.: Center for Cognitive Learning, University of Wisconsin, 1973).

would be assisted by an instructional aide and a clerical aide. The team would help students develop their communication skills and explore careers in the communications cluster.

IGE is now in use in numerous elementary schools and secondary schools. Since the primary emphasis to date has been on the implementation of the model and the development of the curriculum units, there has been only limited summative evaluation. And, according to a report of the Educational Products Information Exchange Institute, those summative evaluations ". . . are narrowly conceived, experimentally and instrumentally inadequate, and not very useful to consumers." [16] Several of IGE's features, however, seem to make much sense, if we consider what we presently know about the needs of both teachers and pupils. The smaller units seem to provide a more personal climate than the large undifferentiated schools. The autonomous instructional teams would seem to be a useful way of organizing the staff. And the use of variable instructional groupings in a block-of-time schedule would seem to provide maximum flexibility for the teacher. I have only two reservations about the IGE model. First, it does not seem to provide sufficient alternatives in the amount of structure provided the pupil, since all pupils must conform to the basic IGE model and cannot opt for a more structured or more open environment. Second, it seems to limit itself unwisely and unnecessarily to a curriculum based on the behavioral objectives or performance outcome model.

THE ALTERNATIVE SCHOOL

A third kind of attempt to revamp the entire school is the alternative school, which actually attempts a redefinition of "school" by reaching beyond the classroom to create learning environments in the community. Such alternative schools also expand the concept of choice: the student can choose not only from among learning experiences in the classroom, but also from among types of schools and school environments.

The recent history of the alternative school movement began with the Parkway Program in Philadelphia, which opened in 1969 with two explicit goals: to provide Philadelphia high school students

16. "Evaluating Instructional Systems," EPIE Report No. 58 (New York: Educational Products Information Exchange Institute, 1974), p. 33.

with an alternative to the regular high school, and to use the entire city as the classroom. By 1975, according to estimates by Smith, there were at least a dozen types of alternative public schools operating in several thousand communities and enrolling at least half a million students.[17]

While there are many ways of categorizing alternative schools, Smith's typology seems more useful than most:

Open schools: provide individualized learning experiences organized around interest or resource centers.

Schools-without-walls: provide learning experiences throughout the community.

Learning centers: provide a concentration of resources in one location available to all students.

Magnet schools: provide opportunity for students to specialize in depth in a particular interest area.

Educational parks: provide a variety of programs on one location.

Continuation schools: provide programs for students whose education has been interrupted.

Multicultural schools: provide a curriculum based on cultural pluralism.

Environmental schools: provide a curriculum focused on the environment.

Free schools: place primary emphasis on student freedom in decision making and learning.

Mini-schools: afford pupils a range of choices within a larger school.

Despite this wide array of types, these alternative schools do have certain elements in common. They are what Fantini calls "schools of choice"—they provide an option different from the conventional schools; they are smaller and consequently more flexible in responding to change; they tend to place more emphasis on student freedom and student choice; they make more extensive use of the community as a classroom; and they use any qualified person as teacher.[18]

Such schools have had a clear impact on the English curriculum, the learning environment, and the concept of "teacher." Curriculum

17. Vernon H. Smith and Robert D. Barr, "Where Should Learning Take Place?" in *Issues in Secondary Education*, Seventy-fifth Yearbook of the National Society for the Study of Education, Part II, ed. William van Til (Chicago: University of Chicago Press, 1976), pp. 153-77.

18. Mario D. Fantini, *Public Schools of Choice* (New York: Simon & Schuster, 1973).

change has in fact been so extensive that it is often difficult to know when students are studying "English." There are many interdisciplinary offerings, such as courses in "Conflict and Violence," "The Nature of Truth," and "Coping with Big Brother." There are mini-courses developed entirely around student interests and/or teacher competency with titles like "Doing Your Own Poetry," "The Novels of Vonnegut," and "Body Language in Home and School." And there are instances of "no curriculum": an adult and some young people meet on Monday and decide they will build a dome, make a film, or picket City Hall. In this last example the experience becomes the curriculum; no one worries too much about objectives, plans, or tests.

Such an open curriculum obviously needs an environment other than the classroom; so for the alternative school, "school" is any place where learning can occur. An observer thus might discover communication being studied in varied spaces and places: an art museum, a library, a township park, a television studio, a newspaper pressroom, and a business office. Even when the alternative school settles down into an ordinary school building, the English "classroom" is likely to be a room stripped of conventional school furniture, with cushions on the floor and a second-hand sofa in the corner.

In addition to expanding the concept of "classroom," alternative schools have also provided leadership in broadening the concept of "English teacher." While many alternative public schools often find themselves limited by teacher union contracts to using only certificated personnel, others have been able to use a wide variety of people to teach—parents, artists and craftsmen, retired people, and students themselves.

It is clearly difficult to measure the impact of such an array of curricula, environments, and people. As a consequence, there have been few reliable studies of alternative schools; those available have in general attested to the success of the alternative schools. A report from the Ford Foundation sums up the results in this way: "How do the students who attend alternative schools fare? Where standard measures of achievement such as test scores and college admissions are applicable, they show that alternative school students perform at least as well as their counterparts in traditional school programs, and usually better. Attendance rates almost without exception exceed those in regular schools." [19] And Smith notes, "Whether the factors involved are humaneness, size, or the different environment, principals of alternative high schools report less absence, less truancy, and less vandalism than conventional high schools in the same districts." [20]

The critics of alternative schools have not been so easily impressed. Broudy, for example, thinks that a "benign technological society" requires a somewhat standardized public school system:

... the current fiddling around with decentralized systems of control, alternatives in curriculum, vouchers for religious and other private schools, are transitional moves designed to preserve differences that are vestiges of a dual system of society and of schooling.[21]

Others have attacked alternative schools for their lack of rigor, their indifference to careful curriculum planning, and their inattention to the academic disciplines.[22]

Despite the attacks of such critics, my own experience leads me to believe that the alternative school movement is not just one more fad. In the early 1960s I was principal of a large high school where we installed a flexible program and tried to make all the students fit it. When the program seemed not to work for about 20 percent of the students, I blamed either the teachers or the students, depending on the audience. In the early 1970s I became the founder and director of two small alternative schools, enrolling only students who wanted our particular form of "free school." And I saw at first hand that offering a choice to the interested made more sense than imposing change on everyone; that a school of 150 had a greater chance of being a humane community than a school of 2000; and that doing independent study in the community was more creative than using a learning package in an "English resource center." While there is clearly a continuing need to reform the large high school, I believe

19. *Matters of Choice: A Ford Foundation Report on Alternative Schools* (New York: Ford Foundation, 1974), p. 6.

20. Smith and Barr, "Where Should Learning Take Place?" p. 166.

21. Harry S. Broudy, *The Real World of the Public Schools* (New York: Harcourt Brace Jovanovich, 1972), p. 229.

22. See, for example, Mortimer Smith, "CBE Views the Alternatives," *Phi Delta Kappan* 54 (March 1973): 441-43.

that part of that reform can best be accomplished by developing a wide variety of small alternative schools, where teachers and students alike can feel that they have more control over their lives and educational fortunes than they would have in a traditional school.

Classroom Models

It is clear from the above that the schoolwide models are primarily concerned with matters of school organization and climate; the classroom models are predictably more concerned with the curriculum and the instructional process. Here again the models and their variations change so rapidly that categorization is difficult. I think, however, that I can make best sense out of such attempts by adapting a schema first proposed by Edling.[23] The categories in table 1 are those proposed by Edling; the terms identifying each cell are those I will use in this paper.

TABLE 1

MODELS FOR CHANGING THE ENGLISH CLASSROOM

Media	Objectives	
	School Determined	Learner Selected
School Determined	Type A Individualized English	Type B Elective English
Learner Selected	Type C Open English	Type D Independent English

INDIVIDUALIZED ENGLISH

In Type A, Individualized English, the learner controls only the pace of learning; the school sets the objectives and specifies the

23. Jack V. Edling, *Individualizing Instruction: A Manual for Administrators* (Corvallis, Ore.: DCE Publications, Oregon State University, 1970).

media. Several "Type A" programs have been developed, including teacher-developed "learning packages" or "unipacks," commercially prepared kits, and comprehensive curriculum materials developed by research laboratories. PLAN, developed by the American Institutes for Research, and Individually Prescribed Instruction (IPI), developed at the University of Pittsburgh's Learning Research and Development Center, are the two major programs of the last sort.[24] While the two programs are somewhat different in design, they are sufficiently similar that a detailed description of one should suffice.

Individually Prescribed Instruction begins with curriculum planning. The substance of what is to be learned is laid out in a linear sequence of articulated units. Each unit of learning in turn is developed into a series of sequential lessons, with outcomes stated in behavioral terms. Placement tests are used to determine where along this sequence the learner is to begin. Preassessment measures tell the teacher which individual lessons to prescribe; postassessment measures determine if the learner is to go on to the next unit or review content not totally mastered.

The IPI concept has been developed into a comprehensive curriculum by Research for Better Schools (RBS), a research and development center. Although RBS originally planned to develop an entire IPI curriculum for kindergarten to grade twelve, reduction in funding forced them to curtail their plans for secondary curricula. In the language arts, IPI curricula and materials are presently available in reading, spelling, and handwriting.

The clear intent of IPI is to individualize learning by enabling each pupil to begin at the level of mastery and to progress at his/her own pace. Thus, an IPI language arts classroom of thirty "fourth-grade" pupils would have a few pupils working on beginning reading lessons, a few working on materials that would be the equivalent of seventh grade, and all the rest spread out in between. Pupils would be working primarily on their own, taking a pretest, having it checked, doing a lesson, taking a posttest, having that checked, and then going on to the next lesson. The teacher and a teacher aide move around the room, working most of the time with individual

24. For a more detailed discussion of PLAN and IPI as well as IGE (Individually Guided Education), see Harriet Talmage, ed., *Systems of Individualized Education* (Berkeley, Calif.: McCutchan Publishing Corporation, 1975).

pupils, occasionally calling a group together for discussion of a common concern or help with a common problem.

Obviously the individualization of IPI focuses primarily on placement and pacing. While the curriculum materials more recently developed do provide for choices in learning activities, most of the IPI materials do not provide options in methodology or choices about the content. The IPI curriculum can therefore be described as a tightly controlled program through which the individual pupil moves at a self-determined pace.

There has been some research on IPI curriculum, especially on the reading and mathematics components, with mixed results. One early study indicated that IPI resulted in no significant difference in pupil achievement, when compared with conventional classroom instruction;[25] a later study reported that IPI pupils achieved as well as or better than non-IPI students on standardized tests, achieved higher than non-IPI students on IPI tests, had a positive attitude towards schools and learning, and demonstrated a change in social behavior.[26]

IPI advocates point out also that the IPI environment results in more active learning, encourages pupils to work together, and alters the role of the teacher from presenter of information to diagnoser and prescriber. These obvious advantages encouraged many districts to adopt IPI programs during the early years of this decade; by 1974, IPI was being used in more than 250 schools across the country.

There were several drawbacks, however, that probably slowed down the adoption rate. For one thing, the per pupil cost for the entire program was higher than that of other models. Critics also were concerned with the seemingly mechanical nature of the teacher-pupil interaction; much of the talk in the IPI classroom seemed to be concerned with questions answered, lessons mastered, and units to be covered. Finally, many teachers felt the curriculum was too controlled by its developer and too much of the learning material was limited to paper and pencil exercises.

25. "A Progress Report: Individually Prescribed Instruction" (Philadelphia: Research for Better Schools, 1969).

26. "Individually Prescribed Instruction-Mathematics Product Development Report No. 17 (IPI-Math)" (Palo Alto, Cal.: American Institute for Research in the Behavioral Sciences, January 1972), p. 35.

Yet an important point had been made: many pupils can profit from a curricular system and learning environment based on IPI principles.

"Mastery learning" is an interesting variation of individualized instruction. Developed by Bloom and his students on the foundations of programmed instruction[27] and incorporating a model of school learning advanced by Carroll,[28] mastery learning is based on a curriculum organized into units of instruction defined by related behavioral objectives. The teacher begins with group instruction for the objectives of a given unit; the teacher then administers one or more criterion-referenced tests to determine mastery of the objectives. Students who do not achieve a satisfactory level of mastery (usually specified as 80-85 percent) are given feedback about errors, corrective techniques, and supplementary materials. After the last unit of the course, a final test covering a sample of course objectives is given for grading purposes.

In describing the mastery model, Mayo identifies these salient features:

1. Students are made aware of course objectives; they thus view learning as cooperative, not competitive.
2. Standards are set in advance and grading is in terms of absolute, not relative, performance.
3. Short diagnostic tests are used at the conclusion of each unit.
4. Additional learning—and additional time—are prescribed for those who need it.[29]

One other important factor of mastery learning is that it provides a variety of methods and media to the student who has not achieved complete mastery.

Thus, an English teacher using mastery learning to teach the concept of *noun* would present the students with the objectives of the unit. The teacher would then explain to the entire group the concept of noun, drawing upon their own language for examples and illustra-

27. Benjamin S. Bloom, "Learning for Mastery," *U.C.L.A. CSEIP Evaluation Comment* 1, no. 2 (1968).

28. John B. Carroll, "Problems of Measurement Related to the Concept of Learning for Mastery," *Educational Horizons* 48 (Spring 1970): 71-80.

29. Samuel T. Mayo, "Mastery Learning and Mastery Testing," *NCME Measurement in Education* 1, no. 3 (1970): 1-4.

tions. The syntactical and lexical features of *noun* would be identified, for the entire group. The class would then be examined with a criterion-referenced test covering all the objectives of the unit. Students who scored above the mastery level would have an opportunity for independent study, perhaps using materials that would explore how nouns function and are identified in other languages. The teacher would return the corrected tests to all students who scored below the mastery level, clarifying individually the errors made on the test. Those students would then have an opportunity to do additional work on the noun; this time, however, they might have an option about method and pace. Some would work in small groups, perhaps tutored by one of the students scoring above the cut-off point. Some would use a programmed text that would provide additional examples. A small group would be playing a game of "Word Class Concentration." Two or three would be listening to cassette tapes in study carrels; the cassette tape would include an explanation by the teacher with additional examples. Students could take the unit test as often as they wished; after achieving the criterion, the student would move on to new work.

What evaluation is there of mastery learning? The evidence indicates that the mastery learning model can be implemented in courses at any level and in any content area. Block, however, notes that the best results have been obtained when the course requires minimal prior learning;[30] other studies indicate that the model best fits content that is highly structured and sequential in nature. Hambleton reports that "the mastery learning model has been used successfully now with more than 100,000 students in elementary, secondary, and college-level courses. . . . Also, if mastery learning is carried out properly, previous research suggests that students will achieve higher scores and have more interest and a better attitude toward school." [31] Bloom, however, is not so sanguine. He notes: "There have been some successes and some dismal failures with this approach." [32]

30. James H. Block, ed., *Mastery Learning: Theory and Practice* (New York: Holt, Rinehart & Winston, 1971).

31. Ronald K. Hambleton, "Testing and Decision-Making Procedures for Selected Individualized Instructional Programs," *Review of Educational Research* 44 (Fall 1974): 387-88.

32. Benjamin S. Bloom et al., *Handbook on Formative and Summative*

ELECTIVE ENGLISH

Type B, Elective English, is exemplified in the numerous English elective programs now being offered. In Type B learning, the learner makes an initial choice of objectives or content by choosing among numerous short-term elective courses. Once the student has selected a course, however, the school typically controls the media and the pace of learning. For example, instead of taking a course called "Sophomore English," the student can choose from among twenty or more offerings that are organized according to genre, theme, skill, or period. Thus an elective English curriculum might offer courses like the following: "Shakespeare's Tragedies," "The Language of Advertising," "Improve Your Composition," and "Contemporary American Novel." Some elective offerings are "phased"—that is, they are open to pupils of several grade levels but are designated for certain achievement levels. Others are designed for particular grades or ability groups.

If the spread of elective courses is any measure of their value, they must be deemed to be of some worth, for they have spread across the nation into a substantial number of school districts. Their evident popularity is no doubt attributable to two enticements: they provide teachers with an opportunity to teach a favorite topic; and they offer pupils a choice of content emphasis. However, some real doubts have already been expressed by numerous critics. Hillocks, who has completed perhaps the most comprehensive survey of elective offerings, points out that they have often resulted in a fragmented curriculum and are put together into a "smorgasbord" offering that lacks design or system.[33] And my own observations lead me to believe that too much of the instruction in elective courses is of a rather conventional sort.

OPEN ENGLISH

Type C, "Open English," is, of course, part of the open education movement. To simplify, open education gives the pupil a choice of methods and media to master objectives set by the teacher but related to pupils' emerging interests.

Evaluation of Student Learning (New York: McGraw-Hill Book Co., 1971), p. 52.

33. George Hillocks, *Alternatives in English: A Critical Appraisal of Elective Programs* (Urbana, Ill.: National Council of Teachers of English, 1972).

Despite the diversity of open education models in American schools, it is still possible to identify the salient aspects of theory and the common attributes of practice in American open education. Barth has identified twenty-nine assumptions about learning and children that characterize open education, among which the following seem to be the most important:

1. Children are innately curious.
2. Active exploration in a rich environment offering a wide array of manipulative materials facilitates children's learning.
3. Children have both the competence and the right to make significant decisions concerning their own learning.
4. When two or more children are interested in exploring the same problem or the same materials, they will often choose to collaborate.
5. Concept formation proceeds very slowly.
6. Children learn at their own rate and in their own style.
7. Children pass through similar stages of intellectual development.
8. Intellectual growth and development take place through a sequence of concrete experiences followed by abstractions.
9. Verbal abstractions should follow direct experience with objects and ideas.
10. Errors are necessarily a part of learning.
11. Objective measures of performance may have a negative effect on learning.
12. Knowledge is a function of one's personal integration of experience and therefore does not fall neatly into separate categories or "disciplines."
13. There is no minimum body of knowledge which is essential for everyone to know.[34]

If we translate Barth's list of assumptions into description of a "typical" open classroom where the English language arts are being learned, we would see a picture something like the following. Four pupils are sitting in the reading corner, reading books they have chosen themselves from a classroom library of multilevel materials. Five are working together in the writing corner. They have examined pictures of old people and are writing short poems about their feelings. Four are in the listening corner, each wearing earphones, listening to disc and cassette recordings of poetry and

34. Roland S. Barth, *Open Education and the American School* (New York: Agathon Press, 1972).

prose. Three are in the game corner, playing a spelling and vocabulary game. In the center of the room a larger group is building a puppet stage, reading the directions, talking informally, and deciding together about the details of the construction. When the stage is finished, they will present a puppet play to their classmates. The teacher moves from group to group, listening, making suggestions for another activity, reminding the pupils to record their progress in their folders.

Such a description obviously portrays an elementary classroom; yet the secondary English classroom that calls itself "open" would not be very different. Some students would be working on a class newspaper; others would be using a programmed text to clear up problems in usage. A few would be sitting in a small group discussing a short story they had read. A small group would be playing *Scrabble*. Several would be sitting at carrels, writing compositions on a current issue. A few students would be tutoring classmates who had difficulty with a recent spelling test. Again, the English teacher would be moving from group to group, providing assistance as needed.

The Hawaii English Program is designed to be used in an open classroom. A total instructional system, the Hawaii program includes at the elementary level close to 700 separate components and activities, including several multimedia and multimodal presentations. Children are trained to work independently and to participate in peer tutoring. Its developers claim that "the structure of the objectives and the management and record-keeping procedures of the system allow teachers to create an environment in which responsible self-activation and self-direction are developed in the learner." [35]

Despite the seeming informality of these open learning environments, there has been careful curriculum planning, at least in the most effective "open" plans. While the curriculum for the open classroom is less concerned with the articulation of learning experiences and with the specifications of behavioral objectives than is the IPI curriculum, there is still a degree of covert control by the

---

35. "Project Aloha: Mainland Demonstration of the Hawaii English Program" (San Jose, Cal.: Berryessa Union Elementary School District, 1973).

teacher. Books have been chosen on the basis of the teacher's insight about pupils' reading interests and needs. The concrete materials have been selected to facilitate certain types of language response. The writing activities have been structured on the basis of the teacher's perceptions of the child's developing competency.

While educational libertarians will scoff at such "structured openness," there is some evidence that open education succeeds in fact only when there is a structured set of learning experiences providing the framework for the informal learning. For example, after surveying and analyzing how "free" and directed schools affected the achievement of disadvantaged pupils, Mills reached this conclusion:

In this regard it is fair to say that directedness has shown itself to be a vital element in the teaching of cognitive skills to disadvantaged children. This is true not only of the programs which are unequivocal about the nature of their directedness but also of the programs which stress freedom. Indeed, it is difficult to find a successful program in which directedness was not part of the teaching process.[36]

INDEPENDENT ENGLISH

Type D, "Independent English," gives the student the greatest amount of choice; the student determines both the objectives or content and the method and media for mastery. This type, of course, does not exist as a separate program offered by an English department to the entire student body. When it is found, independent English is more often an arrangement developed individually between a teacher and a highly motivated student who wants to work completely independently outside the classroom environment. Such independent study, embracing student-determined objectives and media, however, is rarely found; most so-called "independent study," as noted in the discussion of the flexible school, simply provides the student with some unscheduled time for completing teacher-determined work.

Reflecting on the Innovations

So we have been through a decade of widespread change, embracing three quite different approaches to reorganizing the entire

36. Nicolaus Mills, "Free Versus Directed Schools: Benefits for the Disadvantaged?" *IRCD Bulletin* 3 (September 1971): 9.

school and at least four ways to restructure the classroom. It might be useful at this point to look back and attempt to make some generalizations about the kinds of changes proposed and implemented.

1. Classroom Climate. I use this term to connote the amount of personal freedom given to the pupil. In all models there has been a definite move towards a climate of openness—giving the pupil more freedom of movement, more freedom to initiate talk.

2. External Structure. This term is used to designate arrangements of time and space for learning. There has been a general trend toward greater flexibility of time, either through smaller modules of time or through a block-of-time schedule. And there has been a systematic attempt to get beyond the confines of the conventional classroom by using special resource centers, large open spaces, or the community itself.

3. Instructional Personnel. Almost all the proposals involve the use of personnel in addition to regular classroom teachers. A few propose a differentiated staff led by master teachers; all make use of teacher aides; a few involve the use of peers as teachers; the most venturesome use anyone from the community with a competency to share.

4. Instructional Methods and Learning Activities. All models deviate from the conventional mode of teacher explanation through lecture. All involve some type of self-directed learning or independent study. Each one emphasizes what is usually termed "active learning," a phrase that embraces any learning activity in which the pupil does something other than receive information through listening, viewing, and reading; active learning thus includes such diverse activities as working with concrete materials, role playing, gaming and simulation, discussing and debating. Several of the models make extensive use of self-paced learning, with systematic testing and feedback to the learner.

5. Curriculum. Here we find an interesting divergence. Some of the models propose what might be termed an "open" curriculum; that is, one that does not specify all objectives, involves more choice on the part of the student, and requires less control by the teacher. Others propose what could be termed a "closed" curriculum: one that specifies all objectives, offers limited choice to the student, and requires more control by the teacher.

6. Grouping for Learning. In every model there is an attempt to use flexible groups for learning. While some seem to place too much reliance on learning in isolation, there is extensive use of small-group learning activities. In general, groups are organized without regard for conventional grade levels.

7. Materials for Instruction. There is an obvious concern in most of the models for providing a stimuli-rich environment. The single text has given way to multiple print resources covering a wide span of interests and reading levels. The rhetoric at least speaks of multimedia resources that give the student a choice of media.

And what has a decade of such innovation taught us about pupils, environments, and the learning of English? Not too much, obviously, since carefully designed evaluations have been few. We can, however, make some tentative inferences based upon those studies that have been done.

There is, first of all, some persuasive evidence that no single learning climate is best for all pupils. While extremists of the right and left will continue to debate about discipline and freedom, more reasonable people will perceive what the evidence suggests: some pupils at a given point in their development seem to profit from a climate where there is relatively little adult control. Minuchin and her colleagues have produced carefully documented evidence for such a finding in their study on the impact of varied elementary school environments.[37]

Second, there is increasing evidence that, at least at the beginning levels of schooling, some type of structure and direction is needed. The most successful open classrooms, in fact, seem to be those in which there has been careful planning of the curriculum and close monitoring by the teacher. The development of competence in language through schooling cannot be left to chance.

Next, pupils can learn on their own and from each other. There is now extensive evidence that, given the appropriate materials, pupils can indeed acquire much of the basic content of the course without the direct intervention of the teacher. And numerous programs that make systematic use of peer tutoring report success with this age-old process.

These findings do not make the English teacher unnecessary;

37. Patricia Minuchin, Edna Shapiro, and Herbert Zimiles, *Psychological Impact of School Experience* (New York: Basic Books, 1969).

they only suggest that in a time of increasing class size the English teacher needs to find effective ways of using independent study and peer tutoring to share the instructional responsibility.

Finally, the small group seems to be a useful way of organizing the classroom for instruction. In English especially, where the use of oral language is essential, the small group can play a vital role.

Providing for Multiple Options

These findings do not suggest that we can now put together some type of "ideal" English learning environment. In fact, the diversity among individual pupils and the complexity of the task of developing language competency suggest that we should forever abandon such a notion. Instead, it seems more fruitful now to ask how we can provide multiple options in the learning environment so that we can perhaps achieve a better fit between environment, task, and learner.

One way to achieve such a fit is to attempt to match learner with environment. And in recent years both practitioners and scholars have become interested in this problem of matching.

For the practitioner, the problem of matching learner and environment is most easily solved by providing the student with an array of alternative schools, each of which differs in this type of environment, and letting the student choose the one which he or she feels is best. This essentially is the approach advocated by Fantini[38] and actually implemented in the Quincy (Illinois) High School.[39] Both students and teachers at Quincy are able to choose from among seven different "minischools": traditional school, flexible school, open individualized school, fine arts school, career school, work-study school, and special education school.

In another work I have attempted to show how a school of 2000 students could be restructured into seven minischools, varying in terms of climate or program emphasis. Table 2 shows how I see such schools differing along several dimensions.[40]

Obviously, the teaching of English would differ in each of the

38. Fantini, *Public Schools of Choice.*

39. Richard Haugh, *Education by Choice* (Quincy, Ill.: Quincy School District, n.d.).

40. Allan A. Glatthorn, *Alternatives in Education: Schools and Programs* (New York: Dodd, Mead & Co., 1975).

minischools described in table 2. In the "traditional" school, instruction would proceed according to the standard method of lecture and recitation, and the curriculum would be a tightly organized study of language, literature, and composition. In the flexible school, extensive use would be made of large- and small-group instruction in English, supplemented with independent study; the curriculum would include a humanities course at each grade level and a range of English electives. English in the alternative school would make extensive use of community people and community places, with students being encouraged to undertake wide-ranging independent study projects in communication. In the free school, "English" as such would disappear: an adult would work with young people on major creative projects that would involve communication skills; the group would make a film, stage a play, publish a magazine, broadcast a television show.

In the three minischools with a special curricular focus, English would again be something quite different. In the career school, the curricular emphasis would be on the communication skills needed to succeed on the job. In the creative arts school, English would be entirely creative in its thrust. And in the cultural awareness school, the curriculum would focus solely on the literature and language of ethnic minorities.

While such practical solutions have already been implemented, researchers have been concerned with the more complex task of identifying significant differences in learning style and motivation. Among several such attempts, perhaps the most sophisticated has been undertaken by Hunt and his colleagues at the Ontario Institute for Studies in Education.[41] As table 3 indicates, the Hunt model is based upon the notion that children and youth can be found in three separate conceptual levels; and further development in conceptual level is best facilitated by the provision of different learning environments. Hunt has found some evidence that environmental differences can facilitate conceptual development.

There are two obvious ways of applying the Hunt model to the task of creating environments for English. In each case we would begin by identifying conceptual level, perhaps using the

41. David E. Hunt, *Matching Models in Education* (Toronto, Canada: Ontario Institute for Studies in Education, 1971).

TABLE 2

SEVEN PROPOSED ALTERNATIVES FOR A SCHOOL OF 2000 STUDENTS

PROGRAM	APPROX. ENROLLMENT	ENVIRONMENT	DECISION MAKER(S)	CURRICULUM	SCHEDULE	SPACE	TEACHING	GRADING
Traditional	500	Closed	Director	Academic subject	Period	Classroom	Lecture, recitation	Letter grades
Flexible	800	Moderately structured	Director, with staff and student input	Humanities, mini-courses	Modular	Large group seminar rooms, resource center	Lecture, discussion, individual study	Letter grades, with pass-fail option
Alternative	200	Open	Teachers, with student input	Broad fields, mini-courses	College	Seminar rooms, community	Discussion	Pass-fail or credit
Free	50	Free	Consensus	Unplanned projects	None	Community	Facilitator	None
Career	150	Structured	Director, with staff and student input	Careers	Modular	School, community	Master craftsman	Letter grades, with pass-fail option
Creative Arts	150	Open	Teachers, students	Creativity	Block of time	Studios	Artist	Pass-fail
Cultural Awareness	150	Moderately structured	Director	Cultural awareness	Modular	Seminar rooms	Ethnic	Letter grades, with pass-fail option

TABLE 3

CONCEPTUAL LEVELS, DEVELOPMENTAL TASKS, AND OPTIMAL
ENVIRONMENTS (DERIVED FROM *Matching Models in
Education*, BY DAVID E. HUNT)

Stage	Characteristics	Tasks	Optimal Environment
A	Self-centered; seeks immediate gratification; low tolerance for frustration; impulsive. Very concrete conceptual level; closed orientation; an organized phase before cultural standards have been incorporated. In adolescence the person at Stage A is often one who is trying to function at Stage C without having mastered Stage B. Often fails to be independent and consequently will manifest hostility and negativism.	The essential task is to develop the conceptual sophistication and autonomy to move to Stage B.	Needs a clearly organized environment within a normative structure, a highly structured environment with much concrete experience. If the environment is ambiguous or inconsistent, or if there is too much emphasis on autonomy, then normal development will be arrested.
B	Exhibits moral realism; concerned with rules; experiences self through the filter of role prescriptions; sensitive to status and authority of others. At the concrete conceptual level; often manifests an inflexible concreteness.	Needs to define the external boundaries, to learn the generalized standards, the ground rules of the social order.	Needs an environment in which there is an emphasis on autonomy and independence within the normative structure. If the environment is too highly organized and emphasizes compliance to the normative standard, or if the environment requires too much autonomy with an absence of normative structure, then development will be arrested.
C	Dislikes control, but is able to accept some when deemed essential; may show an exaggerated independence of spirit; wants freedom from constraints.	Needs to achieve self-distinctiveness and self-delineation; needs to learn about how one is oneself and to begin to accept responsibility for outcomes; needs to break away from Stage B standards.	Needs an environment which provides for high autonomy with low normative pressure, one which will provide maximum opportunity for independent self-assertion, many opportunities for self-selected individual activities.

TABLE 3 (continued)

CONCEPTUAL LEVELS, DEVELOPMENTAL TASKS, AND OPTIMAL
ENVIRONMENTS (DERIVED FROM *Matching Models in
Education*, BY DAVID E. HUNT)

Stage	Characteristics	Tasks	Optimal Environment
	More highly differentiated in cognitive complexity and more independent in motivation; shows a higher conceptual level—able to deal with abstractions and multiple alternatives.		If environment is too highly structured, or if there is too much emphasis on interpersonal mutuality, then development may be arrested.

paragraph completion test that Hunt has found to be effective. On the basis of the results, we would classify the student population into the three levels. With the classification complete, we could then proceed in one of two ways. One would be to organize a single English class into three learning groups, based on conceptual level, with the teacher differentiating treatment for each group. The other approach would require the English staff to develop four types of English courses:

Standard English (for students at Stage A). This course would present a highly structured curriculum, with separate emphases on language, literature, and composition. It would be taught to class-size groups, primarily through lecture, discussion, and concrete materials.

Individualized English (for students at Stage B). This course would emphasize the basic communication skills of reading and writing. Pupils would be tested and placed at their appropriate level; they would spend most of their time in a "Skills Laboratory," working on individualized learning materials, assisted by an aide or a teacher.

Open English (for students at Stage C). This would be a series of elective courses organized around thematic topics. Students would be able to choose the media and materials with which they would learn, working in an open space environment.

Alternative English (for students at Stage C). This course would develop out of the concerns of students and teachers. It would make extensive use of the community; students would be expected to work on long-term independent study projects.

The staff would then be asked to identify the types of courses they would prefer teaching; teachers would be encouraged to teach two different types of courses for their own growth. The students would then be presented with the four alternatives; their counselors and present English teacher would help them make a selection based upon their conceptual level, their need for structure, and their achievement in English.

All these attempts by practitioner and scholar have been concerned with matching environment and learner. What of the notion of matching task with environment? Do we need different environments for learning to spell, learning to read, learning to write?

One response is to argue that the development of language competency is unitary and cannot be fragmented into discrete "skills." If we see it as a unitary process that develops of its own accord but can be facilitated by a supportive environment, then it is clear that such an environment would be one which encourages the learner to use the spoken and written language with fluency, competency, and creativity. Such a view is supported by Cazden, who after reviewing five major studies on language development among children, concluded that language development proceeds most efficiently, both in functions as well as structure, when motivated by a powerful communicative intent. The child, according to Cazden, is aided by what he is encouraged to say, not simply by what he hears, and adults are necessary for such encouragement. She consequently recommends a group instructional environment that is natural, less didactic, and informal.[42]

Yet it can be argued that, at least for pedagogical efficiency, the subject called English can be analyzed into separate yet related skills; and that these skills might be optimally learned in different modes and environments. Joyce and Weil, who have been looking at environments and the question of learning task and environments, can be helpful here. Although they do not concern themselves spe-

42. Courtney B. Cazden, "Two Paradoxes in the Acquisition of Language Structure and Functions" (Paper presented at a conference sponsored by Developmental Sciences Trust, London, England, January 10-14, 1972), ERIC: ED 063 831.

cifically with English, their *Models of Teaching* can give us a useful perspective for looking at the question.[43] Joyce and Weil begin by specifying four different kinds of education that the child needs: basic education, personalized education, academic inquiry, and dialog. They then review fifteen different models of teaching that they have identified from the literature and try to match teaching models with educational needs. I have tried to show in table 4 how the Joyce-Weil model could be specifically applied to the subject of English. As is evident from the table, we would find ourselves using at least four different kinds of learning environments with all students to provide for the total range of the discipline.

I would like at this point to suggest another approach to the task of fitting learning task with environment. I start with an analysis of the specific tasks involved in the general development of English competency. Then, by examining the research and reviewing expert opinion, I identify those approaches that seem most useful for that specific task. I conclude by deriving from those approaches the general characteristics of an optimal environment for learning English. Table 5 summarizes one such analysis.

This task analysis suggests that the discipline of English can perhaps be optimally mastered by most pupils in a learning environment that comprises five major elements: teacher-talk, small-group learning, peer tutoring, individualized study, and active use of media and materials.

The Next Ten Years

Perhaps now, after this review of current theory and practice, we are ready to look ahead to talk about learning environments of the future. I reject the temptation to fantasize about where our knowledge of the chemistry of learning and of the right and left side of the brain might take us. Instead I choose to consider the reality of the next ten years. The major elements of that future seem both predictable and depressing, but somehow we will survive. And those of us who call ourselves "teacher" will be doing our best to help the children survive by making schools better places for learning and becoming. What will such better places look like for children of

---

43. Bruce Joyce and Marsha Weil, *Models of Teaching* (Englewood Cliffs, N.J.: Prentice-Hall, 1972).

TABLE 4

MODELS OF TEACHING AND THE TEACHING OF ENGLISH
(AFTER JOYCE AND WEIL, *Models of Teaching*)

Type of Education	General Emphasis	Teaching Model Most Applicable	Areas of English Where Applied	Primary Instructional Mode
Basic Education	The basic skills and knowledge needed for functioning in the world	Behavior modification techniques for individualized instruction or advance organizer techniques in teacher-directed learning	Reading, spelling, writing, media competency	Class or individual
Personalized Education	Begins with the person's particular talents and interests; an idiosyncratic approach that helps the learner develop in his/her own terms	Nondirective counseling approaches, synectics groups, or individual tutorials	Reading a favorite author, writing about personal experiences, thinking through personal values	Individual
Academic Inquiry	A process of learning that shows how scientists analyze the human culture by having students use scientific models of inquiry to build and test theories	Group investigation models, or inductive discovery lessons in the Brunerian mode	Doing linguistics; understanding literary analysis; studying communication theory	Small group
Dialog	Dialog on the nature and future of the society; a dialogic examination of the values of the society and the current controversies in that society	T-Group (Training Group) or Socratic discussion sessions	Thematic units on alienation, urbanization, politics	Small group

1984? What kinds of learning environments will increase all our chances of surviving in a fearful old world?

I see first of all thousands of small alternative schools complementing the big conventional school. Some of those alternative

TABLE 5
ENGLISH SKILLS AND ENVIRONMENTAL VARIABLES

General Area	Specific Competency	Optimal Activities and Environment
Writing	Writing well-formed sentences	Direct explication by teacher Individual practice Individual remediation
	Writing expository paragraphs and essays	Direct explication by teacher Individual writing on topic of personal interest Small-group sharing and processing Individual correction
	Writing personal and creative forms	Direct experiencing and use of motivating materials Small-group sharing Individual writing Publishing for an audience
Reading and literary analysis	Improving reading comprehension	Individualized structured lessons Peer tutoring Free reading of high-interest material
	Developing critical reading skills	Direct explication by teacher Small-group discussion and critiquing Individual remediation Peer tutoring
	Developing skills of literary analysis	Direct explication by teacher Individual reading of works of appropriate difficulty and interest Small-group discussion Individual remediation
Language study	Learning basic structure of the language and being able to analyze and identify those structures	Small-group discussion Direct explication by teacher using pupils' language Individual remediation
	Understanding related concepts in language study—dialectology, lexicography, phonology	Independent study units for individuals and small groups
"Mechanics"	Improving spelling	Structured individualized lessons Peer tutoring Individualized remedial lessons based on student's writing

TABLE 5 (continued)

ENGLISH SKILLS AND ENVIRONMENTAL VARIABLES

General Area	Specific Competency	Optimal Activities and Environment
	Using standard punctuation	Structured individualized lessons Peer tutoring Individualized remedial lessons based on student's writing
Media Analysis	Analyzing and evaluating media as an art form	Making own media in laboratory setting Viewing and then responding in small groups
	Critically analyzing techniques used by media to persuade and propagandize	Viewing examples and discussing in small groups Direct explication by teacher
Speaking and Listening	Developing listening skills	Participating in small-group discussions that are recorded Viewing and critiquing small-group discussions
	Improving speaking skills	Participating in small-group discussions Viewing and critiquing small-group discussions
Values and Current Issues	Reflecting on one's own values as they relate to current issues in the society	Role playing Small-group discussions

schools will be conservative in ideology, some very liberal; some highly disciplined, some very permissive. Some will include courses in "Survey of British Literature"; and some, courses in "Dome Building."

There will be all kinds of English classes—some highly structured, some very loose—some stressing "basics," some redefining what is basic. But in all of them we will see children and young people using the language creatively and joyfully: making films and video tapes, acting and playing roles, talking and listening, doing required and unrequired reading, writing poems, and telling stories.

We will see a variety of learning approaches, models, and systems. But in each one we will see some individualized learning and some small-group learning. Working on their own, pupils will be correcting deficiencies, exploring new areas of interest, developing learning autonomy. Working together, they will be sharing what they know, challenging each other, feeling good by being needed.

And at the center, making it all work, holding it all together, will be a teacher, competent, caring, and authentic. For at the least, what will save us is not a new package but a real person. Such a person will be competent—knowing the language, understanding how to vary the environment. That person will also be caring, accepting children for what they are, but believing enough in their potential to set reasonable expectations for growth. And, perhaps most importantly, that person will be authentic. To be an authentic English teacher is simply to be honest—about what one knows, about what one feels, about what one believes, about who one is. In a time of widespread uncertainty and rampant deceit, an honest person may be the only environment we need.

CHAPTER VIII

Evaluating Growth in English

ALAN C. PURVES*

Changing Historical Concerns

If one were to ask most English teachers how they evaluate their students' progress, they would mention tests and papers. English teaching, dealing as it does most frequently with the written word, finds its measure in the written word. The term paper and the essay examination have long predominated as evaluation instruments in English syllabi from elementary school to graduate school. These papers could be used as indices of the pupils' knowledge of and proficiency with the subject matter of English: language, literature, and media. They might alternatively be used as indices of the students' proficiency in the medium of writing itself. In general, judgment of a student's progress would come after the student gave an answer, and would not be involved in the question. A student might be set a topic, such as "Hamlet as a dutiful son," a topic that contains within it no apparent criterion of a correct response. Depending upon what the student wrote in response to that topic and depending upon the teacher's or examiner's sense of what a good response to that topic might be, the student would be judged knowledgeable and proficient.

This form of judgment, magisterial as it may seem, traces its lineage at least to the medieval disputation:

In order to qualify for degrees, a candidate had to uphold or attack from time to time both in his college and in the public schools, certain usually very abstract theses: and his education would be directed to

* Consultant readers for this chapter were Marjorie Drabkin, Coordinator, Alternative High School Reading Programs, New York City Board of Education, and Maude Edmonson, formerly Consultant in Reading, Merced, California.

fitting him to conduct his argument according to the rules of scholastic logic or to weigh it with a sufficiently impressive mass of learning.[1]

Although the medieval disputation was oral and in Latin, its form persisted through the transition from Latinate to vernacular education and from the oral to the written form. Throughout the shifts of rhetoric, from the scholastics to the Senecans, the nineteenth and twentieth century rhetoricians, the absoluteness of what constituted the best means of arguing shifted, but the criterion of effective discourse remained the judgment of the teacher or some external group of examiners.[2]

Besides judging discourse, English teachers have traditionally measured their pupils' knowledge of the material in their courses. Spelling tests, quizzes on literary history and on characters and lines from texts, tests of correct usage, or of grammatical or rhetorical principles and *topoi* have abounded for generations. Much of this kind of testing was on one form or another of rote learning, and, being so, differed from essay examinations in that the answer was prejudged. The correct spelling of *avocado*, the name of the author of *Hohenlinden*, or the meter in which *Tintern Abbey* was written —all these were known by teacher and pupil (presumably) beforehand. If the pupil forgot them, the master judged the pupil to have failed the course. In most cases, rote learning dealt with matters of fact, but quite often matters of conjecture entered into both the instruction and the testing. A point of usage, such as *he don't*, might be judged correct in Boston, incorrect in Chicago. In some cases an even more disputable matter, such as the relative merits of two poems, was the subject of a test. The opinion of the age or of the locality became the criterion of correctness and the object of conning.

1. E. M. W. Tillyard, *Milton* (London: Chatto and Windus, 1956,), p. 14.

2. The earliest formal university examinations—in law at the University of Bologna—consisted of both private and public hearings. The type soon spread to other European countries and from the university to other schools. Written examinations came with the production of paper; the Jesuits were among the first to use them extensively. In England, written examinations at Oxford and Cambridge did not emerge until the beginning of the nineteenth century and they became widespread at the postsecondary level both there and in the United States by the middle of the century. For a more detailed history, see Philip H. DuBois, *A History of Psychological Testing* (Boston: Allyn & Bacon, 1970).

THE RISE OF EXTERNAL TESTING

As might be expected, when the necessity arose for testing to be conducted on a scale larger than that of the classroom, the type of testing changed little. The university entrance examinations, which numbered among the antecedents of most mass achievement testing, contained both questions dealing with pieces of information presumably learned before and questions that called for the marshalling of evidence.[3] In many cases, the tests dealt with texts that the students were assigned to read during the course of the year before the examination, so that university entrance examination helped determine the syllabus of the secondary school English class. College entrance examinations were read by groups mostly from the member colleges. Typically, these graders anathematized the writing capabilities of the candidates even a hundred years ago much as they do today.[4]

At the same time that the rising number of candidates for tertiary education called for interuniversity cooperation on admissions examinations, another phenomenon brought testing out of the individual classroom or school. The American Civil Service began competitive tests in the 1880s. Most of the early tests were practical, not theoretical as had been the Chinese Civil Service examinations, instituted 3000 years earlier. Occasionally on the American tests there were questions of general information, although many complained that this type of question was unfair because it was not specific to the qualifications of the job. The important contribution of these examinations was that they were standardized, particularly in their administration and scoring, so that charges of bias could not readily be brought.[5] Parallel to the development of job aptitude testing in the Civil Service came the growth of psychological testing in the latter part of the nineteenth century, dominated by Galton

---

3. DuBois (*A History of Psychological Testing,* pp. 3-4) also cites the Chinese Civil Service Examinations. See also Michael S. Schudson, "Organizing the 'Meritocracy': A History of the College Entrance Examination Boards," *Harvard Educational Review* 42 (February 1972): 34-69.

4. Schudson, "Organizing the 'Meritocracy.'" See also Arthur N. Applebee, *Tradition and Reform in the Teaching of English: A History* (Urbana, Ill.: National Council of Teachers of English, 1974), especially pp. 29-32.

5. DuBois, *A History of Psychological Testing,* pp. 6-8.

and Pearson in England, Cattell and Thorndike in the United States, and Binet in France. These pioneers developed varieties of means of measuring the "intelligence" and other psychological attributes of both individuals and groups. As Cattell said, "Psychology cannot attain the certainty and exactness of the physical sciences, unless it rests on a foundation of experiment and measurement." [6] The analogue of the mental to the physical sciences has been with us since the last century. What it has meant for psychology, and for testing in general, has been an emphasis on the quantitatively measurable. The importance of numbers and scales for psychologists fitted the demands of those institutions that wanted to use tests and other measuring devices in order to select students on a scientific basis for advanced work. Such methods also fitted the demands of an ever-growing society, one with a larger and larger population that sought access to higher education, and despite a larger and larger number of institutions able to accommodate those students, demand still exceeded supply. Institutions sought more and more accurate means of screening individuals, as well as more and more accurate means of identifying those few individuals whose background might have militated against their being given a chance at attending an elitist college or university.[7]

THE DEVELOPMENT OF EFFICIENT TESTING PROCEDURES

The great breakthrough in large-group testing occurred during World War I with the development of the Army Alpha Test, which included some measures of verbal aptitude (ability to follow oral directions, ability to discern synonyms and antonyms, ability to unscramble sentences, and ability to perceive analogies). The success of the test in selecting and guiding personnel led to an increased sureness among psychologists that they could measure various attributes of the human personality, including intelligence.[8]

The influence of "scientific method" on psychology was paral-

---

6. Quoted by DuBois, *A History of Psychological Testing*, p. 16.

7. For a fuller discussion of the screening function of tests, see Ralph W. Tyler, "Introduction: A Perspective on the Issues," in *Crucial Issues in Testing*, ed. Ralph W. Tyler and Richard M. Wolf (Berkeley, Calif.: McCutchan Publishing Corporation, 1974), especially pp. 4-5.

8. DuBois, *A History of Psychological Testing*, pp. 65ff.

leled by the influence of "technological" thinking upon education. The desire to extend the new model of the factory and the assembly line to other forms of human endeavor grew with the success of the technological-industrial world. People concerned with education began to join the "cult of efficiency" at or shortly after the beginning of the century. They became concerned with monitoring the production of the schools—usually in terms of student learning or achievement. Joseph Rice was one of the pioneers in this field, but it was Thorndike who contributed the most to achievement testing as a means of monitoring the success of the schools. The first tests were in such subjects as spelling and arithmetic, but Thorndike ventured so far as to develop scales for judging handwriting and reading words and sentences. By 1920, there were six standardized achievement tests in English, for grades nine through twelve, of which three were in composition and one in grammar, the other two being in reading and spelling. By the end of that decade there had been copyrighted for those grades a total of ten tests in composition, twenty-seven in grammar, thirteen in literature, eighteen in reading and vocabulary, six in spelling, and two in speech.[9]

One might say that a third sociointellectual force behind the testing movement, besides the rise of scientism and the cry for efficiency in the schools, contributed to the rise in testing, particularly achievement testing: the very democracy of the nation led to a need for a "democratic way to 'sort out' individuals, to identify those who had the ability needed to succeed in professional and managerial positions, to identify the interests and specific aptitudes of the remainder and thus orient them to the 'most appropriate' vocations." [10] One can argue that this very practice was finally undemocratic in that the tests, particularly the early intelligence tests, had built-in sociocultural biases, so that they tended to keep in the middle classes those who were born to or could easily acquire the middle-class standards of language and speech.[11]

9. Ibid., pp. 69-75.

10. James L. Wardrop, *Standardized Testing in the Schools: Uses and Roles* (Monterey, Calif.: Brooks/Cole Publishing Co., 1976), p. 12.

11. A particularly clear exposition of the rise of bias is to be found in Clarence J. Karier, "Testing for Order and Control in the Corporate Liberal State," *Educational Theory* 22 (Spring 1972): 154-80.

From the Army Alpha Test came the impetus to use tests that could be scored by clerks or, later, by machines, rather than by teachers or expert panels as in the original College Board Examinations. The essay achievement tests of the College Entrance Examination Board persisted through the 1930s, but by the end of World War II, the achievement tests had become predominantly "objective." In English there remained a desire on the part of the examiners to have the students actually write an essay which would then be graded, even though various studies showed that multiple-choice questions dealing with matters of language and usage predicted writing scores accurately.[12] This research lent credence to the economics of testing. It is cheaper to administer a multiple-choice examination that can be scored by machine than it is to hire skilled teachers as readers, particularly when the numbers one is testing run into the tens of thousands.

If the practices of teachers examining their students first influenced large-scale examinations, the practices of the mass psychological test came to exert a counter influence on the teacher. Through the 1940s and into the 1960s there appeared many textbook series in language, composition, and literature that had their end-of-unit tests cast in the multiple-choice form. A number of companies sold unit tests on various aspects of English, most of them "objective" in format. Methods books and other guides were available to help teachers make up their own multiple-choice pretests and posttests. Those tests dealt with recall of facts, naturally enough, but testmakers and teachers alike strove to make up easily scorable "objective" [13] questions dealing with complex points of rhetoric, with sensitivity to rhythm and tone in poetry, with taste in literature, and with nuances of interpreting complex texts.[14]

12. Fred I. Godschalk, Frances Swineford, and William E. Coffman, *The Measurement of Writing Ability* (New York: College Entrance Examination Board, 1966). The authors argued, nonetheless, for inclusion of a writing segment to complement the objective test.

13. Many historians and critics of testing have remarked on the misnomer, *objective*. The objective nature of the test is that a machine or a clerk can be programmed to see if the test taker has chosen the answer that the testmaker selected as correct. The testmaker's judgment, of course, is subjective.

14. Cf. Alan C. Purves, "Evaluation of Learning in Literature," in *Handbook of Formative and Summative Evaluation of Student Learning*, ed. B. S. Bloom,

THE ATTACK ON TESTS

The various kinds of achievement tests that were developed in the preceding decades came under attack in the 1960s, and their proliferation was checked somewhat. The main reasons for the attack were both substantive and social, and one has a hard time distinguishing the intellectual from the social critiques. One of the major critics was Banesh Hoffmann, whose *Tyranny of Testing* appeared in 1962.[15] The thrust of his critique was that multiple-choice tests, particularly those developed for the College Entrance Examination Board, were unfair to the able student because the logic of many of the questions was such that the mediocre response was correct, rather than the brilliant one. Hoffmann's criticism of the tests parallels the criticism of the schools by people like Hyman Rickover. In the post-Sputnik clamor, the schools seemed not to be allowing for genius. Later, in the 1960s, the criticism leveled at standardized tests in English was almost antithetical to that of Hoffmann. The tests were discriminatory against the seemingly low-achieving student, particularly the student who came from a social milieu different from that of the testmaker. The tests in composition and usage held as a criterion standard written or "frozen" style; the tests in literature assumed a limited reading list of "classics" or assumed only one form of analytic criticism; the tests in reading used only certain kinds of "lily white" prose.

The outcry against existing tests was heeded on some occasions, not heeded on others. Many testmakers modified their tests somewhat; others made few changes, if any. And many institutions, particularly institutions of higher education, came to discount the importance of test results for admissions purposes, and used such other criteria as race, income, or place of residence. These criteria tended to prevent one usual consequence of basing admissions on test scores alone, which was the homogeneous nature of those who succeeded on the tests. Successful students tended to come from high socioeconomic strata, so that these strata came to perpetuate themselves.

J. T. Hastings, and George Madaus (New York: McGraw-Hill Book Co., 1971), pp. 697-767.

15. Banesh Hoffmann, *The Tyranny of Testing* (New York: Crowell Collier Press, 1962).

That characteristic of test-taking populations came to public attention most strikingly with the publication of the Coleman Report in 1966.[16] From this and subsequent studies that looked at the relationship of achievement on various tests, particularly of reading and other verbal skills, to a number of home and school variables, the most effective predictor of achievement proved to be the home background of the child. On tests of the more basic skills of reading and vocabulary, such factors as parental occupation, education, and income strongly influenced the child's performance; on tests of slightly more complex skills of literary analysis, factors like the number of books and magazines in the home, access to reading, and the sex of the student were more important than purely socioeconomic factors.

CHANGES IN ATTITUDES TOWARD TESTING

One result of such findings, at both the lower secondary and upper secondary level, was dissatisfaction with the measures and the consequent effort to seek new indices of achievement. Teachers and others in the educational enterprise were convinced that the tests that had been used left much to be desired. A number of major changes in testing took shape during the decade of the 1960s, changes that at times seemed mutually contradictory. The first change resulted from the desire of many in education to follow the industrial pattern of schooling even more precisely than they had before. Taking their cue from the production plans instituted by Robert McNamara, first for the Ford Motor Company and then for the Pentagon, certain educational planners sought to adapt those methods to the schools and instruction.[17] A part of their method of "account-

16. James S. Coleman et al., *Equality of Educational Opportunity* (Washington, D.C.: U.S. Government Printing Office, 1966); Frederick Mosteller and Daniel P. Moynihan, *On Equality of Educational Opportunity* (New York: Random House, 1972); Robert Thorndike, *Reading Comprehension Education in Sixteen Countries*, International Studies in Evaluation III (New York: John Wiley & Sons, 1973); Alan C. Purves, *Literature Education in Ten Countries: An Empirical Study*, International Studies in Evaluation II (New York: John Wiley & Sons, 1973).

17. For a particularly thorough history of the growth of Planning-Programming-Budgeting Systems (PPBS) and accountability systems, see Leo Ruth, "Dangers of Systemthink in Education," in *Accountability and the Teaching of English*, ed. Henry B. Maloney (Urbana, Ill.: National Council of Teachers of English, 1972), pp. 63-102.

ability," or "Planning-Programming-Budgeting Systems," or simply the "systems" approach, was the division of the goals of education into single countable bits of student learning. Goals were to be couched in terms of the things that students were to do with the subject matter of English. These things were to be objectively verifiable things and they were labeled "behavioral objectives." [18] The behavioral objective movement encountered a great deal of opposition among English teachers, many of whom saw the insistence on the countable and the observable as a threat to what they held most important in English: development of appreciation, a sense of style, and creativity. For others, however, the movement provided an opportunity to consider more precisely the goals of instruction and to seek new ways to measure growth toward those goals.[19]

A complementary movement was that established under the auspices of the National Assessment of Educational Progress. This program, instituted during the tenure of Francis Keppel as Commissioner of Education and under the early leadership of Ralph W. Tyler, was designed to provide an index of the educational level of the citizenry. Different from the work of Joseph Rice, the National Assessment sought to present its results in terms intelligible to the layman and sought to do so not with scores or percentile ranks but with percentages of people performing satisfactorily on clearly understood tasks (for example, being able to write down a telephone message so that the message could be understood, knowing certain major figures of Greek mythology, being able to read traffic signs). These percentages would be analyzed to show differences among regions, sexes, ethnic groups, and socioeconomic levels for those performing the tasks. Any one person performed only a few tasks in a number of areas, so that one could say little about any individual, but one could talk with greater certainty about groups, which in aggregate performed an entire battery of tasks. The National Assessment program formed an important turning point in educational

18. The most popular apologist for behavioral objectives was and remains Robert F. Mager, *Preparing Objectives for Programmed Instruction* (San Francisco, Calif.: Fearon Publishers, 1962).

19. See the discussions in *On Writing Behavioral Objectives for English*, ed. John Maxwell and Anthony Tovatt (Champaign, Ill.: National Council of Teachers of English, 1970); Maloney, *Accountability and the Teaching of English*; and Henry B. Maloney, ed., *Goal Making for English Teachers* (Urbana, Ill.: National Council of Teachers of English, 1973).

evaluation, because it focused its attention on attainment of individual tasks rather than on total scores, and because it measured both cognitive achievement (which had been often tested) and attitudes, feelings, and interests of people with respect to the subject matter of education and to the instruction in that subject matter. As a result, testmakers were forced to rethink measurement and to come up with new kinds of tasks. Unfortunately, exigencies of time and money prevented the National Assessment from undertaking some of the contemplated experiments in measurement, but the effect of assessment on the thinking of testmakers has been strong.

AFFECTIVE EDUCATION

The fact that the National Assessment focused some attention on emotions, attitudes, and interests coincided with another phenomenon that impinged upon evaluation in English: the "discovery" of affective education. Although earlier educational crosscurrents during the century had stressed the feelings of the children, that emphasis was usually subsumed under the broader goals of citizenship education. In the 1960s, however, whether as a result of the dominance of the schools of psychology of Abraham Maslow and Carl Rogers, whether out of repudiation of the intellectualization of the schools in the post-Sputnik years, or whether as a result of the increased disaffection of secondary school students—first the ghetto students, then the larger number of those concerned by the Vietnam war and the domestic troubles of the decade—teachers, educationists, and lay critics of the schools drew together in a cry against the traditional school curriculum. In English, this movement was given force by the 1966 Anglo-American Seminar on the Teaching of English—otherwise known as the Dartmouth Conference. There, American experts in English learned about the work of David Holbrook, James Britton, and other British teachers of English, people who were less concerned with students learning about the subject than they were with children developing their linguistic power to articulate their experience with the world around them. The concern of the British was with what Britton came to call the expressive uses of language, rather than with the transactional uses.[20]

20. For a full discussion of the general critique of the intellectualized curriculum, see Charles Silberman, *Crisis in the Classroom: The Remaking of American Education* (New York: Random House, 1970); Gerald Weinstein

One major outcome of the concern with the feelings of the student, with the student's response to literature, with the student's expressive uses of language, was, necessarily, a repudiation of most of the standard measures of evaluation. To measure what people knew or to measure their approximation to a standard of usage or rhetoric or criticism became less important than to measure such matters as the sincerity of the student, the nature of the student's responses and interests, and the degree of the student's participation in and satisfaction with school and various language activities. Many of the strongest adherents of the affective or "generative" school of education repudiated any form of evaluation whatsoever.[21] What they were dealing with was virtually unmeasurable, and certainly unmeasurable by any of the normal means of tests, teacher-made or standardized. This argument gained some support from the professional curriculum evaluators who expressed dissatisfaction with the use of traditional testing methods to evaluate curricular programs.[22] As one critic has argued:

Most of today's plans for the evaluation of educational programs are preordinate. They rely on prespecification. . . . There is an important alternative to preordinate evaluation: responsive evaluation. . . . Responsive evaluation is what people do naturally in evaluating things. They observe and react. They examine the thing, the implications of having it, its worth.[23]

An "open" curriculum, one in which the instructional end is not

and Mario D. Fantini, *Toward Humanistic Education: A Curriculum of Affect* (New York: Praeger Publishers, 1970). The two reports of the Dartmouth Conference are Herbert J. Muller, *The Uses of English* (New York: Holt, Rinehart & Winston, 1967); and John Dixon, *Growth through English* (Reading, England: National Association for the Teaching of English, 1967). See also James M. Britton, *Language and Learning* (London: Allen Lane, Penguin, 1970), and chapter 1 of this yearbook.

21. The term "generative" is defined in Alan C. Purves, "Deep Structure in the Curriculum," *Curriculum Theory Network*, in press.

22. See, *inter alia*, Ralph W. Tyler, Robert M. Gagné, and Michael Scriven, *Perspectives of Curriculum Evaluation* (Chicago: Rand McNally & Co., 1967); Alan C. Purves, "Measure What Men Are Doing, Plan for What Man Might Become," in Maxwell and Tovatt, *On Writing Behavioral Objectives for English*, pp. 87-96.

23. Robert M. Stake, "Responsive Evaluation," mimeographed (University of Illinois Center for Instructional Research and Curriculum Evaluation, February 6, 1974).

fully determined—such as a curriculum in the arts or at the upper reaches of the sciences and social sciences—must base its evaluation on the response of the evaluator to what is there, what has been created or discovered. The evaluator may have a plan of observation and may have detailed checklists, but often must make any final evaluation intuitively and holistically.

THE REACTION TO AFFECTIVE EDUCATION

Lest one should think that the "open" curriculum is presently dominant in the teaching of English, recent events have proved otherwise. The realization by minority groups that studies directed at improving their self-image were not simultaneously job-producing; the fear of the middle-class majority that their children might be shut out of further education by the opening of higher education to increasing numbers of minority groups, and the general malaise brought about by the economic downturn have combined to give strength to the group that has been opposed to open education. This group, once silent, is now quite vocal, and since the group in many cases controls the purse strings of the schools, the "back to basics" movement has gained momentum. Groups have now begun to insist on more standardized testing and more teaching of the material that standardized tests measure. One cannot say that the aims of these groups are necessarily wrong,[24] although one may deplore their tactics and their vision of what the standardized tests can do and do do.[25] The demands for basic skills or an educational floor are certainly legitimate demands for any society to place on its educational institutions. There is a question, however, as to what the basic skills might be and whether the tests we have are the appropriate tools for determining that they have been attained.

The Goals of Education for the Future

In the mid-1970s, then, those concerned with the evaluation of student performance and program effectiveness in English are faced with demands placed upon the curriculum which appear to be in

24. See, *inter alia*, Alan C. Purves, "Testing and the Recession," *English Journal* 64 (March 1975): 6-7.

25. See Tyler and Wolf, *Crucial Issues in Testing*, for accounts of the effects of standardized tests on students and the curriculum.

harsh contrast with each other. On the one hand, there is the desire to see English as a skill: reading with understanding and acumen, using language "correctly" in both speech and writing, and producing rhetorically effective communications in various media. On the other hand, there is the desire to see English as one of the arts, if not one of the humanities, to see it as the outlet for the expressive and creative in people. The most significant synthesis of these seeming polarities is to be found in the report of the International Commission on the Development of Education to UNESCO, known as the Faure Report. A first finding is that education must be available to greater and greater numbers of people in order to provide them with the tools to function in a technological society. This goal is described as scientific humanism.

Command of scientific thought and language has become as indispensable to the average man as command of other means of thought and expression. *This must be understood less as an accumulation of knowledge than as a basic grasp of scientific method.*[26]

The second goal is the encouragement of creativity:

Education has the dual power to cultivate and stifle creativity. Recognition of its complex tasks in this domain is one of the most fruitful intellectual achievements of modern psychopedagogical research. These tasks may be described as preserving each individual's originality and creative ingenuity without giving up the need to place him in real life; transmitting culture without overwhelming him with ready-made models; encouraging him to make use of his gifts, aptitudes and personal forms of expression without cultivating his egotism; paying keen attention to each person's specific traits without overlooking the fact that creation is also a collective activity.[27]

The third goal is that related to preparing people for life in society, including

"active participation in the functioning of social structures, and, where necessary, through a personal commitment in the struggle to reform them;" education in economics; and education in world affairs with

26. Edgar Faure et al., *Learning to Be: The World of Education Today and Tomorrow* (Paris: UNESCO, 1972), p. 147, italics Faure's.

27. Ibid., p. 150, italics Faure's.

particular emphasis on peace education and education to respect national
and cultural differences.[28]

The Faure Report proposes several broad steps for achieving
these goals. Among them are the creation of a "learning society" in
which lifelong education is a keystone; the subsuming of formal
schooling in a larger pattern of educational institutions such as social
service agencies and the mass media; the provision of increased
options both between and within institutions; and the provision of
basic education to all through a multiplicity of means.[29]

Although it seems a grand and idealistic plan, the Faure Report
does effect a reconciliation between the demands for a basic education, which allows people to function fully in their society by
providing them with the requisite skills, and the demands for an
education that allows them the freedom of individual creativity.

SCIENTIFIC HUMANISM

When one translates those goals so that they can apply to the
teaching of English (or any native tongue, for that matter), one
can see the breadth of vision that they embody. Scientific humanism
would, I think, translate itself certainly into the goal of literacy,
but beyond that into the development of language as a tool for
survival. This would include, first, the learning of the major dialect
—that dialect which is used for communication through the major
technological media. Second, it would involve practice in the
rhetorics of those media (for example, the rhetorics of television
and radio, as well as of writing) so that one could see the ways by
which the media modify the communicative or the expressive act.
Third, because of the acceleration of change and the explosion of
knowledge, the learning should deal with ways by which people
can cope with change through language. In great measure this is
done through the acquisition of classificatory heuristics so that data
can be assimilated and ordered. One of these heuristic devices is
contained in metalanguage—language about language that enables
people to deal with the language overload and with the manipulatory

28. Ibid., pp. 151-53, italics Faure's.

29. Ibid., pp. 169-93.

uses of language—for with metalanguage people can control language. The fourth goal would be the fostering of humanistic inquiry into the relationship between society, technology, and the individual as it is portrayed in literature.

CREATIVITY

Creativity in language involves the characteristics of intelligence, independence, wit, individuality, tolerance for ambiguity, and openness of mind[30] as these characteristics would manifest themselves in the speech and writing of the individual. Language would be used to help the student find identity, for language is one of the vehicles by which people create their identity—as speakers or as writers. Allied with this would be the encouragement of the imagination, both in expressing oneself and in sharing the expressions of others, particularly as they embody themselves in the various literary forms and media of presentation.

THE SOCIAL GOAL

The social goal of education manifests itself in mother tongue instruction primarily as that instruction helps the individual see the interrelation of language and society. Language is one of the bonds of society; it helps to create cultures and subcultures, and it binds people within a common perspective. Through dialect, language discriminates between subcultures; and instruction should show that dialects are valid language systems. Another aspect of the social goal would be the exploration of the ways in which society uses language—sometimes for good, sometimes for ill—to bind individuals to it.[31] The individual should learn about the ways by which language is used as a societal force.

Four major thrusts of the curriculum emerge from this consideration:

1. The development of people's control over language as a com-

30. These defining terms are derived from Jacob W. Getzels and Philip W. Jackson, *Creativity and Intelligence: Explorations with Gifted Students* (New York: John Wiley & Sons, 1962).

31. For a recent discussion of language and society, see Hugh Rank, ed., *Language and Public Policy* (Urbana, Ill.: National Council of Teachers of English, 1974).

municative device that joins them to others both present and past, and the simultaneous development of people's control over language as a means of asserting their expressiveness and imagination.

2. The development of people's ability to use language to order and to classify the barrage of information that surrounds them.

3. The development of a metalanguage sufficient to enable people to understand how language is used to control them so that they can rise above that control.

4. The development of speculative power so that people can consider the various artistic expressions of the situation of the individual in a technological society.

These thrusts, I would maintain, are to be thought of as survival skills in the most fundamental sense; with these skills the possibility of a democratic and learning society might be obtained.

A Perspective on Evaluation

Given these broad goals, what modes of evaluation might follow? To deal with that question, one must first deal with the twin problems of modes of measurement and criteria. Frequently, although the terms *measurement, testing,* and *evaluation* are used interchangeably, distinctions among them are useful in order to deal with these problems. *Measurement* properly refers to any attempt to describe human behavior (usually in mathematical rather than verbal terms), and includes the ways by which the behavior is elicited and the terms in which it is reported. In education, *testing* usually refers to a formal means of getting people to perform so that their behavior can be measured. The results of testing may be reported in mathematical or verbal terms. *Evaluation* is the assignment of worth to human behavior, and most especially in latter-day educational circles to a group's effort to educate people, which is to say a program.[32] Individuals may be evaluated too, but the term most frequently used to describe that form of evaluation is *grading.*

32. For a discussion of the paradoxes of evaluation, particularly that of the inconsistency between the evaluator's desire to judge and the evaluatee's fear of judgment, see Gene V Glass, "A Paradox about Excellence of Schools and the People in Them," *Educational Researcher* 4 (March 1975): 9-12.

Measurement and evaluation thus become the central terms for the remainder of this essay, although tests and grades will receive side glances.

In general, there are three modes and three references of measurement that would be applicable to English, as shown in figure 1.

Modes of Measurement	References of Measurement	Criterial	Relational	Descriptive
Prespecified Response	Explicit	Multiple-choice achievement test on a specific unit used to determine mastery	Multiple-choice general achievement test used to sort students	Interest inventory with scaled response used to portray a group's reading habits
	Implicit	Open-ended achievement test with teacher's key used to determine mastery	Open-ended achievement test with teacher's key used to sort students	Interest measure asking for book titles which then will be classified to portray a group's reading habits
Formal Performance	Structured	An essay assignment with topic carefully controlled and graded for mastery	A recitation of memorized passages to determine ranks of speakers	An essay assigned on a specific topic and scored for t-unit length
	Unstructured	An essay assignment with open topic graded for mastery	An informal debate with prizes given in order of merit	An open essay on a literary work and analyzed for patterns of response
Naturalistic Observation	Preselected	Examination of library check-outs to determine who has done the assigned task	Taped interviews to determine relative proficiency in "standard" dialect	Examination of selected discussions to determine attitudes of students toward subject
	Unselected	Observation of small-group discussion to determine which students are performing the task satisfactorily	Taped recordings of lunchroom conversation to determine relative proficiency in "standard" dialect	Observation in classroom to determine interaction patterns of students

Fig. 1. Modes and references of measurement.

Note: The cells of the grid contain illustrative examples which are not to be seen as definitive. Obviously, the results of one test based on a single mode of measurement (for example, a multiple-choice achievement test) could be reported under any one of the three modes of reference, depending on purpose and audience.

By modes is meant that means by which the measurement is obtained. By references is meant the ways in which the results of measurement are reported. One of the three major modes of measurement, the prespecified measure, often called the objective measure, is a measure in which the response is presented explicitly, as in a multiple-choice or scaled response measure, or implicitly, as in a short answer measure with an expected correct, preferred, or otherwise precoded response. Examples of the explicit response would be multiple-choice tests in language or literature, attitude or interest inventories, Likert scales, or a semantic differential test. Examples of the implicit response measure would be the in-class quiz, the sentence completion task, or the precoded opinion poll.

The second mode of measurement, the formal performance, differs from the first primarily in that the response is not prespecified although criteria for judging or reporting that response might exist in the head of the measurer. The formal performance would include the essay, poem, film, play, or other piece of writing that an individual might produce, as well as the oral, visual, or filmic recreation of another work. It might also include the testimonial and the interview. The stimulus or the conditions for the performance can be highly structured or they can be completely unstructured. A structured stimulus for an essay might specify the general content of the divisions of that essay (for example, "You will discuss (a) the causes, (b) the first and subsequent appearances, and (c) the results of phenomenon X.") An unstructured stimulus would be "Write about phenomenon X." As with the prespecified measure, there is a continuum from the explicit to the vaguely implicit response, so with the formal measure, the degree of structure preestablished for the response can vary across a wide range. No matter where on the continuum, however, the individual being measured has a broad range of choices as to what to do or to include. The judgment of the nature or the quality of the responses is, by and large, post hoc, although the marker may have some preconception of what to expect or prize.

The third mode of measurement, naturalistic observation, is the attempt to see what people do, not necessarily when they are on their best behavior or when the situation is contrived to elicit their performance. Such observation can take place casually, as when a teacher makes a judgment about students' interest in what they are doing or grades them on their degree of participation in a group activity. It can be more formal in that the observer selects certain key incidents or behaviors and makes note of them. For example, one might check the number of books students take out of the library, evaluate a student's understanding of a book by eavesdropping on a group discussion, or observe the ways in which students undertake a writing assignment to see what strategies of composition they employ.

THE REFERENCES OF MEASUREMENT

The columns of figure 1 differentiate the references of measurement, the ways in which the results of the measure are considered. Criterial reference includes both criterion-referenced and domain-referenced measurement. In either case, there exists some ideal or standard of performance against which each student is measured. A student is described in terms of the distance he has progressed toward that ideal. A criterion-referenced measure specifies the ideal in detailed or minute terms, such as being able to recognize metaphors in poetry; a domain-referenced measure paints a broader picture, such as being able to recognize a variety of figurative language in poetry.[33] In practice, many teachers measure their students in a criterial fashion, considering the performance in relation to some expected answer or in relation to what they consider "good student work" at that level, or a "good answer." The answers provided in the volume *End-of-Year Examinations in English* provide explicit criterial reference for teachers or examiners,[34] as does the system of diagnosis, objectives, treatment, and evaluation used by teachers in elementary language arts programs. In grading papers or examinations, teachers often discover they have criteria, although they might not have thought they did at the outset of a marking session. The research by Diederich in the marking of compositions shows the implicit criteria held by a variety of markers.[35] Diederich has gone on to produce a way of forming explicit criteria that would strike a balance among the implicit predilections of individual graders. He

33. For a fuller discussion of the differences between criterion-referenced and domain-referenced measurement, see *Educational Technology* 14, no. 6 (June 1974): *passim*.

34. Commission on English, *End-of-Year Examinations in English for College-Bound Students, Grades 9-12* (New York: College Entrance Examination Board, 1963).

35. Paul B. Diederich, *Measuring Growth in English* (Urbana, Ill.: National Council of Teachers of English, 1974), pp. 53-58.

does so by having each grader mark a paper on all the major criteria: ideas, organization, wording, style, and mechanics. A further refinement of Diederich's plan, one that gives any group of teachers a means of forming explicit criteria that reflect their particular instructional aims, is set forth by Cohen.[36] While the factors selected for rating the composition in Diederich's formula are scaled, they are dichotomous in Cohen's formula and appear as "yes-no" questions (for example, "Is there an obvious organization?" rather than "Organization: 1, 2, 3, 4, 5"). The dichotomous criteria, Cohen argues, increase the chances for agreement among the readers and are also clearer to students.

Relational referencing is based not on some platonic criterion but on the relation of one student score to some other score or set of scores. In some cases, the reference point is the student's previous score on the same or a similar measure. In many more cases, it is the average score of a larger group of students—perhaps those taking the measure at the same time or perhaps all those similar to the student in terms of some characteristic such as age, sex, grade, or race. This latter kind of referencing, norm-referencing, is the basis of score reporting for most standardized intelligence and achievement tests.[37] Relational referencing finds a place within the classroom in English, where the teacher is looking for a change—if not growth. Using pretests and posttests in language, composition, and literature has become a fairly common practice, and although some few teachers simply average the two tests, most look to the change from the first to the second in order to plot progress. In courses that require frequent compositions, teachers tend to weight the later papers more heavily than the earlier ones, arguing that if all counted equally, they would not be accounting for the beneficial effects of instruction.

36. Arthur Cohen, "Assessing College Students' Ability to Write Compositions," *Research in the Teaching of English* 7 (Winter 1973): 356-71.

37. In recent years norms have come to be confused with criteria, so that people see a sixth-grade norm as an ideal rather than as a description of an average. Groups such as the American Psychological Association and the National Council of Teachers of English have warned against the abuses of norm referencing. For purposes of research, particularly for correlational and regression studies, group means and standard deviations are useful if not necessary; they are subject to great misuse for other kinds of educational decision making.

Many teachers often make either implicit or explicit comparisons among students; the comments of graders and teachers would indicate that they read a number of papers quickly in order to get a sense of the class as a whole, and then begin marking in relation to that general sense. Such a practice is approximated in large-scale readings such as those for the Advanced Placement Examinations in English of the College Entrance Examination Board, where graders are asked to think of papers in relation to papers that are judged as typically good, typically average, and typically poor.

The third form of reference is descriptive, seeking less to evaluate the individual in relation to an ideal or a group (although such relationships may be inferred) than to characterize the individual (or the group) in either a schematic or a nonschematic fashion. Schematic characterizations are usually derived from some a priori formulation of characterizations, such as those employed to classify types of books in reading interest studies (comedy, adventure, romance, etc.) or those used to classify types of sentences or types of responses to literature.[38] Schematic classifications of composition generally follow the designations of classical or neoclassical rhetoricians (such as inductive or deductive order). Some different classifications are beginning to emerge that might be more fruitful to the pedagogy of composition than are the classical descriptors, which are pertinent primarily to that species of composition that is rooted in deductive reasoning as opposed to much of the alogical and analogical writing that is taught in the schools.[39]

Descriptive referenced measurement of language, composition,

38. Such formulations may be exemplified by the classifications of grammarians or students of language such as Kellogg W. Hunt, *Grammatical Structures Written at Three Grade Levels* (Champaign, Ill.: National Council of Teachers of English, 1965). In literature such classification schemes would include those of James R. Squire, *The Responses of Adolescents While Reading Four Short Stories* (Champaign, Ill.: National Council of Teachers of English, 1964); or Alan C. Purves and Victoria Rippere, *Elements of Writing about a Literary Work: A Study of Response to Literature* (Champaign, Ill.: National Council of Teachers of English, 1968).

39. Some examples would include Francis W. Christensen, "A Generative Rhetoric of the Sentence," *College Composition and Communication* 14 (October 1963): 155-61; idem, "A General Use: Rhetoric of the Paragraph," *College Composition and Communication* 16 (October 1965): 144-56; Helmer R. Myklebust, *Development and Disorders of Written Language*, 2 vols. (New York: Grune & Stratton, 1965, 1971); Britton, *Language and Learning*.

and literary response is, of course, a much less common form of
such measurement than are measures that have been used to survey
such diverse phenomena as attitudes toward dialects, values, feelings
about censorship, reading habits, television viewing habits, interests
in leisure activities, and attitudes toward school and English as a
school subject. Measures of the "affective domain," as these phenomena are often classified, tend to be referenced descriptively
perhaps because teachers shy away from setting criteria in the domain and perhaps because relational references, would establish a
"norm" that is not necessarily desirable. More often than not, these
measures are not schematic, as are the analyses of language, composition, or literary response; they portray attitudes toward or interests
in discrete phenomena, and are reported either in terms such as "X
likes to read rather than play cards" or "Y percent of the population reads two books per week."

THE CURRENT STATUS OF TESTS IN THE LIGHT
OF THE POSSIBILITIES

If one were to apply the grid shown in figure 1 to the kinds of
measures most commonly used in schooling, one would find that
the formal performance and the prespecified response are the most
frequent modes and that criterial and relational references occur
most often. The teacher probably employs the formal performance
more than the prespecified response and probably refers either to
a tacit criterion or to comparisons among individuals. Making criteria explicit is not common, particularly in the judging of essays.
The standardized tests frequently used by school administrators
are, of course, relational in their reference, usually pitting the individual student, class, or school against some norm. Occasionally
the results of such tests are misused to describe relationships across
time—as in the reporting of "growth scores" by grade level—although one should bear in mind that the reference group at each
grade level changes so that the relationship between one set of
norms and another is tenuous at best. The infrequent use of systematic naturalistic observation and the equally infrequent descriptive referencing of test results is a lack that has come to be deplored
by many. The need for descriptive referencing is apparent when
one considers the criterial measures that abound. Many of the tests

of language competence, of reading skills, or of literary acumen and taste posit as a criterion the judgment or skills of experts and measure the degree of distance a child is from the experts. Tests of reading comprehension, for instance, will assume that a child's experience is as great as an adult's, so that the child is expected to know background material that is only hinted at in the text. Tests of composition assume that a child of twelve sees fit to use the syntactic complexity common to an adult; and tests of literary taste assume that the criteria of the professional critic or editor are shared (or should be shared) by adolescents. Spurred in part by the research of Piaget in cognitive development, researchers in English have established that criteria may vary according to the age and culture of the child.[40] The research is far from complete; only rough sketches of the stages of competence and the stages of performance have emerged. Still less clear are the interrelationships among skills and between skills and attitudes and interests. The human use of language is highly complex, and too many educational decisions are based on a simplistic approach to that complexity. One may never fully chart the complexities—indeed one could not—but surely educational measurement and evaluation should not be as naive and as dogmatic as they have been, particularly given the challenge that the Faure Report sets forth.

Possibilities for Evaluation in the Learning Environment

If one were to juxtapose the modes and references of measurement with the broad goals of mother-tongue education prompted by the Faure Report (p. 243) one would see that few of the published measurement instruments would suffice.[41] The goals tend to treat the human uses of language in a holistic manner; the tests tend to fragment them. The goals speak to the tension between individual and society; the tests tend to deny the impor-

40. See, *inter alia*, Carol Chomsky, *The Acquisition of Syntax in Children from 5 to 10* (Cambridge, Mass.: M.I.T. Press, 1969); Hunt, *Grammatical Structures Written at Three Grade Levels*; Alan C. Purves, "Research in the Teaching of Literature," *Elementary English* 52 (April 1975): 463-66.

41. For a review of those instruments, see Alfred S. Grommon, ed., *Review of Selected Published Tests in English* (Urbana, Ill.: National Council of Teachers of English, 1976).

tance of the individual. The goals seem to call primarily for formal performance and naturalistic observation; the tests tend to be cast in the mode of the prespecified response. The goals set forth references that are frequently descriptive and critical; the tests tend to be relational and most frequently norm-referenced. One must call for new kinds of measures that would be consonant with goals of education in English as a mother tongue in the learning society.

In the first place, these goals demand new criteria of performance and growth. Even though some of the existing criteria of literacy, of communicative competence, and of understanding of language might exist, they need to be reviewed. To undertake such a review, one must begin at the descriptive naturalistic level. What is it that people do in their daily lives that indicates they have communicative competence, that they can classify phenomena and thus demonstrate control over the information that bombards them? What is it they do that shows their grasp of the relationship of the individual to technocracy? How are individual creativity and imaginative capacity manifested? What are the indices of metalinguistic competence? To each of these questions must be added the overriding question of what are the steps along the road to such kinds of competence, particularly what are the steps for children of different ages and of different subcultures.

From the answers to these questions can emerge not only criteria but curricula. To be sure, the areas under consideration are far from uncharted; psychological research as well as linguistic, rhetorical, and literary research have presented partial answers to many of these questions. What is central, however, is a renewed emphasis on descriptive measurement, much of which would be based upon naturalistic observation, as has earlier been argued. Beyond this thrust, there needs to be consideration of the modes of measurement and their references which will help attest to the progress toward these educational goals. If one were to take the goal of communicative competence and complementary individual expressiveness, one could see that the attainment of these goals must be seen as situational. A person writes or speaks to an audience in a context; the success of that action is determined by the audience, in that context. If, for example, a person seeks to persuade others to share—or at least accept —a point of view or an idea, the criterion of success lies in the behavior of those others. Similarly, if a reader takes up a piece of writing, he does so in a context and the comprehension of that piece of writing is contextually determined. Most traditional measures fail to account for context either in reading or in writing. It is no easy task to take context and audience into consideration in a test situation, although there have been some attempts; in literature, it has been possible to place a comprehension score next to an index of cognitive approach to the literary work, such a cognitive approach being one aspect of the context of reading.[42] The National Assessment of Educational Progress in Writing sought to establish a context for its writing tasks so that the writer had at least a sense of audience other than the testmaker.[43] If it can do nothing else, a test of reading comprehension can deal with a whole selection rather than with an excerpt, the kind that one would not read except on tests.

MEASURING COMMUNICATIVE COMPETENCE

Certainly some aspects of communicative competence can be measured in a prespecified manner, but experience and research tell us that many of the so-called measures of writing competence do not correlate with writing competence as judged by teachers or other audiences.[44] Particularly when one deals with the creative aspects of writing and speaking, the formal performance judged by a reader or group of readers is necessary. There have been some scales and checklists devised to deal with creative (and for that matter expository and descriptive) writing, and these could certainly be employed at those times when there is a need to have the performance measured according to some consistent set of rubrics.[45]

42. Purves, *Literature Education in Ten Countries.*

43. National Assessment of Educational Progress, *Writing: National Results*, Report No. 3 (Denver, Col.: Educational Commission of the States, 1970).

44. See Richard Braddock, Richard Lloyd-Jones, and Lowel Schoer, *Research in Written Composition* (Champaign, Ill.: National Council of Teachers of English, 1963); Grommon, *Review of Selected Published Tests in English.*

45. See Diederich, *Measuring Growth in English*; Cohen, "Assessing College Students' Ability"; Patricia Farrell Alpern, "Can Children Be Helped to Increase the Originality of Their Story Writing?" *Research in the Teaching of English* 7 (Winter 1973): 372-86; Abraham W. Stahl, "Structural Analysis of

MEASURING IMAGINATIVE READING

When it comes to the measurement of the imaginative aspects of reading, particularly the reading of literature, measurement also must look to context. Response to literature has recently come to be seen as a highly complex phenomenon, involving psychological, linguistic, social, and cultural variables.[46] Comprehension of literature must be seen in the light of these variables. A prespecified measure, no matter how good, cannot touch upon some of the most important differences among readers, and measures showing some of the affective aspects should accompany them. Recent research in Sweden has been aimed at developing such measures,[47] and the use of the semantic differential has clearly shown that readers who might have been deemed insensitive are, rather, readers who have not developed the language to express their sensitivity. Formal performances—essays, oral interpretations, filmic translations, and the like—also need to be judged according to complex criteria dealing both with their rhetoric and with the thrust of the performance, which is to say the critical approach used by the individual.

MEASURING LANGUAGE AND CLASSIFICATION

The measurement of the individual's ability to use language to classify phenomena and the measurement of the development of metalanguage have yet to be developed adequately. Again, one is faced with the criterion problem: both areas need work at the conceptual and empirical levels before one can begin to develop criteria or bases for relational referencing of the measures. People classify all the time, but the bases upon which they make their classifications are highly complex, to say the least. Certain measurement techniques,

---

Children's Compositions," *Research in the Teaching of English* 8 (Fall 1974): 184-205.

46. See, *inter alia*, Alan C. Purves and Richard Beach, *Literature and the Reader* (Urbana, Ill.: National Council of Teachers of English, 1972); Norman N. Holland, *Poems in Persons: An Introduction to the Psychoanalysis of Literature* (New York: W. W. Norton & Co., 1973); Purves, *Literature Education in Ten Countries.*

47. See, particularly, Gunnar Hansson, "Some Types of Research on Response to Literature," *Research in the Teaching of English* 7 (Fall 1973): 260-308.

such as latent partition analysis, and measures based on the work of George Kelly,[48] could help establish a ground for further measures of the heuristic capacity of students. Similarly, the criteria for the acquisition and use of metalanguage—language that would help the student to describe dispassionately the voice and point of view of the writer, the semantic and syntactic uses of language to manipulate audiences, and the ways by which discourse is structured—need to be more fully set forth. Much of this work has been done, but two problems need to be dealt with. The first is the delineation of those terms and concepts that are necessary to perform the tasks of understanding the way language is being used. We can imagine, for instance, that the knowledge of the power of repetition in language to affect a reader or a listener is important and necessary; we may question, however, whether it is important to differentiate meters or rhyme schemes, for instance, as subdivisions of repetition. Are there any terms in between the terms of classical prosody and the broad term *repetition* that are necessary and useful? That determination could be made empirically, one supposes; but more probably it could and should be made on an a priori basis.

The second problem is that of determining levels of comprehension of terms and concepts. This step is indeed important when one considers the problem of curriculum and instruction. Often people in education talk about learning difficulties. The term implies the intractability of students, those who cannot or will not master some aspect of content or some skill. Teachers often diagnose these learning difficulties, seeking to determine why the student fails and to provide some treatment that will help the student overcome failure. Let us postulate, however, that difficulty might lie in what is to be learned as well as in the learner. Certain aspects of certain subjects might prove generally intractable. There are, let us say, steep humps as well as easy slopes in the "normal" ascent of children towards the acquisition of a skill or a concept. Anyone who has observed the course of learning to play a musical instrument or some sport can name some of the steep spots, some of the sticking points. Some can even explain why these points should be the steep ones and not others. Let us call these steep places *difficult learnings*. A major task

48. George Kelly, *Psychology of Personal Constructs*, 2 vols. (New York: W. W. Norton & Co., 1956).

for research in measurement is to name these difficult learnings;[49] a second task is to determine why these might be difficult learnings (for example, whether they are so because of the developmental levels of the pupil, because of conceptual complications or procedural complications in the learnings themselves). To illustrate with an example from the area of literature teaching, specifically the teaching of the short story at the junior high school level, most students can read and enjoy and talk about a great number of short stories (excepting perhaps certain highly sophisticated stories). Reading (in the sense of getting the gist of), enjoying, talking about are not then difficult learnings. What might constitute difficult learning is the derivation of principles of character analysis (that is, concepts about characterization), of conflict analysis (that is, concepts about the dynamic relationships within a story), and of plot analysis (that is, concepts about the shifts of relationship through the course of the story), principles that might be applied to any story. These learnings might be difficult because the students have not a sufficient repertoire of stories from which to induce concepts and principles, because the students might not have reached the stage of "formal operations," [50] because the concepts themselves are not clear, or because of a combination of these factors along with others not as yet determined.

MEASURING THE SOCIAL USES OF LANGUAGE

The concept of difficult learning may also apply to the fourth goal, that of dealing with the situation of the individual in a technocratic society as it is portrayed in imaginative literature and the arts generally. This goal has a cognitive side, in particular the development of the ability to generalize across examples to effect some kind of synthetic understanding. To measure this ability requires, most likely, some sort of formal performance. Such formal performance depends in part upon the accumulation of examples, in part upon the development of concepts, in part upon the rhetorical

---

49. In some areas, theoretical work has been done (for example, Harold L. Herber, *Teaching Reading in Content Areas*, Englewood Cliffs, N. J.: Prentice-Hall, 1970), but there needs to be empirical validation of such theory.

50. Cf. Jean Piaget and Barbel Inhelder, *The Growth of Logical Thinking from Childhood to Adolescence* (New York: Basic Books, 1968).

skill, and in part upon the ability to generalize. Research in which I have been engaged recently would suggest that although instruction can play some part in aiding the development in such performance, another equally large part rests upon the maturity level of the individuals. Many younger students—up to the age of fifteen—have not yet acquired the capacity to generalize. Whether they could do so earlier is moot; we do not know entirely whether it is a matter of teaching or a matter of cognitive development that may be independent of teaching. That question, as well as others, must be settled by descriptive referencing and by educational research. The judgment of performances at even the higher levels must also have a descriptive as well as a criterial or relational reference. As in other aspects of mother-tongue learning, so in this most crucial one, there are options left to the individual. What philosophic or conceptual starting point will the individual adopt? What strategies for assimilating previous experience both in reading and in other experiences will the individual use? How will the individual manifest a value system? What value system will it be? In a democratic and diverse society, such as that envisaged by the Faure Report, these questions must remain open, and measurement must adopt a combination of the descriptive reference and one of the other references to determine how well the individual does whatever he chooses to do.

Nowhere is this more true than in the whole matter of values. Value teaching and learning is discussed at length elsewhere in this volume (see chapter 5), and the measurement of values must avoid the trap of adopting dogmatic criteria. That has been the problem of too many of the curricula and measures of value in the past.

The Challenge of the Future

The challenge to measurement in English as a mother tongue over the next years, therefore, is to seek to avoid many of the problems that have beset it in the past: particularly the overreliance on monolithic criteria of performance and on prespecified measures, and the lack of attention to the nature of the individual as the individual uses language in the course of life. To avoid these problems, those concerned with measurement should begin with an open mind, should be able to accommodate and account for diversity in the various uses of language and the order that exists within and above that diversity. With the development of adequate measures, prespecified, formal, and naturalistic, the development of references that are descriptive as well as criterial and relational, the proper evaluation of student growth in English in a learning society can begin. From that evaluation can emerge a more prudent and more useful evaluation of instruction in all phases of the learning society.

CHAPTER IX

Changing Patterns in Teacher Education

WILLIAM A. JENKINS*

Introduction

The past twenty years have seen repeated attempts to improve the preservice and in-service education of teachers of the English language arts. Emphases have changed with the nation's social and cultural concerns, but the education of the teacher, like his classroom teaching, remains almost as it has been.

To a considerable degree, the absence of dramatic change seems related to public attitudes toward teaching and schooling, which tend to insist that education be conservative, basically unchanged and unchanging, with a focus on basic and practical skills. Teaching is viewed by the public (and by a large segment of the teaching profession) as a skill to be developed, almost at the craft level of the carpenter, the electrician, and the plumber. Those who teach are asked to be accountable, economical, and productive. Society is not looking for radical and costly educational innovations, and teachers, mindful of restricted budgets and declining school enrollments, often are more concerned with job security than with change.

Teacher training, more often a reflector than a creator of public attitudes, has tended to adopt an essentially conservative stance. Reforming thrusts, such as those occasionally mounted by professional associations and by selected in-service or preservice teacher education programs, have had only a modest influence. Intervention by federal and state agencies and by teacher unions and teacher associations more often than not tend to reinforce conservative practices.

* Consultant readers for this chapter were Doris V. Gunderson, United States Office of Education, and Bernard J. Weiss, Superintendent, Englewood Public Schools, New Jersey.

WHAT AND HOW DOES THE ENGLISH TEACHER TEACH?

To a considerable degree, improvement in the education of teachers of English language arts has been limited by a lack of a widely accepted definition of English. The attempt in 1965 by the Commission on English of the College Entrance Examination Board to define the subject as language, literature, and composition ignored the important skills of reading and listening and overlooked such concerns as literature for children and adolescents, literature in translation, public speaking, and journalism. The problem of definition is difficult to resolve because the teacher of the English language arts has both a body of knowledge to offer—belles lettres and the nature and history of language—and a set of skills and processes to develop. With a widely accepted definition incorporating both content and skills yet to be developed, those who train teachers find neither direction nor rejection for any approach they wish to take.

Just as the preparation of teachers of the English language arts has been hampered by lack of agreement on what is to be taught, the education of these teachers has been adversely affected by lack of a clear understanding of what teaching is and how one teaches another to teach. Is teaching a craft that an individual learns—a set of techniques to be mastered through trial and error? Does teaching require understanding of a set of behavior patterns, methods, or approaches to imparting knowledge? By not being certain about what he is striving to attain, the teacher educator must necessarily be inefficient and perhaps ineffective.

For the prospective teacher of English, acquiring a body of knowledge is not enough. His objective is to learn how to apply the knowledge in performing certain tasks. Unfortunately, agreement has not been reached on what these tasks are, or even which are basic. Whether the attempt is to develop principles from random experience or to elicit principles from programmed procedures, consensus has not been achieved.

THE CLIMATE FOR CHANGE IN TEACHER EDUCATION

Most teachers of the English language arts, secondary and elementary alike, receive a part of their preparation from a department or school of education, and teacher education departments are generally inhospitable to reform. The education professor, like his colleagues in other disciplines, frequently feels that effecting change derails him as he progresses toward his personal goals. Efforts directed toward effecting change require him to work toward someone else's goals rather than his own. If he is committed to change, he must overcome inertia and resistance. Three problems with which he must wrestle limit his responsiveness: his clientele in the public schools; his liberal arts colleagues on campus; and the structure of the university itself.

The single-client relationship that departments of education have with the schools is probably unique. Sociology professors, for example, teach sociology to a variety of publics. There is no single, unified client group to which they have to answer. But for professors of education, there is such a group—the teachers in the local school system. Most teacher education institutions have not established mutually supportive relationships with local schools. Disagreement focuses on both the goals and means of professional training and particularly on the value of the theory that supports teaching methods and approaches. Moreover, once a teacher has graduated from the teacher education institution, he usually joins the liberal arts professor and the liberal arts graduate in criticizing rather than supporting the institution that educated him. Preparation that does not contribute directly to the teaching act is subject to the severest criticism.

The differences between the liberal arts professor and the professor of education create a sharp division between content and method. Generally speaking, liberal arts professors are not interested in systematic methods of teaching. They are interested in systematic development of a discipline, critiquing this discipline, and perhaps adding knowledge to it. Most liberal arts professors doubt whether methods are reducible to a science. Their attitudes toward those in teacher education who try to develop a science of teaching range from disinterest to overt hostility.

For a brief period in the 1960s—less than a decade—their lack of concern for education programs was superseded by exemplary participation and cooperation. Federal support for teacher education in English, through the medium of institutes and other governmental programs, temporarily provided a new role for the college teacher of English. The institute programs required him to work with his counterpart in teacher education, thereby advancing the idea that professors of English have a responsibility for improving instruction in English at all levels. As long as the impetus of federal programs continued, there was cooperation. Some professors of English, of course, did make changes. Most, however, temporarily adapted to the situation but remained basically uncommitted to the concerns of teacher education. The federal institute programs did set up situations where college professors of English, English teachers, and education professors talked to one another about problems in the teaching of English. But upon withdrawal of the federal support, in the main the dialogue ceased, the responsibility was shrugged off, and the concern evaporated.

Both the liberal arts professor and the teacher educator point to difficulties in changing the university structure that governs their behavior, partially defines their respective roles, and rewards them for certain behaviors and accomplishments. The governance and the established teaching-research patterns of the university in some instances have forced the teacher educator to move off campus to achieve freedom for teaching and experimenting. But moving off campus, it should be noted, tends to separate theory from the practice that the embryonic teacher is given, and can have the effect of reducing the education of teachers to a craft. Unless carefully planned, such experience tends to make prospective teachers something less than self-gauging professionals capable of adapting readily to the learning problems of their students, for it highlights imitation of the successful patterns of teaching that are used by current professionals.

Preservice Education and Certification

Efforts to improve the preservice education of teachers of the English language arts have focused on strengthening the general education and teaching major as well as the professional component. In 1963, a major report, sponsored by the National Council of Teachers of English (NCTE), delineated the preparation required by college as well as elementary school and secondary school teachers of English.[1] One important outcome was encouragement of the

1. Alfred H. Grommon, ed., *The Education of Teachers of English for American Schools and Colleges* (New York: Appleton-Century-Crofts, 1963).

Masters of Arts in Teaching degree, a fifth year program for the preparation of English teachers, sometimes for initial certification and sometimes for permanent certification. Such a degree had earlier been given impetus by Conant's study of the education of American teachers.[2]

Concern about the academic preparation of teachers was enhanced during the same period when a monumental NCTE study, *The National Interest and the Teaching of English*,[3] showed that 25 percent of all elementary school teachers were not college graduates. Moreover, only 40 to 60 percent of high school teachers, depending upon the state in which they practiced, had completed a major in English. Many teachers had completed course work only in freshman composition and sophomore-level literature.

In a companion study, *The National Interest and the Continuing Education of Teachers of English*,[4] the Council reported that 24 percent of the instructional time in grades kindergarten to twelve is spent on English and the language arts, the greatest percentage of time given to any single school subject. Yet less than 8 percent of college preparation time was spent on English and only 20 percent of elementary school teachers and 49 percent of the secondary school teachers had completed a college major in English.

The NCTE in cooperation with the Modern Language Association of America (MLA) pointed convincingly to the need for better preparation, more up-to-date preparation, and a focus on relevancy in the teaching of English. Increased attention to preservice preparation in composition and language study, including the study of black and of Chicano language and literature, was one important result.

Both associations have played an effective and influential role in

2. James B. Conant, *The Education of American Teachers* (New York: McGraw-Hill Book Co., 1963).

3. Committee on National Interest, National Council of Teachers of English, *The National Interest and the Teaching of English: A Report on the Status of the Profession* (Champaign, Ill.: National Council of Teachers of English, 1961).

4. Committee on National Interest, National Council of Teachers of English, *The National Interest and the Continuing Education of Teachers of English*. See also Alfred H. Grommon, ed., *The Education of Teachers of English*; idem, "A History of the Preparation of Teachers of English," *English Journal* 57 (April 1968): 484-524.

bringing about whatever changes have occurred in preparing teachers of the English language arts in the past dozen years. Hardly a study or program reviewed in this chapter has not included NCTE, and many of them included MLA, long (but not recently) the roost of the most conservative of the English flock.

THE ENGLISH TEACHER PREPARATION STUDY (ETPS)

In 1975, NCTE, the MLA, and the National Association of State Directors of Teacher Education and Certification (NASDTEC) joined forces to formulate a definitive set of guidelines for the preparation and certification of English teachers. Developing over a year and a half and involving regional and national study groups of scholars and teachers, the project was headed by William T. Viall, Executive Secretary of NASDTEC, supported by a grant from the U.S. Office of Education, and resulted in a description of desirable competencies for English teachers at both the elementary and secondary levels.[5]

For elementary school teachers, a balanced study of language, literature, and composition beyond the freshman English course was recommended. Supervised teaching and English or language arts methods courses, including the teaching of reading, and a fifth year of study were supported.

For secondary school teachers, the guidelines supported the balanced English major; supervised teaching; English methods, including the teaching of reading at the secondary level; and a fifth year of graduate courses in English and English education. Conferees suggested that plans for the fifth year be flexible and that continuous residence at a college not be required. Consideration of the new media and of censorship in the United States were among topics to be studied.

The ETPS guidelines were intended to assist state departments of education in evaluating programs for the preparation of teachers in institutions seeking accreditation as well as in evaluating individual applicants for certification.

But widespread progress in adopting the guidelines was slow. The

5. William P. Viall et al., "English Teacher Preparation Study: Guidelines for the Preparation of Teachers of English," *English Journal* 56 (September 1967): 884-95.

NCTE's Committee on Certification criticized the lack of orientation to subject matter improvement, which seemed to limit action by state departments of education. Allen pointed out that if the guidelines were to affect English Education curricula for teachers, they should be used to change state certification requirements.[6] Thus, teacher education institutions would be forced to change. He outlined three steps to be taken if the guidelines were to be effective: (a) raise the certification standards to those of the guidelines; (b) incorporate these standards into college programs; and (c) assure implementation and effectiveness of the programs through committees, conferences, and meetings between subfield groups and those in English Education.

While the guidelines continue to offer comprehensive recommendations useful to accrediting agencies, thoughtful analysts noted that they became obsolete almost upon publication. The emphases in English teacher education change rapidly and guidelines that attempt to set only minimum standards for preparation cannot reflect the diversity of programs. Still, guidelines did demonstrate that even minimum standards in English teacher preparation should be under constant review and that the effort needed to keep them abreast of social and professional needs is a major one.[7]

PROFESSIONAL PREPARATION

If the academic preparation of teachers of the English language arts has generated concern, the professional preparation has stimulated even more widespread controversy. For teachers of English, much of the debate has centered on the methods course and the experience of student teachers.

Most professionals agree that future teachers benefit from the study of methods, but even allowing for variation in the preparation of elementary school and secondary school teachers, educators differ in the stress that they would place on general methods as distinct from methods of teaching specialized subject matter. Some advocate separate study of the teaching of writing and the teaching of read-

6. Harold B. Allen, "After the Guidelines—What?" *College English* 30 (May 1969): 680-84.

7. Michael F. Shugrue and Eldonna L. Evertts, "Guidelines for the Preparation of Teachers of English," *English Journal* 56 (September 1967): 884-95.

ing and literature. Others stress the language development of urban children or the familiarization of future teachers with the importance of multiethnic literature. Continued examination of the professional preparation of teachers of English is recorded in the publications of the Conference on English Education (CEE), founded in 1963 to provide for consideration of such issues. During the past decade, particularly strong efforts have been made to eliminate overlap and repetition in methods courses, to avoid presenting set theories to students, and to familiarize prospective teachers with the basic research studies that influence the teaching and learning of English.[8]

During recent decades, too, the wisdom of letting student teaching remain the single clinical experience of prospective teachers has been seriously questioned. Earlier practical experience in the classroom, preceding the study of theoretical matters and methods, has been advocated; so has transformation of the student teaching experience into an internship that more closely resembles the way in which professional preparation is acquired in other fields. Here as elsewhere the different approaches seem to relate to contrasting views of teaching as a craft and teaching as a profession, one viewpoint supporting field-based apprenticeships rooted in practical experiences and the other supporting systematic inquiry into the art and science of teaching and learning. Exemplary programs have been developed, research has been undertaken, and demonstrations of varied approaches have been supported by foundation or governmental agencies, but a consensus has not yet emerged. Basically the student teaching experience has not changed substantially during the past twenty years and its position as the culminating experience of preservice preparation remains virtually unchanged.

But even as the debates on methods courses and student teaching continued, instructional materials and approaches became available to make preservice education more realistic. Analysis of classroom interaction between teacher and students can be examined through videotaped lessons. Modularized instructional packets designed to develop particular teaching skills offer important experiences for the prospective teacher. The Far West Regional Laboratory, sup-

8. David H. Russell, Edmund Farrell, and Margaret J. Early, eds., *Research Design in the Teaching of English: Proceedings of the San Francisco Conference* (Champaign, Ill.: National Council of Teachers of English, 1964).

ported by the National Institute of Education, has concentrated for several years in developing teacher training packages. Particularly promising are the protocol materials developed by universities and educational agencies since 1970 under grants from the U.S. Office of Education.[9] Protocols are printed, filmed, or videotaped exemplifications of concepts not taught effectively under the traditional lecture-discussion method. Designed to be used in a variety of teacher education programs, ranging from the traditional to performance-based, protocol materials offer vignettes of behavior illustrating key concepts for understanding pupils' behavior in the classroom. The main purpose of protocols is to develop knowledge through concept analysis and to link specific behavior to a conceptual base. While not designed specifically for the training of teachers of English, language arts is included in the list of subject areas, and concepts from the teaching of English are among those treated in the protocol materials.[10]

TEACHER CERTIFICATION

Questions regarding responsibility for the certification of teachers have long been unresolved. In recent years, the National Education Association State Standards and Professional Practices Commission has been assigned the legal responsibility for policy making in a few states, a change from its previous unofficial status. Many members of the profession, especially university personnel, find this change unacceptable because college personnel represent a distinct minority on the Commission. Some members of the profession have advocated nationwide licensing standards to be set by the National Education Association and the American Federation of Teachers, a move to prevent teacher qualifications being judged by agencies outside of the profession. Federal accreditation or the training of teachers by school boards and community organizations have been opposed because of the feared low common denominator for certifi-

9. Donald R. Cruickshank, "The Developing Notion of Protocol Materials," *Journal of Teacher Education* 23 (Fall 1972): 281-85.

10. Protocol materials in literature were developed at California State University, Northridge, under the direction of Richard Lid; and in language at the Ohio State University, under the direction of Frank Zidonis. They are available from the National Resource and Dissemination Center at the University of South Florida, Tampa.

cation. Some states, like California, have placed greater licensing responsibility in the hands of the state department of education, less in the hands of the college offering the teacher education curriculum. Many continue to hold the institutions of higher education responsible. A few, like New York, have called for "policy boards" to be set up by local communities to oversee the qualifications of local teachers. Practice varies but, in general, specific certification requirements tend to do little more than establish the minimum requirements for teaching.

Several studies of certification of teachers of English reveal discernible but not definitive trends.[11] Strengthening of subject preparation continues, possibly as a result of the English Teacher Preparation Study. In 1969, for example, West Virginia added a three-hour course requirement in language to help prospective elementary-school teachers develop linguistic flexibility and learn about the nature and structure of the language. Such a basic requirement seems essential, although the attempt to assure the teacher's knowledge of and facility in use of language through the addition of a single course seems unrealistic. Even so, basic requirements have been strengthened to the extent that most states today require elementary-school teachers to complete at least a single course in the language arts and another in reading. Graduate work is usually required in the subject field as well as in professional preparation. In some states, a higher level of preparation is required for those who wish to be full-time teachers of English than for those planning to teach English part-time. But in general, most state certification requirements are set below typical college and university degree requirements even during a period when a surplus of teachers is available.

PERFORMANCE-BASED TEACHER EDUCATION

Performance-based teacher education (PBTE), also referred to as competency-based teacher education, centers on the requisite

---

11. Eldonna L. Evertts, *Selected Annotated Bibliography: English, English Education, and Certification* (Champaign, Ill.: National Council of Teachers of English, ERIC Clearinghouse on the Teaching of English, 1968); Eugene E. Slaughter, "Certification to Teach English in the Elementary or Secondary School, 1964," *College English* 25 (May 1964): 591-604; idem, "Certification Requirements to Teach English in Elementary or Secondary School—1967," *English Journal* 57 (April 1968): 551-64.

competencies that a teacher must have to perform agreed upon tasks. Competency is determined in one of three ways: (a) amount of knowledge imparted to the students; (b) evaluation of the teaching behavior; (c) an assessment of the teacher's ability to teach by examining the achievement of pupils taught by him. Studied by the American Association of Colleges for Teacher Education since 1970, under a grant from the U.S. Office of Education, the approach has been accepted by a large segment of the profession and at this writing more than a dozen states have adopted performance-based or competency-based approaches for ascertaining certification. Many such adoptions were made despite objections from schools of education, who wanted to study the approach prior to its implementation, and, perhaps predictably, several of the states recently have begun to question their precipitous action. But to date none committed to such evaluation has withdrawn from its position.

The subject fields have resisted the approach, and in many instances the objection has been vociferous.[12] Subject matter specialists oppose PBTE because of its limited philosophic and knowledge base. They feel that PBTE threatens to trivialize the curriculum by fragmenting their subjects. They oppose the heavy career or vocational orientation that it seems to suggest, an orientation that for some is a healthy and realistic antidote to the traditional academic emphases of the curriculum.

While some English Education departments are exploring the uses of performance-based evaluation, English departments and English teachers in the main are opposed to the approach. They recognize that performance-based teacher education must necessarily concentrate on the cognitive aspects of learning, and they worry about neglect of the affective. In their view, some of the most important objectives of English teaching are to be found in the affective domain: developing understanding of human values; promoting an ethical and realistic view of life; stimulating life-long habits in reading, writing, and speaking; and inculcating a knowledge and love of wisdom and belles lettres.

Supporters of the performance-based approach point out that

12. For an overview, see Stanley Elam, *Performance-Based Teacher Education: What Is the State of the Art?* (Washington, D.C.: American Association of Colleges for Teacher Education, 1971).

it can help English teachers define their goals in precise terms. It can be used to eliminate "wasted motion" in teacher's efforts and in teacher education programs. And it makes accountability possible by evaluating the teacher's efforts and his pupil's successes.

Part of the resistance stems from the difficulty of validating which of the teacher's activities are basic; which of his approaches the most effective; which of his strategies the most efficient. Judgments based on pupil performance frequently require the use of standardized tests, many of which are outmoded. Suitable instruments for the periodic and incidental evaluation of students' achievement and progress are designed and used by few teachers. Obtaining acceptable data on performance related to teacher behavior thus remains an elusive goal. At this writing, performance-based teacher education appears mainly a promise.

The focus on teaching-learning objectives fostered by PBTE, the shift of emphases from teaching to learning, and the highlighting of the different routes that individuals may follow to develop competency in teaching have stimulated beneficial discussion. If one views the teacher as a person who can facilitate students' cognitive, affective, and psychomotor growth, whether in English or in some other area, ways of assessing successful performance by the teacher should be capable of development. But the present state of the art has not yet yielded widely accepted measures.

In-Service and Continuing Education

Quite possibly the key to implementing significant changes in the schools will come through improved in-service education. Because fewer teachers will be needed in the future, and because most teachers presently in the schools will probably be there for another twenty years, change that can be effected by employing new teachers entering the field will be minimal. Evidence for lack of growth in the teaching profession can be shown by the fact that 700,000 fewer children entered elementary school in 1974 than in 1973. Various estimates indicate that the decrease will continue for a few years, when a plateau will be reached and maintained to 1985, or even until 1990.

Efforts to strengthen in-service education have increased considerably during recent years, spurred on by the Education Professions Development Act, the teacher center movement, and by state and local projects in career education, to mention but three developments. Yet many teachers enter in-service study not out of a desire for knowledge or a wish to improve their teaching, but merely to achieve escalation on the salary schedule. Once the schedule maximum has been reached, in-service work tapers off and no further formal work is taken until there is another chance to advance on the schedule. The underlying problem, and the most basic one, however, is whether or not in-service work can change human behavior and really encourage teachers to change the way they teach. Can it give them new goals? Will it help them evaluate the methods and materials they use? And will it offer them evaluation procedures that they will accept?

For the teacher of the English language arts, the past twenty years have provided numerous opportunities for continuing education. Team teaching approaches were given impetus. Patterns of differentiated staffing were developed. Primarily through support from governmental agencies and by the recruitment of volunteers, programs for the education of paraprofessionals were established. For a time, year-long advanced study as in the John Hay Fellows Program offered special opportunity for a few. Changes in supervision and in audiovisual or multimedia instructional approaches were developed. Minicourses became established as acceptable instructional approaches, and to plan them teachers were granted released time and were required to rethink their instructional goals. Various attempts have been made to redefine the urgent requirements for the continuing education of teachers of English.

A landmark study by Squire and others in 1964[13] pointed to curriculum inadequacies; it offered recommendations for the improvement of English content in institute programs, for changes in methods and in supervision, and commentary on the need for professional libraries and the importance of the professional association to English teachers.

Two years later Olson enumerated priorities to be emphasized in English Language Arts institutes and workshops for teachers of

13. James R. Squire, "The National Study of High School English Programs: Implications for Colleges and Universities," *College English* 27 (May 1966): 613-19.

the culturally disadvantaged.[14] Catalani subsequently found that of nine in-service areas usually included in the education of teachers, recommended criteria and approaches were followed in the areas of organization, administration, funding, and evaluation.[15] Five areas that were not well emphasized in in-service programs were those dealing with objectives, personnel roles, content, inception, and follow-up.

During the 1960s a series of federal interventions stimulated college and school cooperation in improving the in-service education of teachers through subject matter institutes, the development of new instructional materials, and the training of teacher trainers. Of these, the most important were Project English, the National Defense Education Act, and the Education Professions Development Act.

PROJECT ENGLISH

Project English was sponsored by the U.S. Office of Education, beginning in 1962 with the funding of research and development projects in English. Its goals were (a) to support research in English; (b) to study the development of curriculum with both logical sequence and varying rates of children's development in mind; (c) to improve preservice education of English teachers; and (d) to develop a system of disseminating information.

Through some two dozen development and dissemination centers, Project English attempted to make reforms in three "waves": (a) secondary school curricula; (b) elementary school curricula; (c) college and university preparation of teachers. With a centralized materials center, the Project prepared sample units of instruction distributed to approximately 15,000 teachers who were then attending summer institutes, and it supported several significant status studies of in-service needs.

Among the achievements of Project English, Kitzhaber has cited

14. Paul A. Olson, *The Arts of Language, Needed Curricula, and American Development for Institutes in the English Language Arts—Language, Literature, Composition, Speech, and Reading,* Report of a USOE Conference (Lincoln, Neb.: University of Nebraska, 1966).

15. Anne Ramundo Catalani, "A Study of Selected Nationwide Inservice Education Programs for Secondary School Teachers of English, Grades 7-12, from Fall, 1969 through Academic Year 1971-72" (Ph.D. diss., University of Texas at Austin, 1972).

sharper definition of English as a school subject; philosophical integrity for the English curriculum; defensible structures and sequence for English; incorporation of current scholarship and learning theory in the substantive fields of English; the close involvement of experienced teachers in the writing of new curricula; better communication between school and college teachers of English; and profound effects on the making of English textbooks.[16]

In addition, Shugrue found that Project English gave a greater role to linguistics; placed more emphasis on content and sequence in literature; and fostered greater use of the inductive method, audiovisual materials, talk, and drama as motivation for students.[17] At the college level it brought about changes in linguistics, rhetorical systems, and current literary theory, along with television and computer-assisted instruction. Project English was a direct fallout of federal support for revision of curricula in science, foreign languages and mathematics, resulting from the competitive atmosphere created by the Russians' launching of Sputnik. In many respects it became a prototype for succeeding federally sponsored programs in the teaching of English. But federal support for the effort declined by the end of the decade and the Project's hopes were far from fully realized.

THE NATIONAL DEFENSE EDUCATION ACT

Title IX of the National Defense Education Act (NDEA) provided support to colleges and universities for establishing summer and year-long institutes in various facets of English and allowed stipends to be paid to the participants. Title III provided for materials, equipment, and special supervision. The institutes were patterned after those developed earlier by the Commission on English of the College Entrance Examination Board.

Teachers attended the institutes in 1965, 1966, and 1967, by which time the program coverage had been enlarged to include language programs for teachers of the disadvantaged. In 1966, for

16. Albert R. Kitzhaber, "The Government and English Teaching: A Retrospective View," *College Composition and Communication* 18 (October 1967): 135-41.

17. Michael F. Shugrue, *English in a Decade of Change* (New York: Pegasus, 1969).

example, more than 5200 teachers attended, studying linguistics, composition, literary analysis, curriculum reform, new media, historical linguistics, and new grammatical systems.

An exhaustive and detailed but inconclusive study of the NDEA Institutes was made by Donald Gray in 1966.[18] Using survey and observation techniques, Gray reported a set of tentative findings regarding the successes and failures of the institutes and developed a series of recommendations.

He found that teachers planned to put to use much of what they had learned: in literature, to stress close reading in connection with composition and language; in language, to emphasize syntax, not the parts of speech, and to teach usage and the history of language; in composition, to assign frequent, short themes. He also found that subject matter institutes were better than general ones and that older, more experienced teachers and those with few English credits benefited most.

The institutes were disappointing in that they led to little or no experimenting with course offerings or new ways of teaching. An examination of the teaching of the participants did not reveal what they had learned, what they felt they had learned, or whether what they had learned affected their teaching. Not enough lecturers, such as professional writers, were drawn from outside the colleges. Tension in the institutes, as on campus, existed between subject matter advocates and professors of education, creating a distraction. Workshops connecting the courses to the participants' classrooms were the least successful part of the institutes, whether they were based on seminars, demonstrations, discussion, guest lectures, or films. Generally the workshops were not taken seriously nor given graduate credit. Teachers in general displayed little interest in new materials. In fact, they were suspicious of them, except for new books. The workshop staff was not fully involved in planning the institutes, and the teachers were taught the mechanics of using audio-visual materials but were not instructed in their values and uses.

Gray recommended that organizers of future institutes consult

18. Donald J. Gray, *The 1965 NDEA Institutes in English: Report of a Pilot Study to Develop Criteria for Evaluating NDEA Institutes in English* (New York: Modern Language Association of America and the National Council of Teachers of English, 1966).

with teachers and administrators to relate institute experiences to proposed changes in classroom teaching. Program material, he felt, should be integrated rather than taught in discrete courses, and the relationship to English of such fields as drama, speech, sociology, psychology, and anthropology should be demonstrated. He called for more cooperation and mutual acceptance among the professors of English, professors of education, and the public school personnel who staffed the institutes. He felt that the college curriculum should be revised so that the institutes did not teach what teachers should have already learned. Finally, he suggested that the institutes could help elementary teachers more.

The NDEA institutes were not evaluated in depth nor was the long-range impact of the program on participants fully assessed. One can only speculate about the permanent effects. Without a doubt, many teachers were given new motivation for teaching and new awareness of the importance of their roles. The new ideas, skills, and techniques for use in their classrooms that they said they obtained ranged from "hardly any" to "more than I can use." Some new and permanent respect for and appreciation of each other's talents, problems, and expertise developed among the professors of English, the teachers of teachers, and the public school administrators and supervisors who worked together in the institutes. The local school systems, the universities, and the federal educational establishment learned that a special education project such as an institute was costly (almost as much as a medium tank!). Some members of Congress even realized that getting an institute for their states was not unlike having a new dam built there.

THE EDUCATION PROFESSIONS DEVELOPMENTS ACT

The Education Professions Development Act (EPDA) of 1967 provided funds for the improvement of teachers in all areas, at all levels, and beginning in 1969 superseded the NDEA. In EPDA the concentration was on professional education personnel instead of the subject matter specialists, a reversal of the earlier emphasis. EPDA was an amendment of the Higher Education Act of 1965 and provided fellowships for and recruitment of qualified persons for higher education. It supported training for persons serving or preparing to serve as teachers, administrators, or educational specialists at college or university through courses and short-term fellowships. It extended in-service opportunities in schools and for college teachers.

One effect of EPDA was that many school systems began in-service programs. Its effects, in general, were not lasting and few significant developments can be credited to it. One part of it, the Triple-T Program (Trainers of Teacher Trainers) was only incidentally concerned with the teaching of English. Its initial major thrust, the establishment of regional training complexes, held great promise for in-service programs in general, but the promise was empty. Financial support was reduced in 1970 and most of the training complexes did not materialize. As late as 1974, several EPDA projects were still in existence, though funding by that time had been drastically reduced, and much of the training complex activity had evolved into the teacher centers, with the requirement that large portions of their support be provided locally.

REGIONAL PROJECTS

Many of the major developments in continuing education have occurred in regional projects which, if they have not often had national influence, have illuminated continuing local needs. In Philadelphia, for instance, Temple University initiated the Elementary Program for Inner-City Teachers (EPICT) in 1966, emphasizing reading and language arts, and later incorporated many of the school-based learning experiences in its regular training program.[19] The New York State Department of Education initiated the Lackawanna Undergraduate Teacher Education Program to provide a phased introduction of prospective teachers to full teaching responsibility.[20] Impetus for new regional programs had come from federal programs. Two such projects have had a particularly significant impact in the field of English Education.

The Wisconsin Project. The Wisconsin English Language Arts

19. Florence V. Shankman, "Innovations in Teacher-Training for Inner-City Schools," *Reading Teacher* 24 (May 1971): 744-47.

20. Mary Attea, "Teacher Education in Reading and Language Arts: Undergraduate Urban Teacher Education Program (UUTEP) Competency-Based Program, Lackawanna, New York," *Reading Teacher* 27 (November 1973): 138-41.

Curriculum Project, directed by Robert C. Pooley, was a federally-supported, statewide project. It grew out of teacher demand in 1959 for curriculum reform. Every elementary and high school teacher in Wisconsin was eligible to join the program. In-service education was provided through meetings where materials sent from a curriculum center were discussed and evaluated. Forty-eight elementary committees and 89 high school committees, involving 1,183 teachers and administrators were meeting in 1964. Bulletins disseminated information, with a reaction sheet to be filled out by the committee leader. In 1963-64, emphasis was on literature and voluntary reading, kindergarten through grade 12. In 1965 the focus was on the teaching of speaking and writing. In 1965-66 the teaching of English language and grammar were evaluated.

In 1966-67 teachers' experience with the curriculum was verified and final editing preceded publication of the recommended statewide curriculum in English language arts for kindergarten through grade 12.

The Illinois State-Wide Curriculum Study Center. The Illinois State-Wide Curriculum Study Center in the Preparation of Secondary English Teachers (ISCPET) included thirty-three projects. It was supported by U.S. Office of Education funds for five years, beginning in 1964. Both in-service and preservice education of English teachers were studied. Most aspects of the English curriculum and of English teacher education programs were investigated and teachers and administrators from the entire education hierarchy were involved. In making his final report on the project, J. N. Hook, the director, felt that the most important changes resulting from ISCPET were balanced teacher education programs, increased cooperation between English and education departments, and an awareness of the need for in-service education.[21]

ISCPET developed a prototype structure for educators, teachers, and administrators to work together. It developed rating scales for measuring teacher effectiveness. Thirty-three research studies in teacher preparation were completed, and six publications were dis-

---

21. J. N. Hook et al., *Illinois State-Wide Curriculum Study Center in the Preparation of Secondary English Teachers: Final Report* (Urbana, Ill.: Illinois State-Wide Curriculum Study Center in the Preparation of Secondary English Teachers, 1969).

seminated. It developed the *Illinois Test in the Teaching of English*, and disseminated over 100,000 copies of various ISCPET publications.

Three institutions participating in the study completely overhauled their teacher education programs, while fifteen made major changes (most changes were in composition and language.) Three new English methods courses were established, and in ten institutions English and education departments offered courses cooperatively. The National Teacher Examination was used to evaluate and change programs. More than one hundred articles and fourteen dissertations came out of the study, and between ten and twenty thousand English teachers in some way had their teaching affected.

FEDERAL INTERVENTION

As this review has made clear, federal intervention in the preparation and continuing education of teachers of the English language arts increased significantly in 1965 with the support for the NDEA Institute Program, continued with the EPDA Program, and has recently tapered off.

Many of the ideas basic to these federal efforts were congruent with the views of the liberal arts professors, commercial research organizations, and minority group spokesmen. Support generally focussed on academic preparation of teachers, on developing exemplary materials, on demonstrations, and on limited research. Clearly the efforts stimulated ideas, redirected attention to certain urgent needs such as preparation for urban teaching, and provided many teachers with an opportunity to restudy the nature of their subject field. (At the zenith of the institute program, approximately 20,000 elementary and secondary teachers of English were enrolled.) But the federal government, while seeing itself as a catalyst for change, prescribed the change by supporting certain types of proposals and ignoring others. Change, therefore, was of a limited nature, rather than free-flowing and unfettered, and perhaps opportunity for more permanent evolutionary change was lost.

Conclusion

There are those who say that for 300 years the teacher's role has changed very little and that recent changes in teacher education in this century have been only ripples in the education pond. Yet some harbingers of future change have occurred during recent years. It is apparent, for example, that preservice and in-service training are being brought closer together, perhaps out of necessity.

State departments of education are increasingly initiating changes and reforms, as the movement toward performance-based teacher education has indicated. Teacher unions today play a more vigorous role, especially in establishing relationships between teaching conditions and requirements for in-service work. To a considerable extent federal support seems more and more focussed on training related to particular curricular needs, such as career education or bilingual/bicultural education, or to disseminating the results of research and development to schools and teachers as through the ERIC system.

Clearly, also, concern with the changing social, cultural, and instructional setting that has marked the developments of recent years will continue. In his landmark study of the future of English teaching, Farrell sees the following implications for the preparation of teachers of English:

> The panel on English judged the following items among those most necessary in the pre-service education of a secondary teacher of English: learning how to use in his subject field discovery approaches to learning; learning how to reveal clearly to students the social relevance of English; learning how to be a creator and manager of learning strategies and systems; becoming familiar with the processes of language development in children; and taking course work in ancillary fields such as anthropology, sociology, and psychology.
>
> In the panel's opinion, preparation for teaching the disadvantaged should include programs that intensively involve prospective teachers with successful classroom teachers, principals, counselors, and others in the planning, supervision, and evaluation of pre-service experiences. Further, courses should be modified so that techniques and skills essential to teaching in depressed areas can be developed: diagnostic and remedial procedures, methods and materials for individualized instruction, strategies for classroom control, and use of personnel and material sources.[22]

Much of this chapter has considered the role of government at all levels, and its influence on the education of teachers of English.

---

22. Edmund J. Farrell, *Deciding the Future: A Forecast of Responsibilities of Secondary Teachers of English, 1970-2000 A.D.* (Champaign, Ill.: National Council of Teachers of English, 1971), inside back cover.

The period of intensive activity was brief, extending from perhaps 1965 to 1972. Those who watched such activity noted that by 1972 the U.S. Office of Education was requesting legislation which would shift the responsibility for supported programs from the colleges and universities to teachers, making them the primary designers and implementers of the training programs for their profession. Currently, even this support is now being reduced. The economic pullback may be a blessing, at least to colleges and universities, because it can return to them the freedom and responsibility to plan and choose, without direct governmental intervention, quality programs for the education of teachers.

If the teaching profession can accept the notion that education can change but that change will not be revolutionary, adjustments can be made so that teachers can perform their tasks with facility, and students can learn as they always have learned, or better. The key, perhaps, is understanding that change is continuous and evolutionary. Technology has not revolutionized the way in which we teach, nor what we teach. Human relations emphases, semantics, group dynamics, teacher institutes, specialized training programs, and a host of approaches that were supposed to revolutionize education have not done so. And yet each innovation, each important new approach, has made a modicum of difference, produced a miniscule change, a barely perceptible leaning in a new direction. Perhaps this is the nature of education, ever to present a challenge that will never be completely met. Change is fecund, change is pervasive. Perhaps education, like the future, is forever being made.

CHAPTER X

The Future Direction of English Teaching: An Informal Discussion*

What do today's sociocultural, scholarly, and professional trends imply for the future of the teaching of English? To analyze the direction in which curriculum and instruction is moving, the Yearbook Committee invited seven participants to express their diverse views and experiences.

Dorothy Davidson is Associate Commissioner for General Education in the Texas Education Agency. In 1969-70 she was Second Vice-president of the National Council of Teachers of English.

Janet Emig is Professor of English Education at Rutgers, The State University (New Jersey) and is the author of *The Composing Processes of Twelfth Graders,* a 1971 publication of the National Council of Teachers of English. She is also a member of the Council's Commission on Composition.

Theodore Hipple is Professor of Education at the University of Florida, author of *Teaching English in the Secondary School* (1973), and editor of *The Future of Education: 1975-2000* (1975).

Charlotte Huck is Professor of Education at The Ohio State University and coauthor of *Children's Literature in the Elementary School* (1976). She was President of the National Council of Teachers of English for 1975-76.

Daniel A. Lindley, Jr. is Associate Professor of English and Chairman of English Education, University of Illinois at Chicago Circle, and a member of the Committee on Teacher Training in Nonprint Media of the Conference on English Education.

James Moffett is an educational consultant and writer. He is the

---

* Consultant readers for this chapter were Harold Shane, University Professor of Education, Indiana University; Arthur N. Applebee, Tarleton High School, Lancashire, England; and Roy Lahr, Manager of Special Projects, Xerox Corporation.

author of *Student-Centered English and Reading* (1976) and the senior author of *Interaction* (1972).

James R. Squire is Senior Vice-president and Publisher, Ginn and Company. He was formerly Executive Secretary of the National Council of Teachers of English and is Chairman of the Committee for this yearbook of the National Society for the Study of Education.

Dr. Squire served as the moderator for six hours of recorded discussion and has prepared the following abstract based on the transcript of that discussion.

Responding to the Schism in Society

Squire: As each of you looks ahead ten or twenty years, what do you see as the next big wave of curriculum reform in English?

Huck: We seem to be on a collision course between the Skinnerian and the Piagetian points of view. I fear that the Skinnerians are going to win, simply from the standpoint that they offer an easier approach to package and teach; the Piagetian point of view is much more difficult to put into practice. Somehow we are going to have to resolve these differences before any new movement emerges.

Hipple: This is an age of redefinition. We see a redefinition of the institution of marriage and the way the church has an impact on lives. The morals of young people are being redefined. The school may be slow in accepting this redefinition of roles and values because it tends to be a more conservative institution than society itself. I wonder, however, if society isn't trending toward conservatism in a way that will make the school seem more in balance with it. I see all kinds of conservative trends in society at large that suggest that perhaps the school won't be quite so out of step during the future.

Moffett: The schools will probably change very fast within ten to twenty years just because they won't be tolerated if they don't change enough to serve better than they are now serving.

Squire: You are expecting them to change more rapidly during the next ten to twenty years than during the past ten to twenty years?

Moffett: I agree with Charlotte's observations about the sharp conflict between the Skinnerians and the Piagetians and, more broadly, between the technocratic versus the humanistic. Jeanne Dixon, the psychic prophetess who has had an extraordinarily good record, has predicted that there will be a civil war in the 1980s in the United States between forces that want change and the forces that do not. I don't agree that the Skinnerians will win in the end, although I think they are winning now and will continue to win in the years immediately ahead. The technocratic approach simply won't solve the culture's problems and therefore will necessitate a new consensus in the eighties and the nineties.

Squire: Psychology almost seems to be moving away from the Skinnerian view toward cognitive theory. Still the issues posed by these polarized views of learning have been very disturbing to teachers.

Emig: One response to this schism might well be the development of more alternatives in education. Communities may make choices, provide various types of schools and various types of emphases. Parents could indeed select a school for their children that stresses whatever we mean by college preparatory, basic skill, or humanities. This is one possibility. There is also a prior question about who will be going to school in the future. I truly wonder if the same age group will be in whatever we mean by schools. I foresee a vast redefinition. I particularly wonder about the future of the high school as a living community.

Squire: Are you suggesting that our concept of high school is outmoded?

Emig: I think there will be more coming and going of persons of all ages. I think education will indeed be a lifetime affair. If that happens, it seems less likely that there will be a fixed place for the adolescents particularly. The high schools I see are in such a state of dishevelment, I truly wonder about their immediate futures.

Hipple: Such a possibility is closely tied in with the labor movement. The trend toward increasing the age of the compulsory schooling has been related to periods of unemployment, and we seem to be moving through even greater periods of unemployment. Those who are distressed with sixteen- and seventeen-year-old kids getting jobs are going to insist that the schools serve as a holding agency for these kids.

Davidson: Our schools in the next ten years will be focusing attention on mediating the great problems of the society. Instead of fighting one group or another group that is trying to get hold of education, we have an opportunity to respond to the need for a new kind of educational system.

Lindley: I want to get back to the notion of the civil war. I find myself shocked because the idea seems so plausible. Do I hear you saying that the two groups involved will be essentially people who are advocates of change, not necessarily progress, but advocates of changing; and the other group would be advocates of some kind of fixity?

Moffett: That was the way Dixon described it.

Lindley: It is not just liberal-conservative in a political sense at all; it's deeper than that. It is a psychic model of the way the universe is, one model versus another, and the models are irreconcilably different. Well, I find it plausible and that scares me. There's an apocalyptic sense in the time that we live in right now anyway. The Yearbook begins reviewing current developments in the teaching of English about 1952. That was about my first year in college. In those years, it seemed clear that you grew up toward an adult culture into which you were gradually introduced. That was the purpose of the educational enterprise. But starting in the 1960s, people of age twelve, thirteen, and older developed an entirely sufficient culture of their own. And schooling, from that point of view, became irrelevant, particularly English, which was the only place where any kind of culture was being preserved anyway. Music turned into the marching football band and history became a promised democracy. Only in English were there pieces of literature, for example, that represented the culture. And as soon as the kids had a culture, the idea of English that I grew up with was, in effect, vacated. I think that English is going to go around in circles until the watershed between the school cultures and the student cultures can be resolved.

Emig: You don't think the solution of alternatives within a given district might be a possibility?

Davidson: We need help in teaching cultural values through English if we assume such a role.

Lindley: The student's culture is something with which he already lives. I mean, you don't go to Tonga to teach the Tongans Tonga culture.

Davidson: But in order to avert civil disorder, we must understand the various cultures that are operating in our society; and we are closer to them now than we have ever been before.

Hipple: Alternative schools should help the schools respond to new cultural forces. And I believe they are going to come, even though I am a little cynical about the motivations. Many school people will not appreciate having alternative models of schooling within what we are presently calling public schools.

Huck: We have an alternative public school district operating today in a suburb outside of Columbus. It consists of six elementary schools, three of them providing informal classrooms. The teachers elect to go there, and the parents may choose the kind of education they prefer for their children.

Moffett: There are two ways. One is to keep public schools going with some kind of a public tax base and offer alternatives within such schools. The other is to make school attendance noncompulsory. Via that route, public schools are simply dropped. The tax money is retained by parents and put into private schooling or a public voucher system.

Davidson: They need not be only alternative schools. We can offer alternative programs within schools. We need to be careful we do not create alternative systems that perpetuate a narrow point of view, denying individual pupils the opportunity to consider a *diversity* of views.

Moffett: But the alternatives are going to be over a really wide range. I recently attended a conference of the Association of Humanistic Psychology. The theme was reading, writing, and reality; and with respect to reality, participants tried to define the nature of alternative realities. Carl Rogers, in the thematic address, said that, traditionally, schools in just about all cultures have been obliged to perpetuate the official cultural view of reality, and always only a single view. People considered it pointless if schools departed from this version of reality. But such singularity is no longer possible. There are clearly now alternative versions of reality. He was referring to the books of Castaneda and to meditation experiences and a lot of other experiences through which people are perceiving the world quite differently. Rogers believes there is no way in which education can survive unless it accommodates such diverse views. Providing for diverse views represents·a drastic departure from the old cultural role of education, which is to perpetuate society's world view. We are not going to survive if we all see the same things. Our inability to solve the problems of ecology, hunger, pollution and so on, results from an inability to see outside of a single framework. There are going to have to be some alternative realities in order to generate some alternative solutions to the problems.

Davidson: The culture shock in the recent West Virginia school controversy over books resulted in part from trying to explore alternatives. English teachers were trying to help youngsters explore other life-styles. And their parents didn't want them to. It's just that simple, or that complex.

Huck: In thinking about the organization of the schools, we could take advantage of the economic situation and unemployment. We could question the common practice of placing thirty children in school rooms not larger than the average sized house. Rather than close schools, we could keep some schools open, experimenting with school or class sizes that have never been tried before. Think also about economic opportunities for educating preschool and nursery school children. My guess would be that Russia spends more money on preschool education than on high school education. They place a medical doctor in every nursery school, for example. We could make some good out of the economic crunch if we would really stand up for what would constitute good education, particularly for the young children.

Lindley: I think Janet's right that the school is going to have an increasingly disparate kind of audience coming in and out all the time. Certainly we are going to have retired people in large numbers.

Emig: I see a more fluid definition of who teaches and who learns. But, you know, if you can anticipate a kind of CCC movement, WPA, any of these things, why wait until we get to that point and then create an artificial one?

Davidson: One barrier is the increasing militancy in teachers.

Teachers are vying for jobs now and they don't want differentiated staffing. They want the paraprofessionals in the room to assist them and cut down on their pupil-teacher ratios.

Basic Skills

Moffett: Increasingly, we are seeing less and less difference between elementary, secondary, and college schooling. Partially, this trend results from our failure to teach basic skills well, so that now high school English teachers are being required to complete courses in reading as part of their training. The problem of literacy is moving up. I am asked to consult with community colleges about teaching basic skills—beginning reading and writing. In a sense it doesn't make much difference now on which rung of the hierarchy a student is. Basic literacy and skills are of concern at every level. My own feeling is that it is a kind of mechanical problem that we will solve during the next ten years. And the real issue for me is what happens, what do we do with schools, once basic skills are not there to cling to.

Squire: Jimmy Britton claims that the fundamental question in teaching English is language learning in the multiracial, multilinguistic classroom. Are you saying, Jim, you think we are going to have a solution to that within ten years?

Moffett: I am saying we'll have a solution to learning to read and write—basic reading and writing, spelling and punctuation, decoding, and so on. Intrinsically, it is not a difficult problem, but it has appeared so because of institutional problems involved in such teaching in the schools. In fact, such basic teaching has been more accomplished at home than in the school. I think it likely that by the 1980s or 1990s we may put English on an isomorphic alphabet like Unifon[1] in the same way we are shifting to metrication. It's expensive. It's troublesome. It is such a nuisance that it appeared George Bernard Shaw's idea would never come true. But within twenty years computerization will exert tremendous need to have machines translate between speech and print, using an alphabet like Unifon. Furthermore, English is rapidly becoming an international second language. Such requirements will put, then, tre-

1. The Unifon Alphabet Foundation, 230 West Monroe, Chicago, Illinois 60606. John Malone devised the alphabet.

mendous pressure for library services, for publishing, for everything to have an isomorphic alphabet—one symbol for one sound. And when that happens, most basic skill problems will disappear, because they are based on phonemic inconsistencies of English. The kids speaking Italian and Turkish and certain other languages learn to read in a few weeks. If we have an isomorphic alphabet, the problem of basic literacy won't amount to much. The interesting thing to me is what happens when basic skills, which seem to jam the whole school program, are suddenly eliminated. Few teachers may then know how to shift the level of education up.

Squire: A new study suggests that 70 percent of all the time of elementary teachers is spent on language arts. Suppose that Jim is correct and that the skill problem is solved with the isomorphic alphabet. What is going to rush in to fill that vacuum?

Huck: We might have an opportunity to help children with problem solving, thinking about becoming human, and having experience with literature and all of the things they are missing because of the direct approach, which has always been wrong—teaching phonics and all the rest. It might free them to live and become thinking, feeling human beings.

Emig: I wonder if communities are ready for this kind of endeavor. I truly wonder if communities, in light of what we said at the beginning, will be willing to pay for their children to become more human.

Moffett: During the interim period before something like Unifon is adopted, I think we'll simply solve the problem of teaching basic skills through a combination of multimedia approaches and the opportunities of flexible classroom management.

Squire: I suspect too, that the new uses of media in instruction, new opportunities emerging from the open classroom and experiments with creating more conducive learning environments will become merged with alternatives to present class and school organization. Perhaps with new patterns we can triple the amount of instructional time, albeit providing the instruction to groups of three students or five students. I also think, as Charlotte was implying earlier, that the whole thrust of concern with language learning, will inevitably force downward provision for some kind of formal education at the preschool level.

Emig: Teaching of basic skills might be a task involving children of three to, say, nine or ten years old. Do you think that's possible?

Moffett: If you have a really individualized learning environment, then some children will learn at three years old without being forced and some are free to wait until they're psychologically ready, at third grade, maybe . . .

Huck: That's the point—really letting them be free. If we have formal schooling earlier, we must be careful that we don't have formal instruction earlier. Otherwise, we can have the absurdity of a remedial reader at three. Piaget, of course, suggests that we really don't have to teach reading until twelve, at the time of what he calls formal operations. Some of us think that is a little bit late. But to have that kind of freedom!

Squire: Increasingly skills are being stressed with older students, too. We are seeing pressures from our society to develop marketable skills and provide young people with a more realistic career education. We talked about the obsolescence of emphasis on "the culture," at least the majority culture, and the fact that we see a bifurcation between the students' culture and the adult culture being presented in many schools. We have the added complication that the need for schooling may decline if the basic skill problem should be solved as Jim predicts. But against these forces we can see social and economic trends that, short-run surely, long-run possibly, will make society unwilling to turn out large numbers of young people from schools at any earlier age.

Moffett: This conflict between lower school leaving age and the socioeconomic need to have schools retain kids and keep them off the labor market is a good case of the kind of rough polarizing that's happening. Certainly we see a tremendous thrust toward noncompulsory education, a natural outgrowth of the civil libertarian movement in this country. You will recall that the Amish won the Supreme Court decision about not having to force their kids to go to school beyond eighth grade because of conflicts with their religious beliefs. I think the essential concept probably will be extended beyond the religious justification. I've been predicting for some time that compulsory education is probably going to go. This doesn't necessarily mean that the public schools will go. It means rather that another kind of model will emerge.

Lindley: My view is that most people will be in school, not by force of law but by force of economic circumstance.

Squire: What's going to await them in school?

Moffett: One model is the kind that we have in the public library, the public museum, and public sports. All of these are provided and nobody is required to attend. Libraries are generally busy places, particularly if they become media centers as well as book centers. And schools may become like them. This could result in a kind of cross-education among different age groups, adults and older kids, as well as very young kids, down to three.

Hipple: Will they be there because they want to be or because they have nothing else to do?

Moffett: A new kind of accountability may go into effect here, the sort of accountability that's in libraries and museums now, where institutions are judged by use of facilities. That isn't a bad criterion. It means that schools would have to be made interesting, attractive, and really worthwhile. It's a kind of emphasis that isn't there under the present monopoly of required attendance.

Davidson: We can also extend the schools outward to include the museums and the sports arenas and the motion picture theaters.

Huck: Nobody has mentioned enlarging the classroom to include the community, using the work-study approach of the engineering college or the apprenticeship involving a year spent in doing service, whether in the library or in industry. Is that a viable model?

Emig: It's a school-without-walls model. It has succeeded well in Philadelphia, and from what I saw of Metro school in Chicago, I'm convinced of the success of that approach.

Squire: I can remember alternative education in my own life. Drafted into the Army in the middle of my college career, I was projected into a whole different world of people, values, concerns, and responsibilities. The "drop out" experience modified my perspective, and helped me see the value of similar informal educational experiences for all young people. I remember a wise English teacher, when I first started teaching English and was having a terrible time controlling eighth graders, saying "Well, remember, Mr. Squire, that the good Lord went into the wilderness when he was twelve years old." The thought has always stayed with me that there should be a way for each twelve-year-old child to go into his own personal wilderness for a year or two and then come back.

Davidson: Aren't there people who are planning the equivalent of the Australian walk-about for some of the kids in reform schools. The basic notion is that you really give them the experience of climbing mountains and finding out who they are in the process.

The Kettering report on performance in the high schools proposes that we guarantee a certain number of years of education for youngsters. Give them a voucher for so many years, let them out of the high school for a year or so, but guarantee that they can come back and continue.

Moffett: The school today is a kind of place where you should get a pluralistic experience. The more time you spend with people like yourself, the less you have to learn from them. This is an idea that has never been explored in school. I conceive of mixing grades seven through twelve in one school for one thing. And I think having adults in the school provides added experience. It wouldn't make much difference whether somebody is in or out of the school if the school had more pluralism within.

Davidson: We see parents clinging to the kind of culture they want their kids to grow up in. We have white-black groups in inner cities as well as those in suburban districts becoming more and more alike. There is a seeking for one's own kind. We're not going to see schools that are little microcosms of pluralistic society. The school must be responsive to the differences between communities.

Moffett: The fact is that culture tends to be homeostatic; that is, it tends to maintain stasis. Any culture stays together by placing certain constraints and applying sanctions to people outside of it. So if education is to maintain the culture, you have to define education to some extent as offering an alternative to the standard culture, as a way of hoping it will survive. There's a paradox entailed in maintaining a culture.

Developing Values

Lindley: Isn't there really a bigger question? I think of it as the Watergate question, in the sense that I found myself asking over and over again all during the Watergate hearings, "Where did these people find this set of values from which they operated?

Really, where did they find them?" And every time you looked at the educational setting to see whether anything had come out of that, you found that nothing had. The Nixon presidency was like a petri dish, in which the tendencies of those people could simply grow and multiply and prosper within that environment. Mitchell found his place, and Haldeman and Erlichmann found their places; and they did what they did; and none of it had to do with education at all.

Emig: The Watergate people were well-educated, but, of course, we'd say they were partially educated. And the indictment is what was not done by parents and by schools. Where was the development of a sense of responsibility? Where was the sense of responding to the ethics of the situation?

Squire: You can judge the behavior of individuals, but you can also say, in some ways, that the country responded. Janet's argument, extended to the country as a whole, provides support for what the educational system did for the country, however slow and cumbersome the resurgence of ethical and moral responsibility may have been. But despite the educational implications of Watergate, I do think we have some recent evidence of the role of schooling in shaping values. Have you read any of the IEA studies?[2] These demonstrate rather clearly that the literary education provided children does affect their perception of life, the way they look on literature, and the way they look on human values. Now to some extent this may be a reflection of the society that establishes this kind of education.

Emig: I see a connection here with our comments on the responsibility for basic skills. What are schools about? Dwayne Huebner has a wonderful compounded word, "response-ability,"[3] and I can imagine a school having a central kind of concern to teach "response-ability" in dealing with a personal meaning-making affair with literature and with language.

Lindley: An idea of this kind occurred to me as I was reading

2. Alan C. Purves, *Literature Education in Ten Countries: An Empirical Study*, International Studies in Evaluation II (New York: John Wiley & Sons, 1973).

3. Dwayne Huebner, *Language and Meaning* (Washington, D.C.: Association for Supervision & Curriculum Development, 1965).

Schwartz's book, *The Responsive Chord*.[4] He talks about the "principle of resonance," and his thesis is that, if you want to affect anybody by sending a message, you must be sure that the message contains something that person you're trying to affect already knows or recognizes. In fact, this is the only thing the person is going to respond to, or almost the only thing. It seems to me that his observation probably applies in the teaching and learning of literature, too. When a person responds to a work of literature, it is because he recognizes something in there that he already knew. It's not new to him. I think that one of the biggest problems we've had in the teaching of literature in the schools has been the assumption that we are teaching something new.

The Two Hemispheres of the Brain

Moffett: You may know that there's a lot of research going on now on the two hemispheres of the brain. There's been speculation for years, but now for the first time we have hard data emerging from studies of people who have had one or the other hemisphere damaged or have had brain surgery so that the two hemispheres have been cut off from each other. What is emerging from this research relates very much to our concern for values. It goes like this: The left hemisphere tends to specialize in verbal, analytical, linear ratiocination, in the intellectual. The right hemisphere is intuitive, metaphorical, analogical, and holistic. It processes data simultaneously rather than sequentially. The two hemispheres really correspond to the two kinds of computers we've made—the digital and the analogical. So, in a way, man has simply expressed a projection of his two hemispheres. I recommend reading Robert Ornstein's *Psychology of Consciousness*,[5] which summarizes for laymen the research and its implications. The importance of such studies is, I think, that it can now be shown that the operations of the metaphoric mode, the figurative mode in literature, with their resonance, are legitimate mental operations. In other words, they're not frills or nice things you didn't have time to get around to. This is half of the

4. Tony Schwartz, *The Responsive Chord* (Garden City, N.Y.: Doubleday & Co., 1973).

5. Robert Ornstein, *The Psychology of Consciousness* (San Francisco: W. H. Freeman & Co., 1972).

way we work. The culture is tremendously overly oriented to the linear and the analytic, which grows from the technocratic approach. A lot of what McLuhan was saying in his own way applies very much to what this group is saying from a different quarter. Bruner got at this in his own way with *Essays for the Left Hand*,[6] but unfortunately he was partly responsible for the overemphasis on ratiocination. Many believe that our culture is overloaded on that side. One reason we can't solve many problems is that everybody's been educated towards the left, analytic half, which breaks things down, and hence doesn't show the unity of things. The whole brain is a synthesis. The right hemisphere processes information simultaneously and pulls it together into analogs and metaphor. And this is exactly the kind of thing that is needed to solve today's problems, where the intricacies of national and international life, not to mention the intricacies of one's own individual life, are so great that you cannot solve the problems except by this mode.

Emig: The word I get is "balance"—balance between the two.

Moffett: A phrase that comes to my mind is the one that Virginia Woolf used, talking exactly about the same kind of ratiocinative people who shut off the rest of the organism. She said, "The weekly creak and screech of brains rinsed in cold water and wrung dry." She was aiming at just these characters coming out of law school and trying to run the country off the top of their heads only. So unconnected. Not only weren't they solving the problems they were commissioned to solve, they were making a mess of the country and their own personal lives, by not being able to interrelate everything.

Lindley: The great advantage of literature, though, is that you can return to it in its same form. The book is always there. It can be returned to. I think the principle of resonance does apply to, and through, any medium. But the notion of making literature into something special on those grounds seems to me is misplaced. A lot of English teachers have thought that somehow the experiences of literature are something special as compared to the experience of a film or a videotape.

Squire: Much of the power of film comes from its holistic impact. Literature, for many readers, is more difficult to reach and a

6. Jerome S. Bruner, *On Knowing: Essays for the Left Hand* (New York: Atheneum, 1965).

little less immediate. Nevertheless, if we look for too many connections between personal experience and literature, or too superficial connections, we miss some of the real power that literature can have on readers. A marvelous recent statement of this appears in Solzhenitsyn's Nobel Prize lecture describing the ways in which whole nations can transmit to other nations some sense of an experience the second nation has never had through literature or film or other forms of art.[7]

Writing and Composing

Emig: In talking about the teaching and learning of literature, we are, also, talking about the teaching and learning of writing. In this area we must allow for teaching writing in a reflexive or poetic mode, as well as in the transactional or expository mode. I would say, facetiously, that I think it would be very persuasive to the community to say, "Your children are only using 50 percent of their brains. That's very inefficient. It's un-American, really." Perhaps if children were to engage in certain other kinds of activities, they would have access to the other half of their brains. Certain kinds of reading and writing will contribute to this, if they write in the poetic mode, if they read a range of literatures. Perhaps the metaphoric mode is the most efficient method of learning. It coalesces a number of processes at once.

Lindley: It's inefficient to live on half your mind. That's a marvelous way to put it.

Moffett: There's a kind of double standard operating in the field of English. It is all right for kids to read literature, but not to write it. Many young people are asked to do a very narrow kind of expository writing—usually about their reading. And it's strictly left hemisphere stuff and a limited range of that. But as readers in school, they read mainly literature. This is really a double standard. If we had an objective, impartial definition of communications behind English teaching, then it would bring out the balance of sending and receiving as being equal in all modes and open up tremendously the range of ways in which kids can discourse, can

7. Aleksandr Solzhenitsyn, *The Nobel Lecture on Literature*, trans. Thomas P. Whitney (New York: Harper & Row, Publishers, 1972).

write as well as read. There wouldn't be any less literature; there would be more of it. The more they write in these literary modes, the more they understand what they read in them. English teachers need a different way to talk to administrators in offering a rationale for experiences in English. Too often we sound like a dilettantish sort of fairies in trying to talk about poetic things.

Squire: Can English teachers talk to administrators with this kind of rationale until they understand it more deeply themselves? I've been called to high schools with short-course, elective programs to assist administrators in developing a rationale to interpret the programs to the public. The administrators like the new English programs. Enrollments have risen. English, instead of being a problem area, is a most popular one. But administrators cannot easily explain to parents what schools are doing. They have no trouble talking about the math curriculum, the foreign language curriculum, the science curriculum; but they don't know what to tell the parents about the English curriculum, except that it's "turning kids on." Parents want to know what children are learning.

Huck: I think this applies as well to elementary teachers. We must explain the notion that we want to provide a range of discourse. Teachers don't really recognize the differences between modes of discourse and what we are working for in extending children's writing experiences. So much emphasis is placed upon writing stories, but children must be encouraged to write expository prose as well.

Emig: One real problem is our predilection for false dichotomizing—either we are dealing with skills or we're dealing with "expression." There is real traffic between the two parts of the brain, and there's no alternative to this if we are to be living creatures.

Lindley: I have an impression—only an impression—that by the seventh grade or so, the notion of writing for an audience is gone. Little children seem to have an intuitive sense of audience. They have the feeling, just based on faith, that somebody else is going to see that stuff, or hear it, or what not. But by the seventh grade that whole thing is pretty much gone, and the whole thing is just a ritualistic act for the English teacher. On the other hand, the minute a high school student takes on the task of doing a slide-tape presentation or a film, immediately that same intuitive sense of audience returns. I don't know why that is; I just know it's there. You can feel it—vibrantly—in the classroom.

Moffett: If anybody is going to do anything about the teaching of writing, the first priority is going to have to be the rekindling of the sense of audience. Until that's done, nothing else is going to happen.

Emig: Some recent infant studies show that, within the first six to twelve hours of life, infants are already responding to adult speech by coordinated movements, which suggests that there's something quite basic that is requisite to rhetoric, an awareness of another person. And what we're suggesting is, rather than enhancing sense of audience by our activities, somehow, in many of the school activities, we've been deadening what seems to be again a biological kind of correlation.

Squire: You are talking about some kind of a holistic, unified approach rooted in basic communication theory that will undergird all of the school efforts. Yet the movement toward short courses, minicourses, and alternatives seems to be a move toward fragmentation, at least as it is presently being carried over. If an experience in preparing a film-slide is important, really important, for all kids, why is it offered only as one of thirty-eight options?

Moffett: I think the solution is to have all experiences going on within the same room or "pool," so that each can act as audience for the other. Small working parties doing different things at the same time. An elective system, in a sense, is too compartmentalized into separate groups and separate times. You want them, I think, in the same pool so that each group can see what the other is doing and be influenced.

Hipple: I've recently discovered that the mere existence of an elective course in composition or writing has lessened the amount of writing going on in other courses. Teachers feel they don't have to stress writing in the short story elective, in the "British lit." elective, or whatever, because they require students to take an elective course on writing.

Emig: One of the problems is that there are very few teachers who've been successful in teaching composition, and therefore most don't feel comfortable with it. This elective thing offers an out for them. When you ask a principal or consultant today "How are you going to evaluate the basic skills of writing?" they never come up with a thought-through answer. The desire to be free to choose the kind of electives that they wanted to teach and that youngsters want to be taught, has not caused them to face up with, "What eventually do I want the outcome of this program to do, to be?"

Moffett: I think of electives as a way station on the way to real individualization. It's in the right direction, but it doesn't go far enough. It's crude management of an individualization that we will not learn to achieve until we finally make our schools more flexible. A kid takes a certain course for nine or sixteen weeks, an arbitrary time-length, with only one teacher and a handful of other kids. Such courses have too many limitations. There needs to be a bigger pool of resources, so that students can work with several teachers and different kids and benefit from more *ad hoc* groups.

Lindley: I find myself coming back to this in my own methods courses. I guess I would go back to the notion that the reason you teach writing is to illuminate the student's life, an entirely different thing from achieving competence in writing.

Moffett: You are suggesting that the purpose of the teaching of writing for many students is not only to develop basic competence in the ability to communicate in writing, but also to achieve goals of self-expression and control of one's own reactions.

Emig: I hope we'll be able to show within the next twenty years that there are particular, and perhaps unique, cognitive values to writing—that writing is a mode for learning that has unique attributes. I, for one, am interested in devoting some energy to this. For example, in once looking at Bruner's strategies for learning and also looking at the properties of the written, of the analytic mode, I found an incredibly high match between how we learn and the properties of the mode, such as the ability to form generalizations.

Lindley: But Janet, how can you say that writing has some particular or special attribute as a reflexive or intuitive machine when most of the people of the world never write anything and evidently function in a cognitive way? Writing and literacy, in a sense are very specialized and rather aristocratic.

Emig: Again, I'm proceeding introspectively and I come from a very narrow culture.

Moffett: An interesting thing about the two hemispheres of the brain is that both are verbal in kids up to around six or seven years. This is extraordinary. Both halves process ideas verbally and non-verbally until that time. Only after they begin to specialize, around eight or nine years, does one become nonverbal and the other verbal. This change corresponds to a period when there is a tremendous slump in school. After primary schooling, kids who are able to read and to write, suddenly . . . it's almost as if they hadn't learned. Teachers look back at those scores and say, "My God, what happened?" All of a sudden this kid is headed toward being a drop-out. You know how they loved to write stories, and they don't anymore. Well, I think we should connect the change with the fact that after about two or three years into school, the full force of acculturation, stereotyping, and emphasis on the pragmatic, the analytic mode has a real impact on the kid. The way some people explain the sudden specialization of the two hemispheres is that, in order to salvage the metaphorical mode and the holistic, one hemisphere has to dissociate itself from language.[8] This is where the two begin to specialize. In order to survive, the intuitive, the metaphorical has to dissociate itself from language, which means, then, that there's a cut-off between some basic thinking processes and verbalization. It's my own feeling that this is where kids really drop off terribly in school.

Squire: What you're observing, Jim, with respect to young children in school, I've noticed with graduate students, particularly those in English Education and English. You can call this acculturation, you can call it bombardment with unassimilated ideas, whatever, but their writing is dreadful. It's probably at its worst about the time when they're doing their dissertations. A couple of years later the same people can rewrite their ideas beautifully, perhaps because their equilibrium is back in balance.

Moffett: The way I interpret that, Jim, is the tremendous emphasis on the explicit, analytic mode.

Lindley: Can you imagine somebody being allowed to submit his Ph.D. thesis in the metaphoric mode? They'd say, "Get out of here. You've got to be explicit and tell us . . .".

Squire: I think it also results from an enormous amount of un-

8. See, for example, Joseph Chilton Pearce, *Exploring the Crack in the Cosmic Egg* (New York: Julian Press, 1974).

assimilated new knowledge that people can't quite put into focus. The same experience of unassimilation affects students during various periods in their lives. Whenever one moves from comparative balance in his own environment to new experiences and new ideas, new groups, association with new values, ideas being questioned— whenever this happens, it momentarily affects one's command of language.

Huck: Much of this seems related to requiring or assigning tasks just about the time the child begins to develop some power in writing.

Moffett: He's got to sober up and face the real world now and quit writing stories.

Huck: And this happens to the Ph.D. student. He's faced with having to write that damned dissertation. And I know more of them who just can't get to that. They can think of all kinds of other things to do instead.

Emig: The reason I'm concerned about this business about whether or not writing has unique cognitive values, is its justification for staying alive in the curriculum. I guess it's an article of faith. I happen to think there are values. Is this a private opinion?

Squire: Dan was suggesting certainly that the emphasis on achieving a degree of competence in a certain kind of writing for all students may be an impossible, perhaps unnecessary, and certainly low-priority task.

Lindley: I have the impression that the majority of English teachers, especially of the secondary, run-of-the-mill "entry level," really expect that every child ought to be able to write pieces right out of E.B. White's mouth. They expect that kind of lucid, brilliant simplicity that only E.B. White can write.

Hipple: But similarly, Dan, they expect the students will use language as the teachers use language and that they will read literature with the insights that teachers have. Those expectations generally are soundly diminished by the end of the first September . . .

Lindley: I'm only trying to make the case that I just don't agree with Janet that writing has its unique cognitive construction.

Moffett: How about composing?

Lindley: Composing. Absolutely essential, isn't it?

Emig: . . . Across modalities, though.

Lindley: Right, the medium in which the composing is done I take to be absolutely irrelevant. Take, for instance, the fact that a person living in the black slave culture of this country before the Civil War could create in a carved walking stick a preservation of a culture that went back thousands of years, and that that walking stick continued to reflect that culture to the people who could read it. I take this to be the same act. I don't care whether it's symbolic or . . .

Moffett: Universals in the creative process. I agree with you. Composition actually cuts across all the media. Verbalizing is only one kind of composition. One direction we're moving in is toward pluralism in symbolic processes—alternative ways of symbolizing. Suzanne Langer long ago led the way in this direction. Each art as being a "semantic" in the forms and modes of human feeling.

Lindley: What are we doing about it, Jim?

Moffett: Emphasis on media is one thing. I've been consulting recently with National Humanities Faculty, which has various projects under way around the country trying to put the arts and the media and language together, so the humanities is now being construed not just as a kind of core for English and social studies, but a broader spectrum.

Lindley: But the irony of the humanities is that the test of one's experience in the humanities is often whether the person can write about it. This seems to me too narrow a test.

Modes of Symbolization

Squire: Dorothy, in the program of education for "Texas in the Eighties," on which you have worked, what will you be doing about some of these ideas?

Davidson: Our problem is promoting change with teachers educated in single disciplines. What can we do to cross those disciplines and come out with a curriculum that enhances interrelationships? We foresee several curriculums, all coexisting within a comprehensive school with differing time frames put upon them or different pupils entering into them in different ways. The first one, a problem-focused curriculum, would pool together a team of teachers of social studies and science that would try to focus upon learning to work in groups, learning to solve real problems, using the subject matters from whatever disciplines were necessary, particularly science and social studies and health.

Our goal is to develop an informed citizen. This curriculum would begin in elementary and continue in various degrees throughout schooling. The second was the curriculum for humanistic values, also a multidisciplinary approach, which would involve the fine arts, literature, the social sciences.

Hipple: How do you avoid setting up a new kind of dichotomy in a curriculum? It almost sounds as if you're not going to use these humanistic values in solving problems.

Davidson: What we're trying to do is break slowly out of one kind of mode during the next ten years, and perhaps then we will move out some more. The third curriculum for specialization would, for example, keep an English program intact for college entrance. It would try to get the ideas across to youngsters that, for vocational competence, for avocational competence, for continuing-education competence, you have to have a commitment to a single discipline, or a single focus, and that you begin developing that. In other words, if you're going to learn a foreign language, you have to devote eight years of your life to it and focus upon it, or move to a foreign country.

Emig: Is there an alternative perhaps where we could start giving courses called, say, something like "symbolics?"

Davidson: This would be possible in our program. A fourth curriculum would be for personal growth and development, projected as a highly individualized, diagnostic, guidance-supported program.

Lindley: But the whole question of curriculum or the whole question of alternative curricula seems to me to beg the big question. The word curriculum implies a linear organization, as writing implies a linear organization. Schools imply a linear organization. I hate to keep sounding like warmed-over McLuhan. I think at the root of this problem of where writing is, is the McLuhan question; that is, the question of the medium and its fusion with the message. During the last twenty years, with the advent of electronic communication, we have seen over the world an increasing tolerance for the cool and the multisensory. I see a shift—a continuing, ongoing shift. If there is any hope for avoiding Dixon's civil war, it's in the shift of consciousness; that is to say, that the change of consciousness will take everyone willy-nilly along in its tide and will eventually reduce the conflict between the "hot" linear people and the "cool" multisensory orientated people. If this is true, then it seems to me that schools either are going to have to go on with the shift and become "cool," or less linear, or they really will become even more irrelevant than they are now. You can not be struck by anything more powerfully than by going into the school and seeing how the kids don't care about it. The kids will use every tactic in the book to destroy the linear structure of that school. That's what they're doing now. I think we've got to go with the increasing tolerance for "coolness."

Moffett: I don't think we have to decide ahead of time which media are "hot" or "cool." Put all the media out there in an array, a spectrum, competing as well as complementing. Sometimes they work together; sometimes they're alternative to each other. And let kids find out what language can do and what it can't do in which situations, for what subjects, . . . and when you're better off with graphics.

One problem that I don't feel that McLuhan finished thinking through is that print is not just a linear medium. *Moby Dick* is not just a product of the digital hemisphere. It has the metaphorical mode built in. The white whale is not literal. It's a holistic cluster of concepts and meanings.

I think the intuitive side of us has a way of shunting its own mode into the linear processing. It sneaks it in there by figures of speech. It's possible to build into a linear medium, another level of depth, or a "deep" structure, if you want to use the popular term. It's done in literature through metaphor. I don't think that McLuhan allows for that; in other words, a certain mode can be *both* "hot" *and* "cool," in his terms. I think electronic media are linear for one thing; any time you have a succession of images, you have something linear. Any one image may be spatial and simultaneous and holistic, but when you have a succession of them, the medium is linear. So it, too, is both. I wouldn't want us to figure out the curriculum just on the basis of his distinctions. Rather, let's just put them all into play and let the kid work with all of them and let him find out what does what under what circumstances.

Huck: I wouldn't want to limit them either. I think that the use of media, as I'm thinking about school media programs, has been a real copout, particularly for schools in urban situations where it's much easier to hook kids up in the morning and unhook them at night than to teach them to read. I think that there are some communities that are recognizing that this is a real copout. So even as we talk about visual literacy being very important for living today, we must not see it as a substitute for learning to read.

Lindley: But that's what the schools do now. They talk about media. My feeling is that if the kid doesn't do it, he doesn't create media in the school. It's the same old print-oriented analytic mode. Even with *Moby Dick*, we ask the kid to treat it linearly.

Emig: We want something productive to occur, rather than something receptive.

Squire: This is essentially what disturbs me about the term, "media literacy." Some people talk about it as if there are basic skills related to media reception.

Lindley: Media literacy will kill off the media the same way "print literacy" has killed off the study of literature. You can't apply the analytic, new-critical, Brooks and Warren routine on *Lucas Tanner*.

Moffett: What you're bringing up is the issue of evaluation. As we engage kids in the multilevel metaphoric mode, evaluation is going to have to fit that mode, and not just the linear.

Squire: We haven't spent much time on evaluation. The issue of evaluation relates to the problem of trying to communicate to parents what we are doing in schools. Until we can find better ways of evaluating some of the kinds of things we are talking about, so that teachers can assure themselves and kids can be assured that they are making progress, we are going to have difficulty communicating what our programs are about. I'm not thinking of more paper and pencil instruments. I just know that even if we can clarify our own perceptions with respect to linear and nonlinear media and alternate kinds of symbolism, we have to find some way for teachers, for parents, and for kids to know that they're achieving some degrees of growth in language development. I don't see that we are very close to that now, but it is one of the big problems that we face.

Huck: We have some sophisticated measurement tools but the teacher doesn't know how to use them. If you want to measure whether an environment allows children to talk, we don't bother using T-unit or vocabulary-diversity measurement, because most teachers don't know about them. I think we have the measures, and that part of our job is to make them more usable. Miscue analysis, for example, offers a whole range of new kinds of measurements that we could be using, and we fall back invariably on the paper-pencil kind of test.

Moffett: The problem is to detect growth without necessarily using diagnostic tests, but by relying on human judgment. I don't think there's any great mystery about finding out whether basic skills are being delivered. The problem is that we haven't been delivering them and our methods of evaluation make it look somehow as if it takes real sophisticated wizardry to figure out why. You can listen to a kid read aloud for a few minutes and learn an enormous amount. So, evaluation, in a sense, is sort of a red herring, a phony issue, and it's not nearly as difficult as it's made out to be.

Final Thoughts

Squire: Are there any final concerns about the future direction of English teaching that we haven't really dwelled upon?

Huck: I hope we give attention to the very young child in that I think that the child comes to school with the best years of his learning past. We are really giving less attention than we should to the training of those teachers who are apt to be teaching in the nursery school. We don't even have them certified. And yet this is the time of the greatest cognitive learning, the greatest period of language acquisition.

Lindley: Just to summarize how I feel about the whole nonprint or image side of where I think we're going, Walker Evans once said to me, quoting an art teacher he knew, "You know, looking is much tougher than it looks."

Emig: I think we've been talking a great deal about what constitutes the nature of evidence that's persuasive to a range of audiences. If I had a hope for the next twenty years, it is that those of us who are concerned with theory and research would not only ask the important questions but find ways of being persuasive about what we think we know about the best means for learning the teaching of language.

Hipple: Just as Charlotte thinks that schools, learning, and teacher training will be extended downward, I hope that it will be extended upward. All our thrust has been on the present-age children. Maybe it's my Florida background, but parts of St. Petersburg are among the most depressing scenes I've ever seen. Retirees there are living out their lives in quiet desperation, unlike the young people whose desperation is not quite so quiet. I think we need to get these people back into the schools more, both as learners and as workers. This will tie in with something Janet was saying earlier about providing some alternative kinds of modes of instruction in the school. The kid who wants to learn bricklaying is perhaps going to be able to learn it from a guy who is a retired bricklayer. I can't conceive of schooling stopping at grade 14, the community college level. I think we've got to see it extending over a much longer range.

Moffett: I predict that the perceptions about the inner life that are coalescing now will help us to see that language is just the visible surface of a tremendous amount underneath that we have been very naive about and have really ignored. It's much easier to deal with the visible, which is language, than the invisible, which is a whole experiential world and a world of thought and perception that determines what really comes out at the surface level of language.

This relates to teacher training, too. I think we are going to be more concerned with and sophisticated about states of consciousness and states of mind, and how they can be deliberately controlled. People are beginning to learn to control states of mind and body that used to be considered part of the *involuntary* nervous system. This will have a lot to do with reading, for example, because there is a correlation between absorption and proficiency in reading and hypnotic susceptibility. There's a certain state that you go into when you read deeply with comprehension, and speed reading may be definitely related to a certain altered state of consciousness. And writing will be better understood as a kind of regulation of inner speech. The importance, I think, of meditation techniques, and there are many of them, is that they teach control of verbal thinking—to turn it off, or to focus it on something. Verbal composition is simply focused inner speech. I think we're going to learn a lot more about this that will naturally have to enter into teacher training, because the teacher will have to start undergoing the kinds of experiences to learn to control inner states that they will to try to teach their kids. I think the breakthrough in teacher education will come from outside of education. Groups like the Association of Humanistic Psychology or the outfit that the astronaut, Edgar Mitchell, founded, the Institute of Noetic Sciences, are getting more and more interested in education. People outside the field will bring into education kinds of experiences that will make it possible to change and to break the classroom-public-School of Education cycle. Telepathy is one of these things. What happens when telepathy becomes the sort of thing that anybody can learn to do? It's definitely on the way. The whole world of psychic phenomena is just breaking through with tremendous establishment support from M.D.'s, scientists, and others. I would suggest that you look at *Psychic Exploration* by Edgar Mitchell.[9] He has edited an anthology of articles from many different, very well-established fields. There's just simply no joke about so-called "psychic phenomena." How will they affect regular verbal communication? This is a major challenge we face during the next two decades.

Squire: However uncertain many teachers of English may feel about some of the ideas advanced in this discussion, however at variance some may seem with current practice and research, the fact remains that from the radical ideas of today may emerge the major curriculum trends of tomorrow. It is not easy for most of us to predict evolutionary changes in the teaching and learning of reading and writing, much less the consequences that could result from studies of human consciousness. It seems to me that if some of the more radical "abilities" discussed here (e.g., ESP, clairvoyance, unique mind states) do come into common usage and utility, they will serve exactly the same purpose as the more traditional educational practice—to make formal learning safer and more effective than learning from raw experience. Members of the panel have served an important role in identifying current thrusts that need to be carefully watched.

9. Edgar Mitchell, *Psychic Exploration* (New York: G. P. Putnam's Sons, 1974).

CHAPTER XI

Forces at Work: English Teaching in Context, Present to Perhaps

EDMUND J. FARRELL*

Forecasting the Future

Planning for the future was once the business principally of "think tanks" working under covert contracts. Today it is a public enterprise.[1] Scarcely a week passes without the publication of a handful of books outlining the urgent need for more thoughtful planning in the use of human and natural resources or in the structure and performance of social institutions. Since 1967, the World Future Society, located in Washington, D.C., has published *The Futurist: A Journal of Forecasts, Trends and Ideas about the Future* and has offered to its members at discount an ever growing list of books (by 1975, over 130) about possible futures facing the human species. In education alone the outpour of publications having to do with the need for reformation—or even abolition —of schooling has been torrential. In *Alternative Futures for Learning*, itself a 223-page annotated bibliography of publications about possible futures for education, Michael Marien observes that the quantity of such literature nearly doubled between 1966 and 1968 and more than doubled between 1968 and 1970.[2] The twenty-three volumes published between 1967 and 1973 by the Carnegie Com-

---

* The consultant reader for this chapter was Maxwell H. Goldberg, Helmus Distinguished Professor of Humanities and Literature, Converse College, Spartanburg, South Carolina.

1. Examples of such research institutes are the Rand Corporation, Hudson Institute, and Stanford Research Institute. For a discussion of the influence that such organizations have had on American life, see Paul Dickson, *Think Tanks* (New York: Atheneum Publishers, 1971).

2. Michael Marien, *Alternative Futures for Education* (Syracuse, N.Y.: Syracuse University Research Corporation, 1971).

mission on Higher Education are alone a small library, containing thousands of pages and thousands of recommendations for the reform of higher education in the United States. And the Carnegie Commission, though better financed and more prolific than most, was only one among many prestigious commissions, committees, and panels established between 1965 and 1975 to seek the improvement of secondary and postsecondary education.[3]

Why this growing concern about what may lie ahead for mankind? And how is education as an institution affected by permutations or alternations occurring not just within itself but within other areas of the society—or, for that matter, in other areas of the world? More narrowly, to what degree is English, as a subject housed in the institution of education, shaped by winds of change blowing both inside and outside classroom walls?

Many legitimate reasons exist for Americans' concern about the future of their nation and of the human species: phenomenal and continuing growth in world population; proliferation of armaments nationally and internationally; rapid depletion of finite natural resources; harmful, and at times lethal, pollution of the environment; an increasing possibility of pharmacological and genetic control of human behavior; the probability of social and educational apartheid as white suburbs concentrate impoverished blacks, Puerto Ricans, and Mexican Americans in inner cities; an explosive rise in information and communication, which can be conveyed through various media; mounting rates for violence and crime in the United States; possible loss of democratic pluralism and the rise of authoritarian government as the need intensifies to respond quickly to complex problems; evidence of major shifts in values and in sexual roles within the culture; a massive transfer of capital from industrialized nations to member nations of the Organization of Petroleum Exporting Countries (OPEC); the changing nature of work and the place of leisure in the society.

Education as institution and English as subject are markedly sensitive to and influenced by the malaises, aspirations, and commit-

---

3. Others include the Education Commission of the States, the Newman Commission, the President's Commission on School Finance, the Fleischmann Commission, the National Commission on the Reform of Secondary Education, and the Panel on Youth of the President's Science Advisory Committee.

ments of the society at large. During the 1960s schools were temporarily closed by such diverse events as assassinations of national leaders, students' celebrations of "Earth Day," rioting in inner cities, failures of school tax elections, and students' protest against the continued fighting of American armed forces in Vietnam, Laos, and Cambodia. In recent years the subject of English has been forced to respond to the rightful desires of ethnic minorities and women that their contributions to literature be recognized and that their lives and values be represented accurately in textbooks; it has had to accommodate rapid and continuing growth in linguistic scholarship, particularly in psycholinguistics, sociolinguistics, and dialectology; and it has been compelled to broaden its curriculum to include study of film, mass media, and popular culture. Further, legislative demands for responsible justification of tax expenditures have shaped in part both education and English during the past decade, for "accountability" brought with it the writing of performance objectives, massive programs of testing, and new budgetary systems for the schools. At present both education and the profession of English teaching are being adversely affected by inflation and budgetary cutbacks; surpluses of teachers at all levels; declining enrollments of elementary-age students; growing violence in schools, which has necessitated the policing of school halls in many cities; and censorious groups of citizens who attempt to remove from classrooms materials they find objectionable.

In short, education as institution and English as subject exist in an environment which is simultaneously global, national, and local. The explosion of an atomic bomb in India, a decision by OPEC to increase oil prices, the layoff of workers in Detroit, the growth of poppies in Mexico, racial violence attendant upon bussing students in Boston, increased national sales of cassette tape recorders, the burning of books in North Dakota—all to lesser or greater extent contribute to the practices and the tone of contemporary American education, of which English teaching is a part.

No author of a single chapter of a book can do adequate justice to any one of a list of long- or short-range problems and concerns, let alone encompass them all. Even less can he detail the relationship between these matters and the future of English teaching. In limited space, the author cannot begin to explicate the various methods and techniques by which forecasters attempt to determine in the context of present restraints the alternative futures possible to humans.[4] For that matter he cannot presume to enumerate all the options possible among alternative images of the future, for such options are multitudinous. All that he can do in the space allotted is sketch what he believes to be some major areas for concern among the many that should profoundly matter to us all as human beings, citizens, parents, educators, and teachers of English. Of importance finally is not that we acknowledge the presence of complex issues or problems but that we sense fully their gravity with respect to the well-being of human existence. Only out of deeply felt disquietude about the present will come whatever intelligent choices remain available to assure the highest possible quality of life for future generations and for ourselves. Whether any conscious choices can shield mankind from large-scale catastrophes and tragedies in the decades ahead is problematic, but intelligent choices should help mitigate the worst that might befall us, should help us look beyond immediate abysses to the possibilities of better tomorrows.

Population

Because the quality of life is dependent upon adequate availability of food, shelter, clothing, health care, sanitation, transportation, educational facilities, and sufficient "life space" for individuals to realize their potentiality as human beings, the continued growth of population is the most serious problem now confronting mankind. Kahn and Wiener note that from 8000 B.C. to 1650 A.D. world population grew at a rate of 50 percent each thousand years, but that from 1650 to 1965 the rate of millennial growth was 2,000 percent, or forty times greater in the modern age than in the premodern.[5]

4. For a discussion of modes of forecasting, see Erich Jantsch, *Technological Forecasting in Perspective* (Paris: Organization for Economic Cooperation and Development, 1967); Bertrand de Jouvenel, *The Art of Conjecture* (New York: Basic Books, 1967); Daniel Bell, *The Coming of Post-Industrial Society* (New York: Basic Books, 1973); James R. Bright, *A Brief Introduction to Technology Forecasting: Concepts and Exercises* (Austin, Tex.: Permaquid Press, Division of Industrial Management Center, 1411 West Avenue, 78701, 1972).

5. Herman Kahn and Anthony J. Wiener, *The Year 2000: A Framework for Speculation on the Next Thirty-three Years* (New York: Macmillan Co., 1967).

Demographers estimate that it took tens of thousands of years from the evolutionary emergence of *homo sapiens* until 1850 A.D. for the population of the earth to reach one billion, but it took only seventy-five additional years to attain a second billion and a mere thirty-seven years to reach a third billion.

World population, which was 1.5 billion at the start of this century, is now close to 4 billion. With the highest rate of growth in human history (about 2 percent per year), the world is currently adding nearly eighty million people per year and is expected to double its population in less than thirty-five years. Most of the increase will occur in the underdeveloped countries, which already contain almost three-fourths of the earth's population. While death rates in these countries have dropped considerably in the past twenty-five years, so that they now approach the low levels found in the developed countries, birth rates remain twice as high as those of industrialized nations.

Even if population rates stabilized at the rate of replacement by the end of the century, world population would be 8.2 billion in 2050, with more than 90 percent of the additional four-plus billion living in less developed countries. Although many of these countries label as neocolonialism any attempts by affluent nations to persuade them to limit their populations through birth-control programs, what is clear is that the present rate of growth cannot continue indefinitely. As Ansley Coale observes:

Without doubt this period of growth will be a transitory period in the history of the population. If the present rate were to be maintained, the population would double approximately every 35 years, it would be multiplied by 1,000 every 350 years and by a million every 700 years. The consequences of sustained growth at this pace are clearly impossible; in less than 700 years there would be one person for every square foot on the surface of the earth; in less than 1,200 years the human population would outweigh the earth; in less than 6,000 years the mass of humanity would form a sphere expanding at the speed of light.[6]

The problem of adequately providing for the earth's increasing population is compounded by the fact that approximately 37 percent of the present population is under fifteen years of age, with the per-

6. Ansley J. Coale, "The History of the Human Population," *Scientific American* 231 (September 1974): 51.

centage rising to well over 40 in most underdeveloped nations. We have, in short, a mass population of the young, many of whom, though dependent upon others for survival, are capable of reproducing and of creating thereby yet another generation of dependents. Thus swiftly do the numbers rise of those who must look to others for help in meeting life's most basic needs.

Food

Because of better seeds, improved irrigation, development of chemical fertilizers, pesticides, herbicides, and fungicides, and the substitution of mechanical energy for manpower, the efficiency of agriculture in North America permits less than 5 percent of the population to grow enough food to exceed national needs. However, the "problem" of disposing of surplus foods—the dominant agricultural problem in the 1950s for the United States, Canada, Australia, and some European countries—is no more. Adverse weather in 1972 led to a decline in food production in the Soviet Union, China, India, Australia, Southeast Asia, and sections of Africa, and to a decline in world food reserves. (By November 1974 the world's reserves of grains, which had been ample for 95 days in 1961, had dropped to a supply of about 26 days.) Too, the rapid growth of agricultural production in many developed countries began to slow down about 1972. Finally, despite phenomenal agricultural productivity during the two decades preceding 1972, world population had grown almost as rapidly as the production of food.

Greatly increased prices in recent years for fertilizers, oil, and grain have exacerbated the difficulty less developed countries have in feeding their populations. Because they possess neither a capacity to produce commodities for large scale export nor large foreign exchange reserves, poorer nations lack the funds necessary to purchase the food, fuel, and fertilizer they desperately need to prevent the spread of malnutrition and starvation among their populations, malnutrition and starvation already being suffered by close to a half-billion human beings, principally in Africa, Asia, and Latin America.

As Thomas W. Wilson, Jr., rightly points out in his concluding report of a summer workshop conducted by the Program in Environment and Quality of Life, one of a series of programs conducted by the Aspen Institute for Humanistic Studies, "the world food problem cannot be resolved in isolation from the related world problems of population, energy, environment and resources." [7] Agronomists who assert that the earth can feed many times its present population appear to overlook the huge expenditures of money and natural energy, the dislocation of populations, and the disruptions of ecosystems that would be required to put under cultivation enormous numbers of untilled acres. Nor do they seem to attend to vagaries of climatic conditions, including the strong possibility that the earth is entering a cyclical cooling period that will last for decades; the earth's limited supply of fresh water; or the amount of space and mobility needed by persons in order for them to feel most physically free and most fully human. As a means of feeding the hungry and starving, Wilson finds increased yields from land under cultivation, not new acreage, to be most important:

The best hope of raising world food production lies in increased yields from land already under the plow and the greatest prospect of feeding a growing world population therefore lies in narrowing the gaps between the least and the most efficient yields of food per unit of land.[8] (Wilson's italics)

Even though adequately feeding a growing population, at least during the next few decades, will necessitate an increase in the productivity of land already under cultivation, American citizens could alleviate some hunger in poorer nations by reducing consumption of meat, a minor sacrifice that would make available for export millions of additional tons of grain. At present, those in less developed countries eat approximately 400 pounds of grain per capita annually, mainly in the form of bread or gruel, but Americans consume five times that amount per capita, mainly in the form of grain-fed chicken, pork, and beef. While it takes a pound of grain to make a pound of bread, it requires two pounds of grain to produce a pound of chicken, four pounds of grain to make a pound of pork, and ten pounds of grain to produce a pound of beef. Beef consumption in the United States rose from 56 pounds per capita in 1954 to 117 pounds per capita in 1974, an increase that prompted

7. Thomas W. Wilson, Jr., *World Food: The Political Dimension* (Aspen, Col.: Aspen Institute for Humanistic Studies, 1974), p. 11.

8. Ibid., p. 32.

Dr. Lester Brown of the Overseas Development Council to estimate that if Americans reduced meat consumption by only 10 percent for one year, they would free at least 12 million tons of grain, enough to feed 60 million starving persons.[9] Annually we feed our livestock as much grain as all the people in China and India eat in a year; further, because of the inefficiency with which most animals produce protein, the Department of Agriculture has estimated that manure from American livestock contains as much protein as our entire soybean crop.[10]

Ironically, what surpluses of food were available through the Food for Peace program have gone in recent years to South Vietnam, Cambodia, South Korea, Israel, Pakistan, Chile, Jordan, Syria, Egypt and Indonesia—in short, to countries we thought important for military and political reasons rather than to countries in dire want. Once noted for its beneficence to the needy of the world, by 1974 the United Statese ranked fourteenth of sixteen industrial nations, among them most European countries, Japan, Australia, and Canada, in terms of the share of gross national product provided to developing countries through various assistance programs, including food aid.[11] Nevertheless, as sale of U.S. wheat to Russia in 1972 and 1975 testified, even the studied policy of using food assistance to win political friends has been subordinate to the desire to sell surpluses to the highest bidder:

Since World War II, food aid has been a significant element in American foreign policy, regarded as a way both to win friends and to serve development in these countries, while keeping popular discontent within politically manageable bounds. These foreign policy goals, however, have always been secondary to the primary domestic purpose of supporting farm income by providing a market for surpluses. And now that commercial exports sop up almost all our excess production, there is far less political pressure to keep food flowing to hungry countries without a cash return.[12]

9. Boyce Rensberger, *New York Times,* 25 October 1974, p. 1.

10. Frances Moore Lappe, "Fantasies of Famine," *Harper's* 230 (February 1975): 52.

11. Harold G. Shane, "The Coming Global Famine: A Kappan Interview with Lester R. Brown," *Phi Delta Kappan* 56 (September 1974): 36.

12. Stephen S. Rosenfeld, "What Happened to 'America the Beneficent'?" *Saturday Review/World* 1 (18 December 1973): 19.

The absence of a humanitarian impulse aside, the policy of allowing either immediate political or economic goals to dictate allocation of surplus foods to countries other than those in greatest need may ill serve the nation in the long run. With 6 percent of the world's population, the United States has been utilizing 30 to 40 percent of the annual production of the world's natural resources. Since it is dependent upon many less developed nations for such resources and commodities as coffee, bananas, aluminum, manganese, nickel, tin, zinc, and chromium, it is as subject to the politics of scarcity as are less affluent nations.

OPEC is not the sole international cartel determined to make industrialized nations pay dearly for resources that have for long been cheaply obtained. Too, as India, has made clear, an economically depressed nation is nevertheless capable of constructing and detonating a nuclear bomb. Robert Heilbroner speculates on the possibility that malnourished and starving nations, with little to lose, may in time use nuclear weapons to blackmail the industrialized world into redistributing its wealth, including its food.[13] Sheer self-interest, then, should motivate Americans to reduce their consumption, particularly of meat, in order to share their abundance with those in the poorest countries. Beyond such motivation one would hope that through discussion of current events and of literature depicting the lives of oppressed people, teachers of English could help students discover principles that transcend self-interest, principles that morally obligate those in this nation to assist, through both material goods and education for self-determination, deprived human beings with whom they occupy the planet.

Energy

American technology has helped produce one of the highest standards of living in any nation on earth. Most Americans (but certainly not all) have been paid well; have been fed, clothed, and housed well; and have had at their disposal more bathtubs, automobiles, telephones, radios, refrigerators, freezers, television sets, and canned, packaged and bottled foods—in short, more creature

13. Robert Heilbroner, *An Inquiry into the Human Prospect* (New York: W. W. Norton & Co., 1974).

comforts—than other people on earth. But the comforts too often have come at the expense of wasted resources and skewed priorities, both at home and abroad. We have spent as much annually on air conditioning as the combined gross national products of Bolivia, Congo, Liberia, Haiti, and Guinea, while neglecting the proper care of our aged; we have spent six to eight billion dollars annually on cosmetics, toiletries, and fragrances, but less than one-fifth that on subsidizing low-cost housing; we have spent about a third of a billion dollars a year on paper towels for the home, far more than the federal government spent in fiscal 1972 for urban mass transportation.[14]

We have annually spewed into the environment tens of billions of throwaway soft drink and beer containers, and as many as 7 million cars, 100 million tires, and 20 million tons of paper.[15] From World War II to 1974, we doubled our consumption of electrical power every ten years. By 1972, our per capita consumption of energy was 11.6 metric tons of coal equivalent, compared with 5.4 tons for the affluent and industrialized West Germans. Rather than the darlings we have become the wastrels of the Western world, our prodigality dependent on the continued supply of cheap energy provided by oil.

With the oil embargo imposed by OPEC in 1973 and with the cartel's subsequent decisions to raise steeply their prices for exported oil, decades of low-cost energy ended abruptly for Americans, and a new period began of investigating alternative forms of energy—oil shale, offshore oil, solar energy, coal, wind, geothermal energy, nuclear energy, and refuse. With the possible exception of refuse, each alternative poses problems in regard to the time and money it will take for development and the potential harm it can do the environment. What has become obvious of late is that Americans can no longer have energy that is clean, secure, and cheap; energy that is cheap and secure is not clean, and that which is clean and secure is not cheap.

With controversies being waged at present over the detriments

14. "Wastrel of the Western World," *New Republic* 170 (combined issue, 5 and 12 January 1974): 6.

15. "Fighting to Save the Earth from Man," *Time* 95 (2 February 1970): 3.

and benefits of each alternative form of energy, teachers of English have a unique historical opportunity to engage students in research significant to their present and future lives as consumers of power. Such research could help them learn to discriminate between hard evidence and rhetorical ploys, between selflessness and selfishness in human motivation, between causes and effects in nature. Further, it could lead to an understanding of the uses of the library; to the writing of papers and of letters to editors; to discussions and debates; to comprehension of such terms as *connotation, denotation, induction, deduction, inference,* and *fallacy*; to invitations to guest speakers, field trips, and active engagement in civic affairs—in short, to some of the knowledge, attitudes, and behaviors associated with responsible citizenship.

As has been noted, the forms of energy presently being explored are numerous, and the issues attendant to each are complex. Beneath about 16,500 square miles of Colorado, Wyoming, and Utah lies enough oil shale to produce 600 billion to 3,000 billion barrels of oil, more oil than is available from any other source in the world. But companies have been deterred from moving quickly into production because of disputes over the environmental costs of developing oil from shale, inflation, and fear that the energy gained from oil shale will not be worth the energy needed to produce it. The consequence is that the first commercial oil shale plant is not likely to be operational before the mid-1980s—if then.

Similar problems are facing those eager to develop offshore oil. Disputes between the states and the federal government over ownership of the continental shelf beyond the three-mile limit and the concern of citizen groups and legislators about potential environmental damage slowed leasing of offshore property to oil companies. Under the best of circumstances, according to the Department of the Interior, it takes three or more years from initial discovery to the production of offshore oil. Unknown at present are the exact locations and amounts of such oil and the number of problems that may arise in producing it; hence, one may safely guess that many years will pass before full production of offshore oil can help relieve domestic shortages of energy. Too, one can be assured that even if it does become available for business, home, and car, offshore oil will not be purchased cheaply.

A Westinghouse study funded by the National Science Foundation (NSF) has concluded that solar heating and cooling of buildings will be economically competitive in most parts of the country by 1985-90. By the end of the century, according to NSF, solar energy could provide one-third of the energy used to heat and cool buildings, plus 20 to 30 percent of needed electrical power. Although energy from the sun is clean and bounteous, oil companies and electrical utilities were not initially enthusiastic about a resource over which they had no effective control. Recently, however, oil companies have been conducting research in photo-voltaic cells, with the apparent intention of using their patents on the cells to control the market as it develops; too, electrical utilities have considered leasing desert land for the purpose of generating electricity through centralized solar thermal plants. Utilities could also profit from solar energy by "renting" solar heating and cooling equipment for a monthly charge that would include amortization and maintenance of the system, plus a profit. Too, since decentralized solar energy systems would have to rely on centralized electric or gas systems during inclement weather, utilities could profit from maintaining back-up energy systems. In the concluding paragraph of an article on public versus private control of solar energy, Peter Barnes writes:

The way solar energy is controlled will probably be determined within the next decade. The stakes are high, since energy from sunshine will be a multibillion dollar a year business by the end of the century. . . . So far, however, very few cities, states, or federal agencies have given much thought to how to keep the sun a public resource.[16]

With proven coal deposits that will last several hundred years, the United States has an energy resource potentially greater than that of the oil fields in the Middle East. But environmental issues having to do with reclamation of strip-mined land and control of sulfuroxide emission have prevented coal from being quickly exploited as an alternate form of energy. Air pollution standards of the Clean Air Act of 1970, if strictly enforced, would have banned from use nearly half (225 million tons) of the recent annual production of coal. With those standards relaxed, coal production could

16. Peter Barnes, "The Solar Derby," *New Republic* 172 (1 February 1975): 19.

rise to over 2 billion tons by 1985. After that time, technology should be available to convert coal to a gasified or liquified form of oil. Until coal can be converted to a gas or liquid state, many if not most Americans will probably have to suffer the discomforts and hazards to health that accompany air heavily polluted with small particles, especially sulfates.

It is still too early to tell whether either geothermal or wind energy can become efficient and widespread alternate forms of energy. Derived principally from hot water, hot rock, and geopressure (high pressure water), geothermal energy presents some unusual problems. For example, hot water used to produce electricity may cause materials to corrode. Nevertheless, with careful development, it might become an important resource for energy in the western United States, where hot water springs are most common. Though more speculative than hot water and considerably farther from being commercialized, underground deposits of hot rock in formerly active volcanic areas might also become in time a major source of energy. The Atomic Energy Commission's Los Alamos Scientific Laboratory is currently testing the potential power of a deposit lying beneath a dormant volcano near Los Alamos, New Mexico. Windmills, abandoned by American farmers when cheap electricity became available, may grow popular once again. A survey conducted in 1974 by the College of Agriculture of New Mexico State University found that there are about 175,000 water-pumping windmills in the United States, nearly half of them either in good working order or repairable. Because of ranchers' and farmers' expressed desire to save energy and money, the university added to its curriculum a course in how to repair and maintain the mills. Of course, windmills need not be used exclusively on farms or ranches, or even exclusively on land. One person, desiring to exploit most fully the vast amounts of energy generated by wind, has proposed that giant windmills be mounted on buoys at sea, where their blades, turned by ocean winds, could generate electricity to be carried ashore by cable.[17]

Of all forms of energy now utilized or proposed for greater use in the future, nuclear fission is by far the most controversial. Dis-

17. Walter Sullivan, "A Search for Energy Goes Back to Basics," *New York Times,* 3 October 1974, p. 9.

posal of fission wastes from nuclear plants poses extreme hazards. The sixty pounds of cesium-137 produced yearly by a single 1,000 megawatt (electric) nuclear power plant are capable of destroying tens of thousands of humans, for the maximum permissible body burden is about one-trillionth that weight. Those same sixty pounds of cesium-137, which has a half-life of thirty years, have the potential of excluding humans from hundreds of square miles for decades. To date the problem of long-term storage of radioactive wastes has not been resolved.

Fission fuels pose dangers of equal if not greater severity. Neutrons produced in the fissioning of uranium-235, found chiefly in pitchblende, are used to breed new fission fuels, including plutonium-239. Although bred fuels conserve naturally occurring uranium, they not only are radiologically thousands of times more toxic than uranium-235 but are capable of being used in the construction of nuclear explosives. A 1,000 megawatt light water reactor produces 400 to 600 pounds of plutonium annually. The maximum permissible lung burden of plutonium is a hundred-trillionth of this amount, while the air concentration standard for plutonium is one part per million billion. With a radiological half-life of 24,000 years, plutonium-239, unless consumed as fuel, remains as a potential danger for geological times. Moreover, since only ten to twenty pounds of fissionable plutonium is needed to build a nuclear explosive, a single reactor can provide the essential element for a score of bombs.

By 1980, at least thirty nations without nuclear weapons at present will have large nuclear power or research reactors, and an additional two dozen or so countries will have them by 1990. Domestic commercial production of plutonium is projected to exceed fifty tons annually by 1990, with inventories expected to be many times that. The possibility of coercion or catastrophe is great: hijackers or terrorists could blackmail nations; less developed countries could force the industrialized world to share its affluence; sabotage or inadvertent releases of radioactivity could result in national tragedies.[18]

The search for sources of energy other than oil will continue for

18. For a fuller discussion of the hazards of nuclear energy, see *Bulletin of the Atomic Scientists* 30 (October 1974): entire issue; Donald P. Gusaman and Dean E. Abrahamson, "The Dilemma of Fission Power," *Bulletin of the Atomic Scientists* 30 (November 1974): 37-41; J. Gustave Speth, Arthur R.

some time. What has become apparent is that the decision of the thirteen OPEC countries to increase their return on a barrel of oil, less than one dollar at the start of the decade to more than ten dollars by the end of 1974, signaled the beginning of a new world, one in which the United States could no longer rely upon the beneficence of less wealthy oil-possessing countries for cheap energy. As one might anticipate, the world aborning ushered in new problems: the accumulative wealth of the OPEC nations created international banking problems because of difficulties with recycling petrodollars; citizens in the poorest countries of Africa, Asia, and Latin America, unable to afford gasoline for tractors or fertilizers, suffered most deeply from OPEC's decisions; the rate of inflation in industrialized nations rose markedly; other Third World countries, having learned from OPEC, tried to create their own cartels to fix the prices for copper, iron ore, tin, phosphates, rubber, coffee, cocoa, bananas, and pepper; major oil exporting nations, formerly poor and regarded as politically weak, rapidly metamorphosed into major world powers; political and business leaders in the United States were forced to consider the possibilities of zero or modest growth in the nation's use of energy and in its gross national product (GNP).[19]

In sum, the world has entered an era in which natural resources will count for much more than before, conservation will gain a premium over consumption, and more attention will be paid to exploiting resources than curbing pollution. All this will bring many changes in lifestyles: slower gains in real purchasing power, stricter controls on energy use, smaller cars. It remains to be seen to what extent the changes will be accepted by such disparate forces as labor unions, auto manufacturers, and consumer and environmental groups.[20]

Tamplin, and Thomas B. Cochran, "Plutonium Recycle: The Fateful Step," ibid., pp. 15-22; Heilbroner, *An Inquiry into the Human Prospect*, pp. 42-46; *A Time to Choose America's Energy Future*, final report by the Energy Policy Project of the Ford Foundation (Cambridge, Mass.: Ballinger Publishing Co., 1974), pp. 203-24. (Since the scientific and technological breakthroughs necessary for nuclear fusion to occur probably will not take place in this century, its high promise as a major source of energy has not been discussed. The immediate problem for the nation is to develop sources of energy necessary to national vitality, if not to survival, during the next few decades.)

19. For a discussion of three scenarios having to do with future growth in Americans' consumption of energy—high (3.4 percent increase per year), modest (2.0 percent per year), and low (zero growth)—see *A Time to Choose America's Energy Future*.

20. *Time* 105 (6 January 1975): 26.

Though the population of the United States is low and will rise only moderately in comparison to the populations of many less developed countries, Americans need to remember that the average citizen of their nation has been, conservatively, twenty-five times more destructive of the environment than the average citizen of India. Too, as Daniel Bell points out in *The Coming of the Post-Industrial Society*, although industry has emphasized to American workers the importance of such values as thrift, perseverance, sobriety, and delayed gratification for the attainment of goals, it has simultaneously urged those same workers, once away from the place of employment and in their alternate roles as consumers, to be hedonistic and Dionysian in their pursuit of pleasure.[21] The double message has understandably confused most Americans, including young people. A future in which resources are conserved could eliminate confusion by making coherent a system of national values worthy of citizens' respect.

Teachers of English might make easier for students the transition from a society that celebrates rapid consumption of resources to one that honors conservation. Humanists have long argued that the locus of value should be placed upon the individual, not upon the worth of his possessions. From the myth of King Midas to *Something Happened*, from ancient Oriental and Eastern Classics to Thoreau and Eiseley, literature has exposed the vacuousness of materialism and exalted the sacredness of a life lived in communion with nature. Custodians of such a rich tradition of both the mean and the elevated in human behavior, teachers of English would be remiss not to utilize literature to help students develop values that sustain rather than debase life and that fix incomparable worth upon the poorest and most humble of humans.

Weaponry

The prospect of any future existence, let alone its quality, will be dependent, of course, upon nations' abilities to curb their aggressive impulses and not make use of available weaponry. For some years both the United States and Russia have had in storage many times the nuclear power capable of destroying every human being.

21. Bell, *The Coming of Post-Industrial Society*, pp. 477-78.

In June, 1974, for example, the United States was maintaining some 7,000 tactical nuclear warheads in Europe alone, with many more located in Asia and on ships in the Atlantic and Pacific Oceans. At that time, the Soviet Union was thought to have a total of 3,500 short-range missiles and tactical weapons.[22] By 1975, according to calculations of the Center for Defense Information, the United States had a nuclear stockpile equivalent to 615,000 Hiroshimas, or more than fifteen tons of TNT for every person on earth.[23] Nevertheless, the inventory was still accumulating.

The worldwide financial and social costs for support of military force are staggering. The world's outlay for national military forces in dollar equivalents exceeded $240 billion in 1974, more than the combined GNP of Africa, the Middle East, and South Asia, areas in which a third of the world's population lives. The United States was alone responsible for 35 percent of the total. Globally, the military budget consumes more tax revenue than is spent for educating the world's more than one billion school-age children, and it represents twice the amount spent by governments for the health care of a world population of almost four billion. In a ranking of nations from 1 to 132, *World Military and Social Expenditures 1974* showed almost all major military powers standing considerably lower in indicators of social strength than of military strength. The United States, which ranked first militarily, was fourth among the 132 nations in public expenditures per capita for education, fifth in health care, twelfth in number of teachers relative to school-age population, and thirteenth in infant mortality rates. Second in military strength, the Soviet Union was even lower on these same measures.[24]

In the decades ahead, Americans will need to consider carefully a number of questions related to military preparedness. The first is whether the nation, with limited natural and financial resources and with rising social needs, can continue to expend for military pur-

22. Mary Kaldor and Alexander Cockburn, "The Defense Confidence Game," *New York Review of Books* 21 (13 June 1974): 30.

23. Ruth Leger Sevard, "The Arms Race: What It Costs," *New Republic* 172 (combined issue, 4 and 11 January 1975): 10.

24. Ibid.

poses the vast sums annually requested by the Pentagon. In "Defense Spending," an article appearing in the February 1975 issue of *American Heritage*, Allan L. Damon estimates that the United States has spent more on defense in the last two centuries than it has on all other goods and services purchased by federal government. Damon reports that direct military expenditures between 1789 and 1974 total $1.62 trillion, compared with $1.6 trillion for all other governmental costs, such as those for health, education, social security, and operations. The total for *all* military spending between 1789 to 1974, including veterans' benefits, interest on war debts, operation of the Selective Service System, and military projects of the Atomic Energy Commission, is estimated to be $2 trillion. Of that total, $1.3 trillion was spent from 1946 through fiscal 1974, a period of only twenty-eight years. Yet the defense budget requested by President Ford for fiscal 1976 was $104.7 billion, an increase of $8.2 billion in constant dollars over the budget for fiscal 1975.[25] Since weaponry and the means of its deliverance and contravention are capable of becoming ever more sophisticated and expensive, perhaps only the widespread protests of citizens can end the escalation of military spending year after year.

Another question that needs consideration is whether the United States should continue to furnish arms to other nations. International sales of weapons totaled close to $15 billion in 1973, more than twice what they were in 1970. Recognized as the largest arms merchant in the world, the United States sold over eight billion dollars of military hardware in 1974, a five-fold increase from 1970. Not only have Persian Gulf states, suddenly affluent from petroleum profits, been purchasing technologically advanced aircraft, missiles, ships, and tanks, but underdeveloped nations as a whole have been increasing their military budgets at twice the rate of their economic growth. Exportation of arms to other nations not only increases the possibilities of future warfare but frequently leads to regional arms races that upset local balances of power. For example, when Peru ordered Mirage V supersonic fighters from France in 1967, Argentina, Brazil, Colombia, and Venezuela immediately ordered

25. Peter J. Ognibene, "Pentagon Prosperity," *New Republic* 172 (22 February 1975): 10.

similar airplanes; in like vein, Iran's extensive purchase of American aircraft and other military hardware quickly stimulated bids from Saudi Arabia and Kuwait for American, French, and British military equipment.[26]

A final question, one that is deeply troubling, is whether the United States can do anything to control future growth of nuclear arms. In May, 1974, India became the world's sixth nuclear power, joining the United States, the Soviet Union, Britain, France, and China as a nation capable of atomic warfare. Experts believe that Argentina, Brazil, Iran, Israel, Italy, Japan, Pakistan, South Africa, South Korea, and West Germany have the economic and scientific resources to develop atomic bombs before 1980, though they may choose not to do so. Fourteen additional nations are thought capable of becoming atomic powers by the end of the century: Algeria, Bangladesh, Belgium, Chili, Colombia, Indonesia, Libya, North Korea, Portugal, Saudi Arabia, Spain, Switzerland, Turkey, and Venezuela. Plutonium, a byproduct of fission occurring within power generators housed in nuclear reactors, is capable of starting the chain reaction needed to detonate atomic weapons. By September, 1974, there were already 562 power-producing or research reactors in operation or under construction in 33 nations. By 1980, the world's civilian nuclear power industry may have accumulated as much as one million pounds of plutonium with only twenty-two pounds of it needed to destroy a medium-sized city. Directions for constructing an atomic bomb are easily available. (The U.S. Department of Commerce retails for $4.00 a booklet describing in detail the technical problems the United States had in constructing its first bomb). Equally important is that the cost of constructing nuclear warheads can be met by the most impoverished nation if it is willing to divert its resources from other programs.[27] As has already been noted, the possibilities of future nuclear blackmail, terrorism, sabotage, or war are quite high, and there appears at present no means of lowering them.

26. Stanley Karnow, "Weapons for Sale," *New Republic* 170 (23 March 1974): 21.

27. "Mushrooming Spread of Nuclear Power," *Time* 104 (9 September 1974): 28-30.

Biology, Medicine, and Psychology

At the beginning of "Making Babies—the New Biology and the 'Old' Morality," Leon R. Kass, executive secretary of the Committee on the Life Sciences and Social Policy, National Academy of Sciences, comments:

The advent of these new powers for human engineering [that is, transplantation of human and mechanical organs, genetic engineering, electrical and chemical stimulation of the brain] means that some men may be destined to play God, to re-create other men in their own image. This Promethean prospect has captured the imagination of scientist and layman alike, and is being hailed in some quarters as the final solution. But this optimism (not to say hybris) has been tempered by the dim but growing recognition that the use of these new powers will raise profound and difficult moral and political questions—and precisely because the objects on which they are to operate are human beings.[28]

The moral and political questions are indeed difficult. Legalized abortion has forced the medical and legal community to try to specify the time at which a fetus becomes a person, with all the rights to life accorded other individuals. But to date neither juries nor physicians have resolved all the moral and legal questions that have been raised about the commencement of human viability. The discord between law and popular feeling as to when life begins was revealed in 1975 when a doctor in Boston was found guilty of manslaughter for having legally aborted a fetus estimated to be twenty-four weeks old.

Though not as heatedly debated as the determination of life, determination of death has nevertheless proved quite troublesome. With the sustaining of vital processes possible for long periods of time, doctors and relatives are increasingly having to decide when to discontinue life support systems, when to remove tubes, pull electric cords, and allow patients to die peacefully. Too, a growing number of individuals, anticipating the possibility of being kept "alive" some day by such means as artificial respiration and intravenous feeding, have signed statements making known their desire to die naturally if the chances are low of their recovering sufficiently to lead fulfilling lives. Finally, the increasing finesse with which

28. Leon R. Kass, "Making Babies—The New Biology and the 'Old' Morality," *The Public Interest*, no. 26 (Winter 1972): 18-19.

human organs are being transplanted has led to a redefinition of death as the time when the brain, rather than the heart, has ceased functioning. Since legally dead persons with brain damage can nonetheless be maintained for years as warm, respiring, and pulsating bodies, they could come to serve as common objects of medical experiments, a grim possibility examined—and found morally wanting—by Willard Gaylin, a psychiatrist who is president of the Institute of Society, Ethics, and the Life Sciences, an interdisciplinary institute founded in 1969 to examine the ethical, legal, and social implications of advances in the life sciences.[29]

The fact that human organs are not readily available for transplantation, at least not at present, has compelled physicians to decide at times which person among many terminally ill patients should receive a needed heart or a kidney. Such decisions have not always been made by criteria that are ethically as well as medically sound. Too often the answer to the question "Who among many shall live?" has been "The rich and the powerful." And too often it has been prisoners and the poor, those most under coercion and least able to give informed consent, upon whom medical experiments have been performed.

Particularly disquieting to many humanists is evidence that drugs are being unethically used to control human behavior: methylphenidate and amphetamine sulfate have been used to make supposedly hyperkinetic children more docile; succinycholine, which produces a feeling of suffocation when injected into humans, has been used in aversion therapy to make aggressive criminally insane patients more tractable; the hallucinatory (and in at least one case, tragic) effects of LSD on persons who unknowingly ingested the drug have been studied by the Central Intelligence Agency; and to make staff work easier, tranquilizers have been administered in large doses to patients in nursing homes and mental institutions.

In the near future, as psychologist David Krech has predicted, chemicals may be developed that improve humans' memory and accelerate the rate of their learning, but only if ingested regularly. Such a possibility, and its ethical implications, need to be considered

29. Willard Gaylin, "Harvesting the Dead," *Harper's* 249 (September 1974): 23-30.

now by educators, just as the citizenry at large should now be deciding whether all individuals have the right to ingest psychotropic drugs regularly so as to be free of guilt, anxiety, tension, depression, and insomnia. If no individuals have such a right, why have they not? If the right belongs to some but not to all individuals, which some, and why only those?

Another matter having ethical implications is the use of psychosurgery to permit manipulation of humans' behavior. Between 1936 and 1950, lobotomies, which require the severing of fibers between the frontal lobes and lower portions of the brain, were performed on 50,000 patients in the United States. The operation often resulted in convulsive disorders, loss of intelligence and creativity, and postoperative deaths. Found to be less beneficial than conventional treatments of mental illness, lobotomies are rarely performed today. They have been replaced by a more sophisticated form of psychosurgery, one based on new theories of emotion and employing new stereotactic or automated surgical devices. In place of primitive cutting techniques, researchers are employing ultrasound, electricity, and the freezing of tissue to create localized lesions in the amygdala or in other parts of the limbic system of the brain, the section controlling emotions. By 1975 the new techniques were being used on 500 Americans a year.[30]

The implantation into the brain of tiny electrodes capable of inhibiting or intensifying human emotion is still another form of psychosurgery, one that could be widely used, ethically or unethically, as knowledge of the brain becomes more exact. As early as 1967, G. C. Quarton reported that electrical stimulation of the brains of animals had produced alertness, drowsiness, sleep; arrested ongoing behavior; modified the urgency of biological drives; increased and decreased aggressive behavior; caused the animals to continue to press a bar indefinitely when pressing either continued pleasurable stimulation or halted unpleasurable stimulation; caused the animals to alter mood. "In the last few years experiments with implanted electrodes in humans have shown that most of the effects obtained with other mammals are quite feasible in humans."[31]

30. Paul Lowinger, "Psychosurgery," *New Republic* 170 (13 April 1974): 18.

31. G. C. Quarton, "Deliberate Efforts to Control Human Behavior and Modify Personality," *Daedalus* 96 (Summer 1967): 844-45.

Psychotropic drugs and psychosurgery modify in human behavior what is; genetic engineering could determine what will be. Through artificial insemination and the abortion of fetuses whose sloughed off cells reveal Down's syndrome or other genetic defects, our gene pool is being altered. The primary substance of heredity, deoxyribonucleic acid (DNA), has been identified; a gene has been synthesized in the laboratory; and the "genetic code" has been deciphered. In 1974 *Brave New World* seemed to draw closer. In that year Dr. Douglas Bevis from Leeds University, England, reported that after thirty attempts, human embryos conceived in test tubes had been successfully implanted in the wombs of three women, who had then given birth to normal babies. According to Dr. Bevis, researchers had surgically removed eggs from the women (who had been infertile due to diseased, blocked, or missing Fallopian tubes), fertilized the eggs in test tubes with the sperm of their husbands, and then reimplanted them in the women's wombs. The scientific scenario of next steps is that a woman unable to produce normal egg cells will have the fertilized egg of another woman implanted into her uterus; next, a woman unable or unwilling to carry a baby full term will have her fertilized egg implanted into another woman, who will serve as host until the birth; finally, women will be free to select for implantation (or, perhaps, forced to accept) packaged embryos with such characteristics as sex, eye-color, and probably intelligence quotient specified.

The real question is not whether such procedures are possible to perform (they are, or will be) but whether they *should* be performed. At the conclusion of an article on test-tube babies, David Rorvik observes, "We are at a pivotal point in our evolutionary development. For the first time, what we call facts of life need no longer govern us. We possess the knowledge to alter those facts. . . ."[32] If we alter them, we do so only with profound consequences, for at stake is the very definition of what it is to be human, a definition in which teachers of English have a special interest: the literature they teach has been a historical repository of the human enactment, an accumulative definition of what it was to be human in given places and given times, and, by inference, what it has been

32. David Rorvik, "The Embryo Sweepstakes," *New York Times Magazine,* 15 September 1974, p. 62.

to be human across geographic space and historical time, that is, what it has been to be *essentially* human.

The essentiality of humanness includes more, of course, than the rational, verbal, linear, and orderly means by which those living in complex industrialized societies try to manage their lives. As Christian and Eastern mystics, users of psychedelic drugs, practitioners of the occult, and, of late, psychologists like Jerome Bruner and Robert Ornstein have reminded us, there is another major mode of consciousness complementary to the verbal and rational, one which is intuitive and holistic.[33] Popular interest in transcendental meditation; biofeedback training; the meditative practices of Yoga, Zen, and Sufism; mind/body harmony of the martial arts; the "autobiographies" of Black Elk and Carlos Castaneda—all signal what could become a major reorientation in Western ways of perceiving and knowing, a reorientation that could strongly influence the content, pedagogy, and structure of formal education.

If the proper feedback devices are developed, we could include in each person's basic learning experience a training in his or her capacities of self-regulation. We could teach relaxation to students just as we teach baseball. The concept of "physical education" could be expanded to include the mastery of internal states. We could allow people to be more sensitive to the state of their own bodies, and, more in keeping with the intent of the esoteric psychologies, to "Know thyself" in a most intimate way, to master the self, to make oneself more often and more consistently what one wishes.[34]

Not only biofeedback, a process already validated by science, but extrasensory perception (ESP), psychokinesis (PK), and survival phenomena—events presumably influenced by deceased humans or disembodied spirits—have been acknowledged as psychic phenomena worthy of scientific study. In 1969 the Parapsychological Association was formally admitted to the American Association for the Advancement of Science, no sign that all scientists accepted the findings of psychic research but rather a formal recognition of psychic phenomena, or psi, as a valid discipline employing careful

33. See, for example, Jerome Bruner, *On Knowing: Essays for the Left Hand* (New York: Atheneum Publishers, 1965); Robert Ornstein, *The Psychology of Consciousness* (San Francisco, Calif.: W. H. Freeman & Co., 1972).

34. Ornstein, *The Psychology of Consciousness*, p. 203.

scientific procedures. It is yet to be determined whether the study of psi will result in humans who are better able to understand and control their own natures as well as the occurrence of events in nature. But as Albert Rosenfeld, science editor of *Saturday Review*, has argued, in an age in which at least some aspects of acupuncture have been proved medically valid and in which the power to slow one's heart beat at will has been verified in the laboratory, psi warrants careful study.

From the viewpoint of traditional science, the worst that can happen if we give the "mind sciences" an open hearing is that some time and energy will have been wasted (though entertainingly). What is unacceptable will simply not be accepted. On the other hand, if any *new* discoveries are made (or bold ones validated) that might help us surmount our proliferating problems—whether in terms of personal values or global ecologies—we will be the grateful beneficiaries.[35]

Communications

We live at a time when information is printed in such abundance that much of it must be stored on microfiche; when computers are being used daily to print newspapers and books and to catalogue and retrieve library materials; when the New York Times Information Bank can answer—via desktop video terminal, hard-copy printer, and telephone hookup to a computer—their subscribers' most complicated questions; when 40,000 new books and new editions are published in one year (1974) in the United States alone; when Bowker's *Books in Print* lists close to 400,000 titles; when seven million copies of a paperback novel, *The Exorcist*, have been sold within a twelve-month period; when a motion picture, *Jaws*, has grossed in the United States $33 million in admissions in its first seventeen days; when close to 100 percent of American households have television sets, which are turned on an average of six hours daily; when a televised Shakespearean play has commanded an audience estimated to be 25 million; when satellites not only monitor crops, weather, and weaponry, but have made possible live television transmission of an American President's journey to China and Russia; when astronauts have spoken to us live from the moon,

35. Albert Rosenfeld, "Mind and Supermind," *Saturday Review* 2 (22 February 1975): 11.

some 240,000 miles away; when spacecraft, after voyaging millions of miles, have sent back pictures of their atmospheric probes of Venus, Jupiter, and Mars; when 400 million telephone calls are placed daily in the United States; when one corporation has spent in one year as much as 220 million dollars for television advertising; when as many as 400 thousand American students have larked about Europe during a single summer; when films as diverse as *Rashomon* (Japan), *Scenes from a Marriage* (Sweden), *Amarcord* (Italy), *Room at the Top* (England), *The Shop on Main Street* (Czechoslovakia), *War and Peace* (Russia), *Pather Panchali* (India), *Knife in the Water* (Poland), *The Blue Angel* (Germany), and *Bonnie and Clyde* (United States) are appreciated internationally; when airlines worldwide have carried in twelve months 395 million passengers a distance of over 319,500 million passenger-miles.

The rapid technological development of telephone, phonograph, radio, sound-motion picture, television, jet propulsion, cassette tape recorder, miniature camera, computer, transistor, microfilm, holograph, and communication satellite—to mention only a scattering of the means by which modern man communicates with and records the behavior and artifacts of his fellow man—has reduced our conception of the size of the world while simultaneously rendering that conception infinitely more complex. As the world instantaneously feeds in on us via picture, sound, and print, we are forced to attend to more and more information about people, places, and events that would, at best, have been only peripherally important to us decades ago. The devaluation of the dollar can increase overnight the worth of the Swiss franc, and the hand that rules Kuwait today might rock the world tomorrow.

It would be naive for one to believe that education, as institution, has not been and is not being strongly affected by the so-called communications revolution. Through electronic media and means of rapid transportation, persons inside and outside of school can participate vicariously or directly in educational experiences that would have been termed incredible at the turn of this century. In its issue of October 11, 1968, *Life* estimated that for every book the average student reads, he views twenty films; further, according to informed estimates, the average high school graduate has spent

15,000 hours before a television set, 5,000 hours more than he has spent in classrooms. Televised courses such as those offered in the 1960s on NBC's "Sunrise Semester" or those offered in the 1970s by the Open University of Britain have brought college into the home, just as "Sesame Street" and the "Electric Company" transported the elementary classroom into kitchen and den. Programs like Kenneth Clark's "Civilisation" and Jacob Bronowski's "The Ascent of Man," broadcast by public television and viewed with pleasure by millions of nonstudents, have become assigned viewing in hundreds of college courses. Communications satellites have made possible the beaming of live television instruction into remote areas of Appalachia, Alaska, and the Rocky Mountain States; within the next decade, such instruction could be transmitted to the remotest areas of earth. Audio cassettes are enabling physicians, engineers, teachers, and other professionals to keep abreast of that which they profess, and teachers of English have available to them for either private or classroom listening, thousands of recordings and tapes of poetry, drama, essays, and fiction, a great many of them superlatively done. With jet travel has come the development of campuses abroad and with their development, an international flow of students and scholars.

Electronic media, inexpensive paperback books, and means of rapid transportation have already rendered archaic an educational system that fuses chronological age to grade level, that assumes the termination of education at any specified age, that presents the teacher as one whose primary function is that of transmitting information and knowledge—usually from the front of the classroom and via the vocal cords—to a passively receptive audience. As communications technology continues to develop and improve, it will further decentralize both business activities and education. In an article in which he describes the present and possible future uses of communications satellites, Wernher von Braun foresees the average American household of 2024 being equipped with an appliance that combines the features of a television set with those of a desk computer and a Xerox machine:

In addition to serving as a TV set and a printout device for news, the push-button-controlled console will permit its owner to receive facsimile-radioed letters, review the shelves of a nearby grocery store, order food and dry goods, pay bills, balance books, and provide color-video telephone service to any point on earth.[36]

In the near future, domestic satellites could interconnect cable television systems, thereby making possible national networks that would be competitive with commercial networks. Further into the future the technologies of cable, computer, and video cassette may be joined. If they are, the viewer should be able to retrieve programs he has missed or, from a catalog and by means of push-button dialing, have access to an unlimited number of entertainment or educational programs.

One cannot fail to observe that education is much more diffuse today than it was a few decades ago, nor can one miss the signs that education will be yet more diffuse in the future. Programs of nontraditional study are proliferating, many of them with rationales derived, at least in part, from recommendations contained in the reports of the Carnegie Commission, the HEW Task Force on Higher Education, the Commission on Nontraditional Study, the National Commission of the Reform of Secondary Education, and the Panel on Youth of the President's Science Advisory Committee. External degree programs, university without walls, alternative schools, work-study programs, time-shortened degree programs— the experiments appear under innumerable labels but central to each is the belief that education must accommodate itself in highly flexible ways to the different abilities and interests of students and to the emerging needs of the society in which they live.

Pressures in the past decade to diversify and disperse course offerings traditionally found only on campuses and to grant academic credit for particular off-campus "life" experiences have resulted in programs that have awarded credit to thousands of students for courses in which they never enrolled; in courses being taught within prison walls; in experiments at selected American universities with materials developed at the Open University of Britain; in 150 colleges granting credits to servicemen for technical skills learned as part of their military jobs; in college-level courses being printed in newspapers; in the transformation of some public libraries

36. Wernher von Braun, "Space Riders in the Sky," *Saturday Review/World* 1 (24 August 1974): 120.

into community learning centers that serve as "people's universities."[37] To make it possible for older students to attend courses on campus (and in more than one case to assure institutional survival), a number of universities and four-year colleges have followed the lead of community colleges and are now offering evening and weekend degree programs. Too, deference to so-called "senior citizens" has prompted legislators in various geographical areas to waive college tuition fees for those over sixty-five years of age.

In summary, the signs appear clear that education in the future will take place in a variety of settings; will be conducted through a variety of means, both human and technological; and will be open-ended, available to persons of all ages and aptitudes, and for purposes avocational as well as vocational.

Epilogue

Despite the caveats at the outset that no single chapter or book could encompass all the problems or areas of concern related to the quality of human life in the future, one cannot help feeling frustrated that so much has been omitted or only lightly touched upon. Scant space has been given, for example, to possible long-range effects of environmental contamination from such inadvertencies as oil spills, chemical spills, leaks from nuclear reactors, or the emission from aerosol spray cans of flurocarbons that may be depleting the ozone. No attention has been paid to the baneful ways in which polluted industrial environments have shortened the lives of miners or of workers in asbestos, fiberglass, or plastics industries.

Little has been said about racism and the harm it does to institutionalized education and to American idealism, about the fact that by 1975 talk of integration or desegregation had become almost meaningless in cities like Atlanta, Baltimore, Berkeley, Detroit, Washington, D.C., Gary, Newark, Oakland, and San Antonio, cities in which the number of minority students in public schools exceeded 70 percent of total enrollment. Inequitable financing of schools has not been treated, nor has anything been mentioned about inequities in job opportunities or in distribution of income vis-a-vis minorities and whites. Sexism and its pernicious effects on human

37. Edmund J. Farrell, "Perspectives on English in a Vortex of Change," *Phi Delta Kappan* 55 (June 1974): 673.

relationships and human potential have not been discussed, nor has there been speculation about the future of the nuclear family and the rearing of children. Absent, also, are insights into the ways by which automation and cybernation may further alter the nature of work in this society. No adequate account has been given of the continuing rise of domestic violence; no argument has underscored the need to find new methods of providing revenues for essential state and municipal services; no prescience has been offered about the social and financial benefits and risks that may attend continued growth of multinational corporations; no projection, no justification, no condemnation has been made of governmental and military surveillance of citizens.

But enough. Problems and concerns will be with us whether or not they are described in a chapter, a book, or a flurry of tomes. Students, however, may be unaware of or insensitive to many of them. Since this is the case, teachers of English must assume, along with parents and other teachers, responsibility for heightening students' awareness and comprehension of the forces that are helping to shape their present lives and that may, without their eventual intelligent intervention, determine their futures—or at least the manner in which, as adults, they live their tomorrows.

The ways are many by which teachers of English can sensitize students to matters related to the past, the present, and the future—or, rather, possible futures. Remaining space permits only a sample; the reader is encouraged to augment in number, quality, and imagination.

1. *Using media.* (a) By advanced reading of television guides, teachers can alert students to forthcoming programs that treat pressing issues. The programs can then become the subject of classroom discussion and of writing assignments. (b) Individualized reading assignments can be made in such periodicals as *Harper's, Atlantic, Saturday Review, The New Republic, New York Review of Books, American Scholar,* and *Daedalus.* Students can share their reading through small-group discussions and panels. Writing assignments might vary in length from the paragraph to the term paper. Discussion of controversial issues could lead to further research and debates. (c) Students could use tape recorders to interview grandparents and other older acquaintances about changes they have

observed during their lifetimes. Portions of the tapes could be shared in the classroom, and tapes could be exchanged for home listening. (d) Photographs in family albums might be shared for what they reveal about the process of aging and about changes in manners and styles. Discussion and writing could follow.

2. *Exploring the effects of media.* Students could discuss or describe in writing how life in America would differ if each of the following were eliminated: airplanes; quadraphonic and stereophonic records, tapes, and systems; television sets; radios; automobiles; telephones; computers; cameras. Out of such explorations, students should begin to sense how media pervasively affect the values, organization, and commitments of a nation.

3. *Projecting one's life.* Students can be given the following kinds of assignments: (a) Assume that you are seventy years old. Your twelve-year-old grandchild has written asking you to describe the most important events in your life. Write your response. (b) Assume that you are seventy-five years old and that you have kept a diary. Share your entries describing how you spent a typical day at ages thirty, fifty, and seventy-five.

4. *Role playing.* Students are given the following kinds of assignments: (a) Assume that you have decided to campaign for mayor. Write a statement describing what you intend to do to improve your city if you win. (b) Assume that you are a medical doctor who has three patients with terminal kidney cancer. You have available only one machine for dialysis. Discuss your criteria for choosing which patient shall live. (c) Assume that thousands of starving children in India and Bangladesh can be adequately fed if Americans are willing to cut by 10 percent the amount of meat they eat. You are put in charge of a campaign to persuade your fellow citizens that they must make sacrifices so that others may live. Outline the methods of persuasion you would use in your campaign.

5. *Writing scenarios.* Students can be given the following kinds of assignments: (a) Describe in chronological order the national and international events that lead to a banning of all nuclear weapons in 1995. (b) Describe in chronological order the events that lead to India's being economically self-sufficient by the year 2000.

6. *Using literature.* (c) Students can read and discuss various

forms of speculative fiction—dystopian and utopian literature, science fantasy and science fiction—for the imaginative insights into the future such literature offers. Classes might be broken down into small groups, each of which is encouraged to develop its own American Utopia. (b) Students can read and discuss multiethnic literature so that they may come to appreciate and honor life styles and values that differ from their own. (c) Students can read and discuss literature that shows humans living in harmony with, or alienated from, nature. Such literature might include poems of the English nature poets, prose and poetry from the oral tradition of native Americans, and essays of contemporary figures like Joseph Wood Krutch, Edward Hoagland, and Loren Eiseley. Students should come to understand that persons who exploit nature not only risk their peace of mind: they jeopardize the continuance of the human race.

Index

INFORMATION CONCERNING
THE NATIONAL SOCIETY FOR THE STUDY OF EDUCATION

1. *Purpose.* The purpose of the National Society is to promote the investigation and discussion of educational questions. To this end it holds an annual meeting and publishes a series of yearbooks and a series of paperbacks on Contemporary Educational Issues.

2. *Membership.* Any person interested in the purpose of the Society and in receiving its publications may become a member by sending in name, title, address, and a check covering dues and the entrance fee (see items 4 and 5). Graduate students may become members, upon recommendation of a faculty member, at a reduced rate for the first year of membership. Dues for all subsequent years are the same as for other members.

Membership is not transferable. It is limited to individuals and may not be held by libraries, schools, or other institutions, either directly or indirectly.

3. *Period of Membership.* Membership is for the calendar year and terminates automatically on December 31, unless dues for the ensuing year are paid as indicated in item 6. Applicants for membership may not date their entrance back of the current calendar year.

4. *Categories of Membership.* The following categories of membership have been established:

Regular. Annual dues are $13.00. The member receives a clothbound copy of each part of the current yearbook.

Comprehensive. Annual dues are $27.00. The member receives a clothbound copy of the current yearbook *and* all volumes in the current year's paperback series on Contemporary Educational Issues.

Special Memberships for Retired Members and Graduate Students.

Retired members. Persons who are retired or who are sixty-five years of age *and* who have been members of the Society continuously for at least ten years may retain their Regular Membership upon payment of annual dues of $10.00 or their Comprehensive Membership upon payment of annual dues of $20.00.

Graduate Students. Graduate students may pay annual dues of $10.00 for Regular Membership or $20.00 for Comprehensive Membership for their first year of membership, plus the $1.00 entrance fee in either case.

Life Memberships. Persons sixty years of age or above may become life members on payment of a fee based on the average life expectancy of their age group. Regular life members may take out a Comprehensive Membership for any year upon payment of an additional fee of $10.00. For further information apply to the Secretary-Treasurer.

5. *Privileges of Membership.* Members receive the publications of the Society as described above. All members are entitled to vote, to participate in meetings of the Society, and (under certain conditions) to hold office.

6. *Entrance Fee.* New members are required to pay an entrance fee of one dollar, in addition to the dues, for the first year of membership.

7. *Payment of Dues.* Statements of dues are rendered in October for the following calendar year. Any member so notified whose dues remain unpaid on January 1 thereby loses membership and can be reinstated only by paying the dues plus a reinstatement fee of fifty cents ($.50).

School warrants and vouchers from institutions must be accompanied by definite information concerning the name and address of the person for whom the membership fee is being paid. Statements of dues are rendered on our own form only. The Secretary's office cannot undertake to fill out special invoice forms of any kind or to affix a notary's affidavit to statements or receipts.

Cancelled checks serve as receipts. Members desiring an additional receipt must enclose a stamped and addressed envelope therefor.

8. *Distribution of Yearbooks to Members.* The yearbooks, normally ready prior to the February meeting of the Society, will be mailed from the office of the distributor only to members whose dues for that year have been paid.

9. *Commercial Sales.* The distribution of all yearbooks prior to the current year, and also of those of the current year not regularly mailed to members in exchange for their dues, is in the hands of the distributor, not of the Secretary. Orders may be placed with the University of Chicago Press, Chicago, Illinois 60637, which distributes the yearbooks of the Society. Orders for paperbacks in the series on Contemporary Educational Issues should be placed with the designated publisher of that series. The list of the Society's publications is printed in each yearbook.

10. *Yearbooks.* The yearbooks are issued about one month before the February meeting. Published in two volumes, each of which contains 300 to 400 pages, the yearbooks are planned to be of immediate practical value as well as representative of sound scholarship and scientific investigation.

11. *Series on Contemporary Educational Issues.* This series, in paperback format, is designed to supplement the yearbooks by timely publications on topics of current interest. There will usually be three of these volumes each year.

12. *Meetings.* The annual meeting, at which the yearbooks are presented and critiqued, is held as a rule in February at the same time and place as the meeting of the American Association of School Administrators. Members will be notified of other meetings.

Applications for membership will be handled promptly at any time. New members will receive the yearbook scheduled for publication during the calendar year in which application for Regular Membership is made. New members who elect to take out the Comprehensive membership will receive both the yearbook and the paperbacks scheduled for publication during the year in which application is made.

KENNETH J. REHAGE, Secretary-Treasurer

5835 Kimbark Avenue
Chicago, Illinois 60637

PUBLICATIONS OF THE NATIONAL SOCIETY FOR THE STUDY OF EDUCATION

1. The Yearbooks

NOTICE: Many of the early yearbooks of this series are now out of print. In the following list, those titles to which an asterisk is prefixed are not available for purchase.

*First Yearbook, 1902, Part I—*Some Principles in the Teaching of History.* Lucy M. Salmon.

*First Yearbook, 1902, Part II—*The Progress of Geography in the Schools.* W. M. Davis and H. M. Wilson.

*Second Yearbook, 1903, Part I—*The Course of Study in History in the Common School.* Isabel Lawrence, C. A. McMurray, Frank McMurry, E. C. Page, and E. J. Rice.

*Second Yearbook, 1903, Part II—*The Relation of Theory to Pratice in Education.* M. J. Holmes, J. A. Keith, and Levi Seeley.

*Third Yearbook, 1904, Part I—*The Relation of Theory to Practice in the Education of Teachers.* John Dewey, Sarah C. Brooks, F. M. McMurry, et al.

*Third Yearbook, 1904, Part II—*Nature Study.* W. S. Jackman.

*Fourth Yearbook, 1905, Part I—*The Education and Training of Secondary Teachers.* E. C. Elliott, E. G. Dexter, M. J. Holmes, et al.

*Fourth Yearbook, 1905, Part II—*The Place of Vocational Subjects in the High-School Curriculum.* J. S. Brown, G. B. Morrison, and Ellen Richards.

*Fifth Yearbook, 1906, Part I—*On the Teaching of English in Elementary and High Schools.* G. P. Brown and Emerson Davis.

*Fifth Yearbook, 1906, Part II—*The Certification of Teachers.* E. P. Cubberley.

*Sixth Yearbook, 1907, Part I—*Vocational Studies for College Entrance.* C. A. Herrick, H. W. Holmes, T. deLaguna, V. Prettyman, and W. J. S. Bryan.

*Sixth Yearbook, 1907, Part II—*The Kindergarten and Its Relation to Elementary Education.* Ada Van Stone Harris, E. A. Kirkpatrick, Marie Kraus-Boelté, Patty S. Hill, Harriette M. Mills, and Nina Vandewalker.

*Seventh Yearbook, 1908, Part I—*The Relation of Superintendents and Principals to the Training and Professional Improvement of Their Teachers.* Charles D. Lowry.

*Seventh Yearbook, 1908, Part II—*The Co-ordination of the Kindergarten and the Elementary School.* B. J. Gregory, Jennie B. Merrill, Bertha Payne, and Margaret Giddings.

*Eighth Yearbook, 1909, Part I—*Education with Reference to Sex: Pathological, Economic, and Social Aspects.* C. R. Henderson.

*Eighth Yearbook, 1909, Part II—*Education with Reference to Sex: Agencies and Methods.* C. R. Henderson and Helen C. Putnam.

*Ninth Yearbook, 1910, Part I—*Health and Education.* T. D. Wood.

*Ninth Yearbook, 1910, Part II—*The Nurses in Education.* T. D. Wood, et al.

*Tenth Yearbook, 1911, Part I—*The City School as a Community Center.* H. C. Leipziger, Sarah E. Hyre, R. D. Warden. C. Ward Crampton, E. W. Stitt, E. J. Ward, Mrs. T. C. Grice, and C. A. Perry.

*Tenth Yearbook, 1911, Part II—*The Rural School as a Community Center.* B. H. Crocheron, Jessie Field, F. W. Howe, E. C. Bishop, A. B. Graham, O. J. Kern, M. T. Scudder, and B. M. Davis.

*Eleventh Yearbook, 1912, Part I—*Industrial Education: Typical Experiments Described and Interpreted.* J. F. Barker, M. Bloomfield, B. W. Johnson, P. Johnson, L. M. Leavitt, G. A. Mirick, M. W. Murray, C. F. Perry, A. L. Stafford, and H. B. Wilson.

*Eleventh Yearbook, 1912, Part II—*Agricultural Education in Secondary Schools.* A. C. Monahan, R. W. Stimson, D. J. Crosby, W. H. French, H. F. Button, F. R. Crane, W. R. Hart, and G. F. Warren.

*Twelfth Yearbook, 1913, Part I—*The Supervision of City Schools.* Franklin Bobbitt, J. W. Hall, and J. D. Wolcott.

*Twelfth Yearbook, 1913, Part II—*The Supervision of Rural Schools.* A. C. Monahan, L. J. Hanifan, J. E. Warren, Wallace Lund, U. J. Hoffman, A. S. Cook, E. M. Rapp, Jackson Davis, J. D. Wolcott.

*Thirteenth Yearbook, 1914, Part I—*Some Aspects of High-School Instruction and Administration.* H. C. Morrison, E. R. Breslich, W. A. Jessup, and L. D. Coffman.

*Thirteenth Yearbook, 1914, Part II—*Plans for Organizing School Surveys, with a Summary of Typical School Surveys.* Charles H. Judd and Henry L. Smith.

*Fourteenth Yearbook, 1915, Part I—*Minimum Essentials in Elementary School Subjects—Standards and Current Practices.* H. B. Wilson, H. W. Holmes, F. E. Thompson, R. G. Jones, S. A. Courtis, W. S. Gray, F. N. Freeman, H. C. Pryor, J. F. Hosic, W. A. Jessup, and W. C. Bagley.

*Fourteenth Yearbook, 1915, Part II—*Methods for Measuring Teachers' Efficiency.* Arthur C. Boyce.

*Fifteenth Yearbook, 1916, Part I—*Standards and Tests for the Measurement of the Efficiency of Schools and School Systems.* G. D. Strayer, Bird T. Baldwin, B. R. Buckingham, F. W. Ballou, D. C. Bliss, H. G. Childs, S. A. Courtis, E. P. Cubberley, C. H. Judd, George Melcher, E. E. Oberholtzer, J. B. Sears, Daniel Starch, M. R. Trabue, and G. M. Whipple.

*Fifteenth Yearbook, 1916, Part II—*The Relationship between Persistence in School and Home Conditions.* Charles E. Holley.
*Fifteenth Yearbook, 1916, Part III—*The Junior High School.* Aubrey A. Douglas.
*Sixteenth Yearbook, 1917, Part I—*Second Report of the Committee on Minimum Essentials in Elementary-School Subjects.* W. C. Bagley, W. W. Charters, F. N. Freeman, W. S. Gray, Ernest Horn, J. H. Hoskinson, W. S. Monroe, C. F. Munson, H. C. Pryor, L. W. Rapeer, G. M. Wilson, and H. B. Wilson.
*Sixteenth Yearbook, 1917, Part II—*The Efficiency of College Students as Conditioned by Age at Entrance and Size of High School.* B. F. Pittenger.
*Seventeenth Yearbook, 1918, Part I—*Third Report of the Committee on Economy of Time in Education.* W. C. Bagley, B. B. Bassett, M. E. Branom, Alice Camerer, J. E. Dealey, C. A. Ellwood, E. B. Greene, A. B. Hart, J. F. Hosic, E. T. Housh, W. H. Mace, L. R. Marston, H. C. McKown, H. E. Mitchell, W. V. Reavis, D. Snedden, and H. B. Wilson.
*Seventeenth Yearbook, 1918, Part II—*The Measurement of Educational Products.* E. J. Ashbaugh, W. A. Averill, L. P. Ayers, F. W. Ballou, Edna Bryner, B. R. Buckingham, S. A. Courtis, M. E. Haggerty, C. H. Judd, George Melcher, W. S. Monroe, E. A. Nifenecker, and E. L. Thorndike.
*Eighteenth Yearbook, 1919, Part I—*The Professional Preparation of High-School Teachers.* G. N. Cade, S. S. Colvin, Charles Fordyce, H. H. Foster, T. S. Gosling, W. S. Gray, L. V. Koos, A. R. Mead, H. L. Miller, F. C. Whitcomb, and Clifford Woody.
*Eighteenth Yearbook, 1919, Part II—*Fourth Report of Committee on Economy of Time in Education.* F. C. Ayer, F. N. Freeman, W. S. Gray, Ernest Horn, W. S. Monroe, and C. E. Seashore.
*Nineteenth Yearbook, 1920, Part I—*New Materials of Instruction.* Prepared by the Society's Committee on Materials of Instruction.
*Nineteenth Yearbook, 1920, Part II—*Classroom Problems in the Education of Gifted Children.* T. S. Henry.
*Twentieth Yearbook, 1921, Part I—*New Materials of Instruction.* Second Report by Society's Committee.
*Twentieth Yearbook, 1921, Part II—*Report of the Society's Committee on Silent Reading.* M. A. Burgess, S. A. Courtis, C. E. Germane, W. S. Gray, H. A. Greene, Regina R. Heller, J. H. Hoover, J. A. O'Brien, J. L. Packer, Daniel Starch, W. W. Theisen, G. A. Yoakam, and representatives of other school systems.
*Twenty-first Yearbook, 1922, Parts I and II—*Intelligence Tests and Their Use.* Part I—*The Nature, History, and General Principles of Intelligence Testing.* E. L. Thorndike, S. S. Colvin, Harold Rugg, G. M. Whipple, Part II—*The Administrative Use of Intelligence Tests.* H. W. Holmes, W. K. Layton, Helen Davis, Agnes L. Rogers, Rudolf Pintner, M. R. Trabue, W. S. Miller, Bessie L. Gambrill, and others. The two parts are bound together.
*Twenty-second Yearbook, 1923, Part I—*English Composition: Its Aims, Methods and Measurements.* Earl Hudelson.
*Twenty-second Yearbook, 1923, Part II—*The Social Studies in the Elementary and Secondary School.* A. S. Barr, J. J. Coss, Henry Harap, R. W. Hatch, H. C. Hill, Ernest Horn, C. H. Judd, L. C. Marshall, F. M. McMurry, Earle Rugg, H. O. Rugg, Emma Schweppe, Mabel Snedaker, and C. W. Washburne.
*Twenty-third Yearbook, 1924, Part I—*The Education of Gifted Children.* Report of the Society's Committee. Guy M. Whipple, Chairman.
*Twenty-third Yearbook, 1924, Part II—*Vocational Guidance and Vocational Education for Industries.* A. H. Edgerton and others.
*Twenty-fourth Yearbook, 1925, Part I—*Report of the National Committee on Reading.* W. S. Gray, Chairman, F. W. Ballou, Rose L. Hardy, Ernest Horn, Francis Jenkins, S. A. Leonard, Estaline Wilson, and Laura Zirbes.
*Twenty-fourth Yearbook, 1925, Part II—*Adapting the Schools to Individual Differences.* Report of the Society's Committee. Carleton W. Washburne, Chairman.
*Twenty-fifth Yearbook, 1926, Part I—*The Present Status of Safety Education.* Report of the Society's Committee. Guy M. Whipple, Chairman.
*Twenty-fifth Yearbook, 1926, Part II—*Extra-Curricular Activities.* Report of the Society's Committee. Leonard V. Koos, Chairman.
*Twenty-sixth Yearbook, 1927, Part I—*Curriculum-making: Past and Present.* Report of the Society's Committee. Harold O. Rugg, Chairman.
*Twenty-sixth Yearbook, 1927, Part II—*The Foundations of Curriculum-making.* Prepared by individual members of the Society's Committee. Harold O. Rugg, Chairman.
*Twenty-seventh Yearbook, 1928, Part I—*Nature and Nurture: Their Influence upon Intelligence.* Prepared by the Society's Committee. Lewis M. Terman, Chairman.
*Twenty-seventh Yearbook, 1928, Part II—*Nature and Nurture: Their Influence upon Achievement.* Prepared by the Society's Committee. Lewis M. Terman, Chairman.
Twenty-eighth Yearbook, 1929, Parts I and II—*Preschool and Parental Education,* Part I—*Organization and Development.* Part II—*Research and Method.* Prepared by the Society's Committee. Lois H. Meek, Chairman. Bound in one volume. Cloth.
*Twenty-ninth Yearbook, 1930, Parts I and II—*Report of the Society's Committee on Arithmetic.* Part I—*Some Aspects of Modern Thought on Arithmetic.* Part II—*Research in Arithmetic.* Prepared by the Society's Committee. F. B. Knight, Chairman. Bound in one volume.
*Thirtieth Yearbook, 1931— Part I—*The Status of Rural Education.* First Report of the Society's Committee on Rural Education. Orville G. Brim, Chairman.
Thirtieth Yearbook, 1931, Part II—*The Textbook in American Education.* Report of the Society's Committee on the Textbook, J. B. Edmonson, Chairman. Cloth, Paper.

Fifty-first Yearbook, 1952, Part I—*General Education*. Prepared by the Society's Committee. T. R. McConnell, Chairman. Cloth, Paper.

Fifty-first Yearbook, 1952, Part II—*Education in Rural Communities*. Prepared by the Society's Committee. Ruth Strang, Chairman. Cloth, Paper.

*Fifty-second Yearbook, 1953, Part I—*Adapting the Secondary-School Program to the Needs of Youth*. Prepared by the Society's Committee: William G. Brink, Chairman.

Fifty-second Yearbook, 1953, Part II—*The Community School*. Prepared by the Society's Committee. Maurice F. Seay, Chairman. Cloth.

Fifty-third Yearbook, 1954, Part I—*Citizen Co-operation for Better Public Schools*. Prepared by the Society's Committee. Edgar L. Morphet, Chairman. Cloth, Paper.

Fifty-third Yearbook, 1954, Part II—*Mass Media and Education*. Prepared by the Society's Committee. Edgar Dale, Chairman. Paper.

*Fifty-fourth Yearbook, 1955, Part I—*Modern Philosophies and Education*. Prepared by the Society's Committee. John S. Brubacher, Chairman.

Fifty-fourth Yearbook, 1955, Part II—*Mental Health in Modern Education*. Prepared by the Society's Committee. Paul A. Witty, Chairman. Paper.

*Fifty-fifth Yearbook, 1956, Part I—*The Public Junior College*. Prepared by the Society's Committee. B. Lamar Johnson, Chairman.

Fifty-fifth Yearbook, 1956, Part II—*Adult Reading*. Prepared by the Society's Committee. David H. Clift, Chairman. Paper.

Fifty-sixth Yearbook, 1957, Part I—*In-service Education of Teachers, Supervisors, and Administrators*. Prepared by the Society's Committee. Stephen M. Corey, Chairman. Cloth, Paper.

Fifty-sixth Yearbook, 1957, Part II—*Social Studies in the Elementary School*. Prepared by the Society's Committee. Ralph C. Preston, Chairman. Cloth, Paper.

Fifty-seventh Yearbook, 1958, Part I—*Basic Concepts in Music Education*. Prepared by the Society's Committee. Thurber H. Madison, Chairman. Cloth.

Fifty-seventh Yearbook, 1958, Part II—*Education for the Gifted*. Prepared by the Society's Committee. Robert J. Havighurst, Chairman. Cloth, Paper.

Fifty-seventh Yearbook, 1958, Part III—*The Integration of Educational Experiences*. Prepared by the Society's Committee. Paul L. Dressel, Chairman. Cloth.

Fifty-eighth Yearbook, 1959, Part I—*Community Education: Principles and Practices from World-wide Experience*. Prepared by the Society's Committee. C. O. Arndt, Chairman. Cloth, Paper.

Fifty-eighth Yearbook, 1959, Part II—*Personnel Services in Education*. Prepared by the Society's Committee. Melvene D. Hardee, Chairman. Paper.

*Fifty-ninth Yearbook, 1960, Part I—*Rethinking Science Education*. Prepared by the Society's Committee. J. Darrell Barnard, Chairman.

Fifty-ninth Yearbook, 1960, Part II—*The Dynamics of Instructional Groups*. Prepared by the Society's Committee. Gale E. Jensen, Chairman. Cloth.

Sixtieth Yearbook, 1961, Part I—*Development in and through Reading*. Prepared by the Society's Committee. Paul A. Witty, Chairman. Cloth, Paper.

Sixtieth Yearbook, 1961, Part II—*Social Forces Influencing American Education*. Prepared by the Society's Committee. Ralph W. Tyler, Chairman. Cloth.

Sixty-first Yearbook, 1962, Part I—*Individualizing Instruction*. Prepared by the Society's Committee. Fred T. Tyler, Chairman. Cloth.

Sixty-first Yearbook, 1962, Part II—*Education for the Professions*. Prepared by the Society's Committee. G. Lester Anderson, Chairman. Cloth.

Sixty-second Yearbook, 1963, Part I—*Child Psychology*. Prepared by the Society's Committee. Harold W. Stevenson, Editor. Cloth.

Sixty-second Yearbook, 1963, Part II—*The Impact and Improvement of School Testing Programs*. Prepared by the Society's Committee. Warren G. Findley, Editor. Cloth.

Sixty-third Yearbook, 1964, Part I—*Theories of Learning and Instruction*. Prepared by the Society's Committee. Ernest R. Hilgard, Editor. Paper.

Sixty-third Yearbook, 1964, Part II—*Behavioral Science and Educational Administration*. Prepared by the Society' Committee. Daniel E. Griffiths, Editor. Paper.

Sixty-fourth Yearbook, 1965, Part I—*Vocational Education*. Prepared by the Society's Committee. Melvin L. Barlow, Editor. Cloth.

Sixty-fourth Yearbook, 1965, Part II—*Art Education*. Prepared by the Society's Committee. W. Reid Hastie, Editor. Cloth.

Sixty-fifth Yearbook, 1966, Part I—*Social Deviancy among Youth*. Prepared by the Society's Committee. William W. Wattenberg, Editor. Cloth.

Sixty-fifth Yearbook, 1966, Part II—*The Changing American School*. Prepared by the Society's Committee. John I. Goodlad, Editor. Cloth.

Sixty-sixth Yearbook, 1967, Part I—*The Educationally Retarded and Disadvantaged*. Prepared by the Society's Committee. Paul A. Witty, Editor. Cloth.

Sixty-sixth Yearbook, 1967, Part II—*Programed Instruction*. Prepared by the Society's Committee. Phil C. Lange, Editor. Cloth.

Sixty-seventh Yearbook, 1968, Part I—*Metropolitanism: Its Challenge to Education*. Prepared by the Society's Committee. Robert J. Havighurst, Editor. Cloth.

Sixty-seventh Yearbook, 1968, Part II—*Innovation and Change in Reading Instruction*. Prepared by the Society's Committee. Helen M. Robinson, Editor. Cloth.

Sixty-eighth Yearbook, 1969, Part I—*The United States and International Education*. Prepared by the Society's Committee. Harold G. Shane, Editor. Cloth.

Sixty-eighth Yearbook, 1969, Part II—*Educational Evaluation: New Roles, New Means*. Prepared by the Society's Committee. Ralph W. Tyler, Editor. Paper.

Sixty-ninth Yearbook, 1970, Part I—*Mathematics Education*. Prepared by the Society's Committee. Edward G. Begle, Editor. Cloth.

Sixty-ninth Yearbook, 1970, Part II—*Linguistics in School Programs*. Prepared by the Society's Committee. Albert H. Marckwardt, Editor. Cloth.

Seventieth Yearbook, 1971, Part I—*The Curriculum: Retrospect and Prospect.* Prepared by the Society's Committee. Robert M. McClure, Editor. Paper.
Seventieth Yearbook, 1971, Part II—*Leaders in American Education.* Prepared by the Society's Committee. Robert J. Havighurst, Editor. Cloth.
Seventy-first Yearbook, 1972, Part I—*Philosophical Redirection of Educational Research.* Prepared by the Society's Committee. Lawrence G. Thomas, Editor. Cloth.
Seventy-first Yearbook, 1972, Part II—*Early Childhood Education.* Prepared by the Society's Committee. Ira J. Gordon, Editor. Cloth, Paper.
Seventy-second Yearbook, 1973, Part I—*Behavior Modification in Education.* Prepared by the Society's Committee. Carl E. Thoresen, Editor. Cloth.
Seventy-second Yearbook, 1973, Part II—*The Elementary School in the United States.* Prepared by the Society's Committee. John I. Goodlad and Harold G. Shane, Editors. Cloth.
Seventy-third Yearbook, 1974, Part I—*Media and Symbols: The Forms of Expression, Communication, and Education.* Prepared by the Society's Committee. David R. Olson, Editor. Cloth.
Seventy-third Yearbook, 1974, Part II—*Uses of the Sociology of Education.* Prepared by the Society's Committee. C. Wayne Gordon, Editor. Cloth.
Seventy-fourth Yearbook, 1975, Part I—*Youth.* Prepared by the Society's Committee. Robert J. Havighurst and Philip H. Dreyer, Editors. Cloth.
Seventy-fourth Yearbook, 1975, Part II—*Teacher Education.* Prepared by the Society's Committee. Kevin Ryan, Editor. Cloth.
Seventy-fifth Yearbook, 1976, Part I—*Psychology of Teaching Methods.* Prepared by the Society's Committee. N. L. Gage, Editor. Cloth.
Seventy-fifth Yearbook, 1976, Part II—*Issues in Secondary Education.* Prepared by the Society's Committee. William Van Til, Editor. Cloth.
Seventy-sixth Yearbook, 1977, Part I—*The Teaching of English.* Prepared by the Society's Committee. James R. Squire, Editor. Cloth.
Seventy-sixth Yearbook, 1977, Part I—*The Politics of Education.* Prepared by the Society's Committee. Jay D. Scribner, Editor. Cloth.

Yearbooks of the National Society are distributed by

THE UNIVERSITY OF CHICAGO PRESS, CHICAGO, ILLINOIS 60637

Please direct inquiries regarding prices of volumes still available to the University of Chicago Press. Orders for these volumes should be sent to the University of Chicago Press, not to the offices of the National Society.

2. The Series on Contemporary Educational Issues

In addition to its Yearbooks the Society now publishes volumes in a series on Contemporary Educational Issues. These volumes are prepared under the supervision of the Society's Commission on an Expanded Publication Program.

The 1977 Titles

> *Early Childhood Education: Perspectives and Issues* (Bernard Spodek and Herbert J. Walberg, eds.)
>
> *The Future of Big City Schools: Desegregation Policies and Magnet Alternatives* (Daniel U. Levine and Robert J. Havighurst, eds.)
>
> *Educational Administration: The Developing Decades* (Luvern L. Cunningham, Walter G. Hack, and Raphael O. Nystrand, eds.)

The 1976 Titles

> *Prospects for Research and Development in Education* (Ralph W. Tyler, ed.)
>
> *Public Testimony on Public Schools* (Commission on Educational Governance)
>
> *Counseling Children and Adolescents* (William M. Walsh, ed.)

The 1975 Titles

> *Schooling and the Rights of Children* (Vernon Haubrich and Michael Apple, eds.)
>
> *Systems of Individualized Education* (Harriet Talmage, ed.)
>
> *Educational Policy and International Assessment: Implications of the IEA Assessment of Achievement* (Alan Purves and Daniel U. Levine, eds.)

The 1974 Titles

> *Crucial Issues in Testing* (Ralph W. Tyler and Richard M. Wolf, eds.)
>
> *Conflicting Conceptions of Curriculum* (Elliott Eisner and Elizabeth Vallance, eds.)
>
> *Cultural Pluralism* (Edgar G. Epps, ed.)
>
> *Rethinking Educational Equality* (Andrew T. Kopan and Herbert J. Walberg, eds.)

All of the above volumes may be ordered from

McCutchan Publishing Corporation
2526 Grove Street
Berkeley, California 94704

The 1972 Titles

> *Black Students in White Schools* (Edgar G. Epps, ed.)
>
> *Flexibility in School Programs* (W. J. Congreve and G. L. Rinehart, eds.)
>
> *Performance Contracting—1969-1971* (J. A. Mecklenburger)
>
> *The Potential of Educational Futures* (Michael Marien and W. L. Ziegler, eds.)
>
> *Sex Differences and Discrimination in Education* (Scarvia Anderson, ed.)

The 1971 Titles

Accountability in Education (Leon M. Lessinger and Ralph W. Tyler, eds.)

Farewell to Schools? ? ? (D. U. Levine and R. J. Havighurst, eds.)

Models for Integrated Education (D. U. Levine, ed.)

PYGMALION *Reconsidered* (J. D. Elashoff and R. E. Snow)

Reactions to Silberman's CRISIS IN THE CLASSROOM (A. Harry Passow, ed.)

Titles in the 1971 and 1972 series may be ordered from
Charles A. Jones Publishing Company
Worthington, Ohio 43085